THOR
THE MIGHTY AVENGER

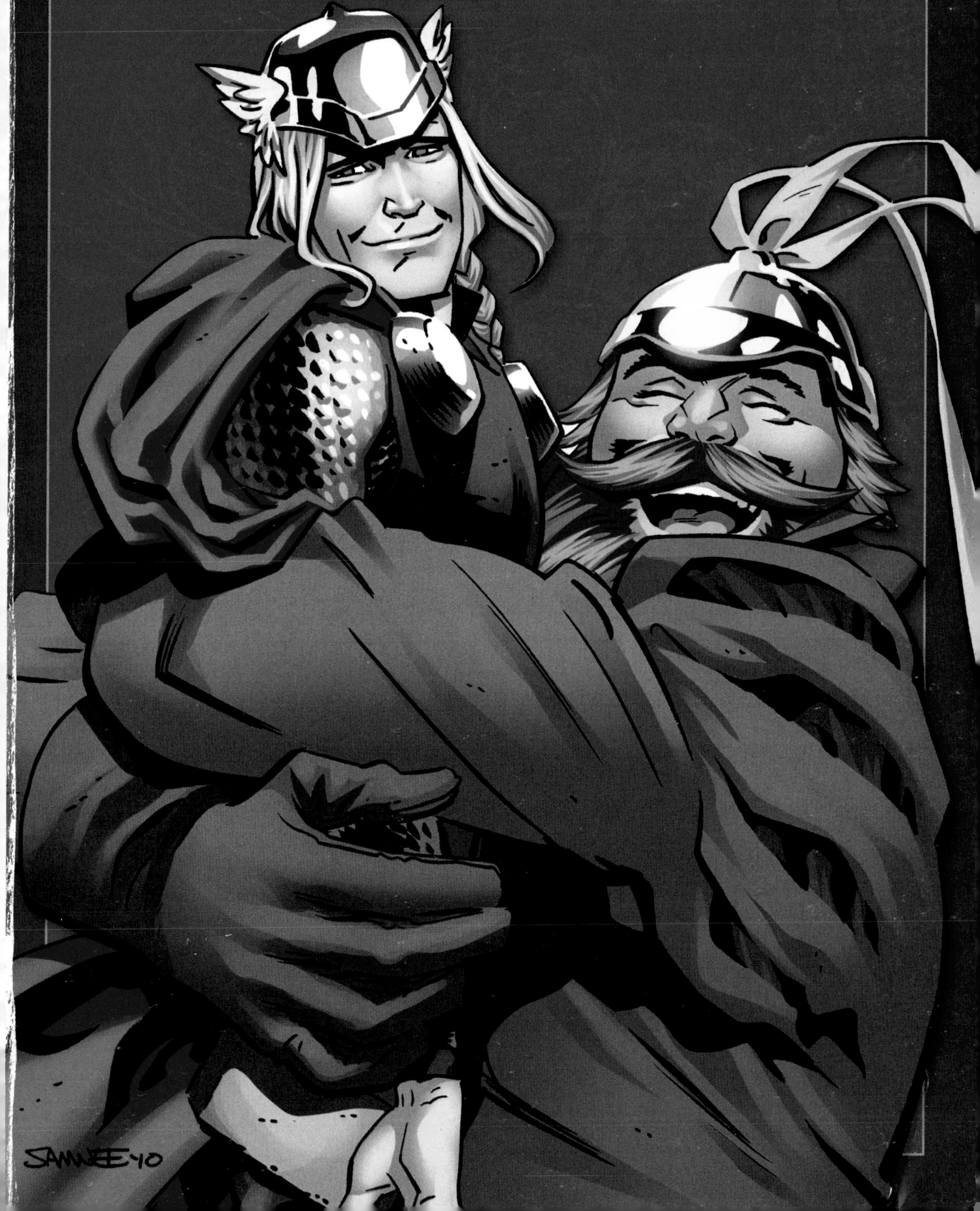
SAMNEE '10

THOR
THE MIGHTY AVENGER

Writer **ROGER LANGRIDGE**

Artist **CHRIS SAMNEE**

Color Artist **MATTHEW WILSON**

Letterer **VIRTUAL CALLIGRAPHY'S RUS WOOTON**

Cover Artists **CHRIS SAMNEE & MATTHEW WILSON**
WITH CHRISTINA STRAIN (#4)

Assistant Editor **MICHAEL HORWITZ**

Editors **NATHAN COSBY & SANA AMANAT**
WITH MICHAEL HORWITZ (*FREE COMIC BOOK DAY 2011*)

Collection Editor **CORY LEVINE**
Assistant Editors **ALEX STARBUCK & NELSON RIBEIRO**
Editors, Special Projects **JENNIFER GRÜNWALD & MARK D. BEAZLEY**
Senior Editor, Special Projects **JEFF YOUNGQUIST**
SVP of Print & Digital Publishing Sales **DAVID GABRIEL**
Book Design **ARLENE SO**

Editor In Chief **AXEL ALONSO**
Chief Creative Officer **JOE QUESADA**
Publisher **DAN BUCKLEY**
Executive Producer **ALAN FINE**

YA
Graphic
Fic
Thor

(192)

THOR: THE MIGHTY AVENGER — THE COMPLETE COLLECTION. Contains material originally published in magazine form as THOR THE MIGHTY AVENGER #1-8 and FREE COMIC BOOK DAY 2011 (THOR THE MIGHTY AVENGER). First printing 2013. ISBN# 978-0-7851-8381-5. Published by MARVEL WORLDWIDE, INC., a subsidiary of MARVEL ENTERTAINMENT, LLC. OFFICE OF PUBLICATION: 135 West 50th Street, New York, NY 10020. Copyright © 2010, 2011 and 2013 Marvel Characters, Inc. All rights reserved. All characters featured in this issue and the distinctive names and likenesses thereof, and all related indicia are trademarks of Marvel Characters, Inc. No similarity between any of the names, characters, persons, and/or institutions in this magazine with those of any living or dead person or institution is intended, and any such similarity which may exist is purely coincidental. **Printed in the U.S.A.** ALAN FINE, EVP - Office of the President, Marvel Worldwide, Inc. and EVP & CMO Marvel Characters B.V.; DAN BUCKLEY, Publisher & President - Print, Animation & Digital Divisions; JOE QUESADA, Chief Creative Officer; TOM BREVOORT, SVP of Publishing; DAVID BOGART, SVP of Operations & Procurement, Publishing; RUWAN JAYATILLEKE, SVP & Associate Publisher, Publishing; C.B. CEBULSKI, SVP of Creator & Content Development; DAVID GABRIEL, SVP of Print & Digital Publishing Sales; JIM O'KEEFE, VP of Operations & Logistics; DAN CARR, Executive Director of Publishing Technology; SUSAN CRESPI, Editorial Operations Manager; ALEX MORALES, Publishing Operations Manager; STAN LEE, Chairman Emeritus. For information regarding advertising in Marvel Comics or on Marvel.com, please contact Niza Disla, Director of Marvel Partnerships, at ndisla@marvel.com. For Marvel subscription inquiries, please call 800-217-9158. **Manufactured between 12/27/2012 and 1/29/2013 by QUAD/GRAPHICS, DUBUQUE, IA, USA.**

10 9 8 7 6 5 4 3 2 1

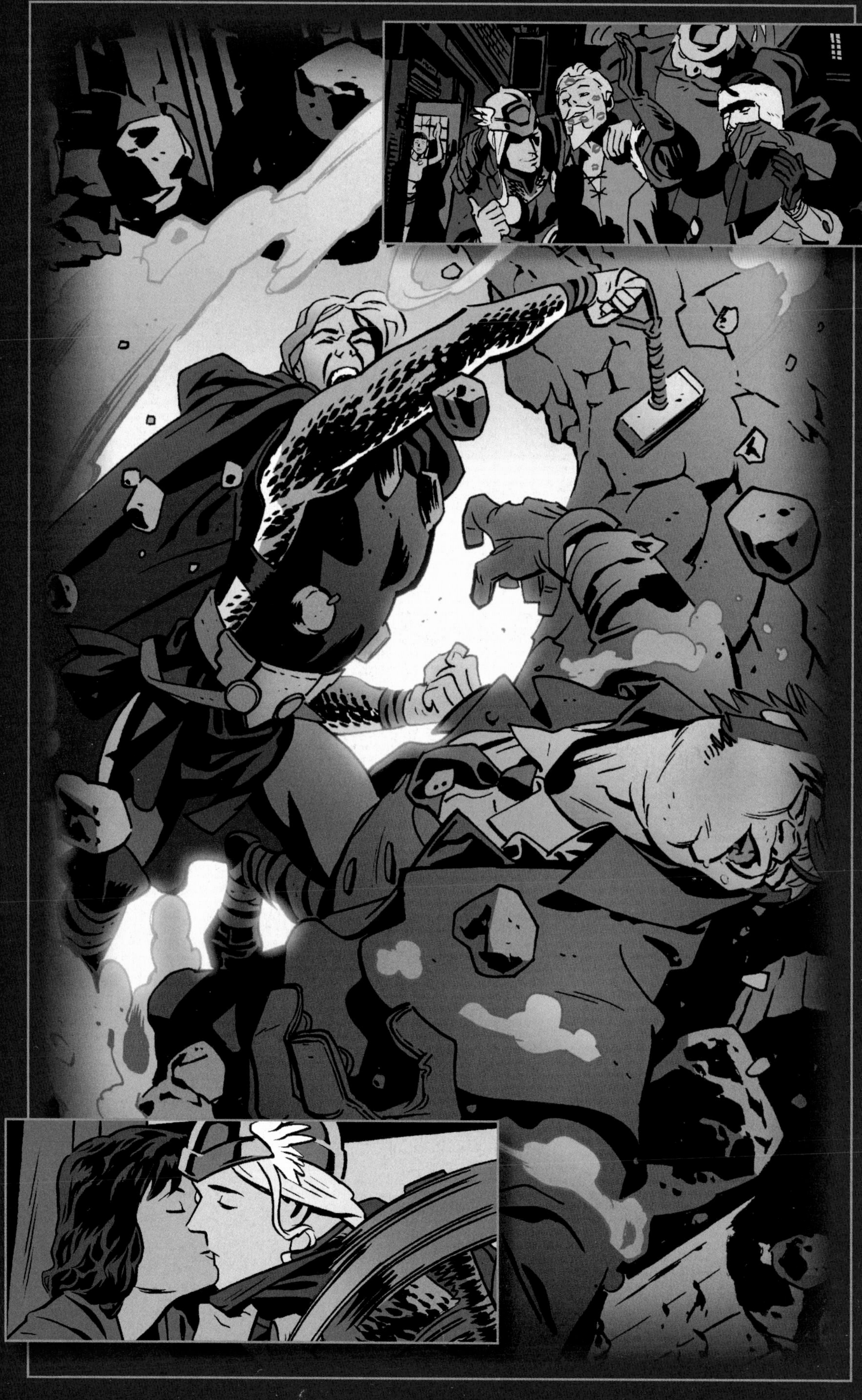

THOR THE MIGHTY AVENGER #1

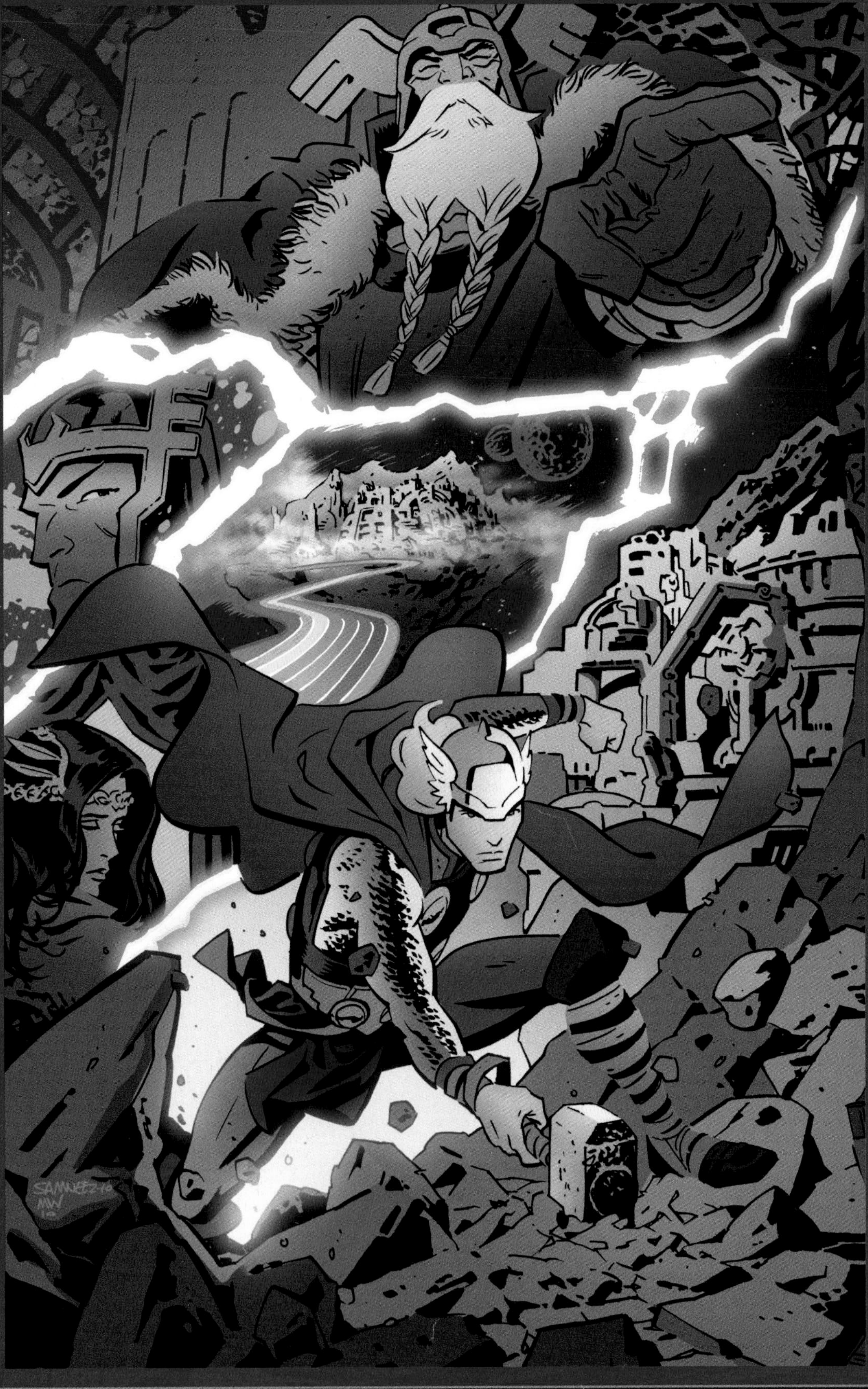

BERGEN, OKLAHOMA. LAST THURSDAY.

RRRRRMMMMBBBBBLLL

KRA-BOOOOOOMMM!

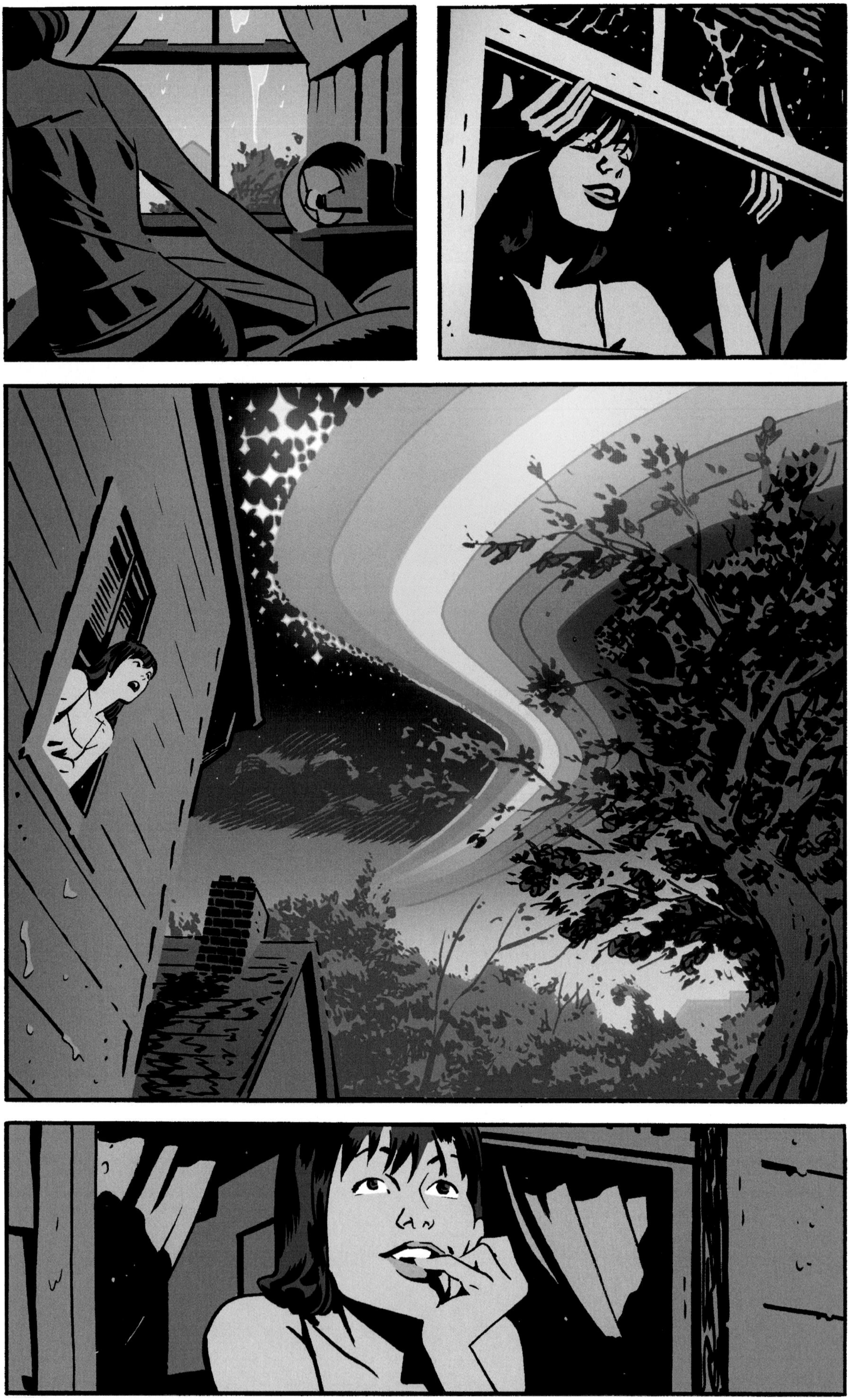

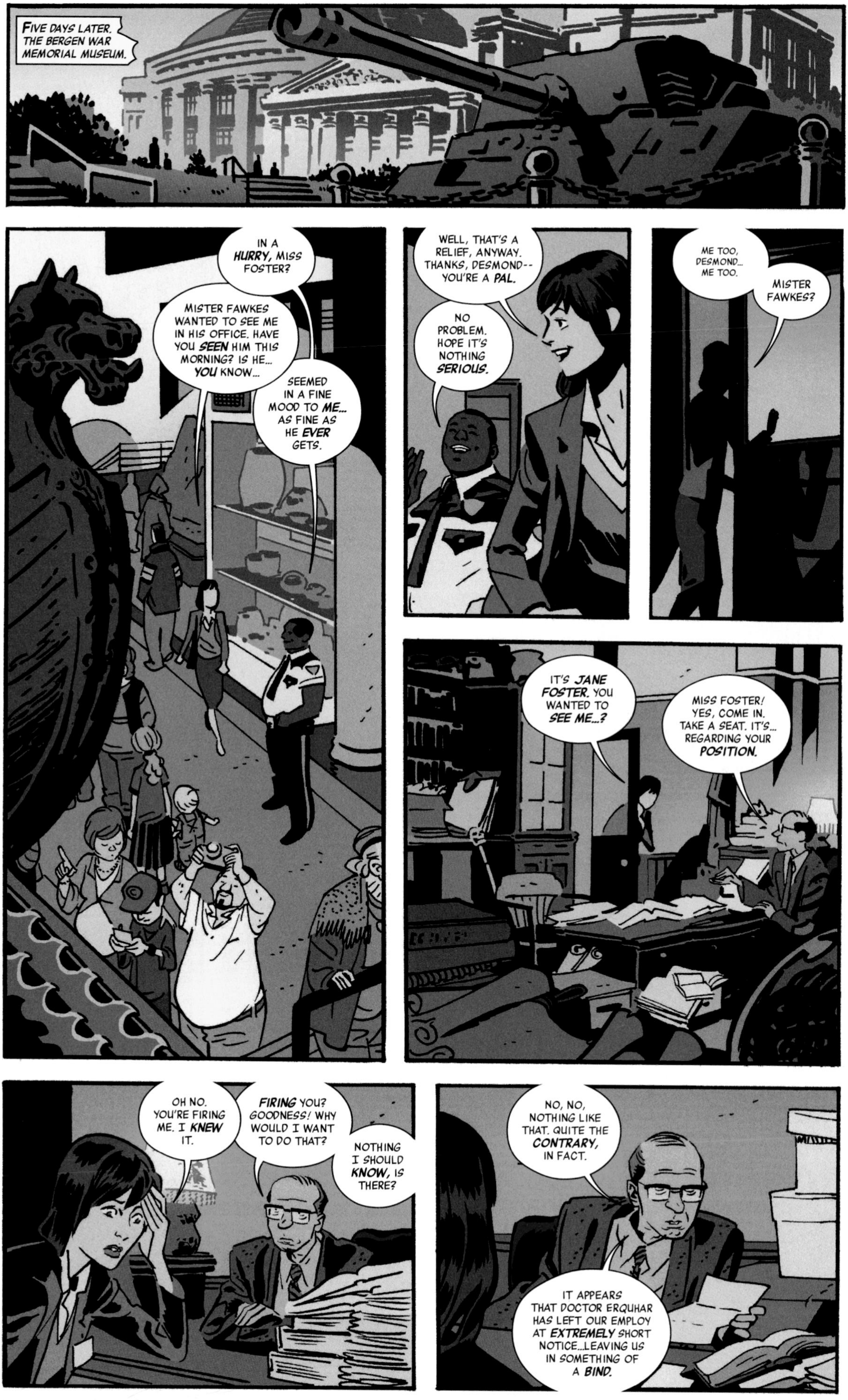

FIVE DAYS LATER. THE BERGEN WAR MEMORIAL MUSEUM.
IN A HURRY, MISS FOSTER?
MISTER FAWKES WANTED TO SEE ME IN HIS OFFICE. HAVE YOU SEEN HIM THIS MORNING? IS HE... YOU KNOW...
SEEMED IN A FINE MOOD TO ME... AS FINE AS HE EVER GETS.
WELL, THAT'S A RELIEF, ANYWAY. THANKS, DESMOND-- YOU'RE A PAL.
NO PROBLEM. HOPE IT'S NOTHING SERIOUS.
ME TOO, DESMOND... ME TOO.
MISTER FAWKES?
IT'S JANE FOSTER. YOU WANTED TO SEE ME...?
MISS FOSTER! YES, COME IN. TAKE A SEAT. IT'S... REGARDING YOUR POSITION.
OH NO. YOU'RE FIRING ME. I KNEW IT.
FIRING YOU? GOODNESS! WHY WOULD I WANT TO DO THAT?
NOTHING I SHOULD KNOW, IS THERE?
NO, NO, NOTHING LIKE THAT. QUITE THE CONTRARY, IN FACT.
IT APPEARS THAT DOCTOR ERQUHAR HAS LEFT OUR EMPLOY AT EXTREMELY SHORT NOTICE...LEAVING US IN SOMETHING OF A BIND.

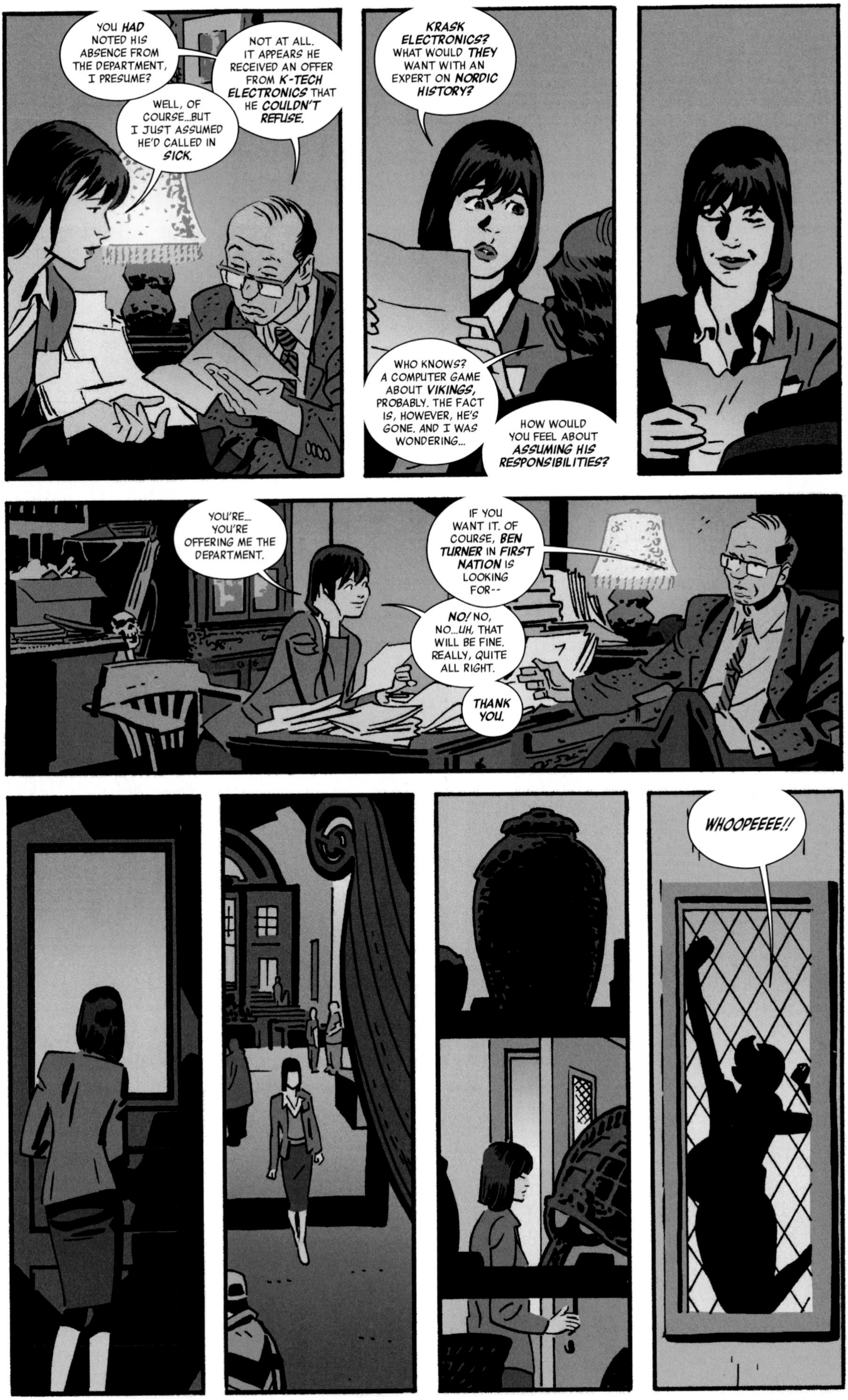
YOU HAD NOTED HIS ABSENCE FROM THE DEPARTMENT, I PRESUME?
NOT AT ALL. IT APPEARS HE RECEIVED AN OFFER FROM K-TECH ELECTRONICS THAT HE COULDN'T REFUSE.
WELL, OF COURSE...BUT I JUST ASSUMED HE'D CALLED IN SICK.
KRASK ELECTRONICS? WHAT WOULD THEY WANT WITH AN EXPERT ON NORDIC HISTORY?
WHO KNOWS? A COMPUTER GAME ABOUT VIKINGS, PROBABLY. THE FACT IS, HOWEVER, HE'S GONE. AND I WAS WONDERING...
HOW WOULD YOU FEEL ABOUT ASSUMING HIS RESPONSIBILITIES?
YOU'RE... YOU'RE OFFERING ME THE DEPARTMENT.
IF YOU WANT IT. OF COURSE, BEN TURNER IN FIRST NATION IS LOOKING FOR--
NO! NO, NO...UH, THAT WILL BE FINE. REALLY, QUITE ALL RIGHT.
THANK YOU.
WHOOPEEEE!!

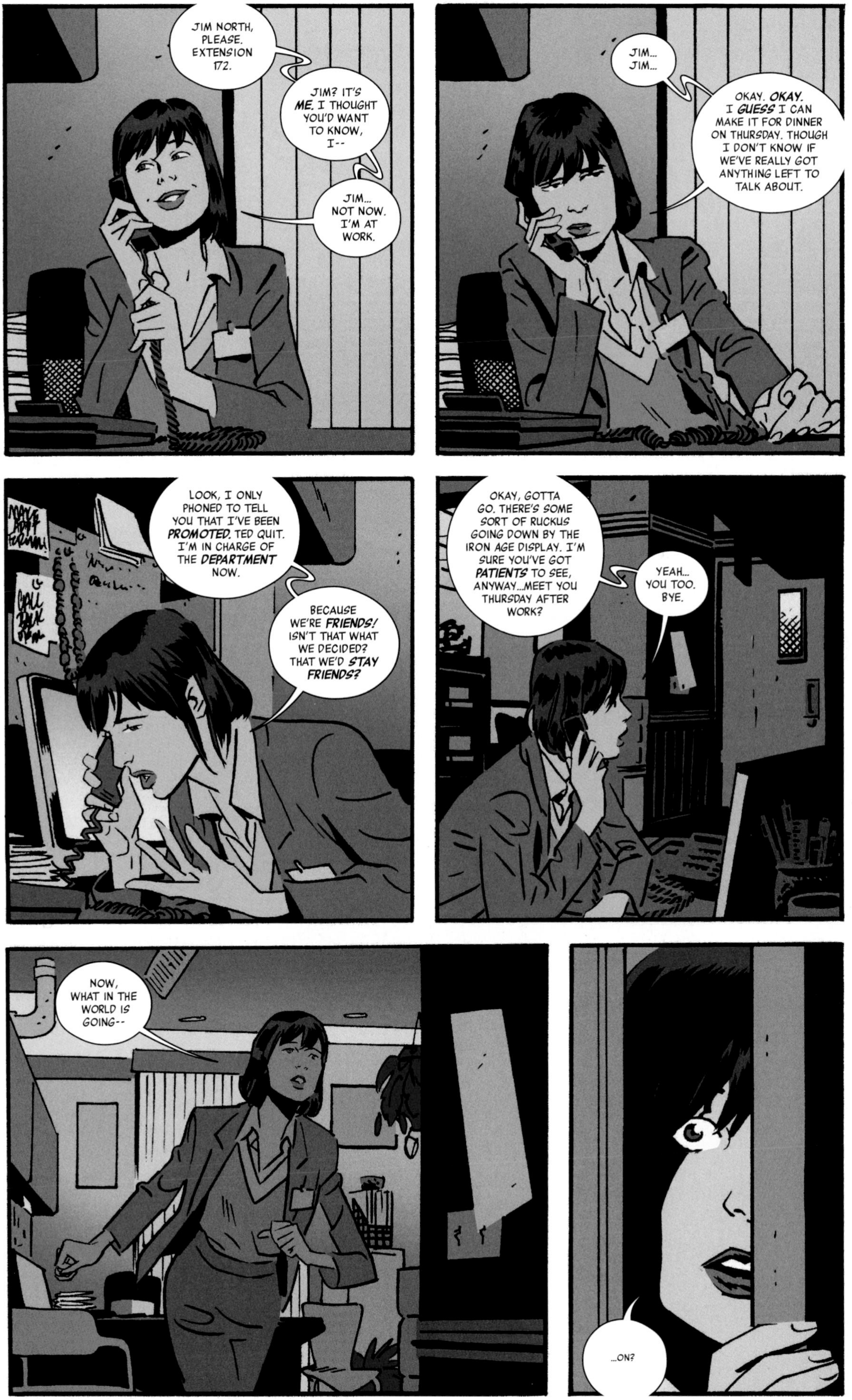
JIM NORTH, PLEASE. EXTENSION 172.
JIM? IT'S ME. I THOUGHT YOU'D WANT TO KNOW, I--
JIM... NOT NOW. I'M AT WORK.
JIM... JIM...
OKAY. OKAY. I GUESS I CAN MAKE IT FOR DINNER ON THURSDAY. THOUGH I DON'T KNOW IF WE'VE REALLY GOT ANYTHING LEFT TO TALK ABOUT.
LOOK, I ONLY PHONED TO TELL YOU THAT I'VE BEEN PROMOTED. TED QUIT. I'M IN CHARGE OF THE DEPARTMENT NOW.
BECAUSE WE'RE FRIENDS! ISN'T THAT WHAT WE DECIDED? THAT WE'D STAY FRIENDS?
OKAY, GOTTA GO. THERE'S SOME SORT OF RUCKUS GOING DOWN BY THE IRON AGE DISPLAY. I'M SURE YOU'VE GOT PATIENTS TO SEE, ANYWAY...MEET YOU THURSDAY AFTER WORK?
YEAH... YOU TOO. BYE.
NOW, WHAT IN THE WORLD IS GOING--
...ON?

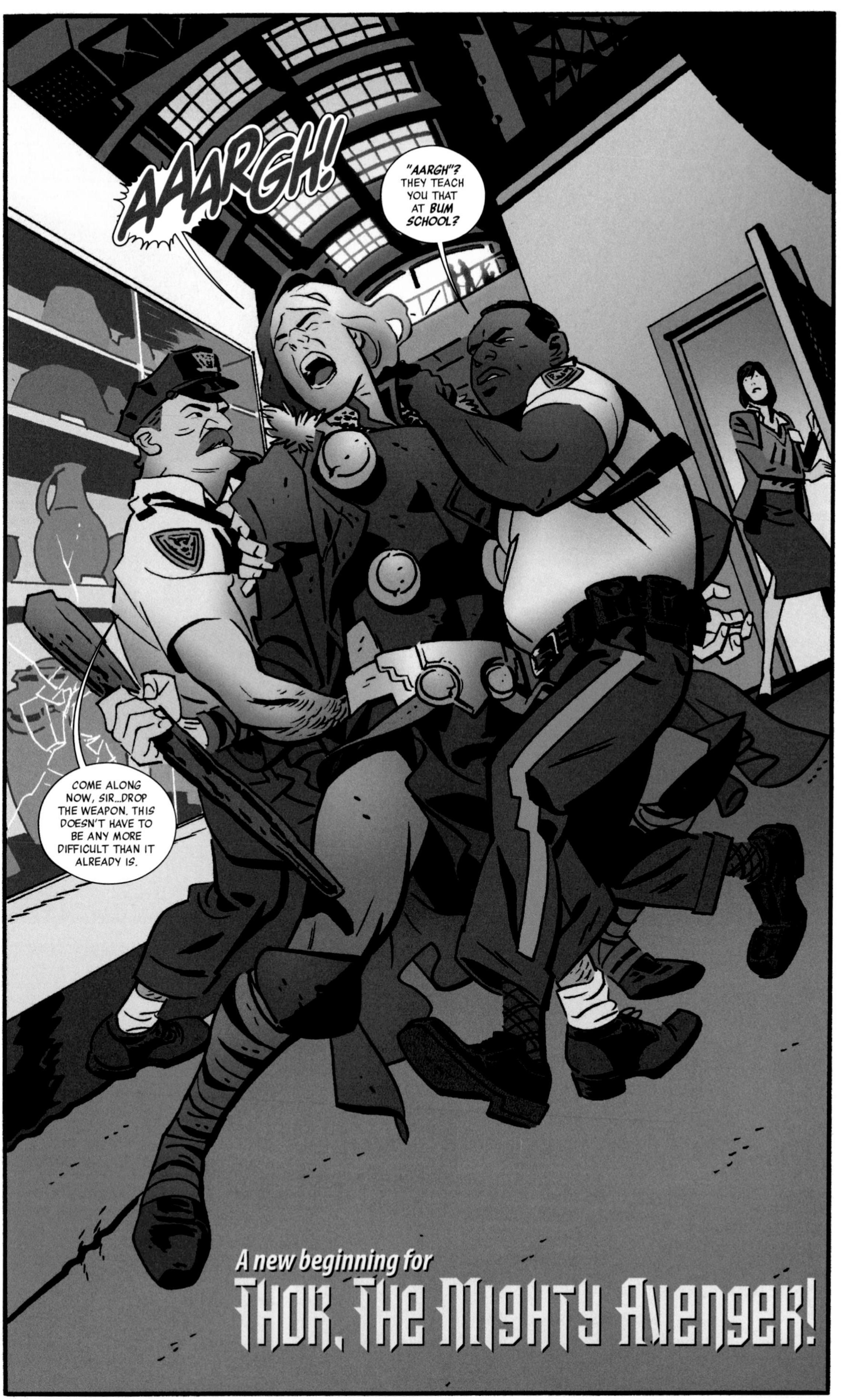
AAARGH!
"AARGH"? THEY TEACH YOU THAT AT BUM SCHOOL?
COME ALONG NOW, SIR...DROP THE WEAPON. THIS DOESN'T HAVE TO BE ANY MORE DIFFICULT THAN IT ALREADY IS.
A new beginning for
THOR, THE MIGHTY AVENGER!

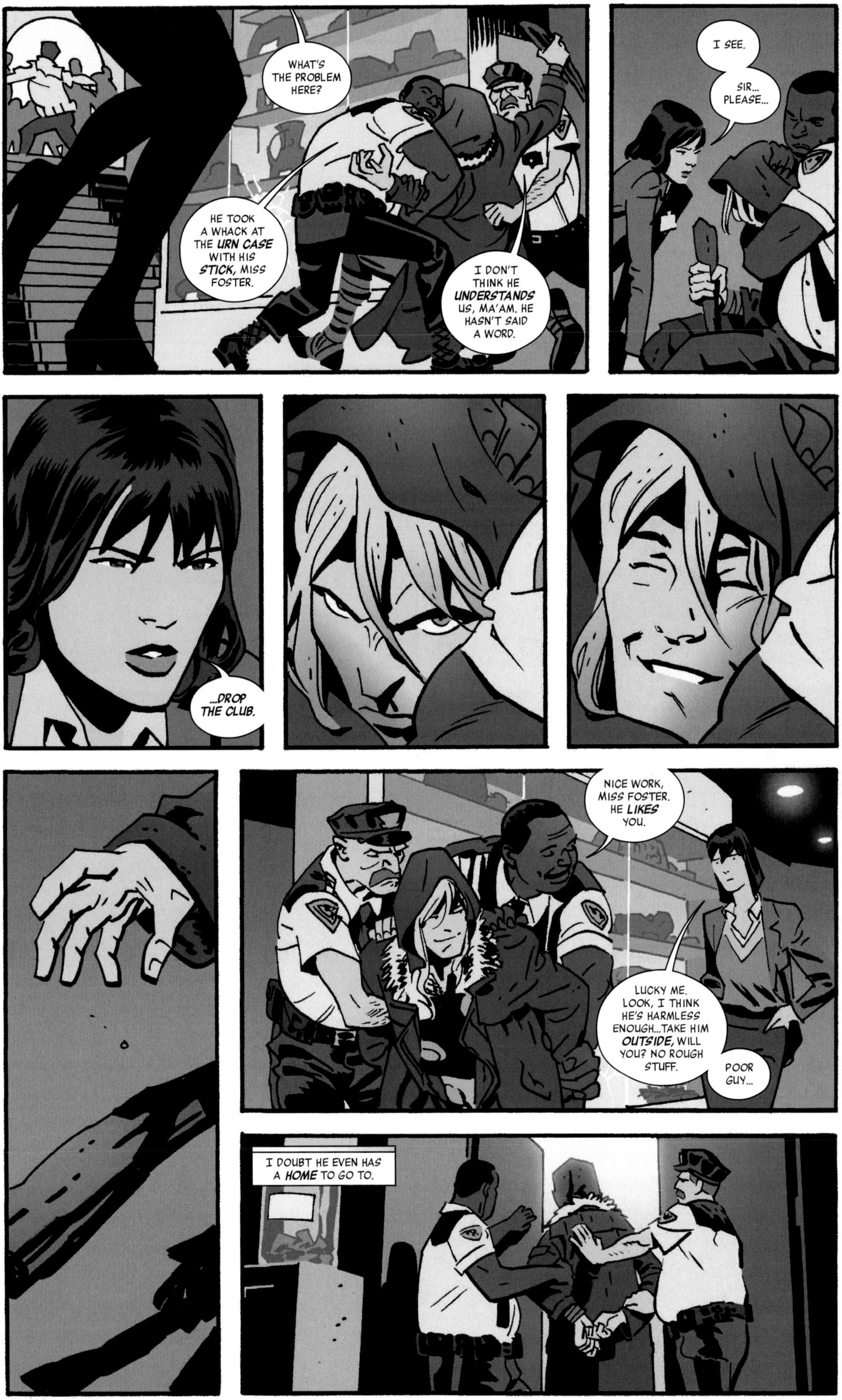

WHAT'S THE PROBLEM HERE?
HE TOOK A WHACK AT THE URN CASE WITH HIS STICK, MISS FOSTER.
I DON'T THINK HE UNDERSTANDS US, MA'AM. HE HASN'T SAID A WORD.
I SEE.
SIR... PLEASE...
...DROP THE CLUB.
NICE WORK, MISS FOSTER. HE LIKES YOU.
LUCKY ME. LOOK, I THINK HE'S HARMLESS ENOUGH...TAKE HIM OUTSIDE, WILL YOU? NO ROUGH STUFF.
POOR GUY...
I DOUBT HE EVEN HAS A HOME TO GO TO.

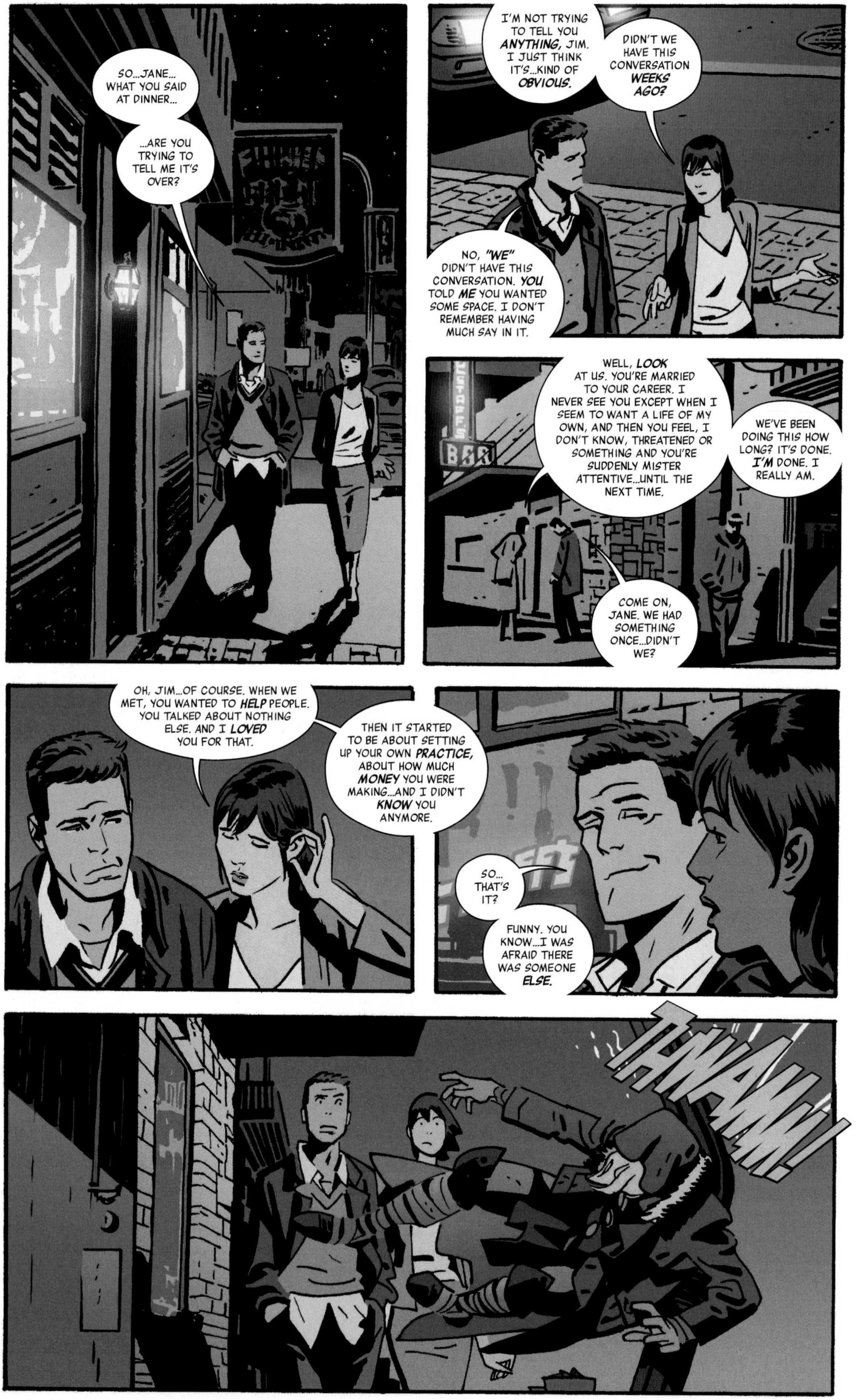
SO...JANE... WHAT YOU SAID AT DINNER...
...ARE YOU TRYING TO TELL ME IT'S OVER?
I'M NOT TRYING TO TELL YOU ANYTHING, JIM. I JUST THINK IT'S...KIND OF OBVIOUS.
DIDN'T WE HAVE THIS CONVERSATION WEEKS AGO?
NO, "WE" DIDN'T HAVE THIS CONVERSATION. YOU TOLD ME YOU WANTED SOME SPACE. I DON'T REMEMBER HAVING MUCH SAY IN IT.
BAR
WELL, LOOK AT US. YOU'RE MARRIED TO YOUR CAREER. I NEVER SEE YOU EXCEPT WHEN I SEEM TO WANT A LIFE OF MY OWN, AND THEN YOU FEEL, I DON'T KNOW, THREATENED OR SOMETHING AND YOU'RE SUDDENLY MISTER ATTENTIVE...UNTIL THE NEXT TIME.
WE'VE BEEN DOING THIS HOW LONG? IT'S DONE. I'M DONE. I REALLY AM.
COME ON, JANE. WE HAD SOMETHING ONCE...DIDN'T WE?
OH, JIM...OF COURSE. WHEN WE MET, YOU WANTED TO HELP PEOPLE. YOU TALKED ABOUT NOTHING ELSE. AND I LOVED YOU FOR THAT.
THEN IT STARTED TO BE ABOUT SETTING UP YOUR OWN PRACTICE, ABOUT HOW MUCH MONEY YOU WERE MAKING...AND I DIDN'T KNOW YOU ANYMORE.
SO... THAT'S IT?
FUNNY. YOU KNOW...I WAS AFRAID THERE WAS SOMEONE ELSE.
THWAMM!

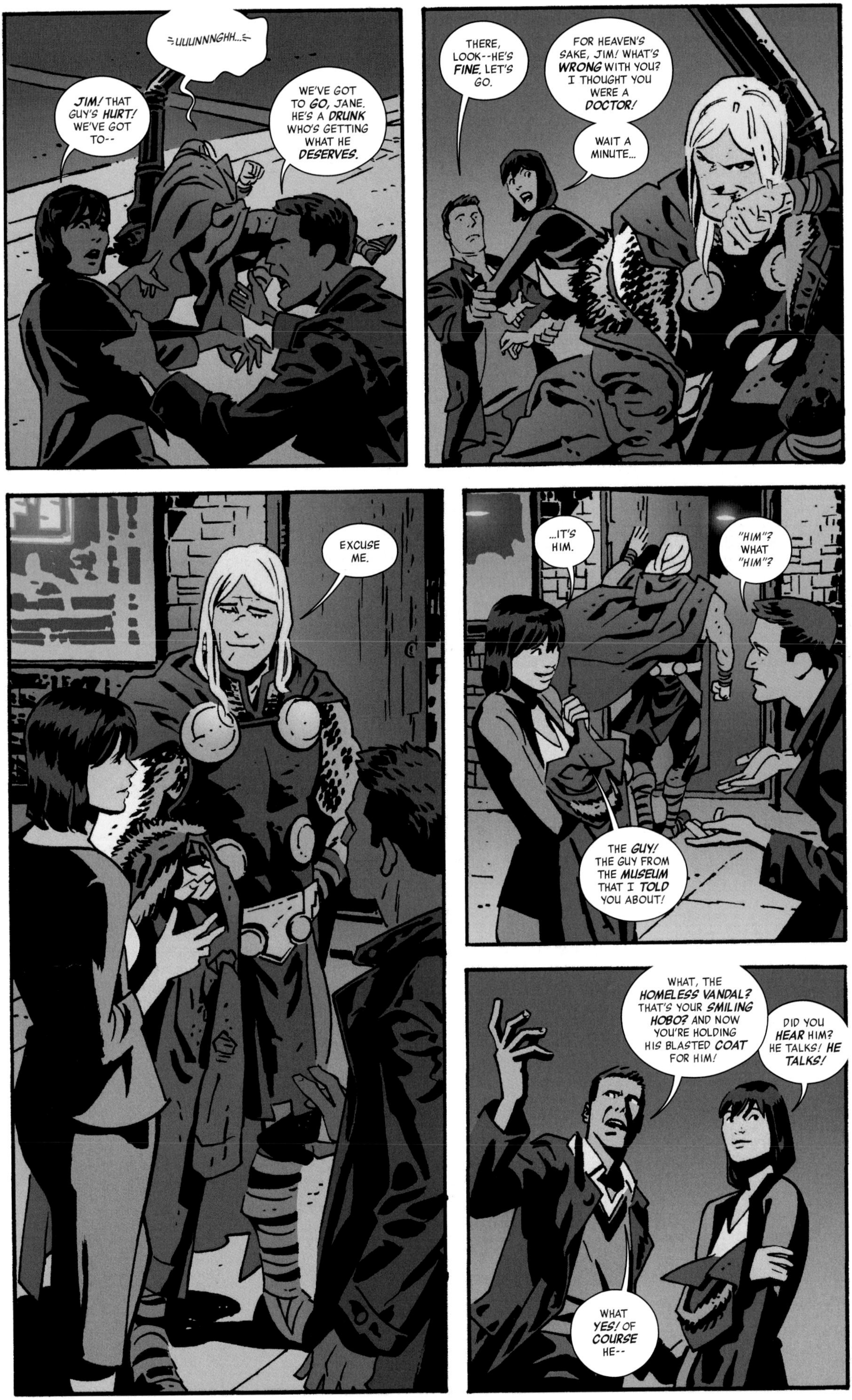

≈UUUNNNGHH...≈
JIM! THAT GUY'S HURT! WE'VE GOT TO--
WE'VE GOT TO GO, JANE. HE'S A DRUNK WHO'S GETTING WHAT HE DESERVES.
THERE, LOOK--HE'S FINE. LET'S GO.
FOR HEAVEN'S SAKE, JIM! WHAT'S WRONG WITH YOU? I THOUGHT YOU WERE A DOCTOR!
WAIT A MINUTE...
EXCUSE ME.
...IT'S HIM.
"HIM"? WHAT "HIM"?
THE GUY! THE GUY FROM THE MUSEUM THAT I TOLD YOU ABOUT!
WHAT, THE HOMELESS VANDAL? THAT'S YOUR SMILING HOBO? AND NOW YOU'RE HOLDING HIS BLASTED COAT FOR HIM!
DID YOU HEAR HIM? HE TALKS! HE TALKS!
WHAT YES! OF COURSE HE--

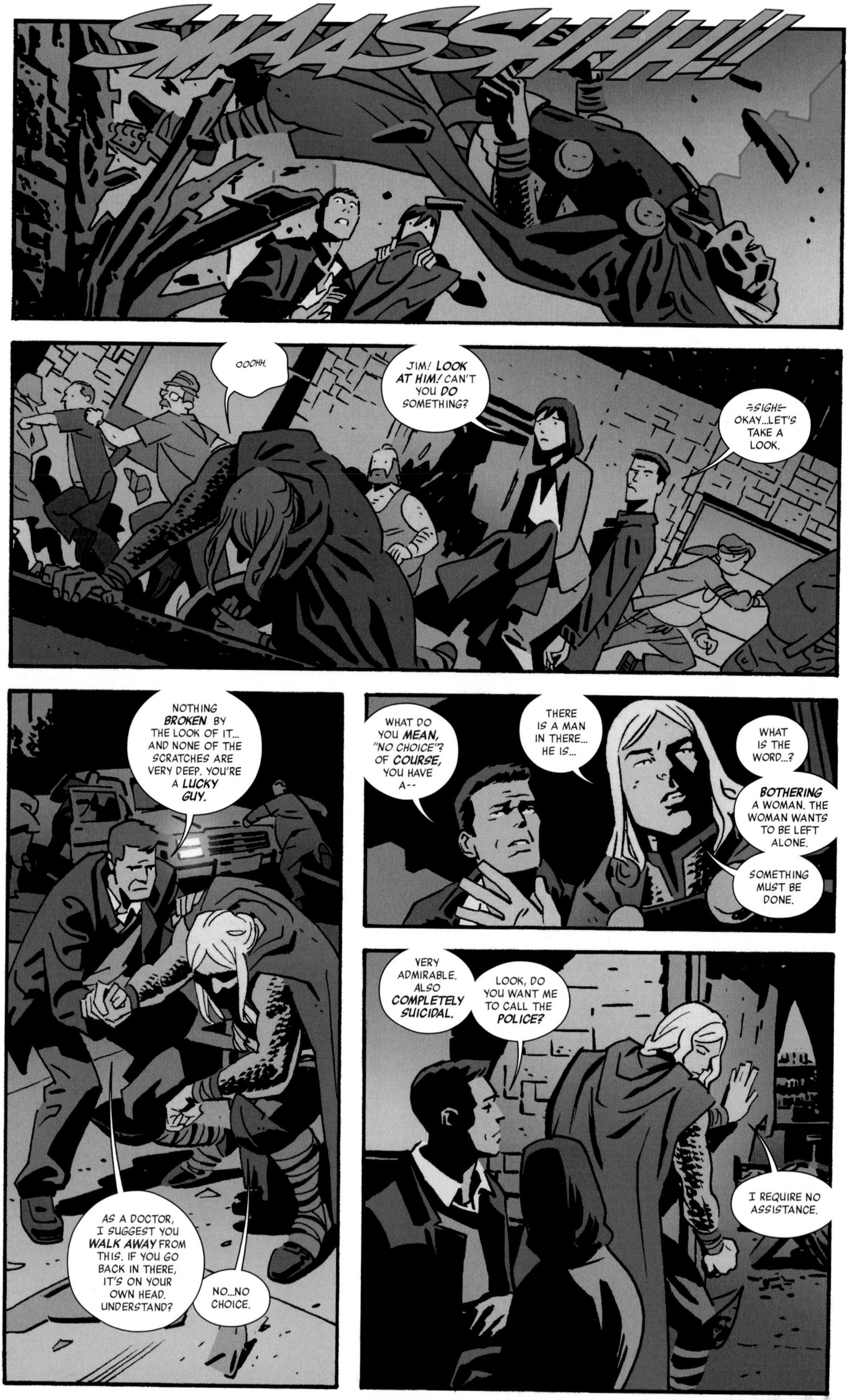
SWAASSHHH!!!
OOOHH.
JIM! LOOK AT HIM! CAN'T YOU DO SOMETHING?
=SIGH= OKAY...LET'S TAKE A LOOK.
NOTHING BROKEN BY THE LOOK OF IT... AND NONE OF THE SCRATCHES ARE VERY DEEP. YOU'RE A LUCKY GUY.
AS A DOCTOR, I SUGGEST YOU WALK AWAY FROM THIS. IF YOU GO BACK IN THERE, IT'S ON YOUR OWN HEAD. UNDERSTAND?
NO...NO CHOICE.
WHAT DO YOU MEAN, "NO CHOICE"? OF COURSE, YOU HAVE A--
THERE IS A MAN IN THERE... HE IS...
WHAT IS THE WORD...?
BOTHERING A WOMAN. THE WOMAN WANTS TO BE LEFT ALONE.
SOMETHING MUST BE DONE.
VERY ADMIRABLE. ALSO COMPLETELY SUICIDAL.
LOOK, DO YOU WANT ME TO CALL THE POLICE?
I REQUIRE NO ASSISTANCE.

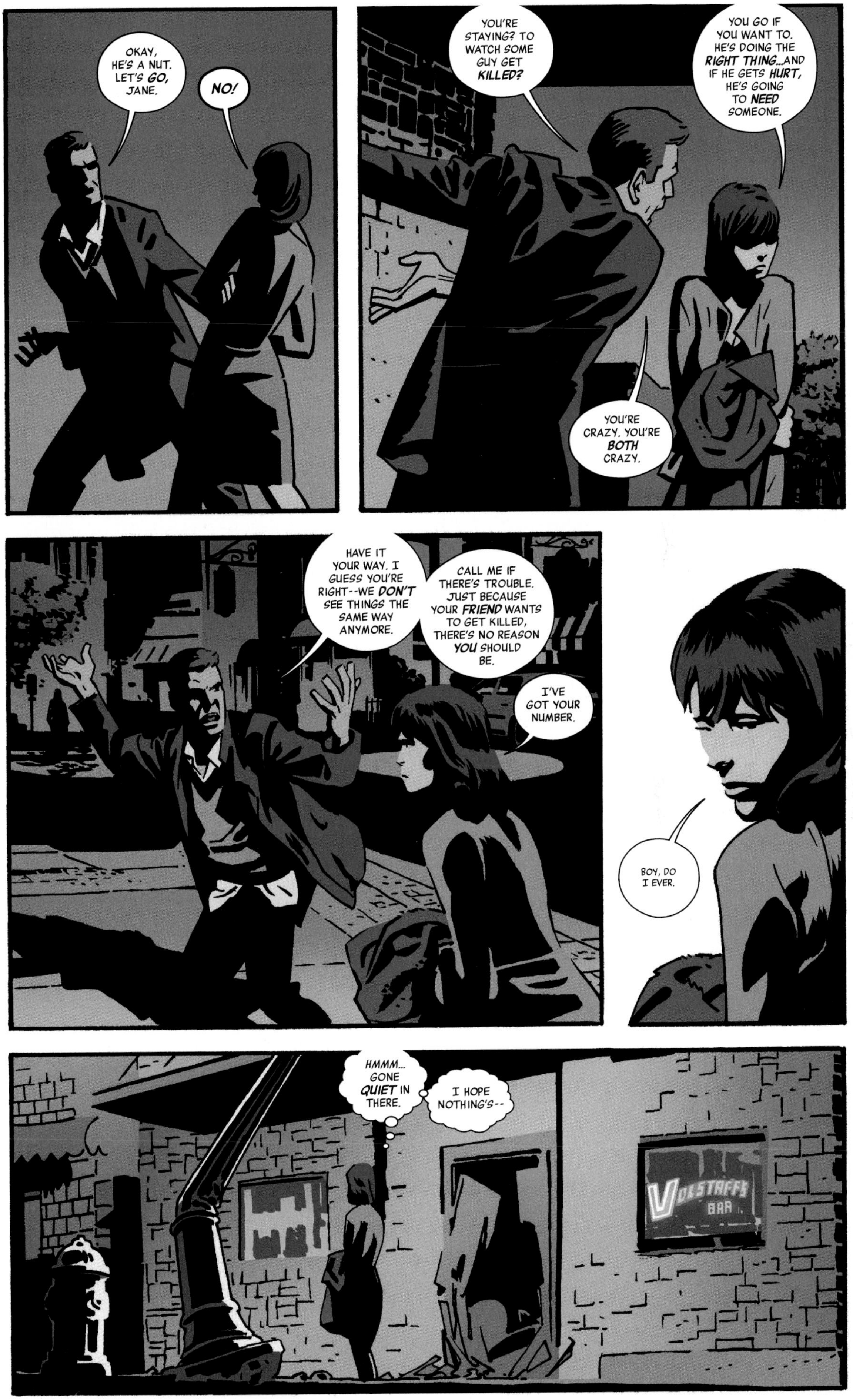
OKAY, HE'S A NUT. LET'S GO, JANE.
NO!
YOU'RE STAYING? TO WATCH SOME GUY GET KILLED?
YOU GO IF YOU WANT TO. HE'S DOING THE RIGHT THING...AND IF HE GETS HURT, HE'S GOING TO NEED SOMEONE.
YOU'RE CRAZY. YOU'RE BOTH CRAZY.
HAVE IT YOUR WAY. I GUESS YOU'RE RIGHT--WE DON'T SEE THINGS THE SAME WAY ANYMORE.
CALL ME IF THERE'S TROUBLE. JUST BECAUSE YOUR FRIEND WANTS TO GET KILLED, THERE'S NO REASON YOU SHOULD BE.
I'VE GOT YOUR NUMBER.
BOY, DO I EVER.
HMMM... GONE QUIET IN THERE.
I HOPE NOTHING'S--
VOLSTAFFS BAR

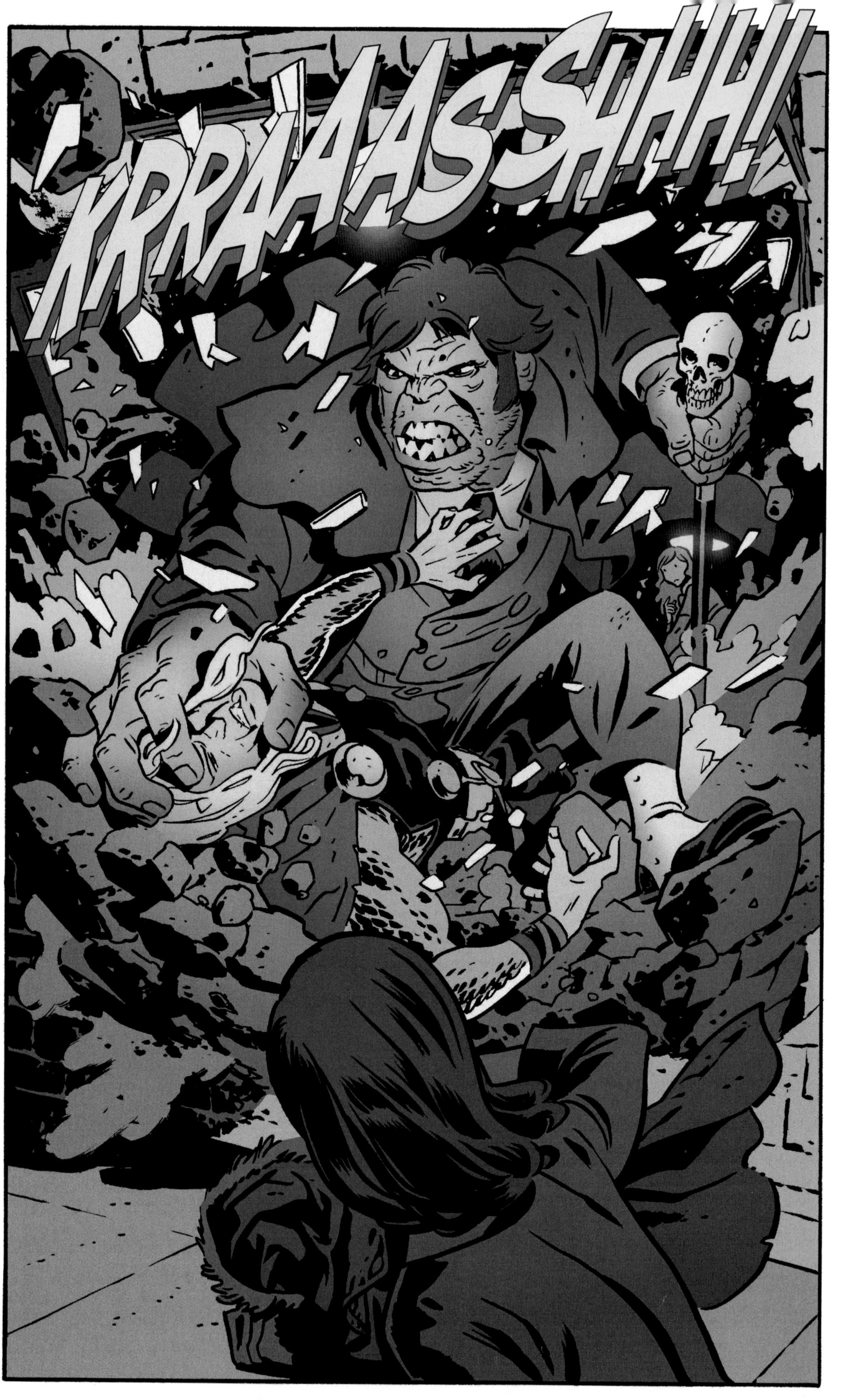
KRRAAAASSHHH!!

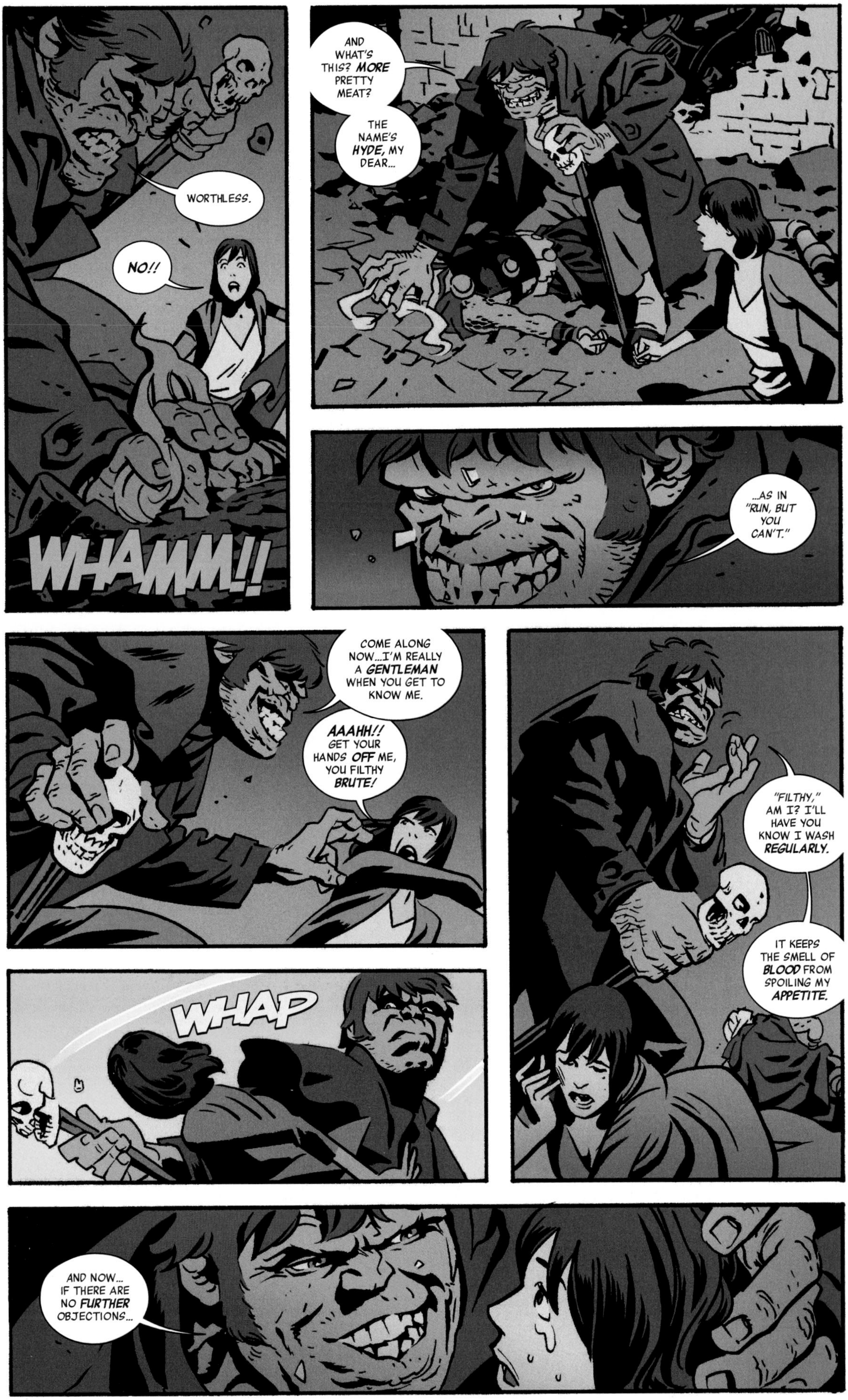
WORTHLESS.
NO!!
WHAMM!!
AND WHAT'S THIS? MORE PRETTY MEAT?
THE NAME'S HYDE, MY DEAR...
...AS IN "RUN, BUT YOU CAN'T."
COME ALONG NOW...I'M REALLY A GENTLEMAN WHEN YOU GET TO KNOW ME.
AAAHH!! GET YOUR HANDS OFF ME, YOU FILTHY BRUTE!
WHAP
"FILTHY," AM I? I'LL HAVE YOU KNOW I WASH REGULARLY.
IT KEEPS THE SMELL OF BLOOD FROM SPOILING MY APPETITE.
AND NOW... IF THERE ARE NO FURTHER OBJECTIONS...

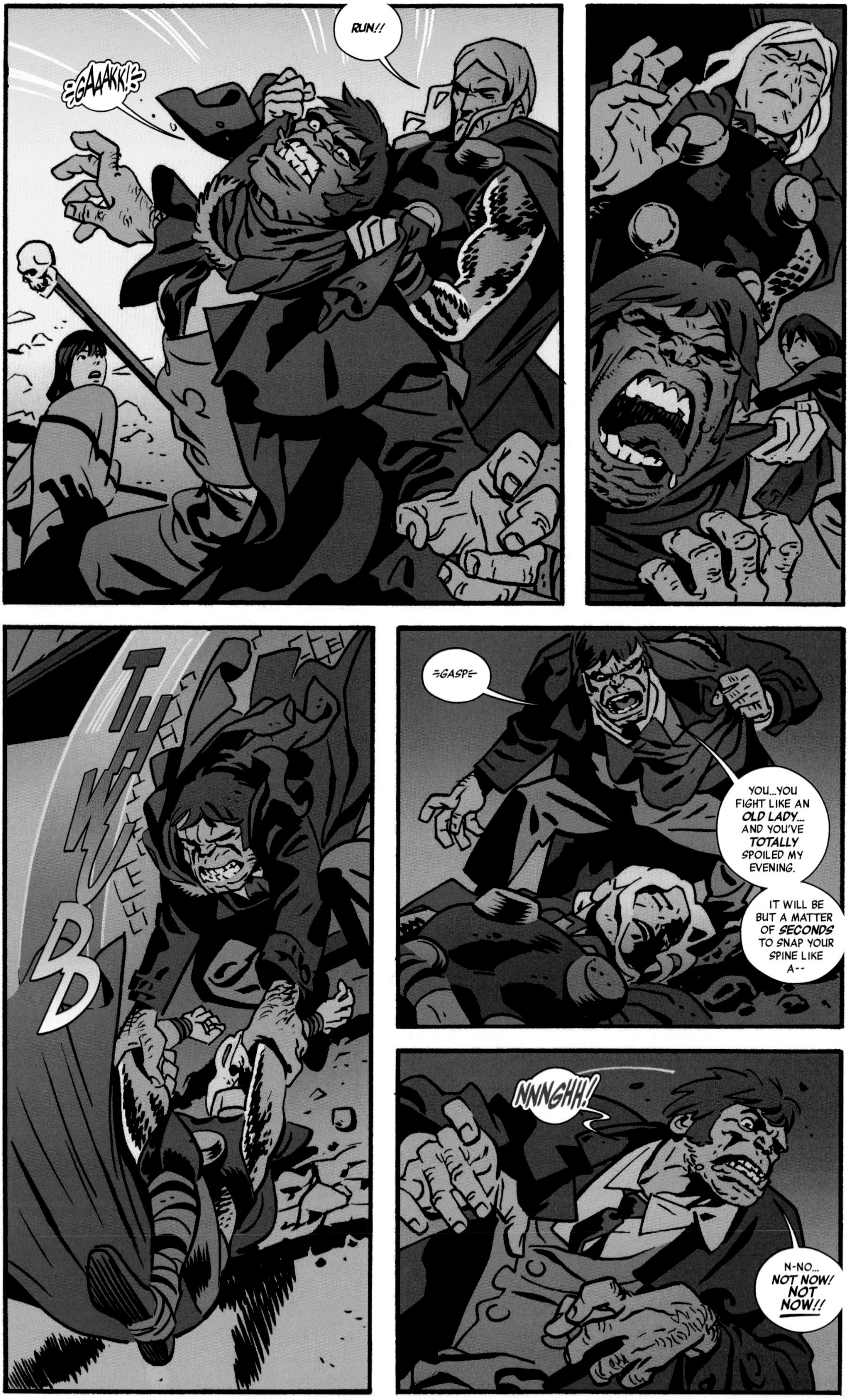
RUN!!
GAAAKK!
THWUBB
GASP
YOU...YOU FIGHT LIKE AN OLD LADY... AND YOU'VE TOTALLY SPOILED MY EVENING.
IT WILL BE BUT A MATTER OF SECONDS TO SNAP YOUR SPINE LIKE A--
NNNGHH!
N-NO... NOT NOW! NOT NOW!!

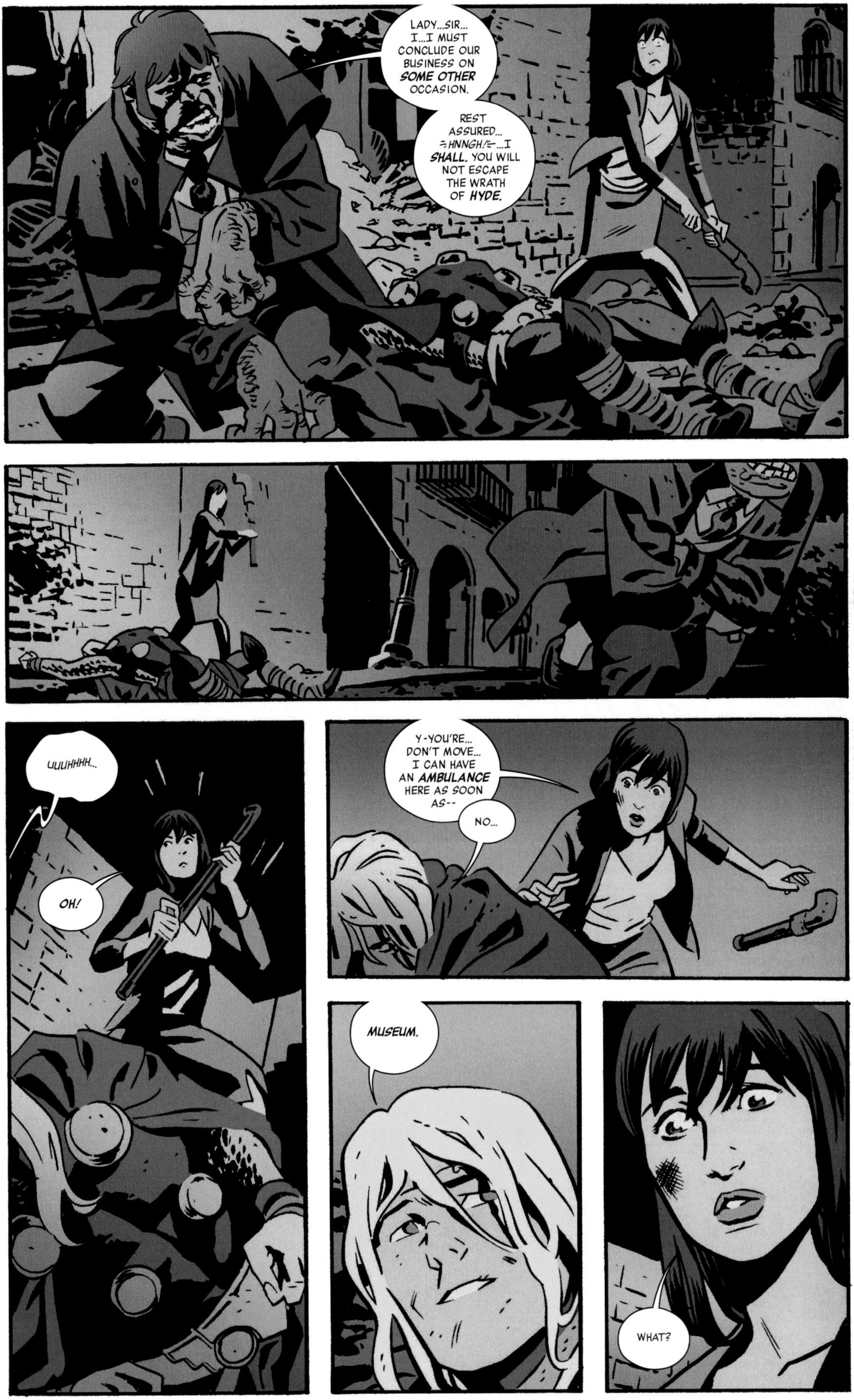
LADY...SIR... I...I MUST CONCLUDE OUR BUSINESS ON SOME OTHER OCCASION.
REST ASSURED... =HNNGH!= ...I SHALL. YOU WILL NOT ESCAPE THE WRATH OF HYDE.
UUUHHHH...
OH!
Y-YOU'RE... DON'T MOVE... I CAN HAVE AN AMBULANCE HERE AS SOON AS--
NO...
MUSEUM.
WHAT?

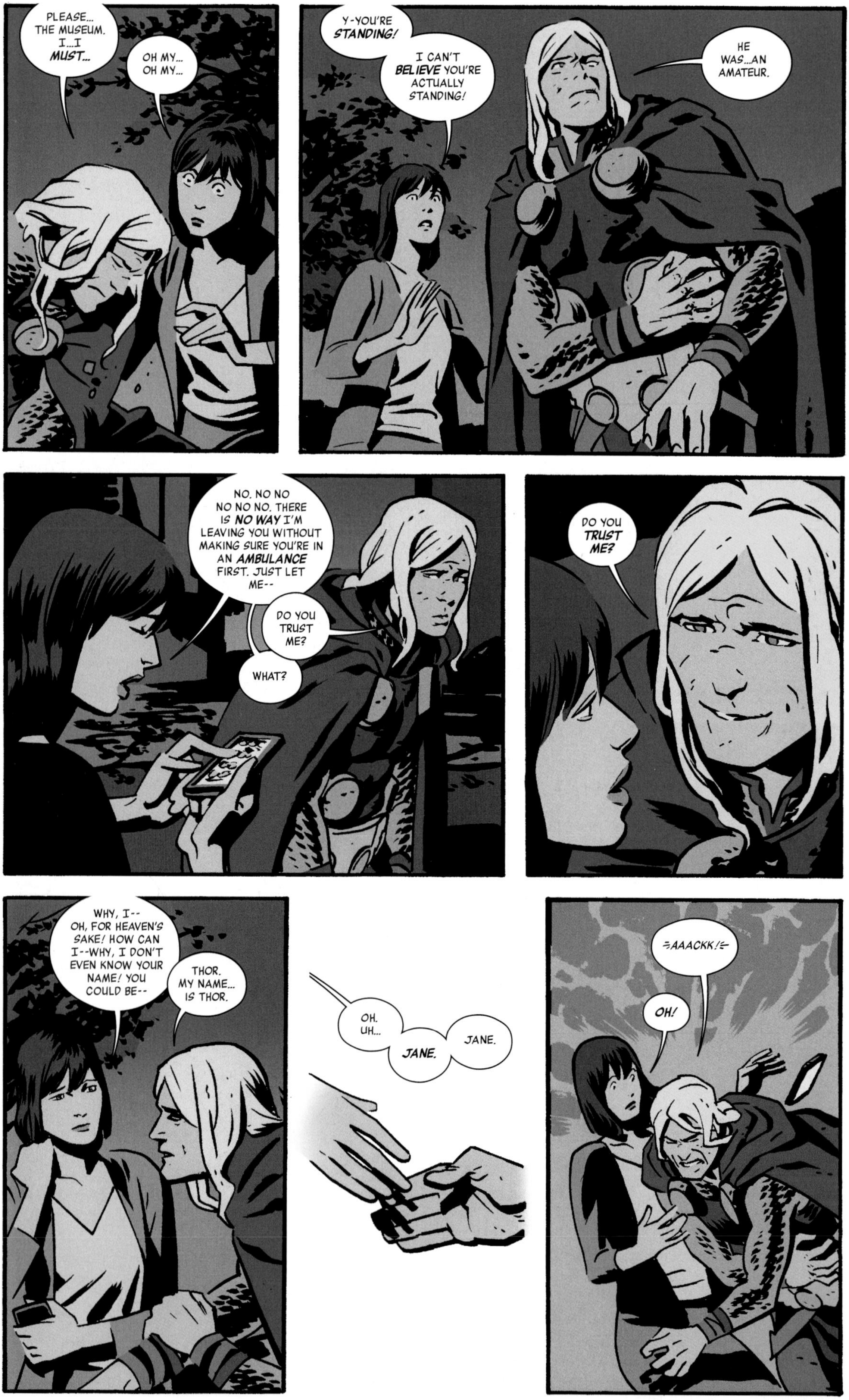
PLEASE... THE MUSEUM. I...I MUST...
OH MY... OH MY...
Y-YOU'RE STANDING!
I CAN'T BELIEVE YOU'RE ACTUALLY STANDING!
HE WAS...AN AMATEUR.
NO. NO NO NO NO NO. THERE IS NO WAY I'M LEAVING YOU WITHOUT MAKING SURE YOU'RE IN AN AMBULANCE FIRST. JUST LET ME--
DO YOU TRUST ME?
WHAT?
DO YOU TRUST ME?
WHY, I-- OH, FOR HEAVEN'S SAKE! HOW CAN I--WHY, I DON'T EVEN KNOW YOUR NAME! YOU COULD BE--
THOR. MY NAME... IS THOR.
OH. UH...
JANE.
JANE.
AAACKK!
OH!

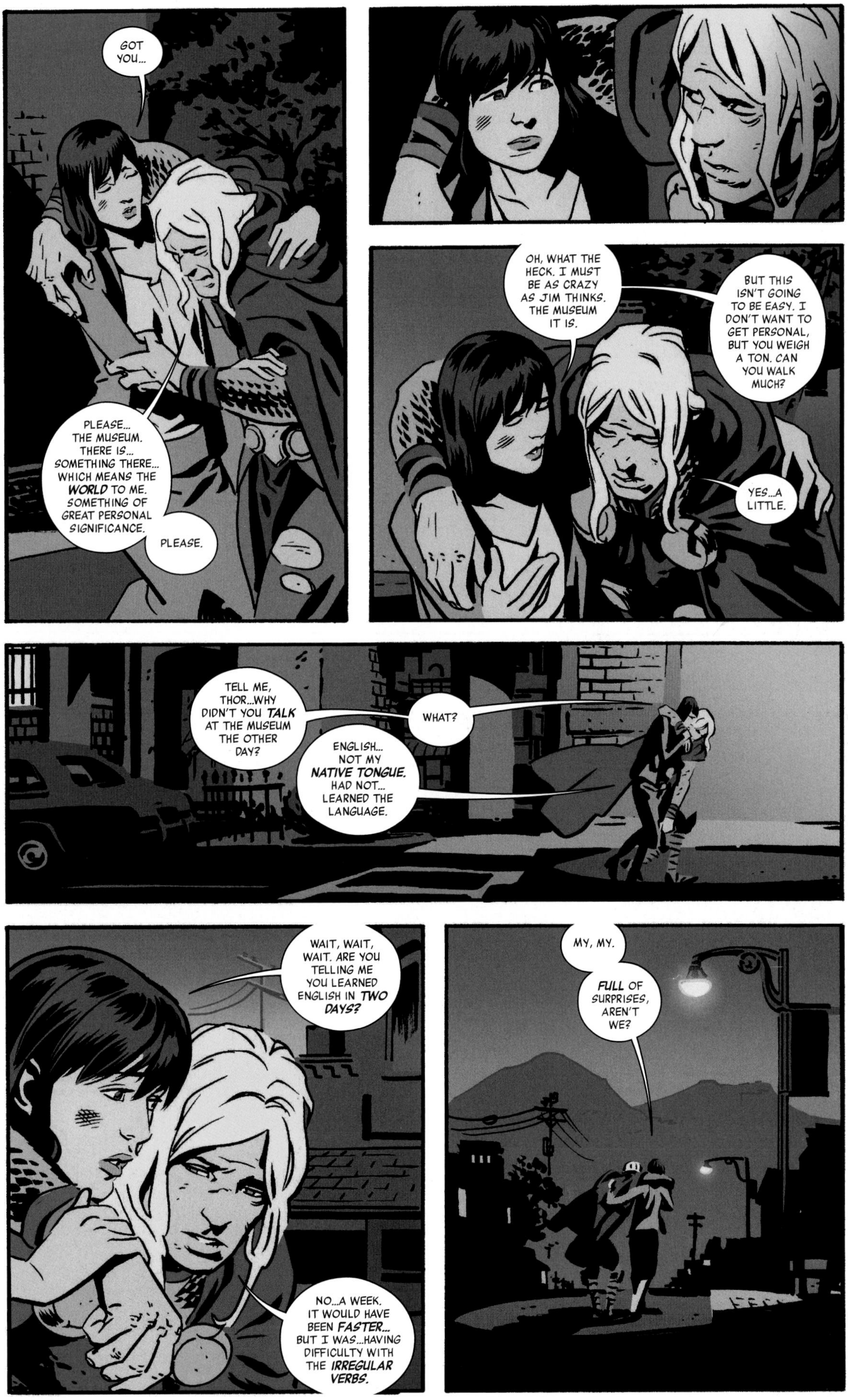
GOT YOU...
PLEASE... THE MUSEUM. THERE IS... SOMETHING THERE... WHICH MEANS THE WORLD TO ME. SOMETHING OF GREAT PERSONAL SIGNIFICANCE.
PLEASE.
OH, WHAT THE HECK. I MUST BE AS CRAZY AS JIM THINKS. THE MUSEUM IT IS.
BUT THIS ISN'T GOING TO BE EASY. I DON'T WANT TO GET PERSONAL, BUT YOU WEIGH A TON. CAN YOU WALK MUCH?
YES...A LITTLE.
TELL ME, THOR...WHY DIDN'T YOU TALK AT THE MUSEUM THE OTHER DAY?
WHAT?
ENGLISH... NOT MY NATIVE TONGUE. HAD NOT... LEARNED THE LANGUAGE.
WAIT, WAIT, WAIT. ARE YOU TELLING ME YOU LEARNED ENGLISH IN TWO DAYS?
NO...A WEEK. IT WOULD HAVE BEEN FASTER... BUT I WAS...HAVING DIFFICULTY WITH THE IRREGULAR VERBS.
MY, MY.
FULL OF SURPRISES, AREN'T WE?

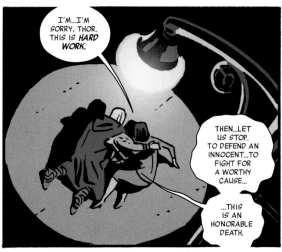

I'M...I'M SORRY, THOR. THIS IS *HARD WORK*.

THEN...LET US *STOP*. TO DEFEND AN *INNOCENT*...TO FIGHT FOR A *WORTHY CAUSE*...

...THIS IS AN *HONORABLE DEATH*.

DEATH? YOU'RE *DYING?*

I... FEAR AS MUCH.

AND THE MUSEUM...THAT'S, WHAT, YOUR *FINAL WISH?*

IT CONTAINS... RELICS. MY *HERITAGE*. BUT IT...MATTERS NOT. NOT ANYMORE.

THANK YOU, JANE... FOR YOUR *KINDNESS*.

NO! NO, SIR-- YOU'RE NOT GETTING OFF *THAT* EASILY! GET UP! *GET UP!* WE'LL GET YOU THERE IF IT *KILLS* ME!

NNNNGHH! COME *ON!* COME ON, YOU BIG *LUMP!* COME OOONNN!!

NOW WHAT...?

GET IN AND BRING YOUR FRIEND.

J-JIM?

YOU DIDN'T *REALLY* THINK I WAS GOING TO LEAVE YOU BEHIND, DID YOU?

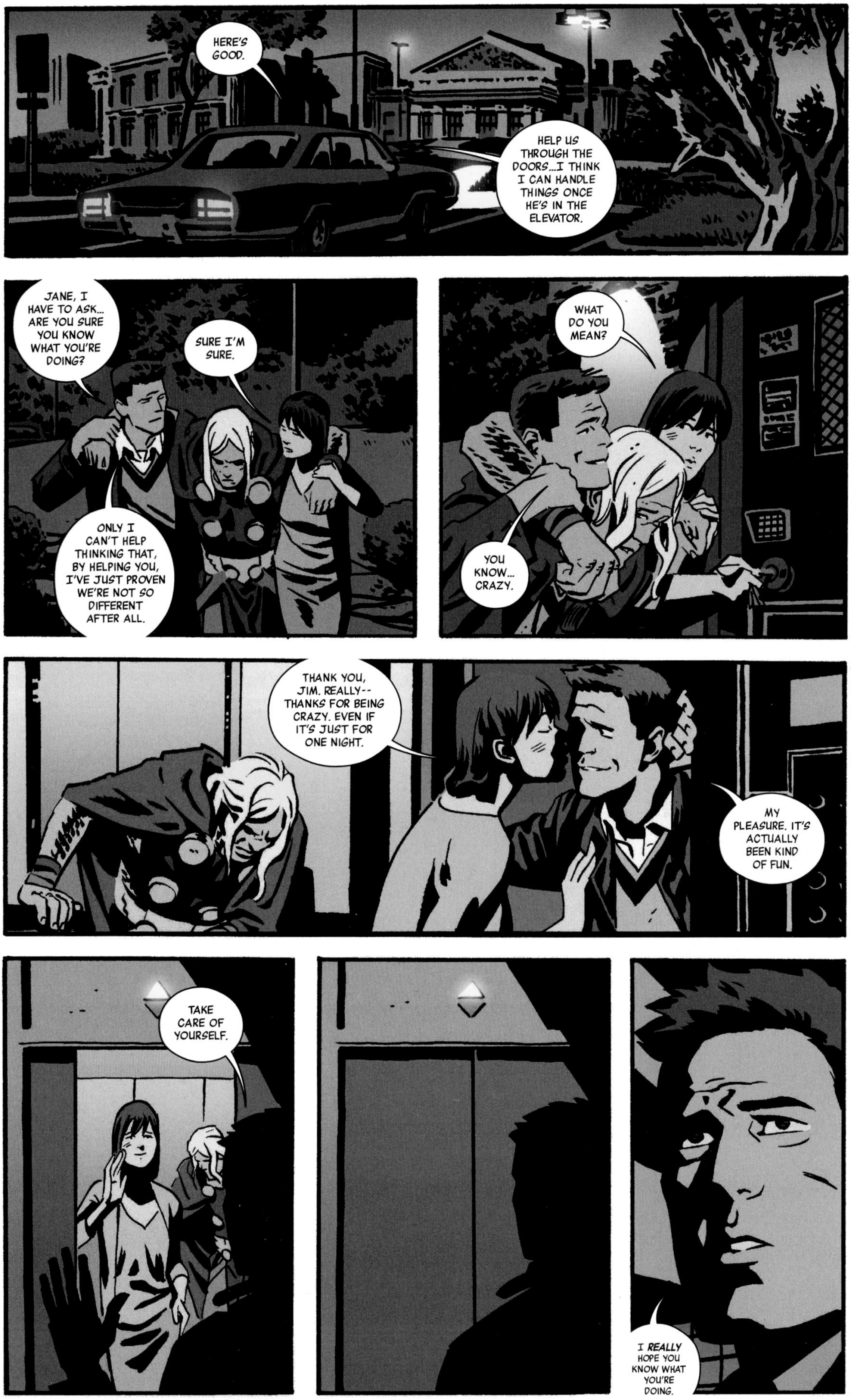
HERE'S GOOD.
HELP US THROUGH THE DOORS...I THINK I CAN HANDLE THINGS ONCE HE'S IN THE ELEVATOR.
JANE, I HAVE TO ASK... ARE YOU SURE YOU KNOW WHAT YOU'RE DOING?
SURE I'M SURE.
ONLY I CAN'T HELP THINKING THAT, BY HELPING YOU, I'VE JUST PROVEN WE'RE NOT SO DIFFERENT AFTER ALL.
WHAT DO YOU MEAN?
YOU KNOW... CRAZY.
THANK YOU, JIM. REALLY-- THANKS FOR BEING CRAZY. EVEN IF IT'S JUST FOR ONE NIGHT.
MY PLEASURE. IT'S ACTUALLY BEEN KIND OF FUN.
TAKE CARE OF YOURSELF.
I *REALLY* HOPE YOU KNOW WHAT YOU'RE DOING.

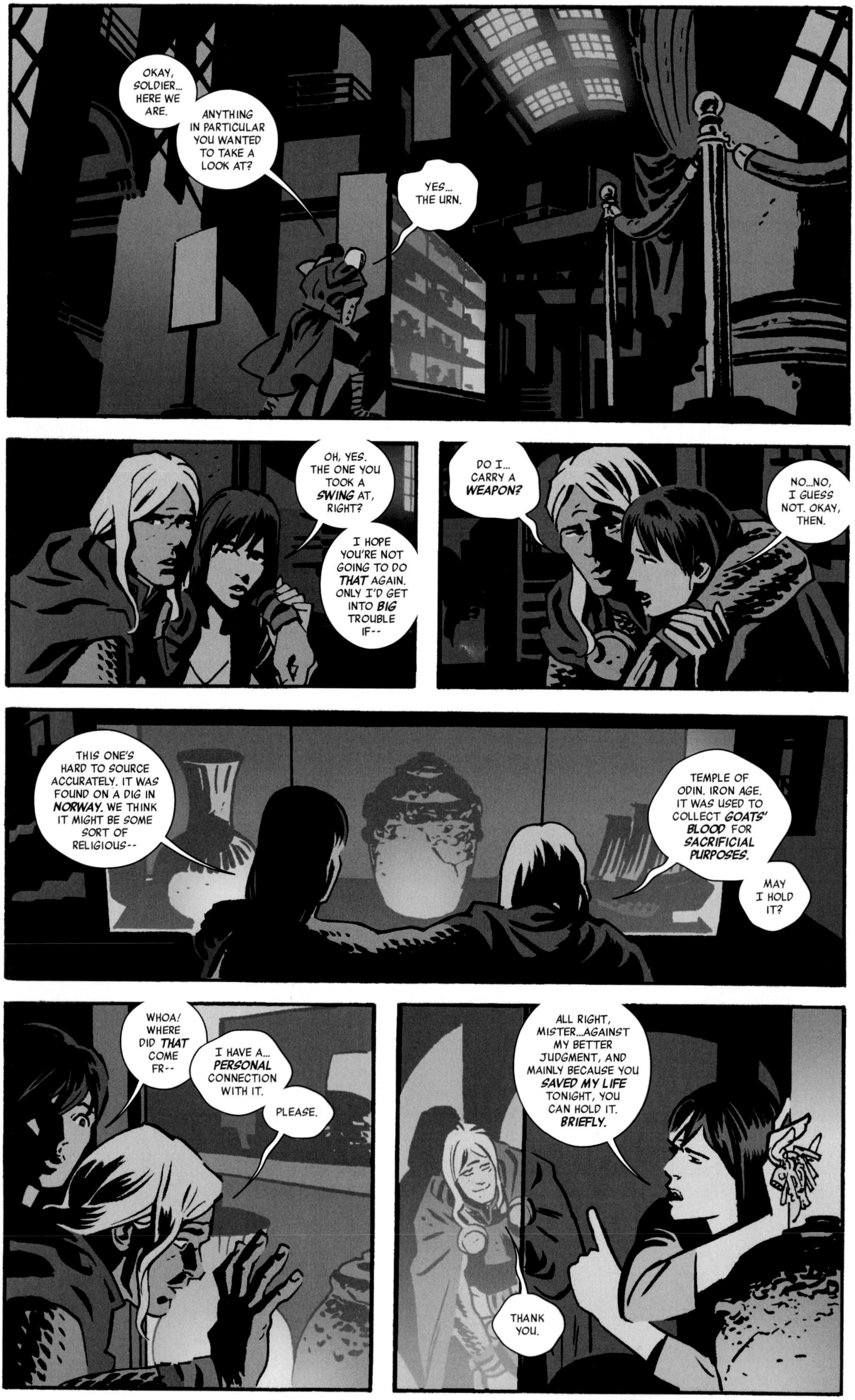
OKAY, SOLDIER... HERE WE ARE.
ANYTHING IN PARTICULAR YOU WANTED TO TAKE A LOOK AT?
YES... THE URN.
OH, YES. THE ONE YOU TOOK A SWING AT, RIGHT?
I HOPE YOU'RE NOT GOING TO DO THAT AGAIN. ONLY I'D GET INTO BIG TROUBLE IF--
DO I... CARRY A WEAPON?
NO...NO, I GUESS NOT. OKAY, THEN.
THIS ONE'S HARD TO SOURCE ACCURATELY. IT WAS FOUND ON A DIG IN NORWAY. WE THINK IT MIGHT BE SOME SORT OF RELIGIOUS--
TEMPLE OF ODIN. IRON AGE. IT WAS USED TO COLLECT GOATS' BLOOD FOR SACRIFICIAL PURPOSES.
MAY I HOLD IT?
WHOA! WHERE DID THAT COME FR--
I HAVE A... PERSONAL CONNECTION WITH IT.
PLEASE.
ALL RIGHT, MISTER...AGAINST MY BETTER JUDGMENT, AND MAINLY BECAUSE YOU SAVED MY LIFE TONIGHT, YOU CAN HOLD IT. BRIEFLY.
THANK YOU.

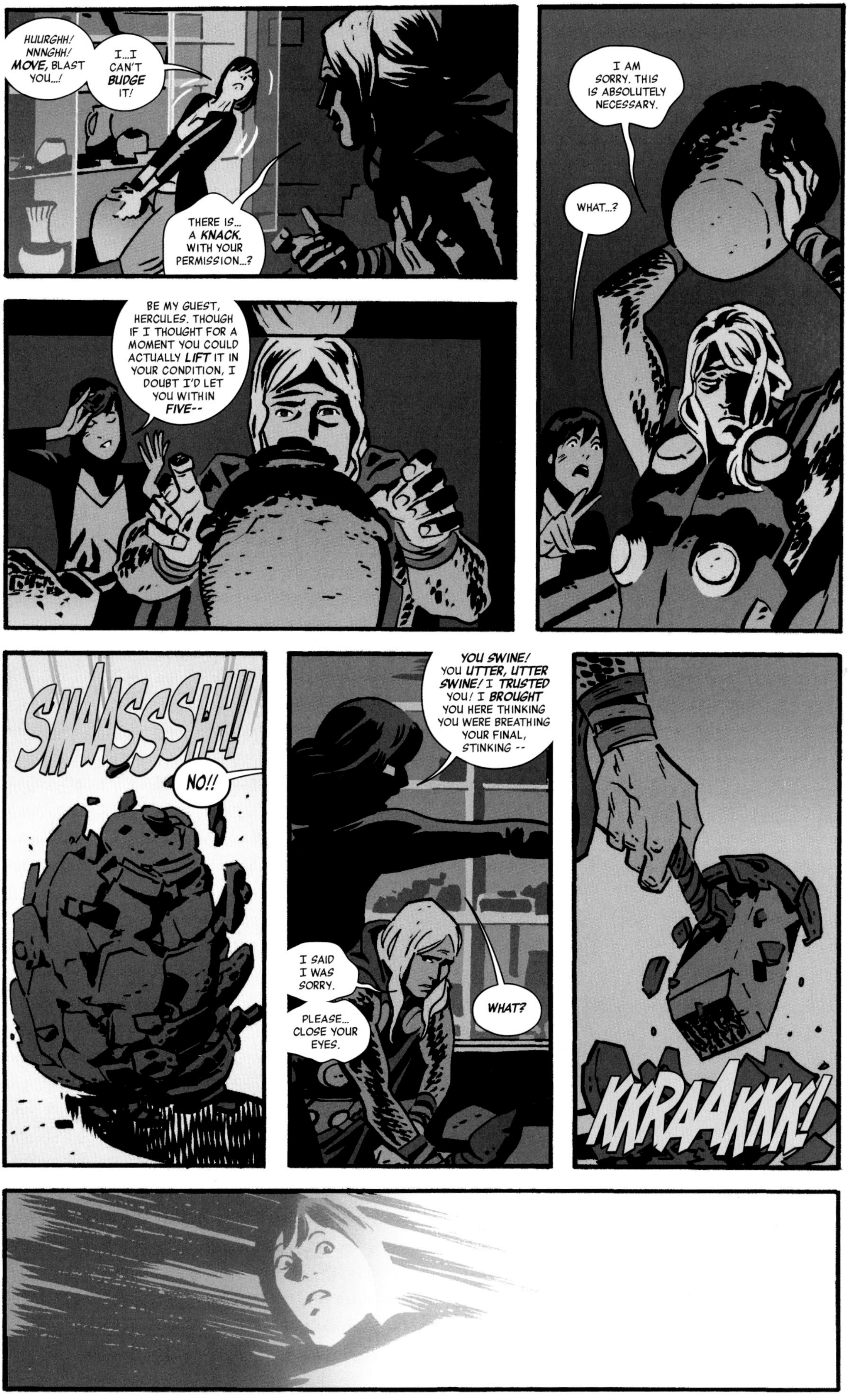
HUURGHH! NNNGHH! MOVE, BLAST YOU...!
I...I CAN'T BUDGE IT!
THERE IS... A KNACK. WITH YOUR PERMISSION...?
I AM SORRY. THIS IS ABSOLUTELY NECESSARY.
WHAT...?
BE MY GUEST, HERCULES. THOUGH IF I THOUGHT FOR A MOMENT YOU COULD ACTUALLY LIFT IT IN YOUR CONDITION, I DOUBT I'D LET YOU WITHIN FIVE--
SHAASSSHH!
NO!!
YOU SWINE! YOU UTTER, UTTER SWINE! I TRUSTED YOU! I BROUGHT YOU HERE THINKING YOU WERE BREATHING YOUR FINAL, STINKING --
I SAID I WAS SORRY.
PLEASE... CLOSE YOUR EYES.
WHAT?
KKRAAKKK!

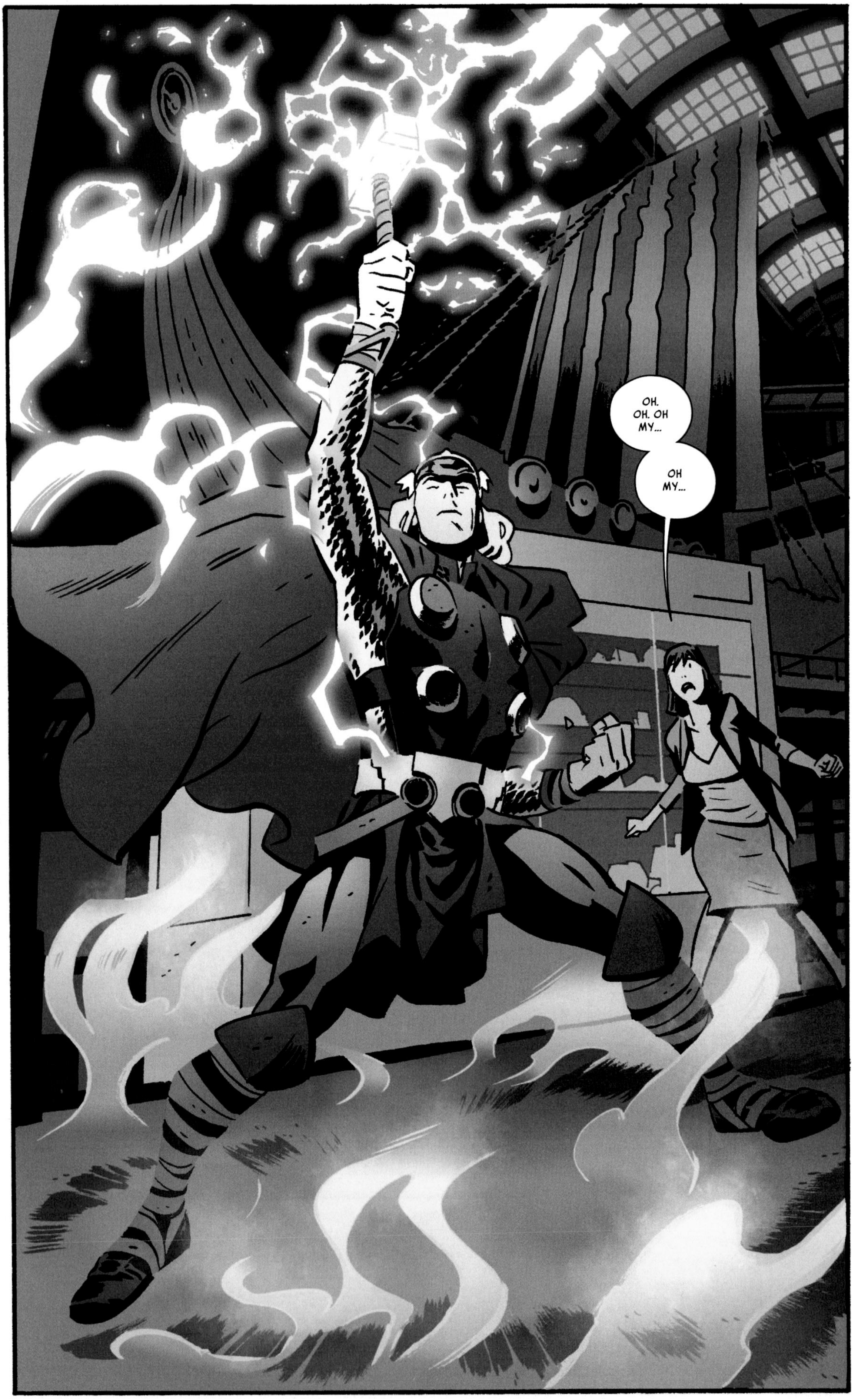
OH. OH. OH MY...
OH MY...

THOR THE MIGHTY AVENGER #2

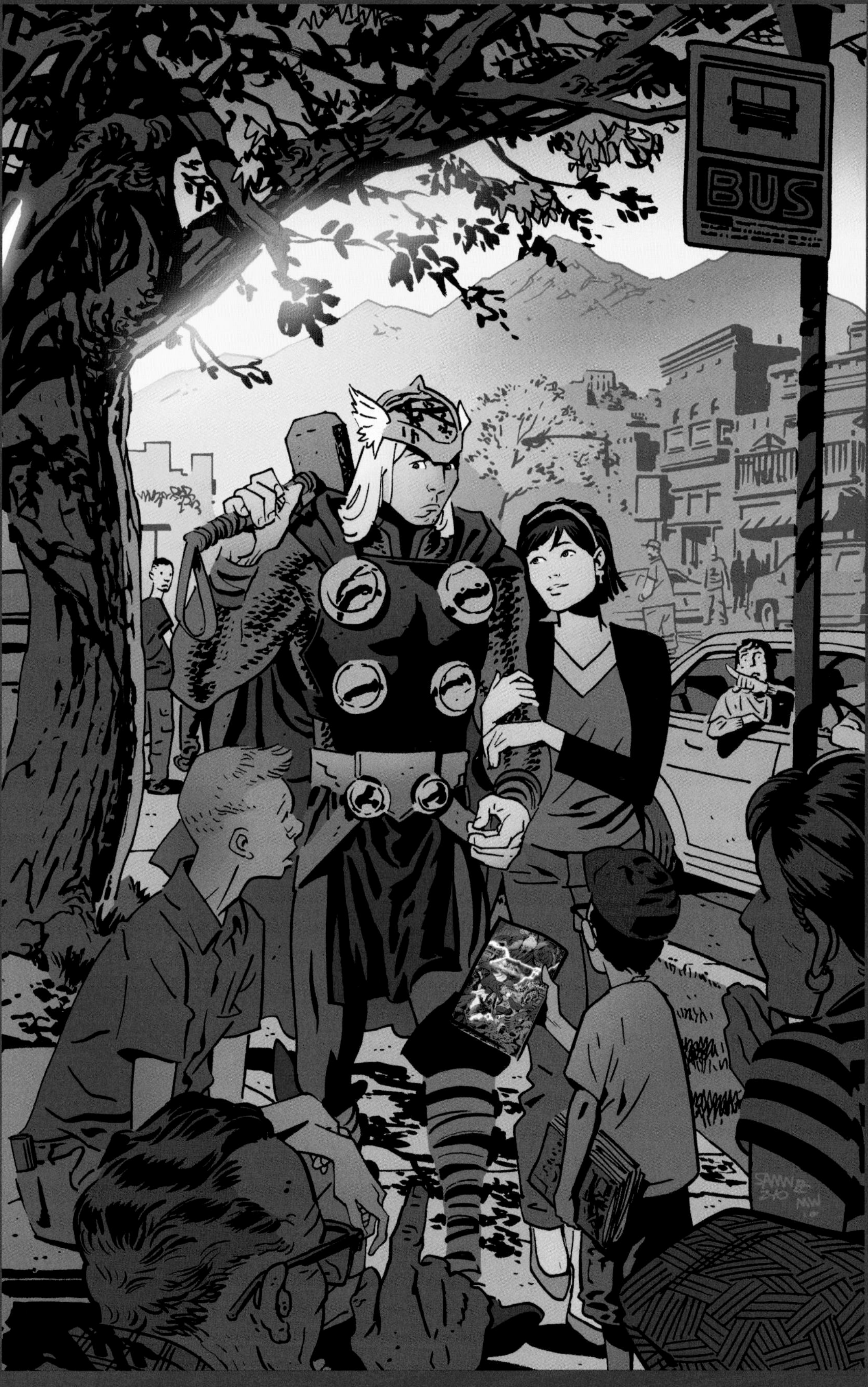
BUS

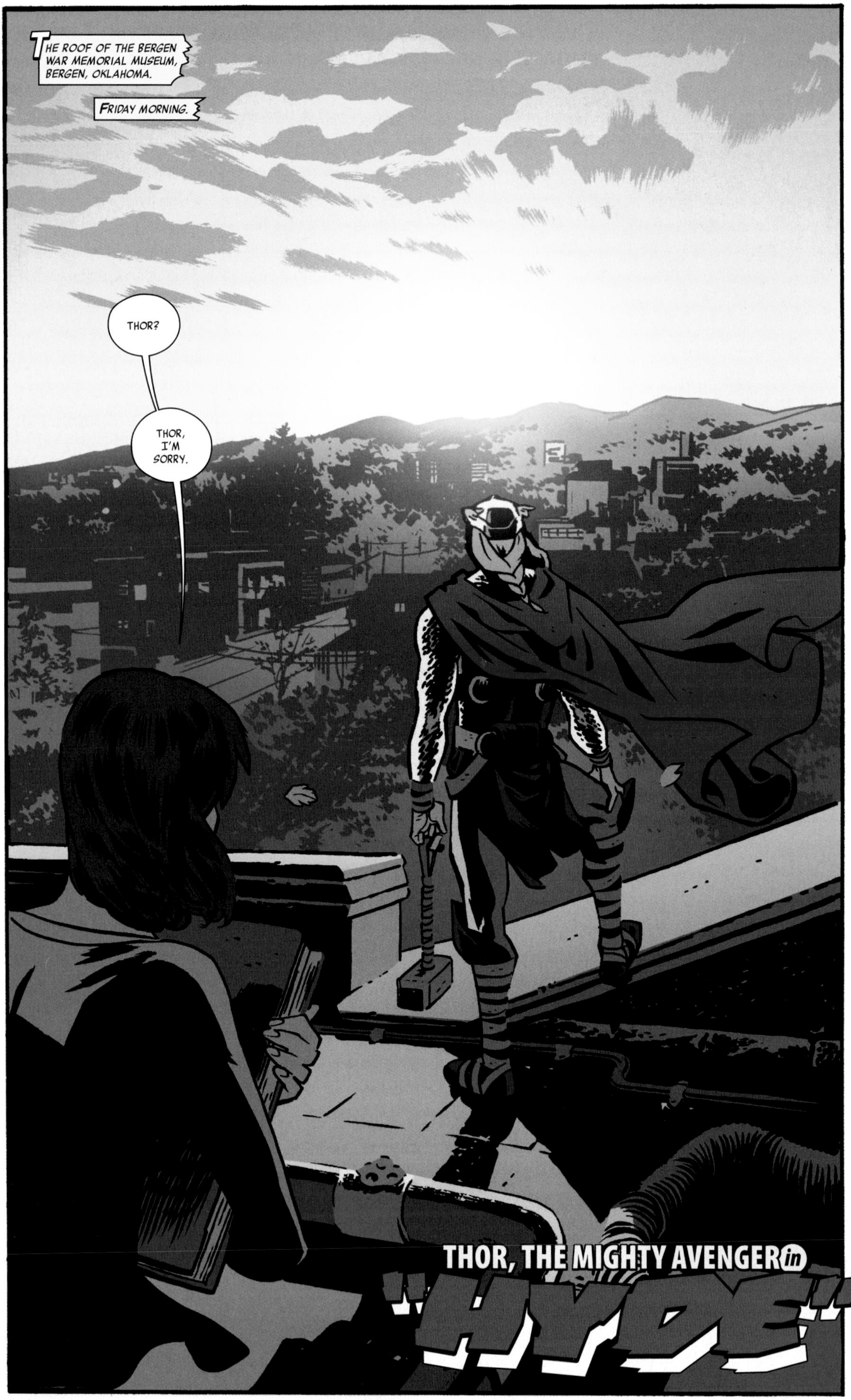

THE ROOF OF THE BERGEN WAR MEMORIAL MUSEUM, BERGEN, OKLAHOMA.
FRIDAY MORNING.
THOR?
THOR, I'M SORRY.
THOR, THE MIGHTY AVENGER in
"HYDE"

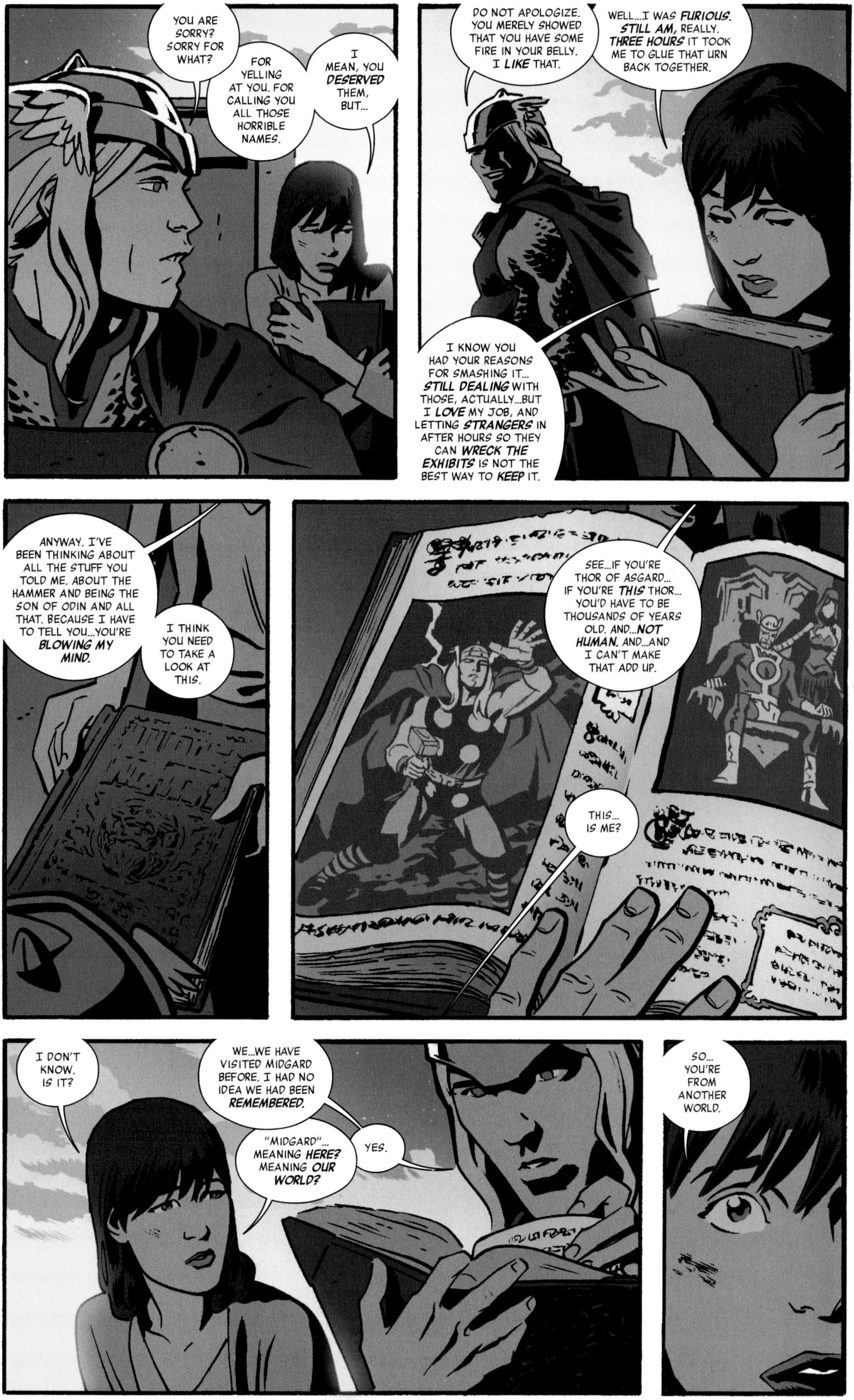
YOU ARE SORRY? SORRY FOR WHAT?
FOR YELLING AT YOU. FOR CALLING YOU ALL THOSE HORRIBLE NAMES.
I MEAN, YOU DESERVED THEM, BUT...
DO NOT APOLOGIZE. YOU MERELY SHOWED THAT YOU HAVE SOME FIRE IN YOUR BELLY. I LIKE THAT.
WELL...I WAS FURIOUS. STILL AM, REALLY. THREE HOURS IT TOOK ME TO GLUE THAT URN BACK TOGETHER.
I KNOW YOU HAD YOUR REASONS FOR SMASHING IT... STILL DEALING WITH THOSE, ACTUALLY...BUT I LOVE MY JOB, AND LETTING STRANGERS IN AFTER HOURS SO THEY CAN WRECK THE EXHIBITS IS NOT THE BEST WAY TO KEEP IT.
ANYWAY. I'VE BEEN THINKING ABOUT ALL THE STUFF YOU TOLD ME. ABOUT THE HAMMER AND BEING THE SON OF ODIN AND ALL THAT. BECAUSE I HAVE TO TELL YOU...YOU'RE BLOWING MY MIND.
I THINK YOU NEED TO TAKE A LOOK AT THIS.
SEE...IF YOU'RE THOR OF ASGARD... IF YOU'RE THIS THOR... YOU'D HAVE TO BE THOUSANDS OF YEARS OLD. AND...NOT HUMAN. AND...AND I CAN'T MAKE THAT ADD UP.
THIS... IS ME?
I DON'T KNOW. IS IT?
WE...WE HAVE VISITED MIDGARD BEFORE. I HAD NO IDEA WE HAD BEEN REMEMBERED.
"MIDGARD"... MEANING HERE? MEANING OUR WORLD?
YES.
SO... YOU'RE FROM ANOTHER WORLD.

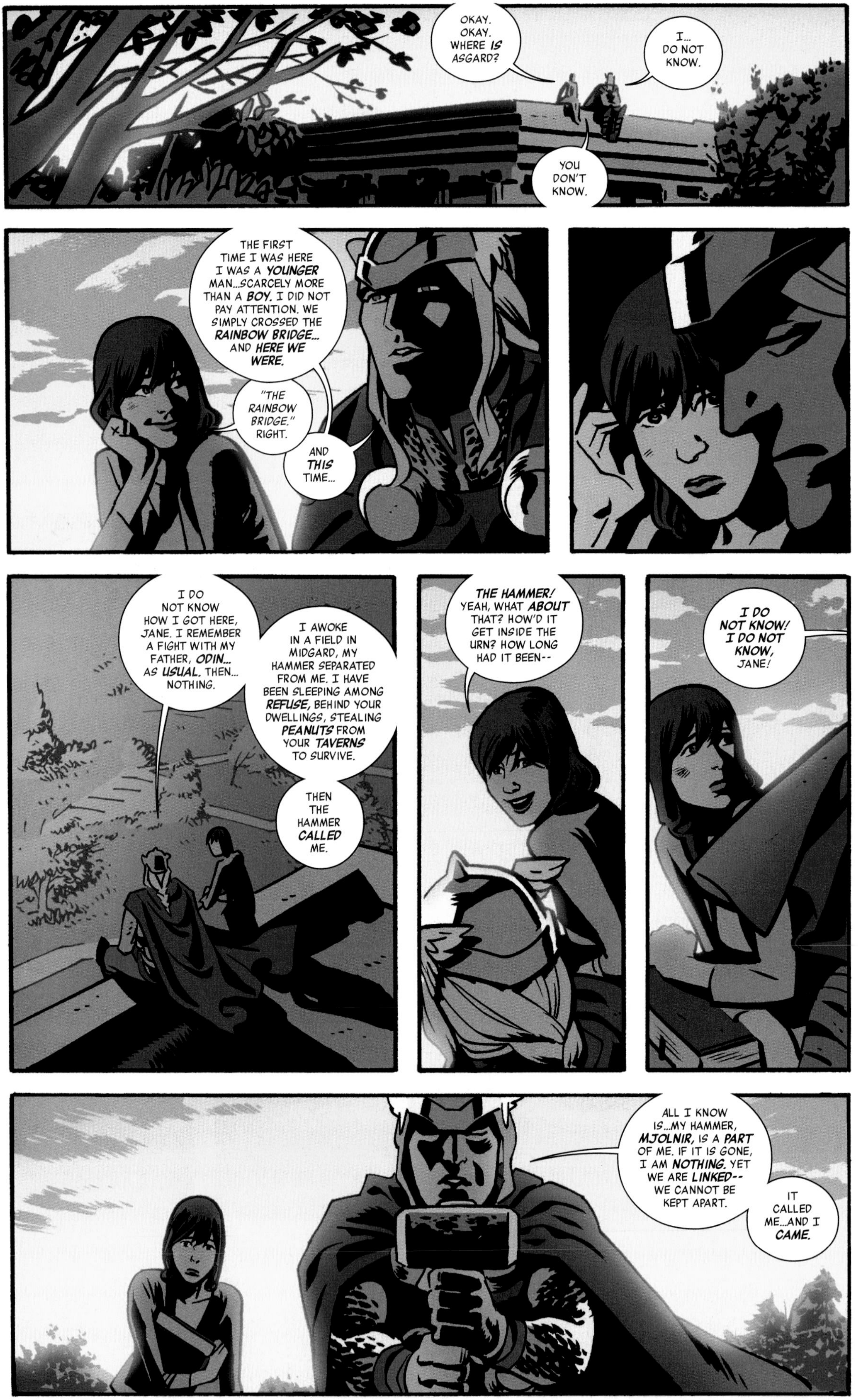
OKAY. OKAY. WHERE IS ASGARD?
I... DO NOT KNOW.
YOU DON'T KNOW.
THE FIRST TIME I WAS HERE I WAS A YOUNGER MAN...SCARCELY MORE THAN A BOY. I DID NOT PAY ATTENTION. WE SIMPLY CROSSED THE RAINBOW BRIDGE... AND HERE WE WERE.
"THE RAINBOW BRIDGE." RIGHT.
AND THIS TIME...
I DO NOT KNOW HOW I GOT HERE, JANE. I REMEMBER A FIGHT WITH MY FATHER, ODIN... AS USUAL. THEN... NOTHING.
I AWOKE IN A FIELD IN MIDGARD, MY HAMMER SEPARATED FROM ME. I HAVE BEEN SLEEPING AMONG REFUSE, BEHIND YOUR DWELLINGS, STEALING PEANUTS FROM YOUR TAVERNS TO SURVIVE.
THEN THE HAMMER CALLED ME.
THE HAMMER! YEAH, WHAT ABOUT THAT? HOW'D IT GET INSIDE THE URN? HOW LONG HAD IT BEEN--
I DO NOT KNOW! I DO NOT KNOW, JANE!
ALL I KNOW IS...MY HAMMER, MJOLNIR, IS A PART OF ME. IF IT IS GONE, I AM NOTHING. YET WE ARE LINKED-- WE CANNOT BE KEPT APART.
IT CALLED ME...AND I CAME.

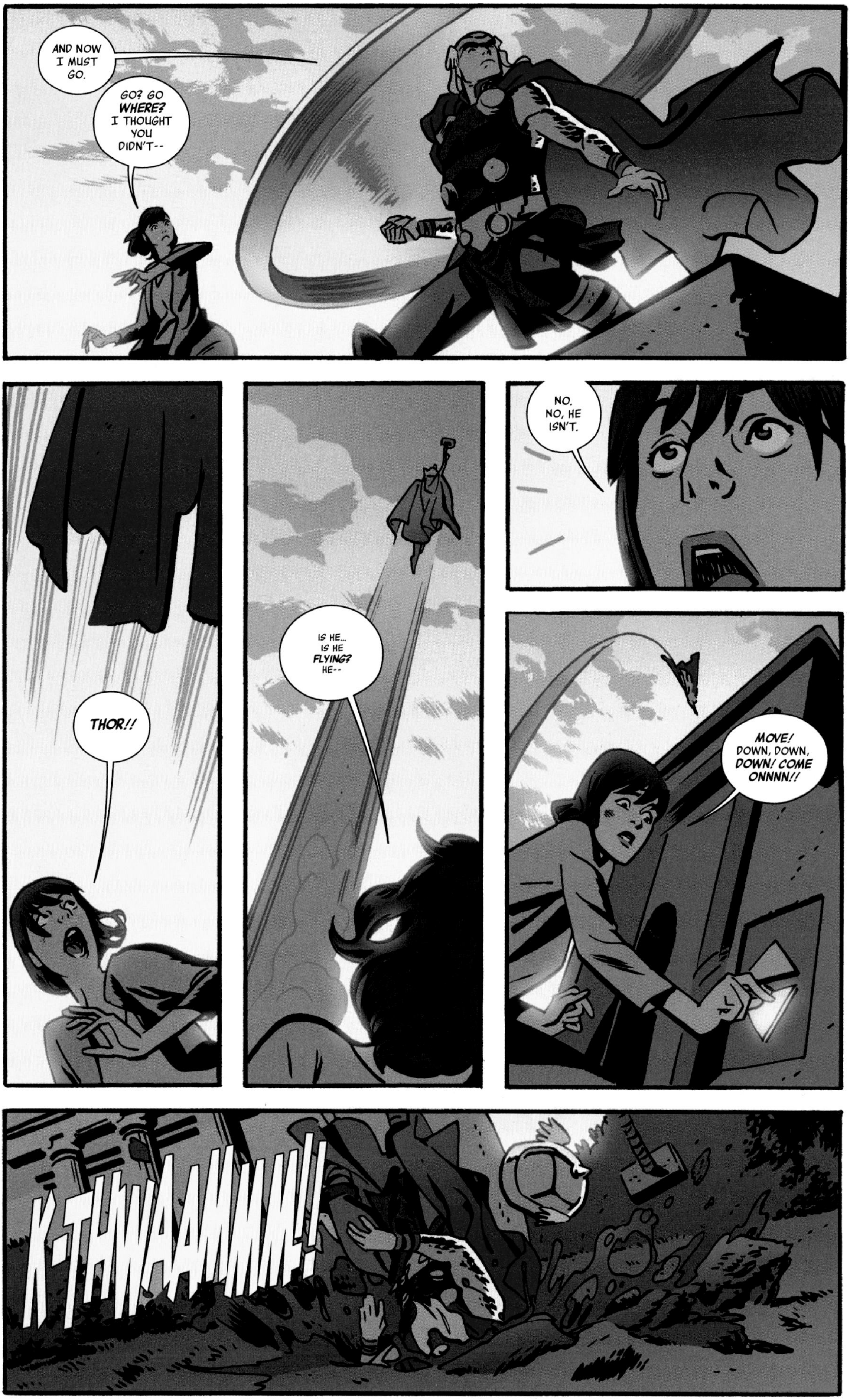
AND NOW I MUST GO.
GO? GO WHERE? I THOUGHT YOU DIDN'T--
THOR!!
IS HE... IS HE FLYING? HE--
NO. NO, HE ISN'T.
MOVE! DOWN, DOWN, DOWN! COME ONNNN!!
K-THWAAMMM!!

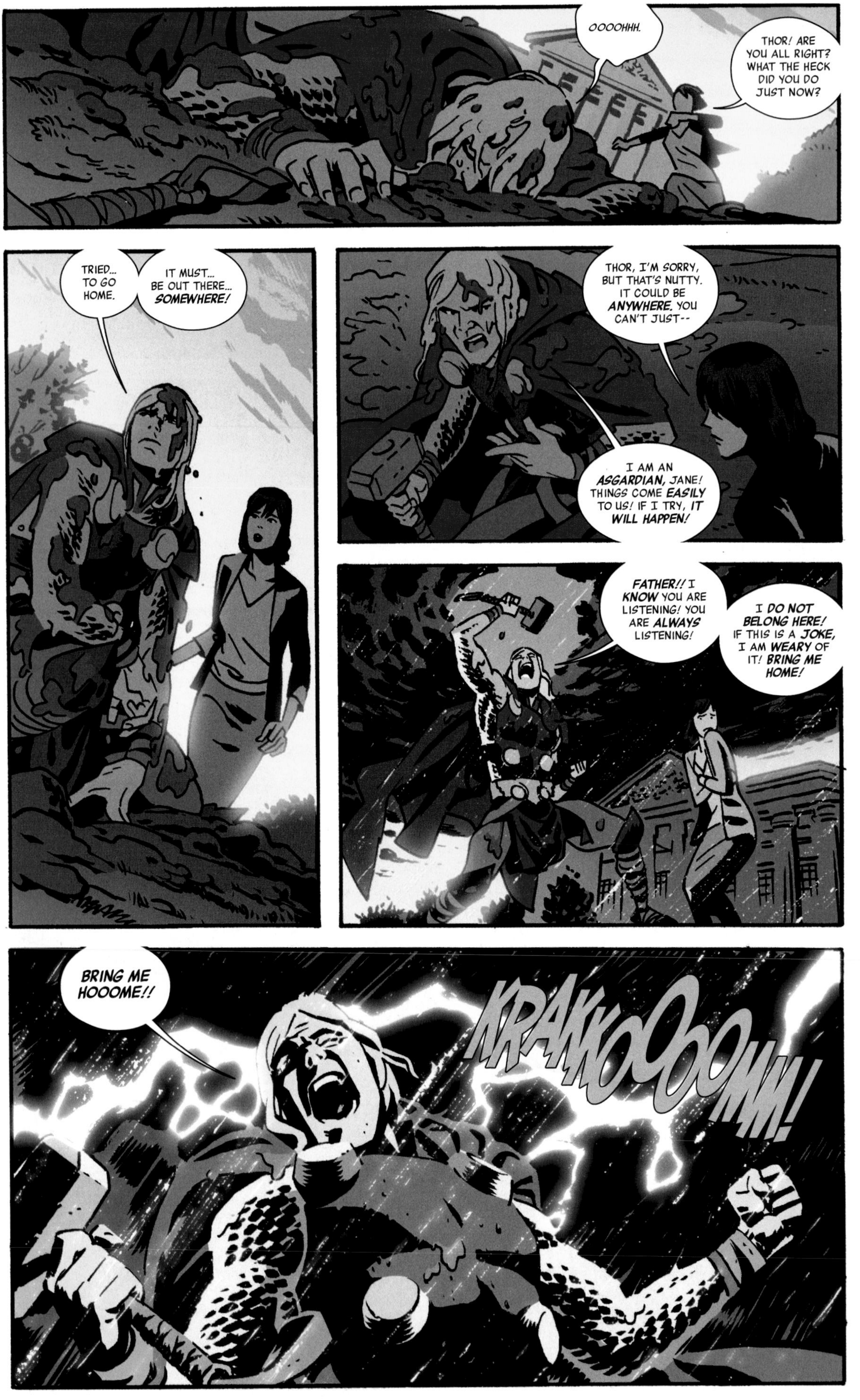
OOOOHHH.
THOR! ARE YOU ALL RIGHT? WHAT THE HECK DID YOU DO JUST NOW?
TRIED... TO GO HOME.
IT MUST... BE OUT THERE... SOMEWHERE!
THOR, I'M SORRY, BUT THAT'S NUTTY. IT COULD BE ANYWHERE. YOU CAN'T JUST--
I AM AN ASGARDIAN, JANE! THINGS COME EASILY TO US! IF I TRY, IT WILL HAPPEN!
FATHER!! I KNOW YOU ARE LISTENING! YOU ARE ALWAYS LISTENING!
I DO NOT BELONG HERE! IF THIS IS A JOKE, I AM WEARY OF IT! BRING ME HOME!
BRING ME HOOOME!!
KRAKKOOOOMM!

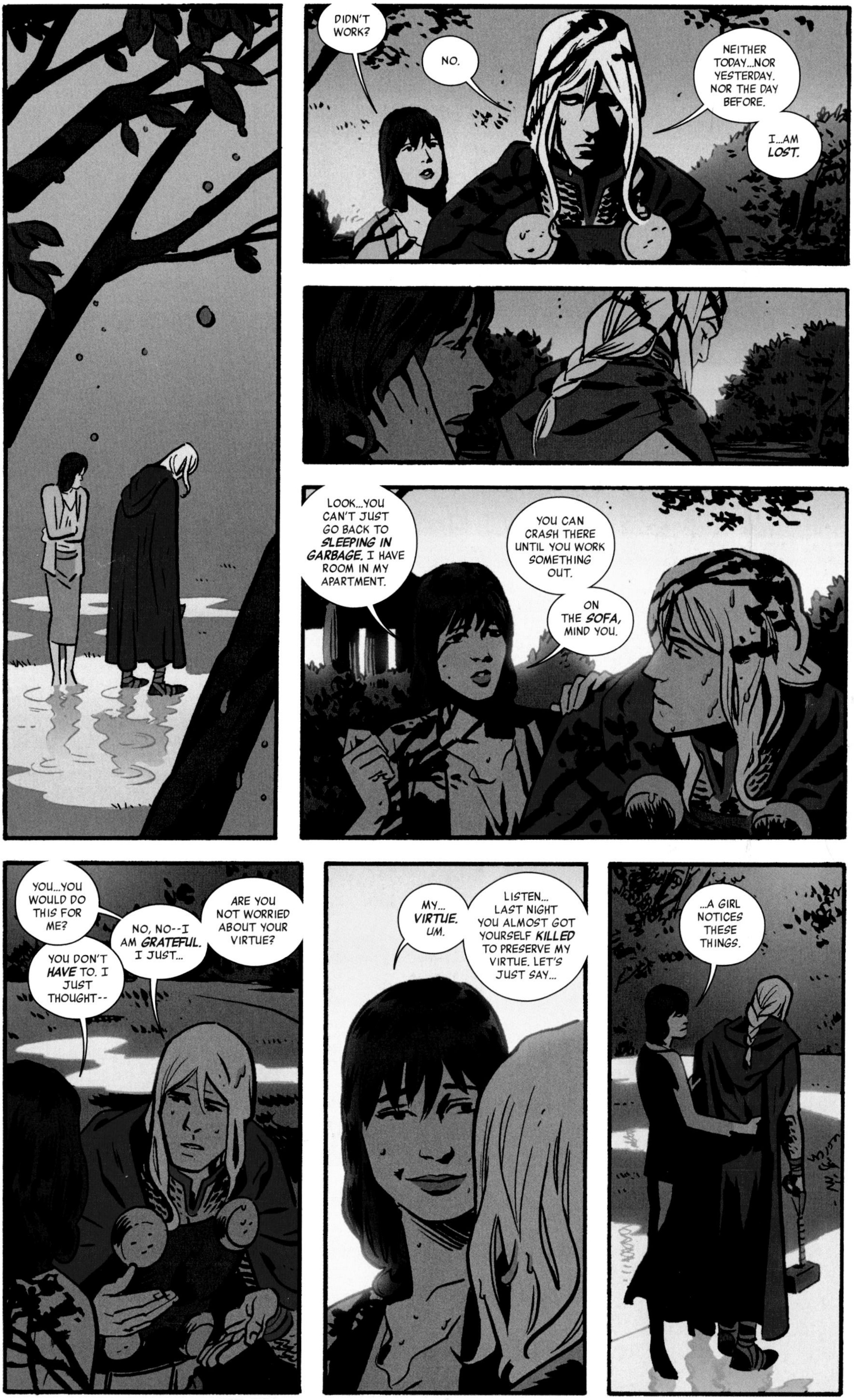

DIDN'T WORK?
NO.
NEITHER TODAY...NOR YESTERDAY. NOR THE DAY BEFORE.
I...AM LOST.
LOOK...YOU CAN'T JUST GO BACK TO SLEEPING IN GARBAGE. I HAVE ROOM IN MY APARTMENT.
YOU CAN CRASH THERE UNTIL YOU WORK SOMETHING OUT.
ON THE SOFA, MIND YOU.
YOU...YOU WOULD DO THIS FOR ME?
YOU DON'T HAVE TO. I JUST THOUGHT--
NO, NO--I AM GRATEFUL. I JUST...
ARE YOU NOT WORRIED ABOUT YOUR VIRTUE?
MY... VIRTUE. UM.
LISTEN... LAST NIGHT YOU ALMOST GOT YOURSELF KILLED TO PRESERVE MY VIRTUE. LET'S JUST SAY...
...A GIRL NOTICES THESE THINGS.

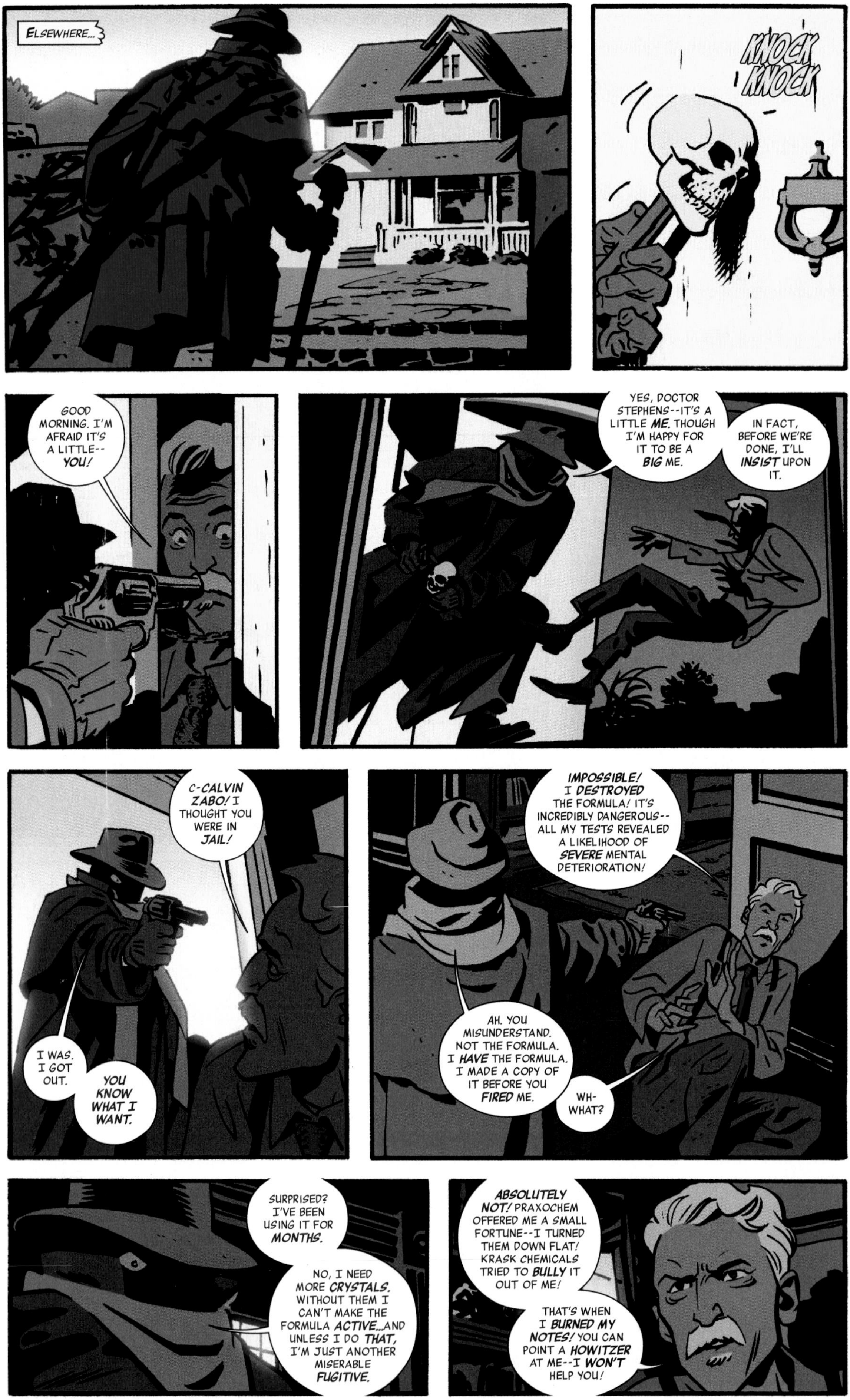

ELSEWHERE...
KNOCK KNOCK
GOOD MORNING. I'M AFRAID IT'S A LITTLE-- YOU!
YES, DOCTOR STEPHENS--IT'S A LITTLE ME. THOUGH I'M HAPPY FOR IT TO BE A BIG ME.
IN FACT, BEFORE WE'RE DONE, I'LL INSIST UPON IT.
C-CALVIN ZABO! I THOUGHT YOU WERE IN JAIL!
I WAS. I GOT OUT.
YOU KNOW WHAT I WANT.
IMPOSSIBLE! I DESTROYED THE FORMULA! IT'S INCREDIBLY DANGEROUS--ALL MY TESTS REVEALED A LIKELIHOOD OF SEVERE MENTAL DETERIORATION!
AH. YOU MISUNDERSTAND. NOT THE FORMULA. I HAVE THE FORMULA. I MADE A COPY OF IT BEFORE YOU FIRED ME.
WH-WHAT?
SURPRISED? I'VE BEEN USING IT FOR MONTHS.
NO, I NEED MORE CRYSTALS. WITHOUT THEM I CAN'T MAKE THE FORMULA ACTIVE...AND UNLESS I DO THAT, I'M JUST ANOTHER MISERABLE FUGITIVE.
ABSOLUTELY NOT! PRAXOCHEM OFFERED ME A SMALL FORTUNE--I TURNED THEM DOWN FLAT! KRASK CHEMICALS TRIED TO BULLY IT OUT OF ME!
THAT'S WHEN I BURNED MY NOTES! YOU CAN POINT A HOWITZER AT ME--I WON'T HELP YOU!

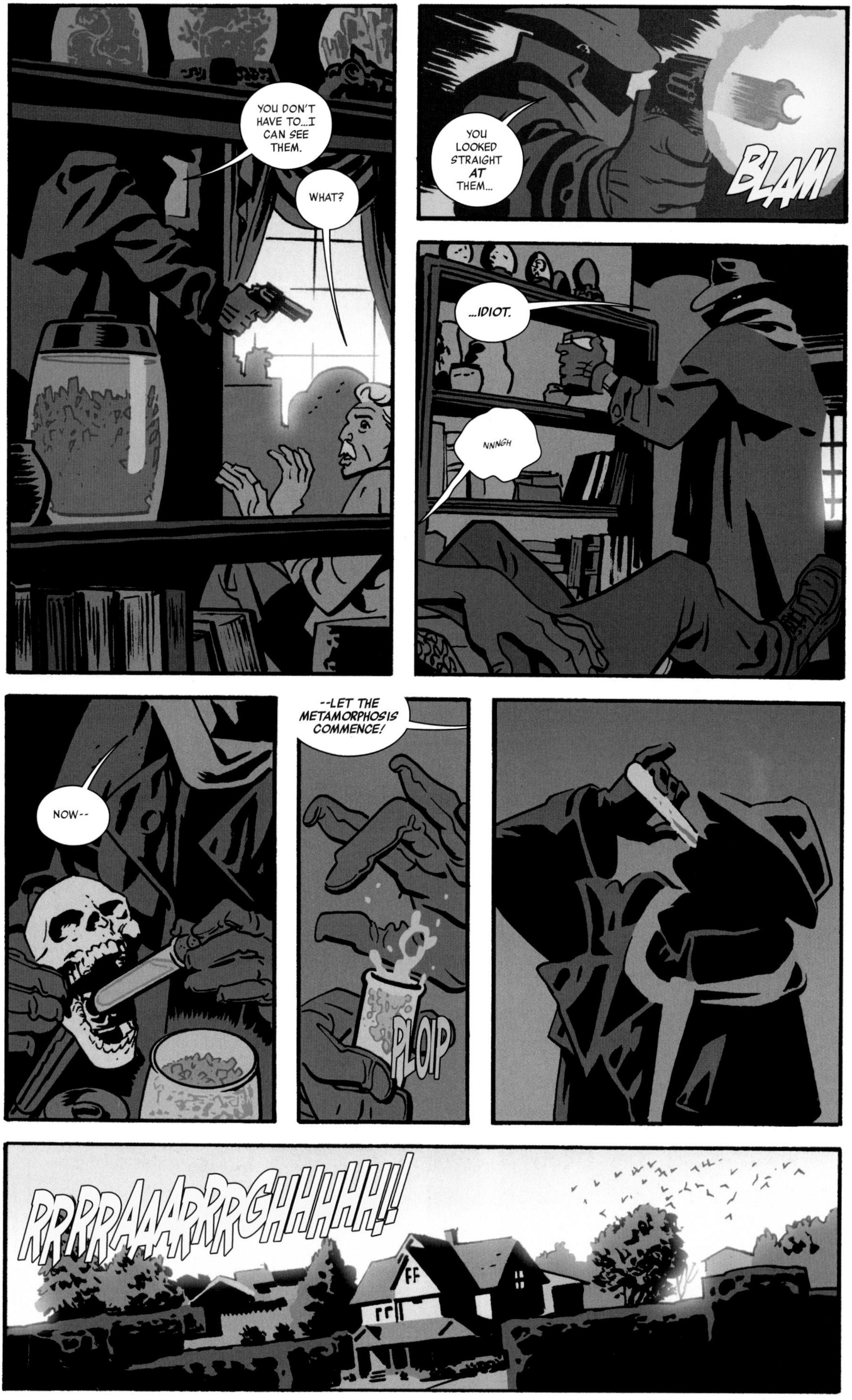
YOU DON'T HAVE TO...I CAN SEE THEM.
WHAT?
YOU LOOKED STRAIGHT AT THEM...
BLAM
...IDIOT.
NNNGH
NOW--
--LET THE METAMORPHOSIS COMMENCE!
PLOIP
RRRRAAAARRRGHHHHHH!!

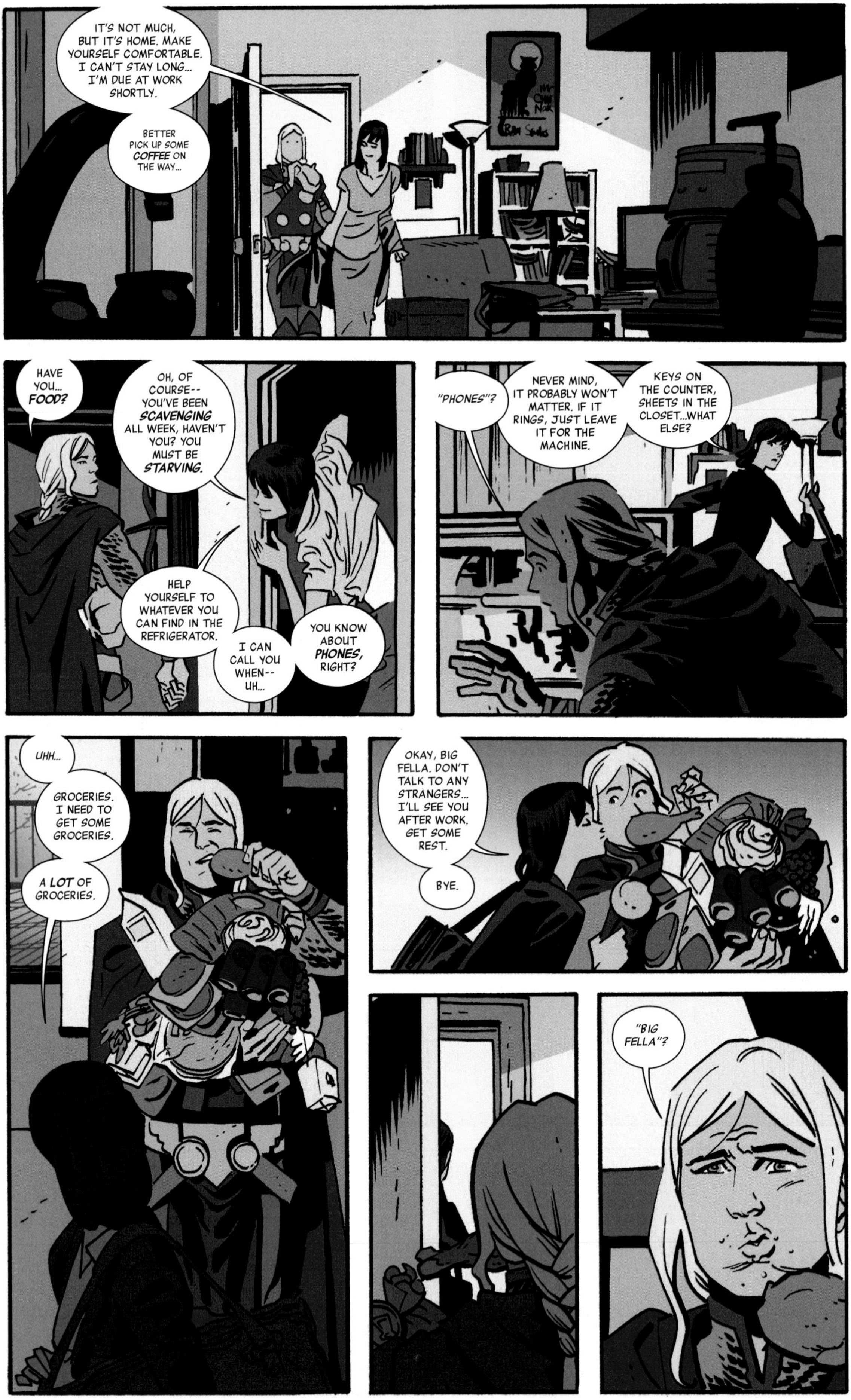
IT'S NOT MUCH, BUT IT'S HOME. MAKE YOURSELF COMFORTABLE. I CAN'T STAY LONG... I'M DUE AT WORK SHORTLY.
BETTER PICK UP SOME COFFEE ON THE WAY...
HAVE YOU... FOOD?
OH, OF COURSE-- YOU'VE BEEN SCAVENGING ALL WEEK, HAVEN'T YOU? YOU MUST BE STARVING.
HELP YOURSELF TO WHATEVER YOU CAN FIND IN THE REFRIGERATOR.
I CAN CALL YOU WHEN-- UH...
YOU KNOW ABOUT PHONES, RIGHT?
"PHONES"?
NEVER MIND, IT PROBABLY WON'T MATTER. IF IT RINGS, JUST LEAVE IT FOR THE MACHINE.
KEYS ON THE COUNTER, SHEETS IN THE CLOSET...WHAT ELSE?
UHH...
GROCERIES. I NEED TO GET SOME GROCERIES.
A LOT OF GROCERIES.
OKAY, BIG FELLA. DON'T TALK TO ANY STRANGERS... I'LL SEE YOU AFTER WORK. GET SOME REST.
BYE.
"BIG FELLA"?

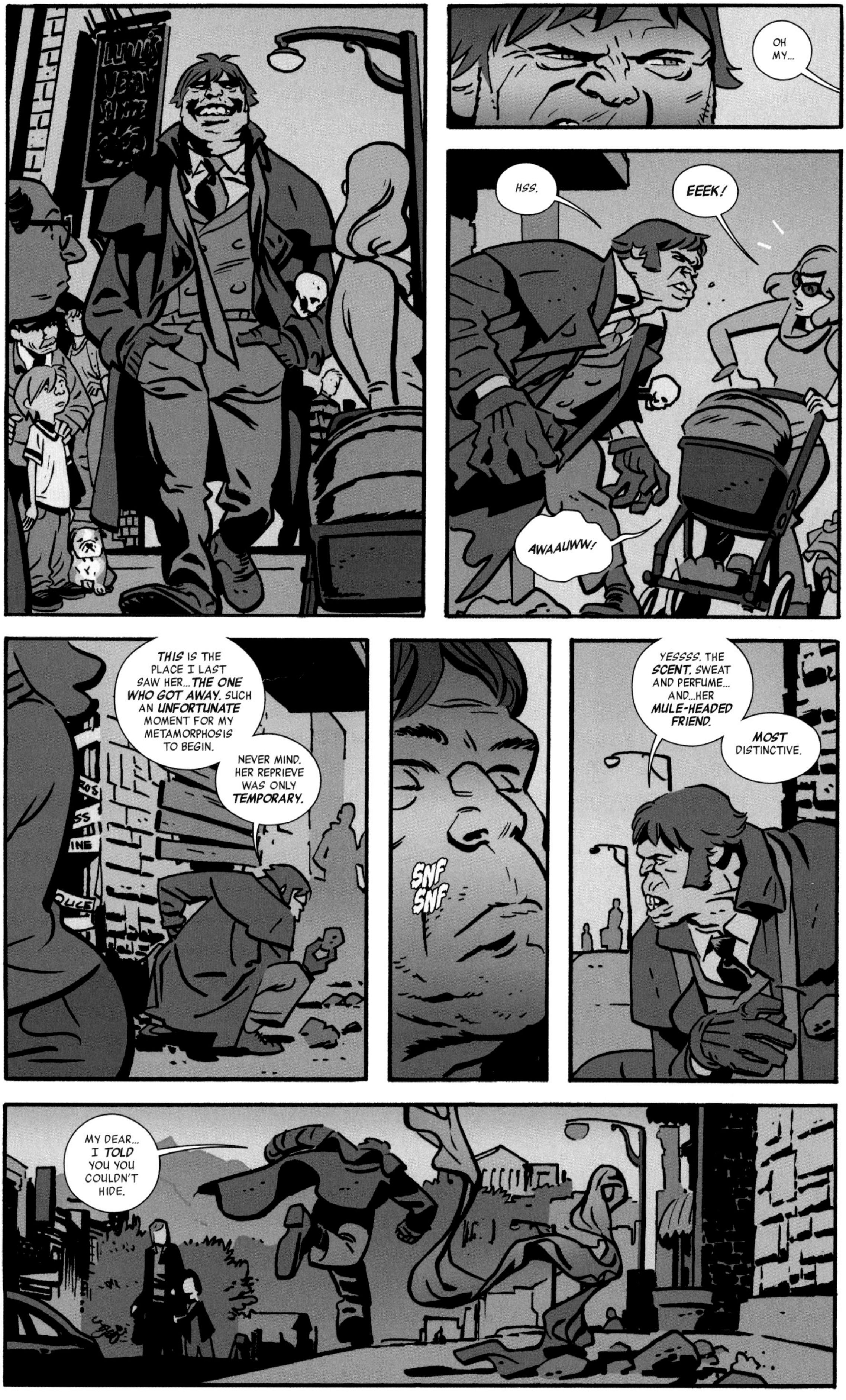

OH MY...
HSS.
EEEK!
AWAAUWW!
THIS IS THE PLACE I LAST SAW HER...THE ONE WHO GOT AWAY. SUCH AN UNFORTUNATE MOMENT FOR MY METAMORPHOSIS TO BEGIN.
NEVER MIND. HER REPRIEVE WAS ONLY TEMPORARY.
SNF SNF
YESSSS. THE SCENT. SWEAT AND PERFUME... AND...HER MULE-HEADED FRIEND.
MOST DISTINCTIVE.
MY DEAR... I TOLD YOU YOU COULDN'T HIDE.

...STARK INDUSTRIES TODAY, MARKING THEIR THIRD NEW DESIGN THIS YEAR...

...DO YOU SUPPOSE THERE IS SUCH A PLACE, TOTO? THERE MUST BE. IT'S NOT A PLACE YOU CAN GET TO BY A BOAT OR A TRAIN...

...IT'S FAR, FAR AWAY... BEHIND THE MOON...BEHIND THE RAIN...

BRRRRRRRRRR

BRRRRRRRRRR

CLICK

THOR, IT'S JANE! CAN YOU HEAR ME? PICK UP THE PHONE!

ALL RIGHT, DON'T PICK UP THE PHONE. LISTEN--IT'S THAT "HYDE" GUY! THE ONE FROM THE BAR! HE'S HERE AT THE MUSEUM-- AND I THINK HE'S LOOK

BEEEEEEEEEEEEEE

CHK-POW

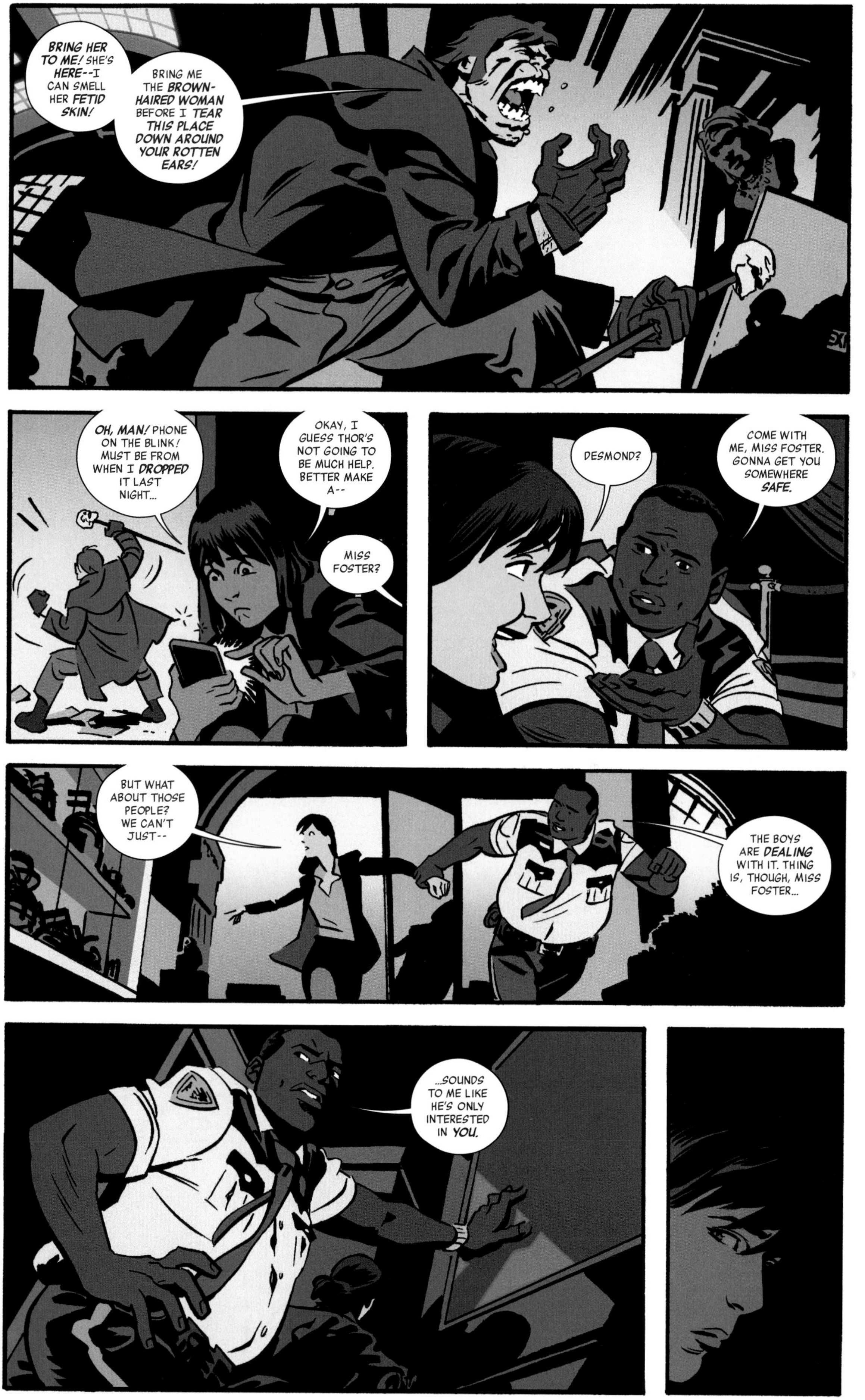
BRING HER TO ME! SHE'S HERE--I CAN SMELL HER FETID SKIN!
BRING ME THE BROWN-HAIRED WOMAN BEFORE I TEAR THIS PLACE DOWN AROUND YOUR ROTTEN EARS!
OH, MAN! PHONE ON THE BLINK! MUST BE FROM WHEN I DROPPED IT LAST NIGHT...
OKAY, I GUESS THOR'S NOT GOING TO BE MUCH HELP. BETTER MAKE A--
MISS FOSTER?
DESMOND?
COME WITH ME, MISS FOSTER. GONNA GET YOU SOMEWHERE SAFE.
BUT WHAT ABOUT THOSE PEOPLE? WE CAN'T JUST--
THE BOYS ARE DEALING WITH IT. THING IS, THOUGH, MISS FOSTER...
...SOUNDS TO ME LIKE HE'S ONLY INTERESTED IN YOU.

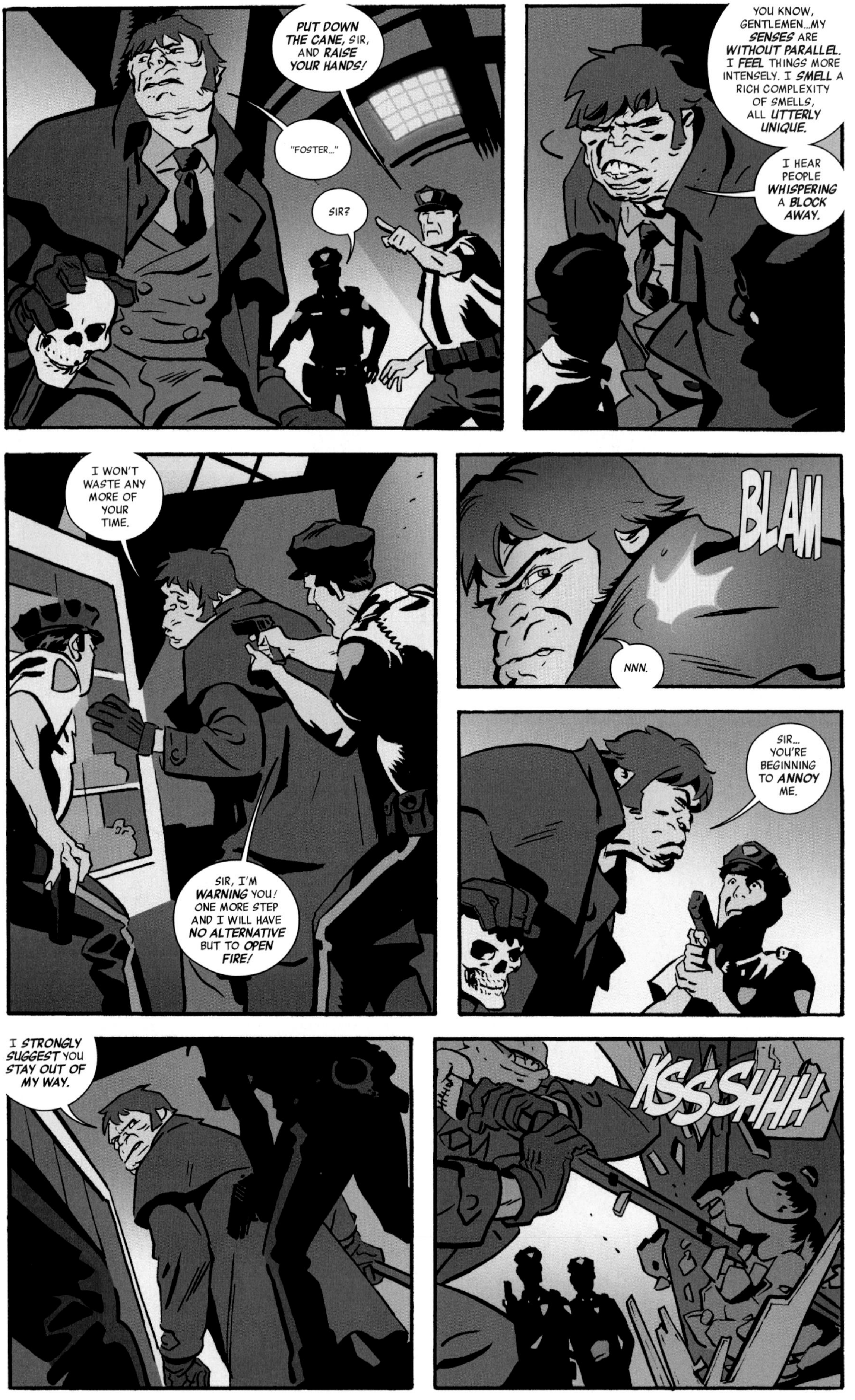
PUT DOWN THE CANE, SIR, AND RAISE YOUR HANDS!
"FOSTER..."
SIR?
YOU KNOW, GENTLEMEN...MY SENSES ARE WITHOUT PARALLEL. I FEEL THINGS MORE INTENSELY. I SMELL A RICH COMPLEXITY OF SMELLS, ALL UTTERLY UNIQUE.
I HEAR PEOPLE WHISPERING A BLOCK AWAY.
I WON'T WASTE ANY MORE OF YOUR TIME.
SIR, I'M WARNING YOU! ONE MORE STEP AND I WILL HAVE NO ALTERNATIVE BUT TO OPEN FIRE!
BLAM
NNN.
SIR... YOU'RE BEGINNING TO ANNOY ME.
I STRONGLY SUGGEST YOU STAY OUT OF MY WAY.
KSSSHHH

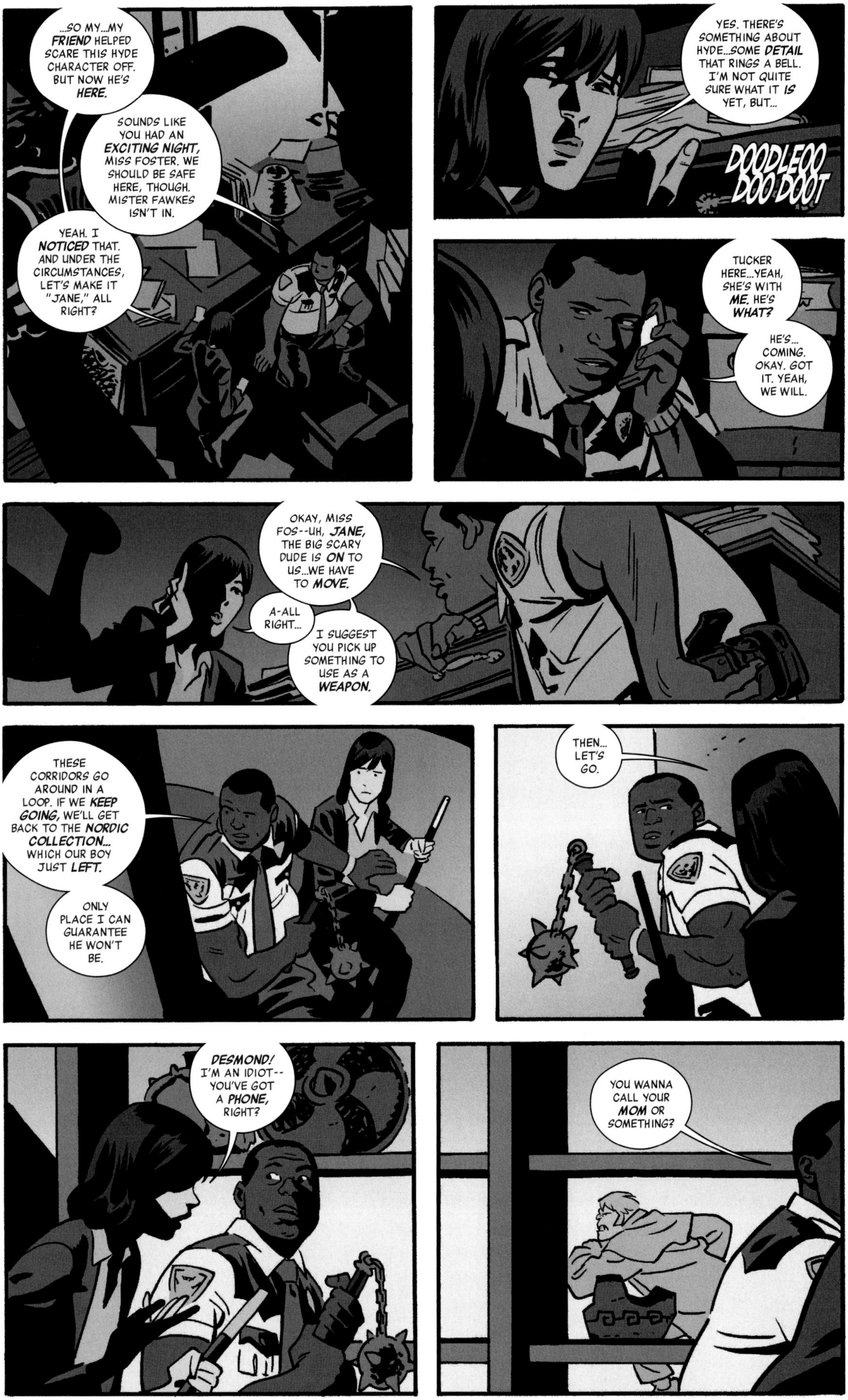

...SO MY...MY FRIEND HELPED SCARE THIS HYDE CHARACTER OFF. BUT NOW HE'S HERE.
SOUNDS LIKE YOU HAD AN EXCITING NIGHT, MISS FOSTER. WE SHOULD BE SAFE HERE, THOUGH. MISTER FAWKES ISN'T IN.
YEAH. I NOTICED THAT. AND UNDER THE CIRCUMSTANCES, LET'S MAKE IT "JANE," ALL RIGHT?
YES. THERE'S SOMETHING ABOUT HYDE...SOME DETAIL THAT RINGS A BELL. I'M NOT QUITE SURE WHAT IT IS YET, BUT...
DOODLEOO DOO DOOT
TUCKER HERE...YEAH, SHE'S WITH ME. HE'S WHAT?
HE'S... COMING. OKAY. GOT IT. YEAH, WE WILL.
OKAY, MISS FOS--UH, JANE, THE BIG SCARY DUDE IS ON TO US...WE HAVE TO MOVE.
A-ALL RIGHT...
I SUGGEST YOU PICK UP SOMETHING TO USE AS A WEAPON.
THESE CORRIDORS GO AROUND IN A LOOP. IF WE KEEP GOING, WE'LL GET BACK TO THE NORDIC COLLECTION... WHICH OUR BOY JUST LEFT.
ONLY PLACE I CAN GUARANTEE HE WON'T BE.
THEN... LET'S GO.
DESMOND! I'M AN IDIOT-- YOU'VE GOT A PHONE, RIGHT?
YOU WANNA CALL YOUR MOM OR SOMETHING?

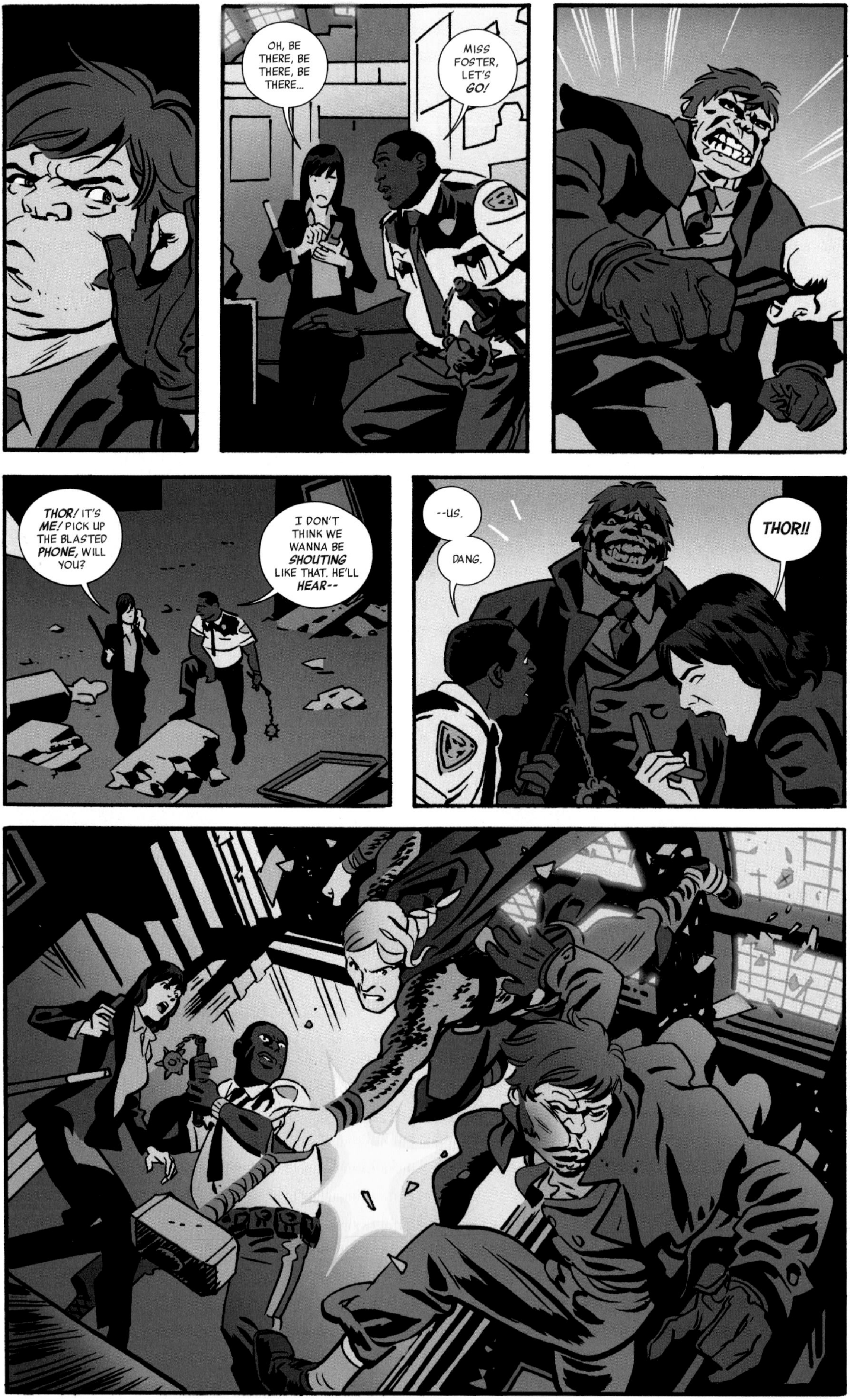
OH, BE THERE, BE THERE, BE THERE...
MISS FOSTER, LET'S GO!
THOR! IT'S ME! PICK UP THE BLASTED PHONE, WILL YOU?
I DON'T THINK WE WANNA BE SHOUTING LIKE THAT. HE'LL HEAR--
--US.
DANG.
THOR!!

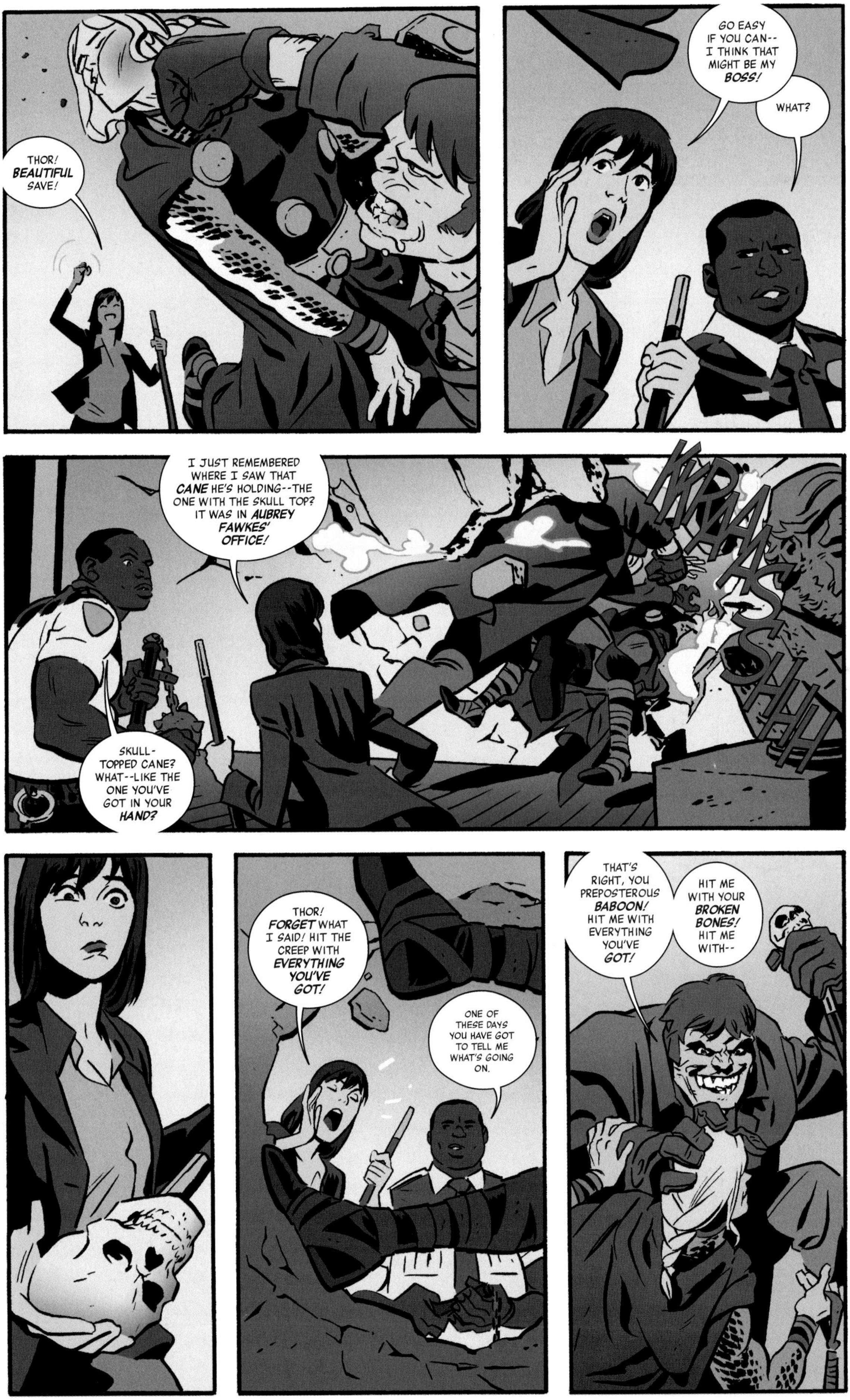
THOR! BEAUTIFUL SAVE!
GO EASY IF YOU CAN-- I THINK THAT MIGHT BE MY BOSS!
WHAT?
I JUST REMEMBERED WHERE I SAW THAT CANE HE'S HOLDING--THE ONE WITH THE SKULL TOP? IT WAS IN AUBREY FAWKES' OFFICE!
KKRAAASSHHH
SKULL-TOPPED CANE? WHAT--LIKE THE ONE YOU'VE GOT IN YOUR HAND?
THOR! FORGET WHAT I SAID! HIT THE CREEP WITH EVERYTHING YOU'VE GOT!
ONE OF THESE DAYS YOU HAVE GOT TO TELL ME WHAT'S GOING ON.
THAT'S RIGHT, YOU PREPOSTEROUS BABOON! HIT ME WITH EVERYTHING YOU'VE GOT!
HIT ME WITH YOUR BROKEN BONES! HIT ME WITH--

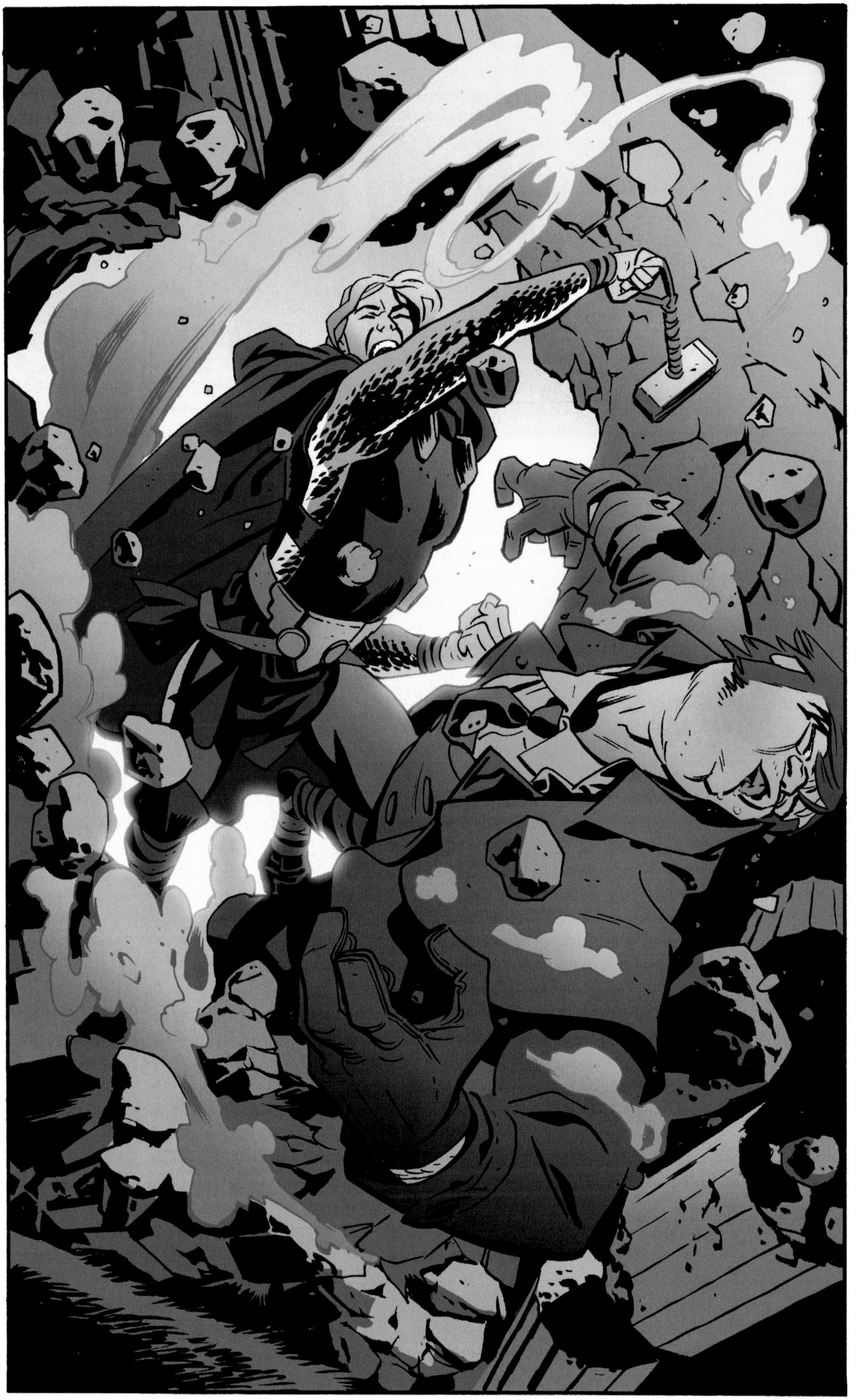

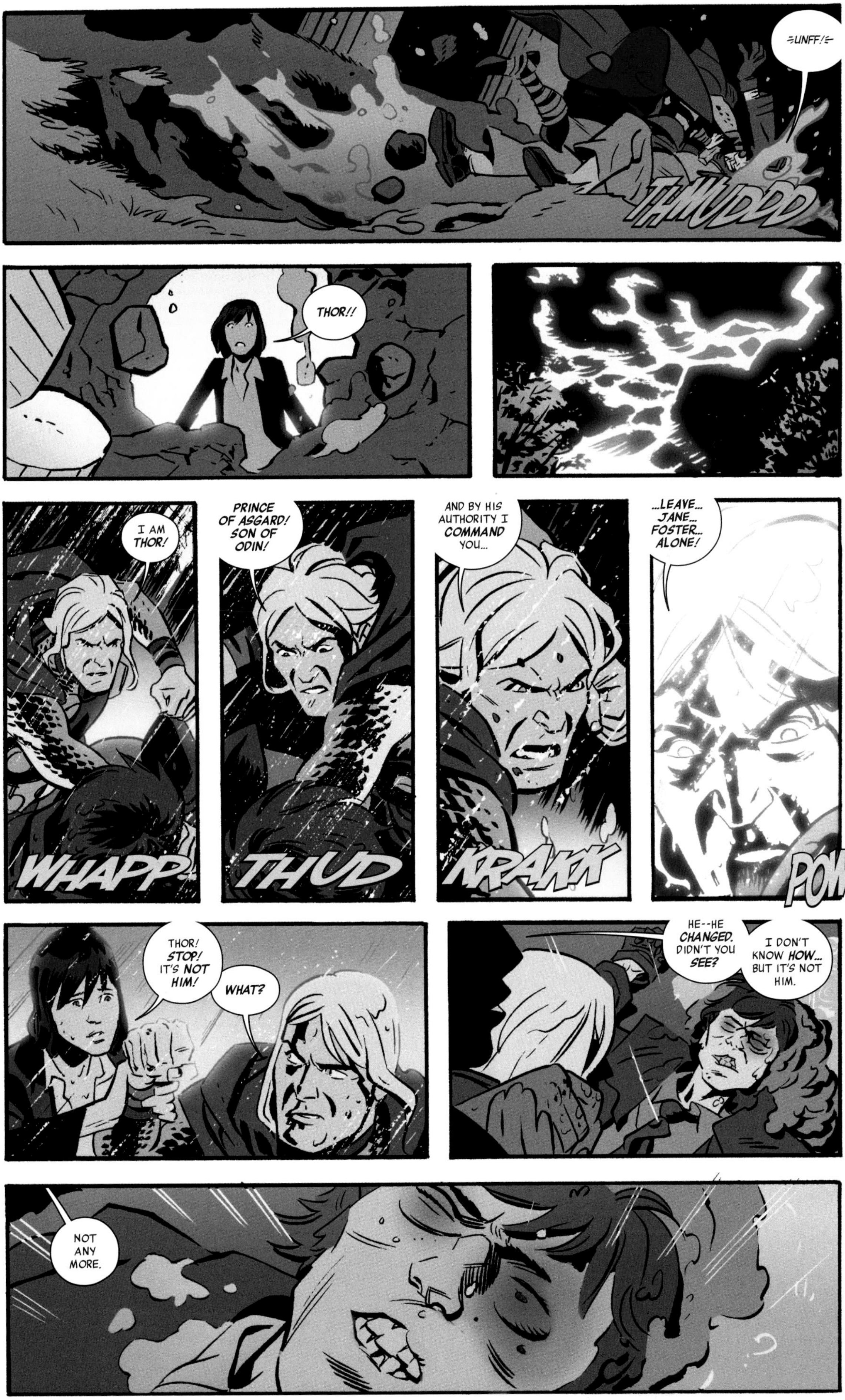
=UNFF!=
THWUDDD
THOR!!
I AM THOR!
WHAPP
PRINCE OF ASGARD! SON OF ODIN!
THUD
AND BY HIS AUTHORITY I COMMAND YOU...
KRAKK
...LEAVE... JANE... FOSTER... ALONE!
POW
THOR! STOP! IT'S NOT HIM!
WHAT?
HE--HE CHANGED. DIDN'T YOU SEE?
I DON'T KNOW HOW... BUT IT'S NOT HIM.
NOT ANY MORE.

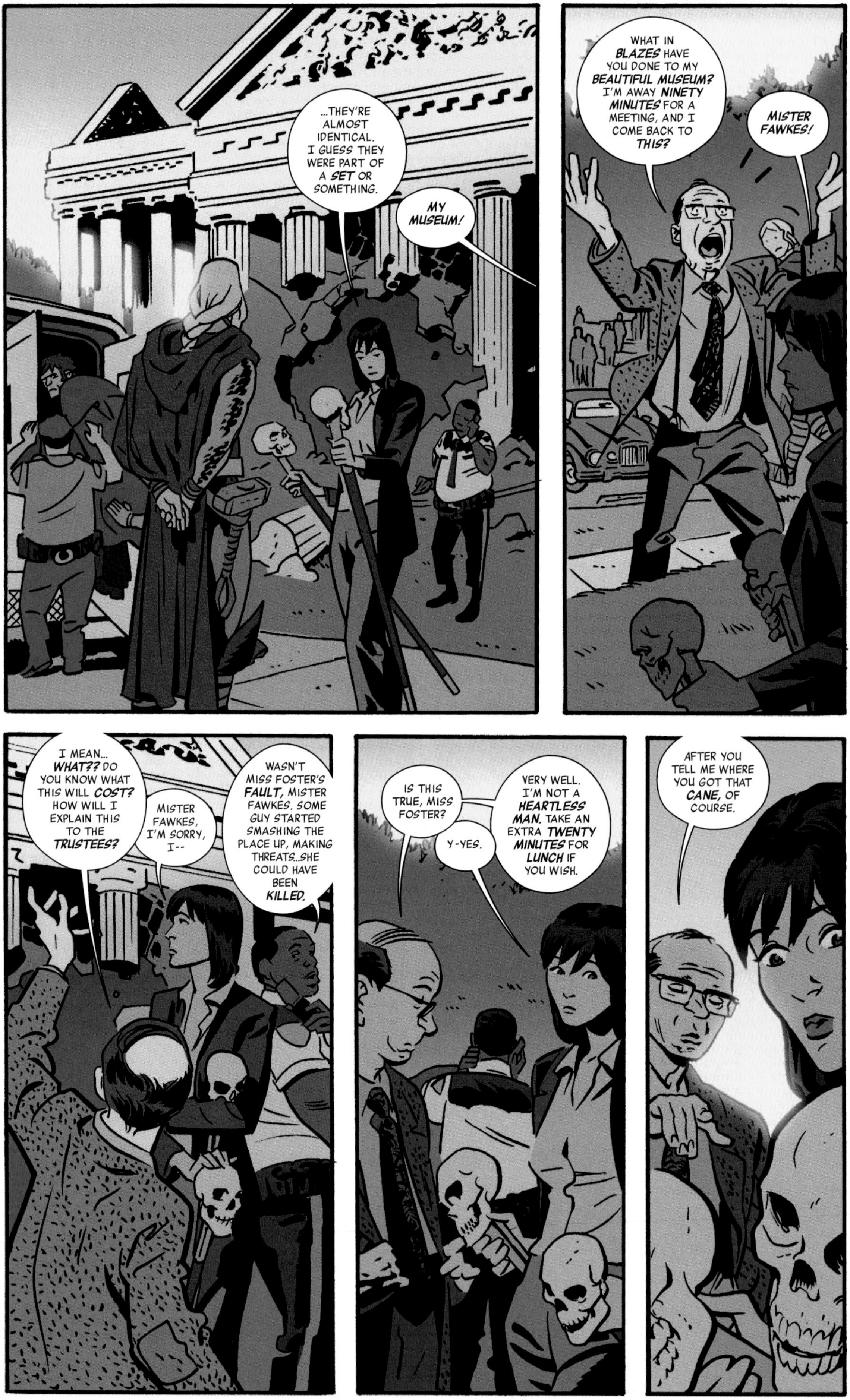
...THEY'RE ALMOST IDENTICAL. I GUESS THEY WERE PART OF A SET OR SOMETHING.
MY MUSEUM!
WHAT IN BLAZES HAVE YOU DONE TO MY BEAUTIFUL MUSEUM? I'M AWAY NINETY MINUTES FOR A MEETING, AND I COME BACK TO THIS?
MISTER FAWKES!
I MEAN... WHAT?? DO YOU KNOW WHAT THIS WILL COST? HOW WILL I EXPLAIN THIS TO THE TRUSTEES?
MISTER FAWKES, I'M SORRY, I--
WASN'T MISS FOSTER'S FAULT, MISTER FAWKES. SOME GUY STARTED SMASHING THE PLACE UP, MAKING THREATS...SHE COULD HAVE BEEN KILLED.
IS THIS TRUE, MISS FOSTER?
Y-YES.
VERY WELL. I'M NOT A HEARTLESS MAN. TAKE AN EXTRA TWENTY MINUTES FOR LUNCH IF YOU WISH.
AFTER YOU TELL ME WHERE YOU GOT THAT CANE, OF COURSE.

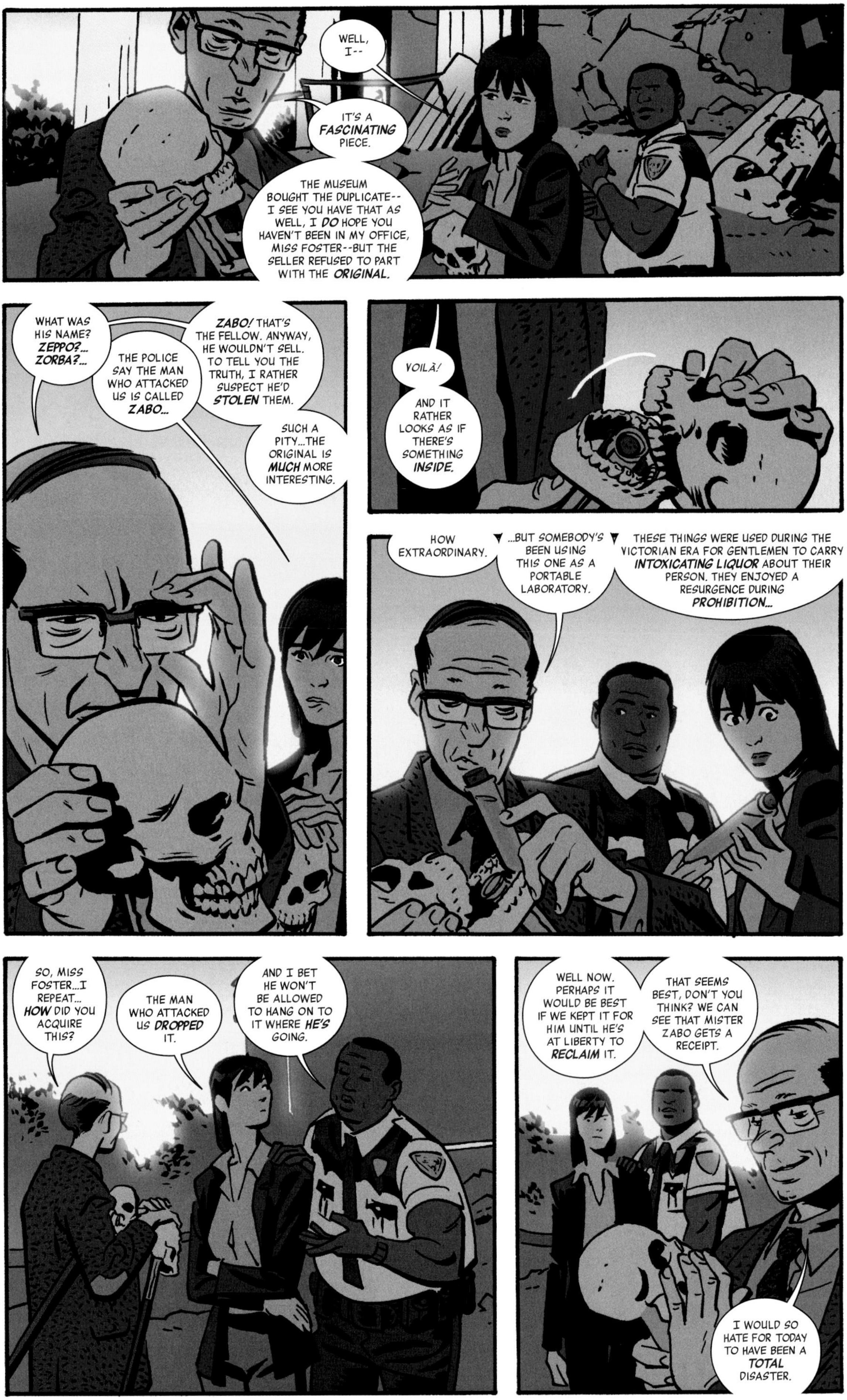
WELL, I--
IT'S A FASCINATING PIECE.
THE MUSEUM BOUGHT THE DUPLICATE-- I SEE YOU HAVE THAT AS WELL, I DO HOPE YOU HAVEN'T BEEN IN MY OFFICE, MISS FOSTER--BUT THE SELLER REFUSED TO PART WITH THE ORIGINAL.
WHAT WAS HIS NAME? ZEPPO?... ZORBA?...
THE POLICE SAY THE MAN WHO ATTACKED US IS CALLED ZABO...
ZABO! THAT'S THE FELLOW. ANYWAY, HE WOULDN'T SELL. TO TELL YOU THE TRUTH, I RATHER SUSPECT HE'D STOLEN THEM.
SUCH A PITY...THE ORIGINAL IS MUCH MORE INTERESTING.
VOILÀ!
AND IT RATHER LOOKS AS IF THERE'S SOMETHING INSIDE.
HOW EXTRAORDINARY.
...BUT SOMEBODY'S BEEN USING THIS ONE AS A PORTABLE LABORATORY.
THESE THINGS WERE USED DURING THE VICTORIAN ERA FOR GENTLEMEN TO CARRY INTOXICATING LIQUOR ABOUT THEIR PERSON. THEY ENJOYED A RESURGENCE DURING PROHIBITION...
SO, MISS FOSTER...I REPEAT... HOW DID YOU ACQUIRE THIS?
THE MAN WHO ATTACKED US DROPPED IT.
AND I BET HE WON'T BE ALLOWED TO HANG ON TO IT WHERE HE'S GOING.
WELL NOW. PERHAPS IT WOULD BE BEST IF WE KEPT IT FOR HIM UNTIL HE'S AT LIBERTY TO RECLAIM IT.
THAT SEEMS BEST, DON'T YOU THINK? WE CAN SEE THAT MISTER ZABO GETS A RECEIPT.
I WOULD SO HATE FOR TODAY TO HAVE BEEN A TOTAL DISASTER.

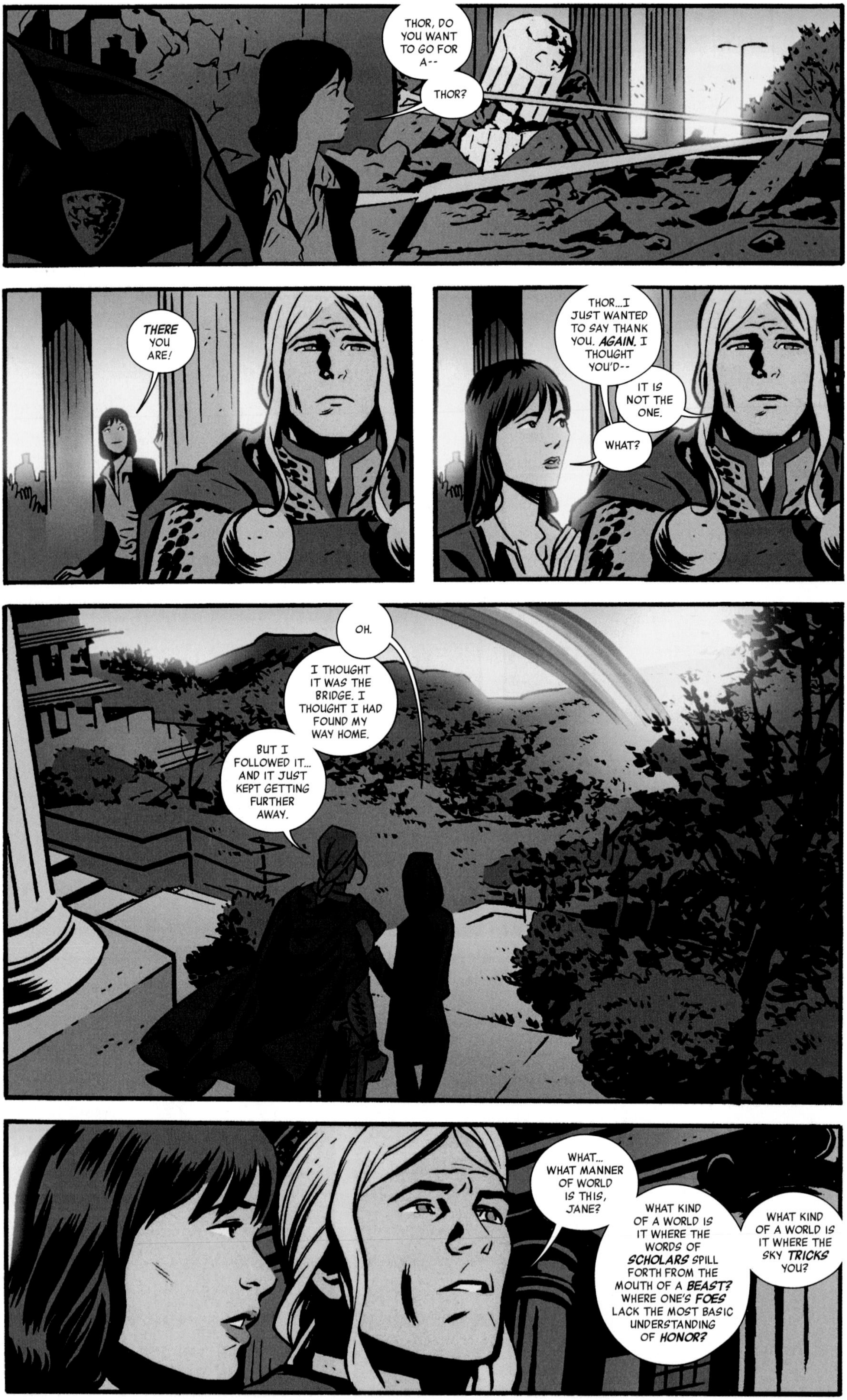
THOR, DO YOU WANT TO GO FOR A--
THOR?
THERE YOU ARE!
THOR...I JUST WANTED TO SAY THANK YOU. AGAIN. I THOUGHT YOU'D--
IT IS NOT THE ONE.
WHAT?
OH.
I THOUGHT IT WAS THE BRIDGE. I THOUGHT I HAD FOUND MY WAY HOME.
BUT I FOLLOWED IT... AND IT JUST KEPT GETTING FURTHER AWAY.
WHAT... WHAT MANNER OF WORLD IS THIS, JANE?
WHAT KIND OF A WORLD IS IT WHERE THE WORDS OF SCHOLARS SPILL FORTH FROM THE MOUTH OF A BEAST? WHERE ONE'S FOES LACK THE MOST BASIC UNDERSTANDING OF HONOR?
WHAT KIND OF A WORLD IS IT WHERE THE SKY TRICKS YOU?

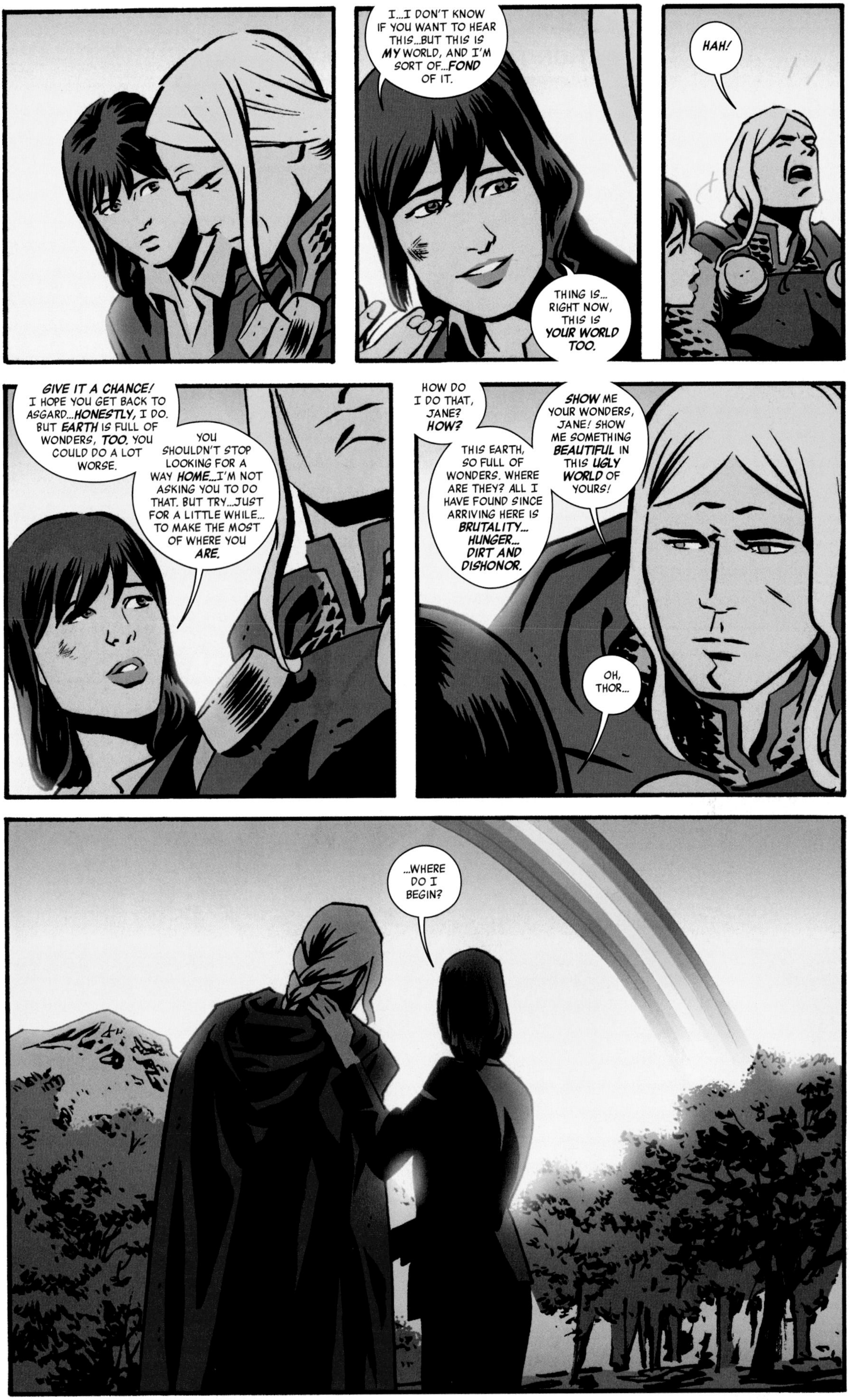
I...I DON'T KNOW IF YOU WANT TO HEAR THIS...BUT THIS IS MY WORLD, AND I'M SORT OF...FOND OF IT.
THING IS... RIGHT NOW, THIS IS YOUR WORLD TOO.
HAH!
GIVE IT A CHANCE! I HOPE YOU GET BACK TO ASGARD...HONESTLY, I DO. BUT EARTH IS FULL OF WONDERS, TOO. YOU COULD DO A LOT WORSE.
YOU SHOULDN'T STOP LOOKING FOR A WAY HOME...I'M NOT ASKING YOU TO DO THAT. BUT TRY...JUST FOR A LITTLE WHILE... TO MAKE THE MOST OF WHERE YOU ARE.
HOW DO I DO THAT, JANE? HOW?
THIS EARTH, SO FULL OF WONDERS. WHERE ARE THEY? ALL I HAVE FOUND SINCE ARRIVING HERE IS BRUTALITY... HUNGER... DIRT AND DISHONOR.
SHOW ME YOUR WONDERS, JANE! SHOW ME SOMETHING BEAUTIFUL IN THIS UGLY WORLD OF YOURS!
OH, THOR...
...WHERE DO I BEGIN?

THOR THE MIGHTY AVENGER #3

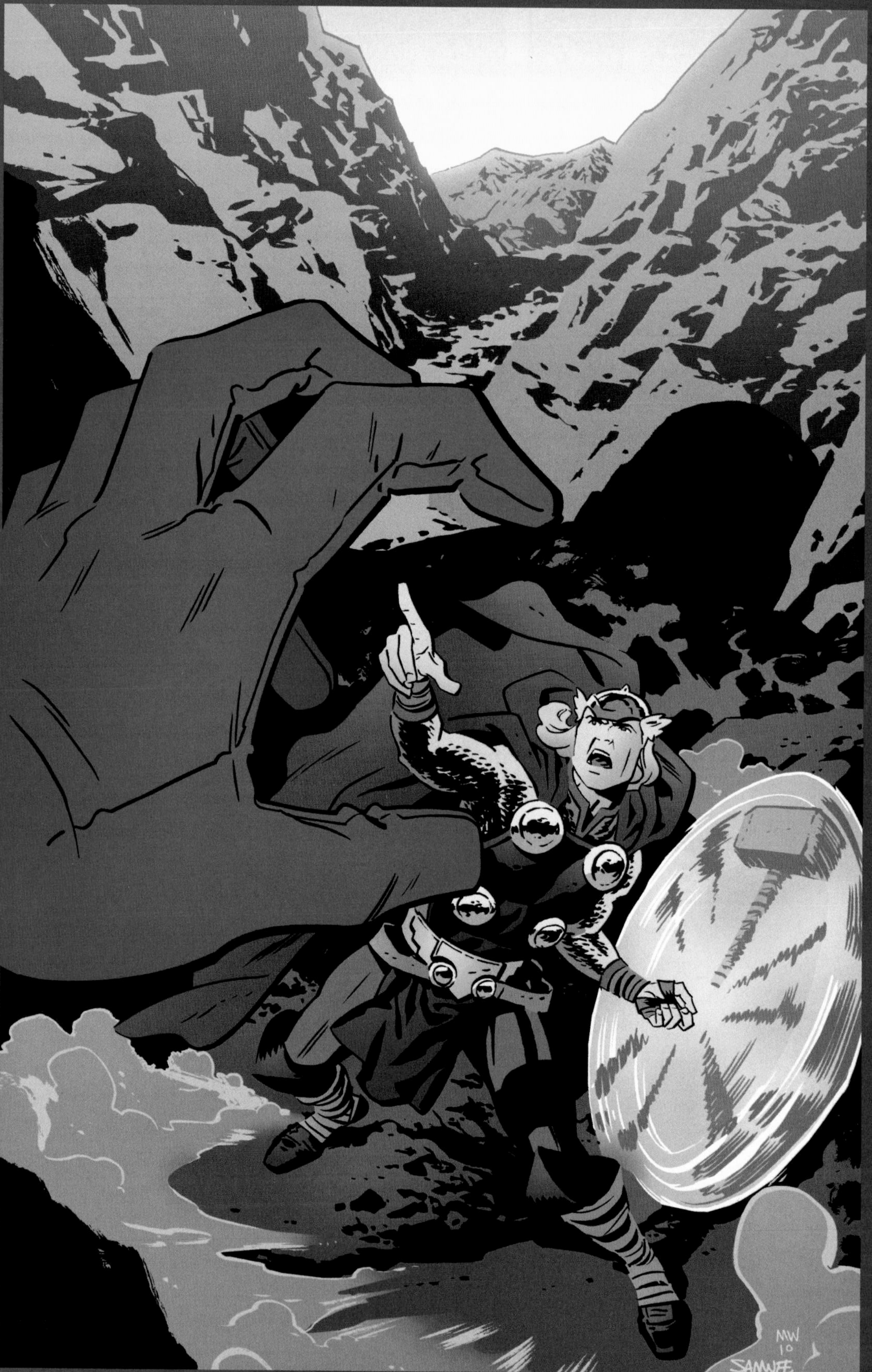
MW
10
SAMWEE

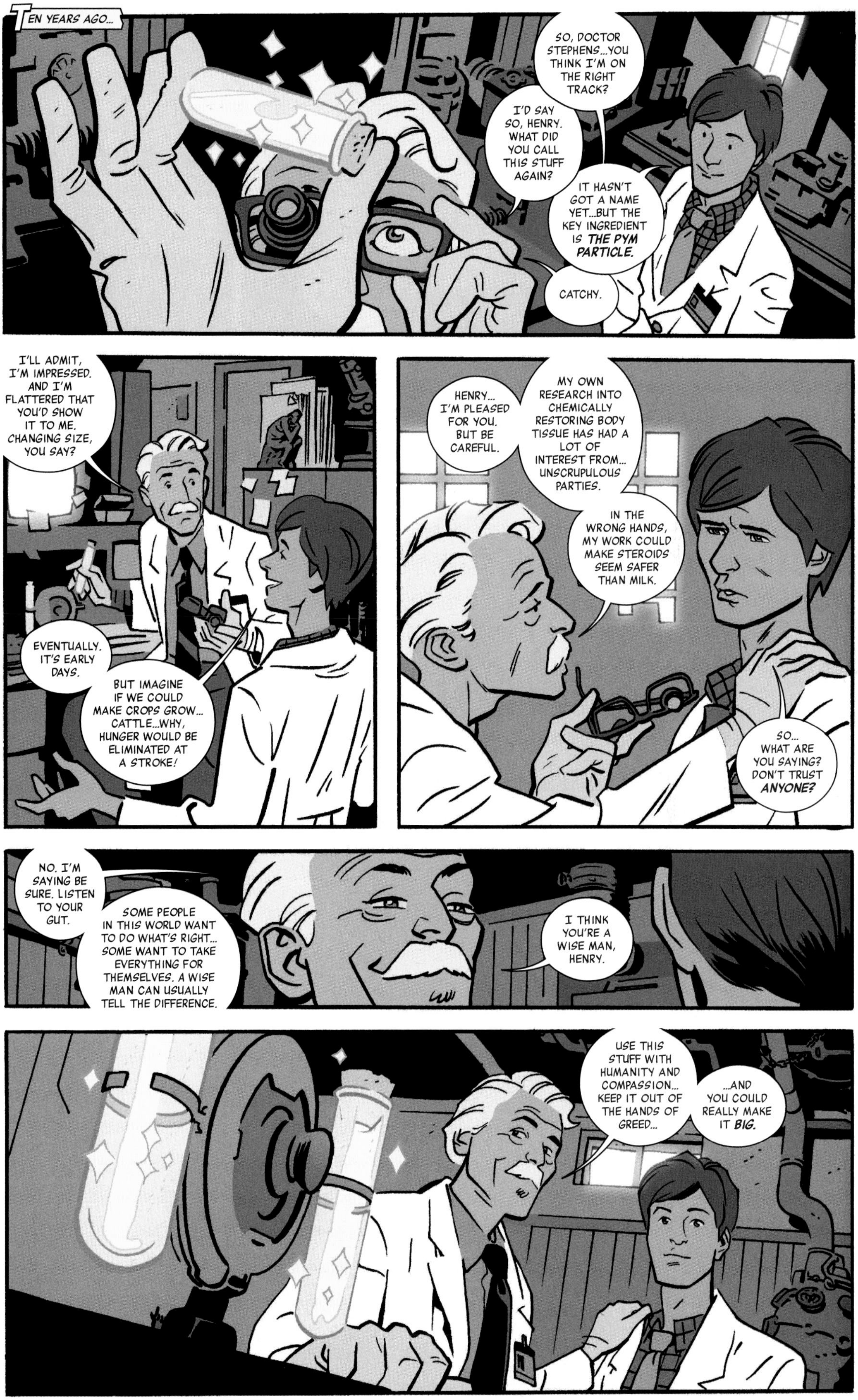
TEN YEARS AGO...
SO, DOCTOR STEPHENS...YOU THINK I'M ON THE RIGHT TRACK?
I'D SAY SO, HENRY. WHAT DID YOU CALL THIS STUFF AGAIN?
IT HASN'T GOT A NAME YET...BUT THE KEY INGREDIENT IS THE PYM PARTICLE.
CATCHY.
I'LL ADMIT, I'M IMPRESSED. AND I'M FLATTERED THAT YOU'D SHOW IT TO ME. CHANGING SIZE, YOU SAY?
EVENTUALLY. IT'S EARLY DAYS.
BUT IMAGINE IF WE COULD MAKE CROPS GROW... CATTLE...WHY, HUNGER WOULD BE ELIMINATED AT A STROKE!
HENRY... I'M PLEASED FOR YOU. BUT BE CAREFUL.
MY OWN RESEARCH INTO CHEMICALLY RESTORING BODY TISSUE HAS HAD A LOT OF INTEREST FROM... UNSCRUPULOUS PARTIES.
IN THE WRONG HANDS, MY WORK COULD MAKE STEROIDS SEEM SAFER THAN MILK.
SO... WHAT ARE YOU SAYING? DON'T TRUST ANYONE?
NO. I'M SAYING BE SURE. LISTEN TO YOUR GUT.
SOME PEOPLE IN THIS WORLD WANT TO DO WHAT'S RIGHT... SOME WANT TO TAKE EVERYTHING FOR THEMSELVES. A WISE MAN CAN USUALLY TELL THE DIFFERENCE.
I THINK YOU'RE A WISE MAN, HENRY.
USE THIS STUFF WITH HUMANITY AND COMPASSION... KEEP IT OUT OF THE HANDS OF GREED...
...AND YOU COULD REALLY MAKE IT BIG.

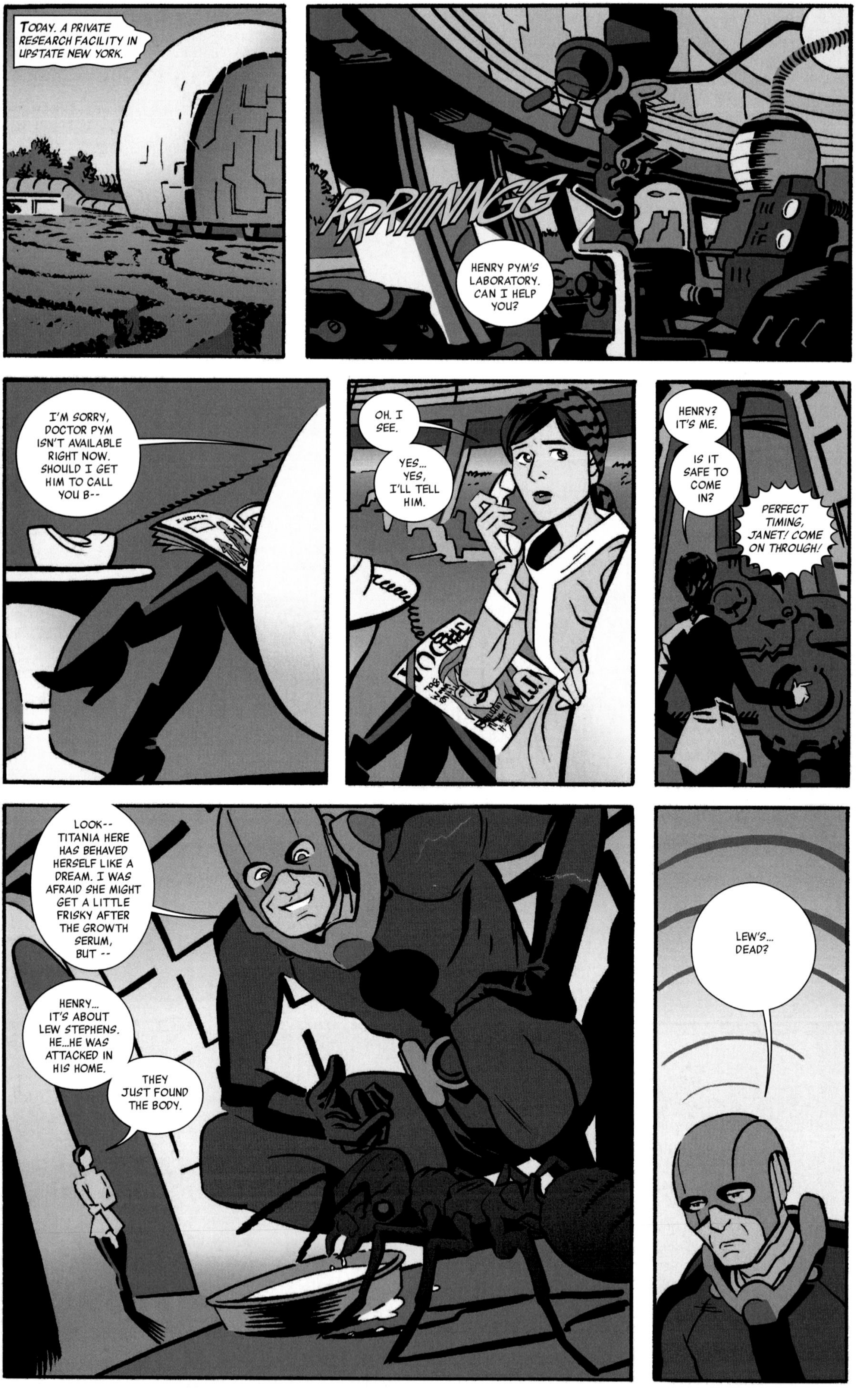
TODAY. A PRIVATE RESEARCH FACILITY IN UPSTATE NEW YORK.
RRRIIINNGG
HENRY PYM'S LABORATORY. CAN I HELP YOU?
I'M SORRY, DOCTOR PYM ISN'T AVAILABLE RIGHT NOW. SHOULD I GET HIM TO CALL YOU B--
OH. I SEE.
YES... YES, I'LL TELL HIM.
HENRY? IT'S ME.
IS IT SAFE TO COME IN?
PERFECT TIMING, JANET! COME ON THROUGH!
LOOK-- TITANIA HERE HAS BEHAVED HERSELF LIKE A DREAM. I WAS AFRAID SHE MIGHT GET A LITTLE FRISKY AFTER THE GROWTH SERUM, BUT --
HENRY... IT'S ABOUT LEW STEPHENS. HE...HE WAS ATTACKED IN HIS HOME.
THEY JUST FOUND THE BODY.
LEW'S... DEAD?

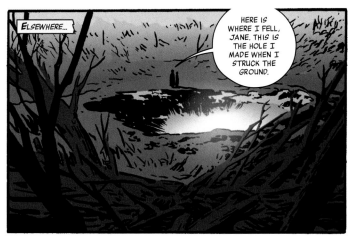

HERE IS WHERE I FELL, JANE. THIS IS THE HOLE I MADE WHEN I STRUCK THE GROUND.

W-WHAT'S THAT LIGHT?

I DO NOT KNOW. PERHAPS... ANSWERS?

LET US FIND OUT!

THOR!

AAAGHH!!

THE LIGHT... IT HURTS LIKE A THOUSAND SPEARS!

TAKE MY HAND, THOR! I WON'T LET GO! I WON'T LET GO!

JANE! JAAAAAANE!!

NNNGHH!

THWUDD

MY SON...

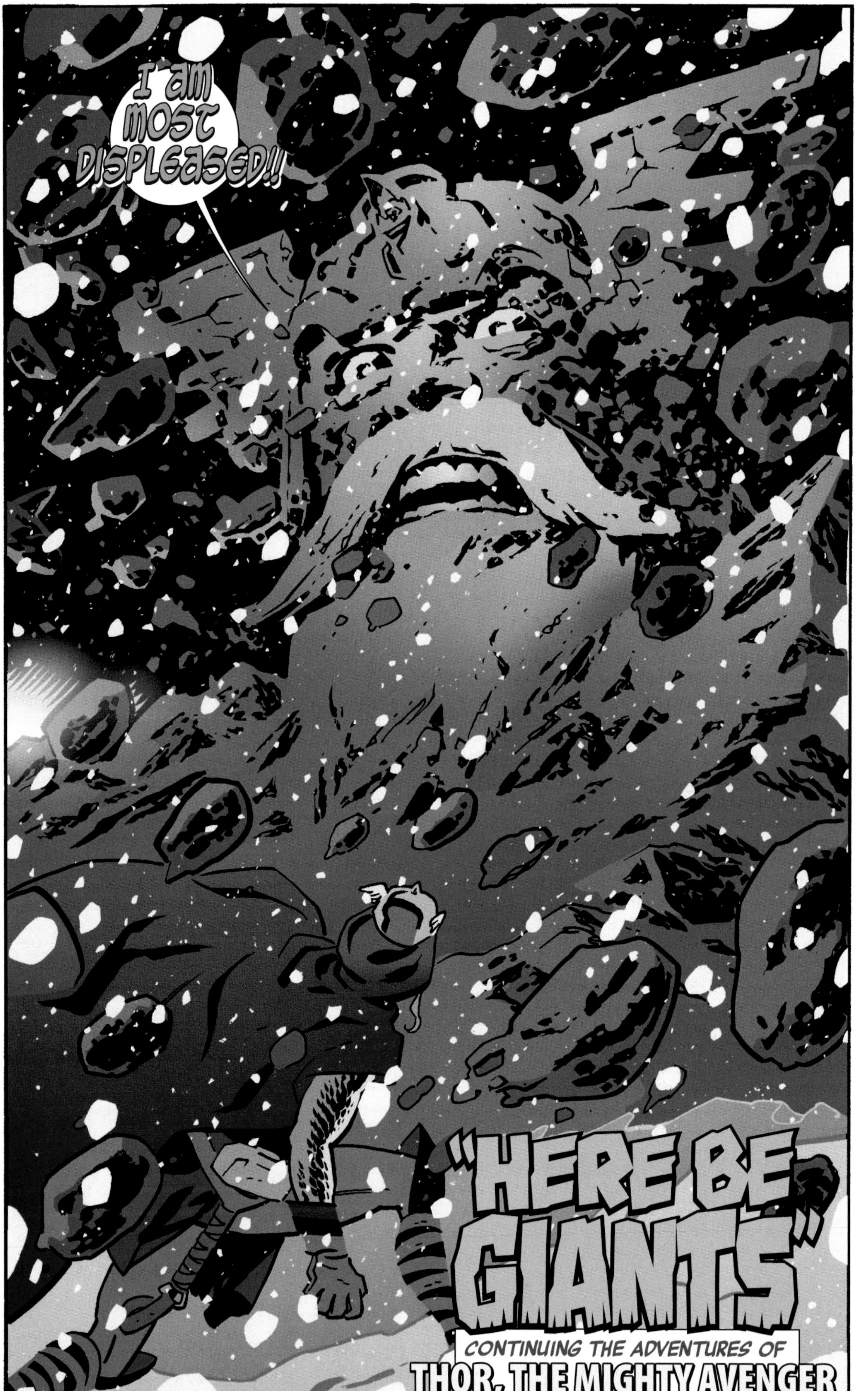
I am most DISPLEASED!!
"HERE BE GIANTS"
CONTINUING THE ADVENTURES OF
THOR, THE MIGHTY AVENGER

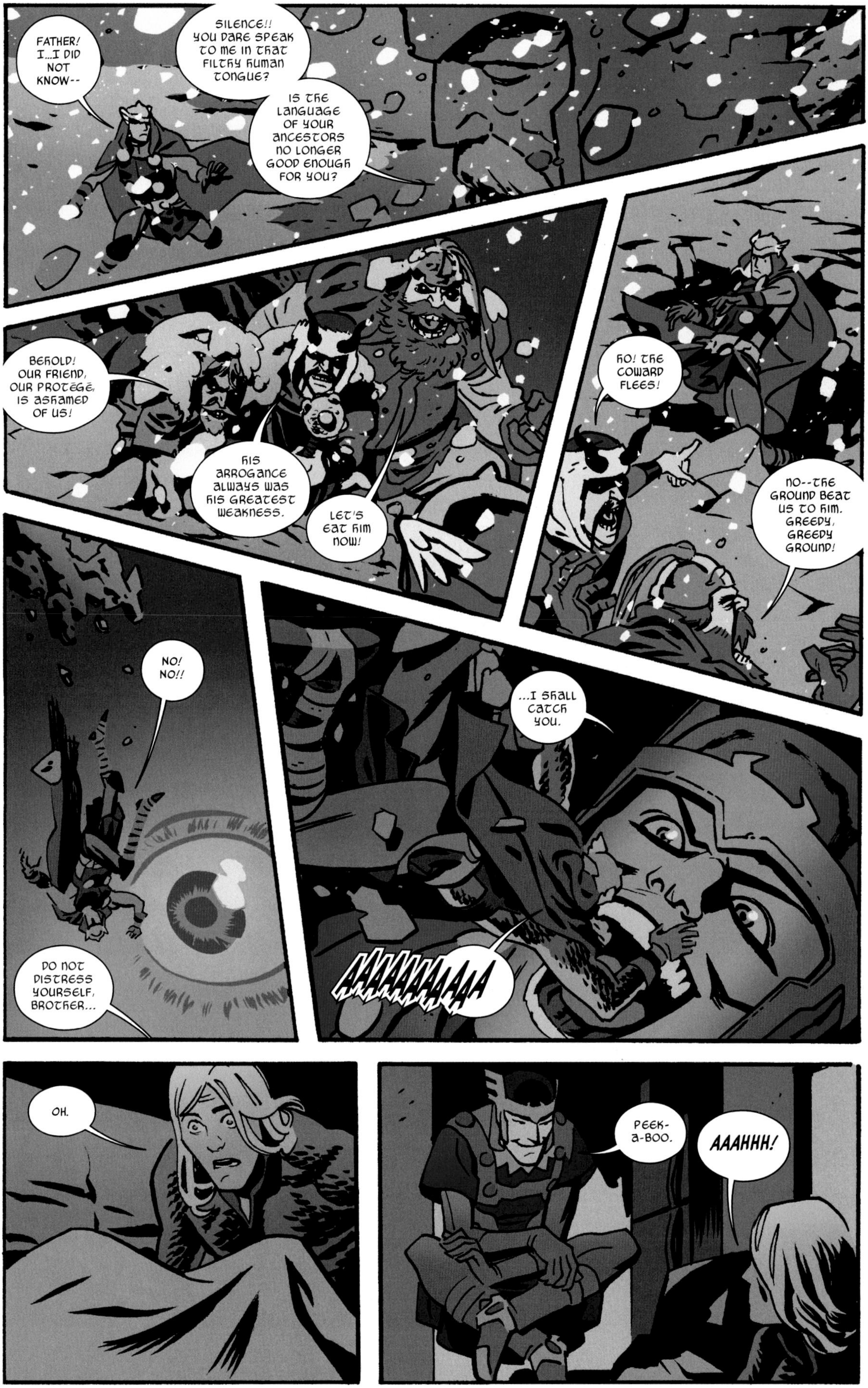
FATHER! I...I DID NOT KNOW--
SILENCE!! YOU DARE SPEAK TO ME IN THAT FILTHY HUMAN TONGUE?
IS THE LANGUAGE OF YOUR ANCESTORS NO LONGER GOOD ENOUGH FOR YOU?
BEHOLD! OUR FRIEND, OUR PROTÉGÉ, IS ASHAMED OF US!
HIS ARROGANCE ALWAYS WAS HIS GREATEST WEAKNESS.
LET'S EAT HIM NOW!
HO! THE COWARD FLEES!
NO--THE GROUND BEAT US TO HIM. GREEDY, GREEDY GROUND!
NO! NO!!
DO NOT DISTRESS YOURSELF, BROTHER...
...I SHALL CATCH YOU.
AAAAAAAAAA
OH.
PEEK-A-BOO.
AAAHHH!

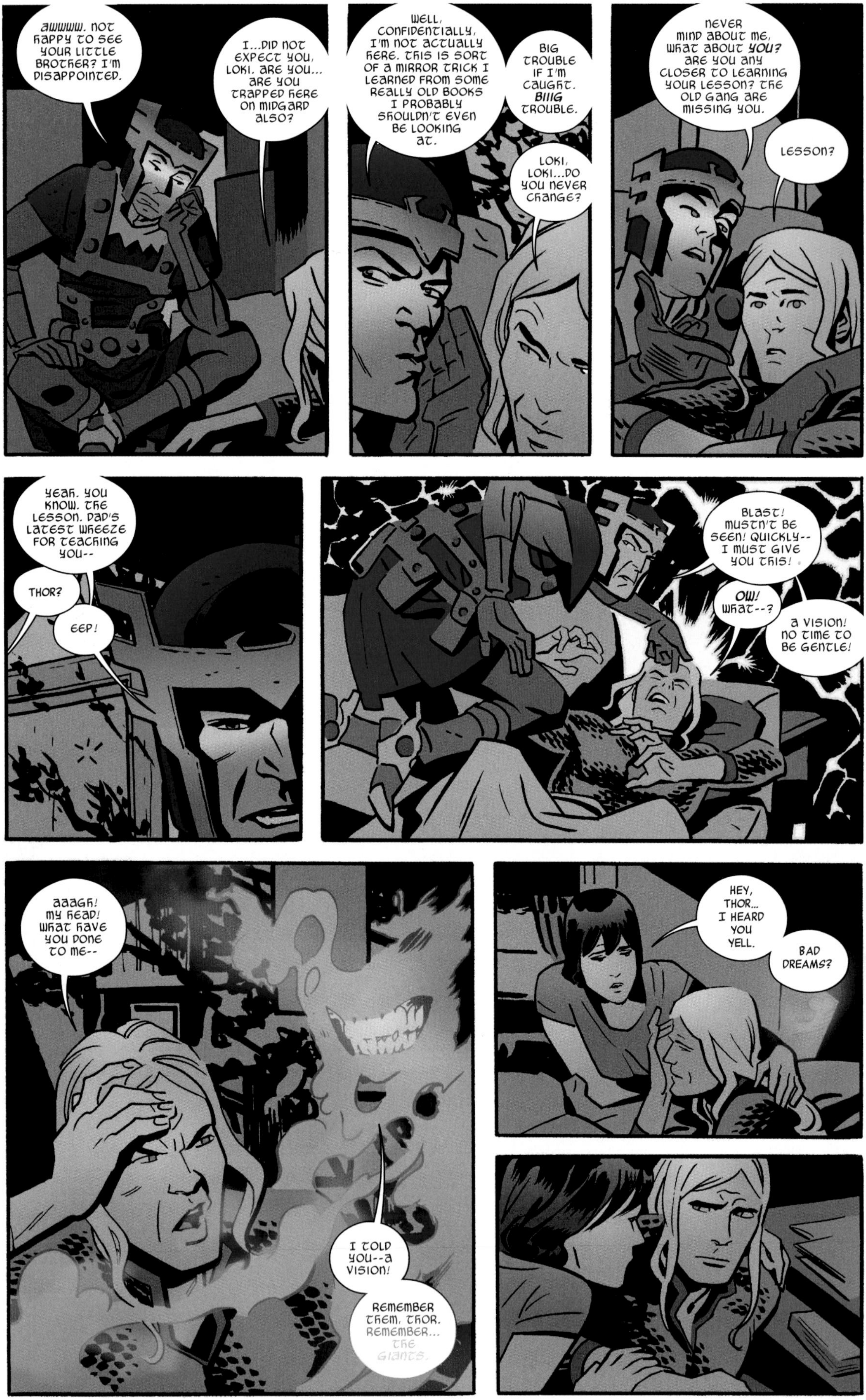
AWWWW. NOT HAPPY TO SEE YOUR LITTLE BROTHER? I'M DISAPPOINTED.
I...DID NOT EXPECT YOU, LOKI. ARE YOU... ARE YOU TRAPPED HERE ON MIDGARD ALSO?
WELL, CONFIDENTIALLY, I'M NOT ACTUALLY HERE. THIS IS SORT OF A MIRROR TRICK I LEARNED FROM SOME REALLY OLD BOOKS I PROBABLY SHOULDN'T EVEN BE LOOKING AT.
BIG TROUBLE IF I'M CAUGHT. BIIIG TROUBLE.
LOKI, LOKI...DO YOU NEVER CHANGE?
NEVER MIND ABOUT ME, WHAT ABOUT YOU? ARE YOU ANY CLOSER TO LEARNING YOUR LESSON? THE OLD GANG ARE MISSING YOU.
LESSON?
YEAH. YOU KNOW. THE LESSON. DAD'S LATEST WHEEZE FOR TEACHING YOU--
THOR?
EEP!
BLAST! MUSTN'T BE SEEN! QUICKLY-- I MUST GIVE YOU THIS!
OW! WHAT--?
A VISION! NO TIME TO BE GENTLE!
AAAGH! MY HEAD! WHAT HAVE YOU DONE TO ME--
I TOLD YOU--A VISION!
REMEMBER THEM, THOR. REMEMBER... THE GIANTS.
HEY, THOR... I HEARD YOU YELL.
BAD DREAMS?

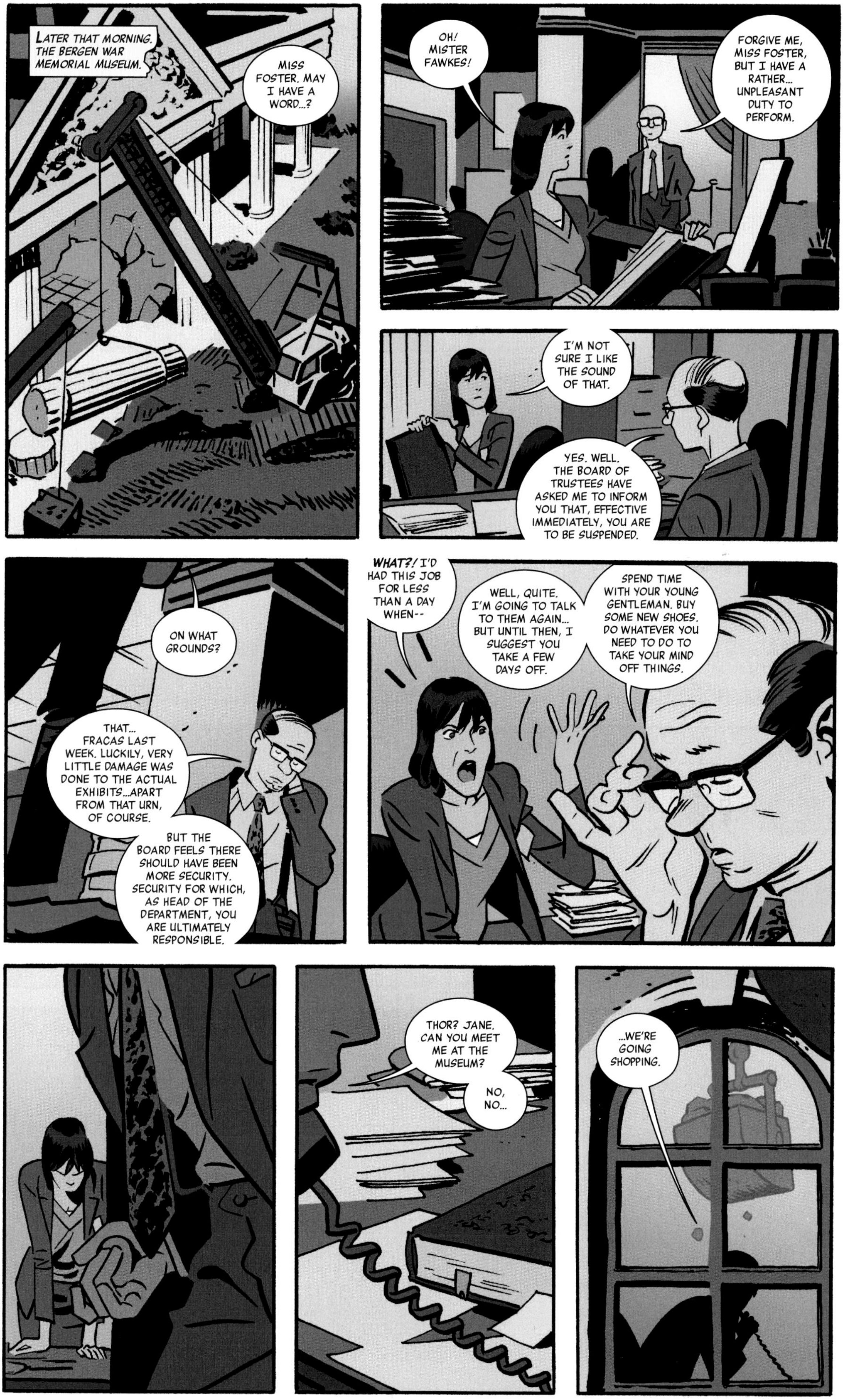
LATER THAT MORNING. THE BERGEN WAR MEMORIAL MUSEUM.
MISS FOSTER. MAY I HAVE A WORD...?
OH! MISTER FAWKES!
FORGIVE ME, MISS FOSTER, BUT I HAVE A RATHER... UNPLEASANT DUTY TO PERFORM.
I'M NOT SURE I LIKE THE SOUND OF THAT.
YES. WELL. THE BOARD OF TRUSTEES HAVE ASKED ME TO INFORM YOU THAT, EFFECTIVE IMMEDIATELY, YOU ARE TO BE SUSPENDED.
ON WHAT GROUNDS?
THAT... FRACAS LAST WEEK. LUCKILY, VERY LITTLE DAMAGE WAS DONE TO THE ACTUAL EXHIBITS...APART FROM THAT URN, OF COURSE.
BUT THE BOARD FEELS THERE SHOULD HAVE BEEN MORE SECURITY. SECURITY FOR WHICH, AS HEAD OF THE DEPARTMENT, YOU ARE ULTIMATELY RESPONSIBLE.
WHAT?! I'D HAD THIS JOB FOR LESS THAN A DAY WHEN--
WELL, QUITE. I'M GOING TO TALK TO THEM AGAIN... BUT UNTIL THEN, I SUGGEST YOU TAKE A FEW DAYS OFF.
SPEND TIME WITH YOUR YOUNG GENTLEMAN. BUY SOME NEW SHOES. DO WHATEVER YOU NEED TO DO TO TAKE YOUR MIND OFF THINGS.
THOR? JANE. CAN YOU MEET ME AT THE MUSEUM?
NO, NO...
...WE'RE GOING SHOPPING.

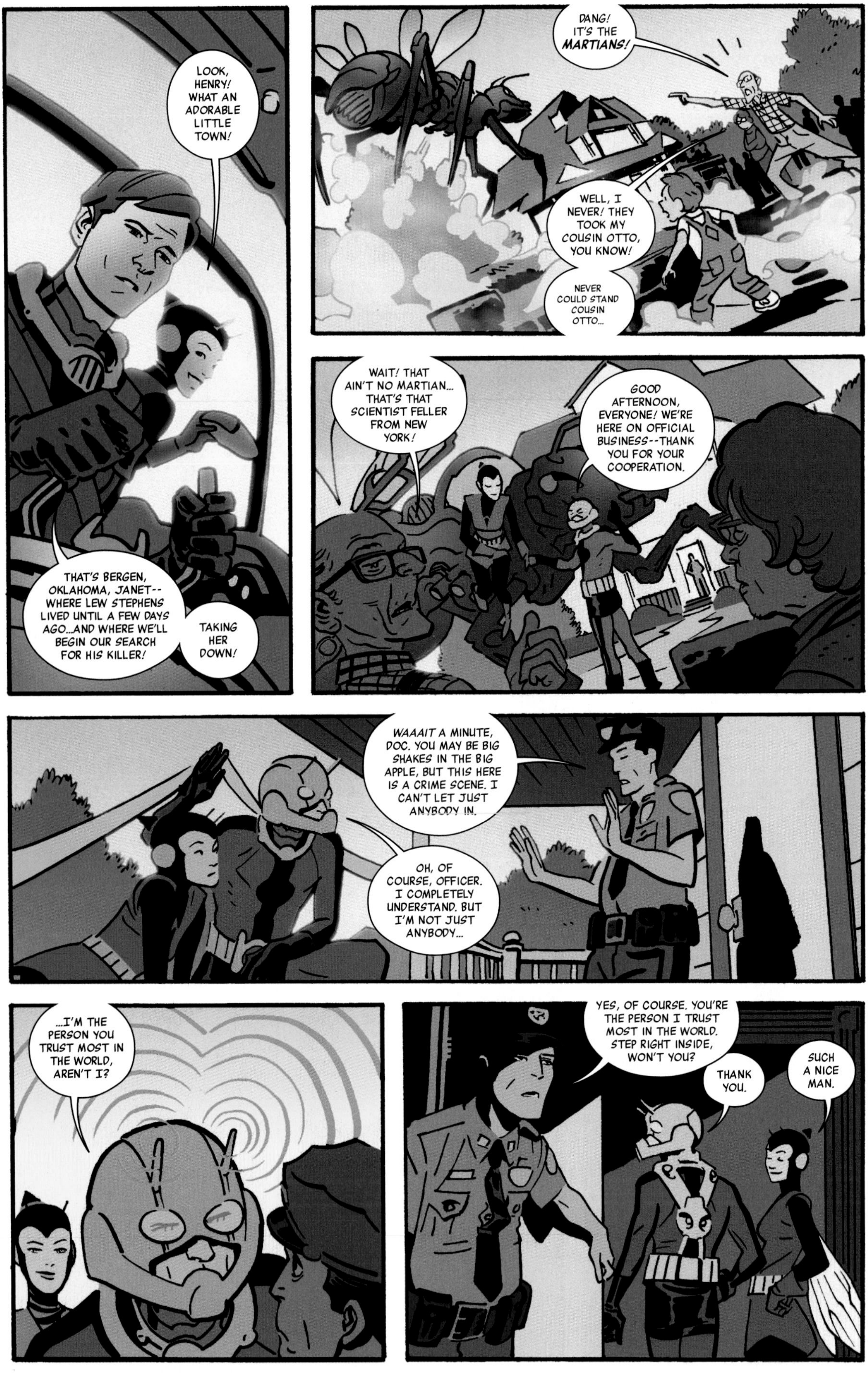
LOOK, HENRY! WHAT AN ADORABLE LITTLE TOWN!
THAT'S BERGEN, OKLAHOMA, JANET--WHERE LEW STEPHENS LIVED UNTIL A FEW DAYS AGO...AND WHERE WE'LL BEGIN OUR SEARCH FOR HIS KILLER!
TAKING HER DOWN!
DANG! IT'S THE MARTIANS!
WELL, I NEVER! THEY TOOK MY COUSIN OTTO, YOU KNOW!
NEVER COULD STAND COUSIN OTTO...
WAIT! THAT AIN'T NO MARTIAN... THAT'S THAT SCIENTIST FELLER FROM NEW YORK!
GOOD AFTERNOON, EVERYONE! WE'RE HERE ON OFFICIAL BUSINESS--THANK YOU FOR YOUR COOPERATION.
WAAAIT A MINUTE, DOC. YOU MAY BE BIG SHAKES IN THE BIG APPLE, BUT THIS HERE IS A CRIME SCENE. I CAN'T LET JUST ANYBODY IN.
OH, OF COURSE, OFFICER. I COMPLETELY UNDERSTAND. BUT I'M NOT JUST ANYBODY...
...I'M THE PERSON YOU TRUST MOST IN THE WORLD, AREN'T I?
YES, OF COURSE. YOU'RE THE PERSON I TRUST MOST IN THE WORLD. STEP RIGHT INSIDE, WON'T YOU?
THANK YOU.
SUCH A NICE MAN.

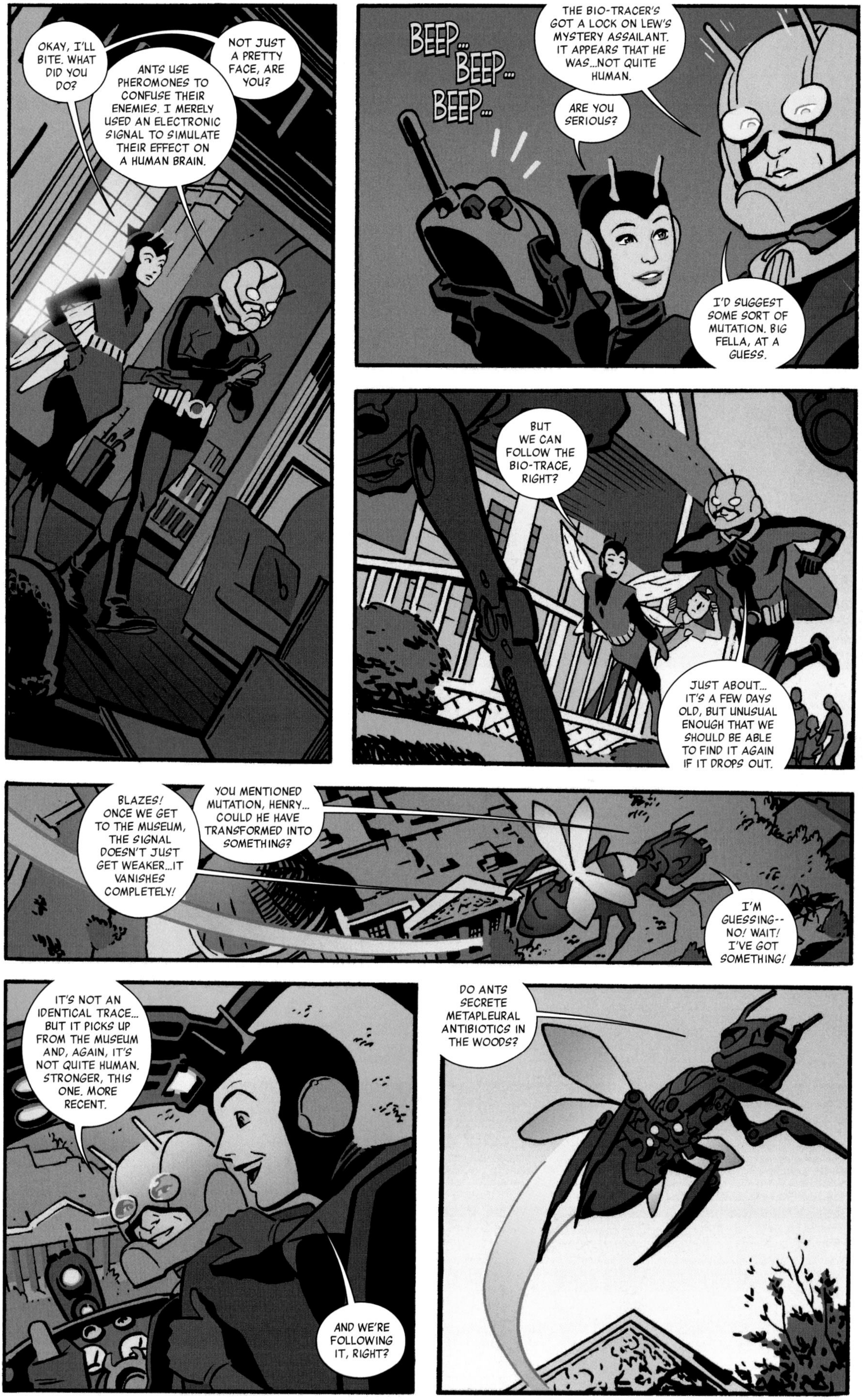
OKAY, I'LL BITE. WHAT DID YOU DO?
NOT JUST A PRETTY FACE, ARE YOU?
ANTS USE PHEROMONES TO CONFUSE THEIR ENEMIES. I MERELY USED AN ELECTRONIC SIGNAL TO SIMULATE THEIR EFFECT ON A HUMAN BRAIN.
BEEP... BEEP... BEEP...
THE BIO-TRACER'S GOT A LOCK ON LEW'S MYSTERY ASSAILANT. IT APPEARS THAT HE WAS...NOT QUITE HUMAN.
ARE YOU SERIOUS?
I'D SUGGEST SOME SORT OF MUTATION. BIG FELLA, AT A GUESS.
BUT WE CAN FOLLOW THE BIO-TRACE, RIGHT?
JUST ABOUT... IT'S A FEW DAYS OLD, BUT UNUSUAL ENOUGH THAT WE SHOULD BE ABLE TO FIND IT AGAIN IF IT DROPS OUT.
BLAZES! ONCE WE GET TO THE MUSEUM, THE SIGNAL DOESN'T JUST GET WEAKER...IT VANISHES COMPLETELY!
YOU MENTIONED MUTATION, HENRY... COULD HE HAVE TRANSFORMED INTO SOMETHING?
I'M GUESSING-- NO! WAIT! I'VE GOT SOMETHING!
IT'S NOT AN IDENTICAL TRACE... BUT IT PICKS UP FROM THE MUSEUM AND, AGAIN, IT'S NOT QUITE HUMAN. STRONGER, THIS ONE. MORE RECENT.
AND WE'RE FOLLOWING IT, RIGHT?
DO ANTS SECRETE METAPLEURAL ANTIBIOTICS IN THE WOODS?

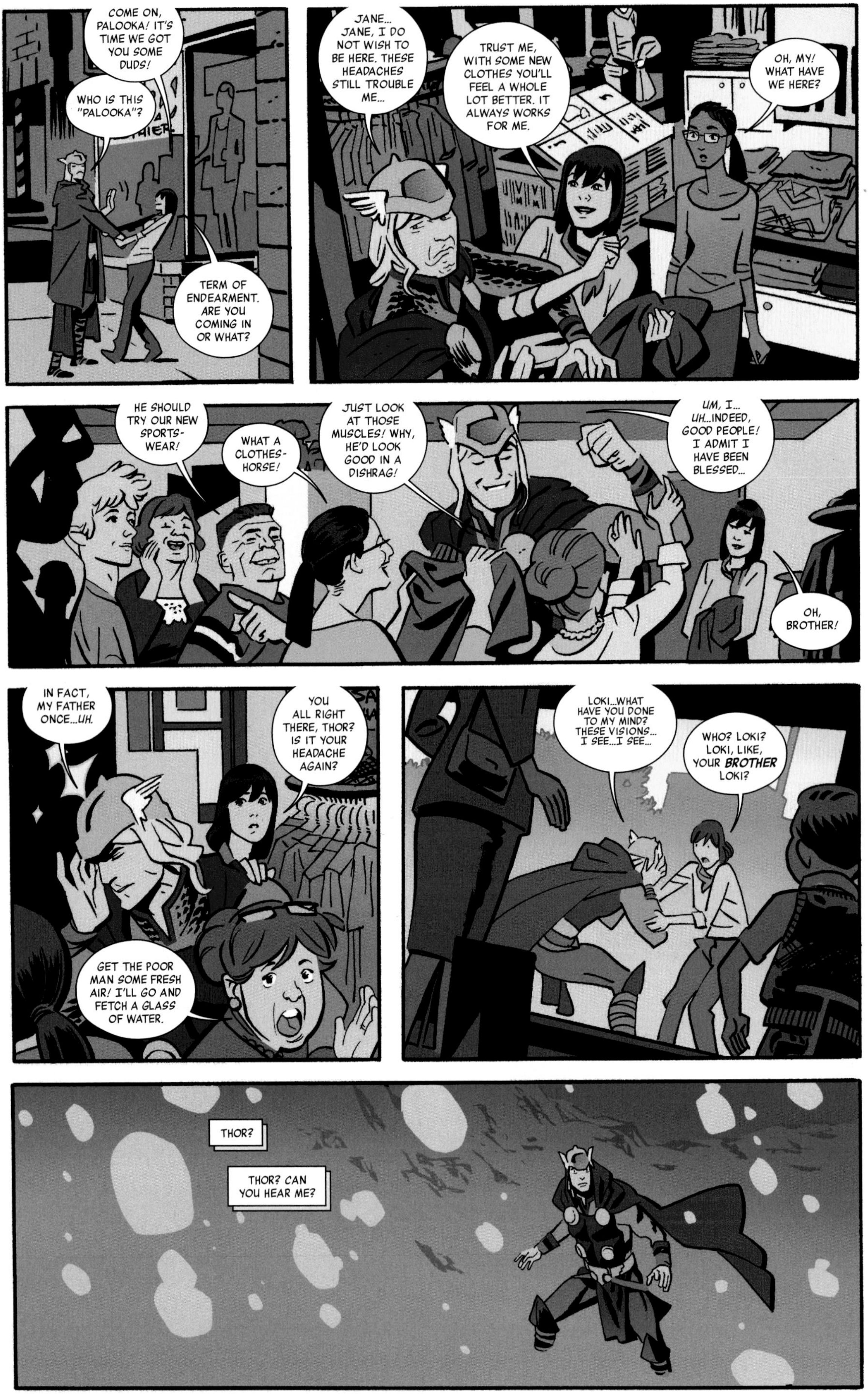
COME ON, PALOOKA! IT'S TIME WE GOT YOU SOME DUDS!
WHO IS THIS "PALOOKA"?
TERM OF ENDEARMENT. ARE YOU COMING IN OR WHAT?
JANE... JANE, I DO NOT WISH TO BE HERE. THESE HEADACHES STILL TROUBLE ME...
TRUST ME, WITH SOME NEW CLOTHES YOU'LL FEEL A WHOLE LOT BETTER. IT ALWAYS WORKS FOR ME.
OH, MY! WHAT HAVE WE HERE?
HE SHOULD TRY OUR NEW SPORTS-WEAR!
WHAT A CLOTHES-HORSE!
JUST LOOK AT THOSE MUSCLES! WHY, HE'D LOOK GOOD IN A DISHRAG!
UM, I... UH...INDEED, GOOD PEOPLE! I ADMIT I HAVE BEEN BLESSED...
OH, BROTHER!
IN FACT, MY FATHER ONCE...UH.
YOU ALL RIGHT THERE, THOR? IS IT YOUR HEADACHE AGAIN?
GET THE POOR MAN SOME FRESH AIR! I'LL GO AND FETCH A GLASS OF WATER.
LOKI...WHAT HAVE YOU DONE TO MY MIND? THESE VISIONS... I SEE...I SEE...
WHO? LOKI? LOKI, LIKE, YOUR BROTHER LOKI?
THOR?
THOR? CAN YOU HEAR ME?

OUR QUARRY IS DIRECTLY BELOW US, JANET. INITIATING AUTOMATIC LANDING PROCEDURE!

HENRY... ARE YOU SURE ABOUT THIS?

IF IT COMES TO A CONFRONTATION, I'LL BE ABLE TO GET US AWAY FROM THE BUSY STREETS EASILY ENOUGH.

THAT'S NOT WHAT I MEANT. I'M CONCERNED ABOUT HOW EMOTIONALLY INVOLVED YOU ARE.

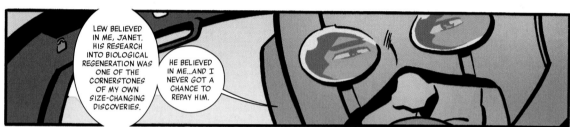

LEW BELIEVED IN ME, JANET. HIS RESEARCH INTO BIOLOGICAL REGENERATION WAS ONE OF THE CORNERSTONES OF MY OWN SIZE-CHANGING DISCOVERIES.

HE BELIEVED IN ME...AND I NEVER GOT A CHANCE TO REPAY HIM.

YOU'RE REPAYING HIM NOW, DARLING. JUST REMEMBER YOU'RE A SCIENTIST. STAY OBJECTIVE. YOU'RE HERE TO SERVE JUSTICE, NOT VENGEANCE.

I'D HATE TO SEE YOU LOSE CONTROL.

TIME TO TACKLE THIS GUY. I'LL GIANT-SIZE MYSELF UP FIRST...NO POINT TAKING CHANCES.

GOOD LUCK, HENRY. I'LL PARK THIS RIG AND JOIN YOU IN A MINUTE.

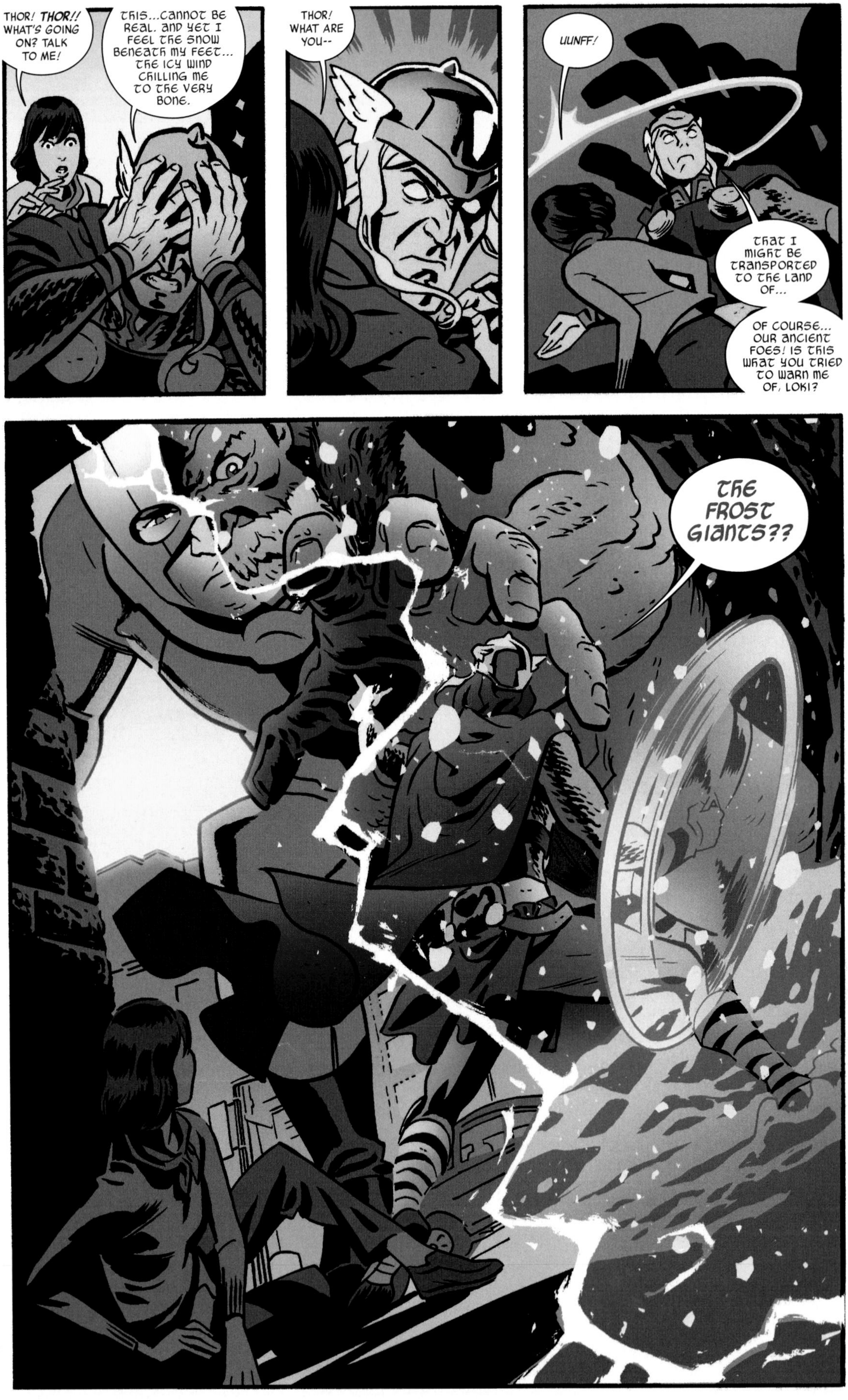
THOR! THOR!! WHAT'S GOING ON? TALK TO ME!
THIS...CANNOT BE REAL. AND YET I FEEL THE SNOW BENEATH MY FEET... THE ICY WIND CHILLING ME TO THE VERY BONE.
THOR! WHAT ARE YOU--
UUNFF!
THAT I MIGHT BE TRANSPORTED TO THE LAND OF...
OF COURSE... OUR ANCIENT FOES! IS THIS WHAT YOU TRIED TO WARN ME OF, LOKI?
THE FROST GIANTS??

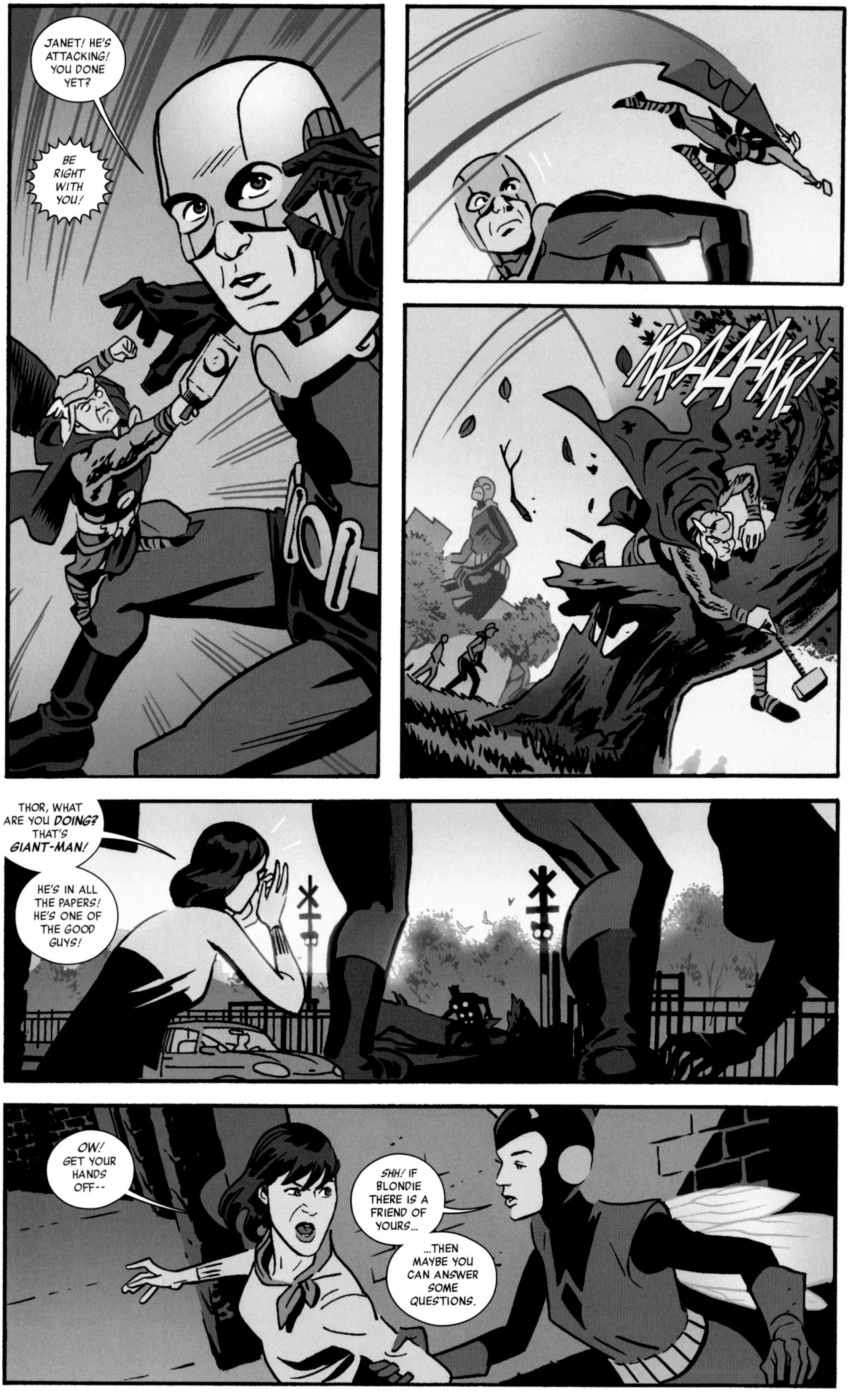
JANET! HE'S ATTACKING! YOU DONE YET?
BE RIGHT WITH YOU!
KRAAAKK!
THOR, WHAT ARE YOU DOING? THAT'S GIANT-MAN!
HE'S IN ALL THE PAPERS! HE'S ONE OF THE GOOD GUYS!
OW! GET YOUR HANDS OFF--
SHH! IF BLONDIE THERE IS A FRIEND OF YOURS...
...THEN MAYBE YOU CAN ANSWER SOME QUESTIONS.

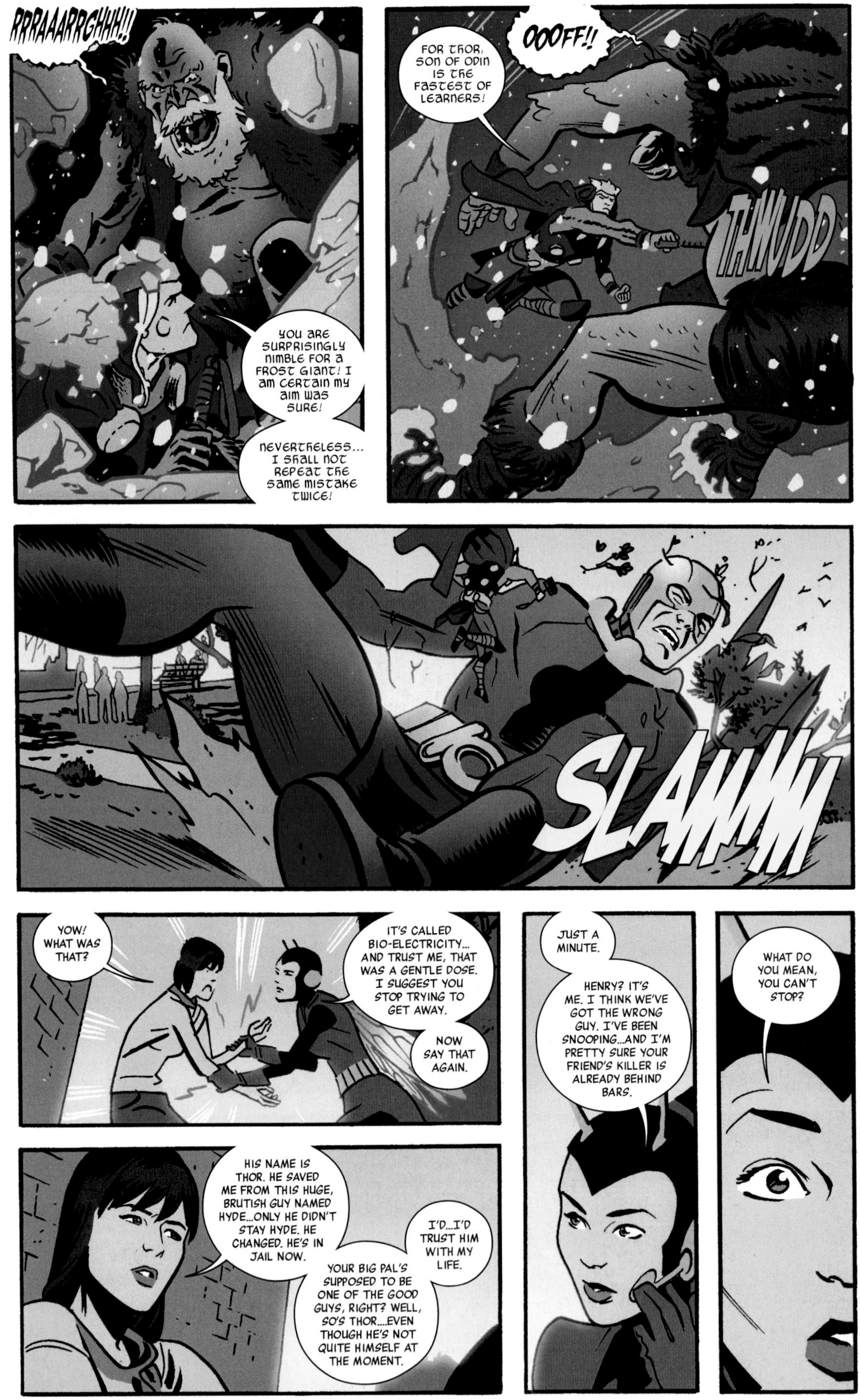
RRRAAARRGHHH!!
YOU ARE SURPRISINGLY NIMBLE FOR A FROST GIANT! I AM CERTAIN MY AIM WAS SURE!
NEVERTHELESS... I SHALL NOT REPEAT THE SAME MISTAKE TWICE!
OOOFF!!
FOR THOR, SON OF ODIN IS THE FASTEST OF LEARNERS!
THWUDD
SLAMMM
YOW! WHAT WAS THAT?
IT'S CALLED BIO-ELECTRICITY... AND TRUST ME, THAT WAS A GENTLE DOSE. I SUGGEST YOU STOP TRYING TO GET AWAY.
NOW SAY THAT AGAIN.
HIS NAME IS THOR. HE SAVED ME FROM THIS HUGE, BRUTISH GUY NAMED HYDE...ONLY HE DIDN'T STAY HYDE. HE CHANGED. HE'S IN JAIL NOW.
I'D...I'D TRUST HIM WITH MY LIFE.
YOUR BIG PAL'S SUPPOSED TO BE ONE OF THE GOOD GUYS, RIGHT? WELL, SO'S THOR....EVEN THOUGH HE'S NOT QUITE HIMSELF AT THE MOMENT.
JUST A MINUTE.
HENRY? IT'S ME. I THINK WE'VE GOT THE WRONG GUY. I'VE BEEN SNOOPING...AND I'M PRETTY SURE YOUR FRIEND'S KILLER IS ALREADY BEHIND BARS.
WHAT DO YOU MEAN, YOU CAN'T STOP?

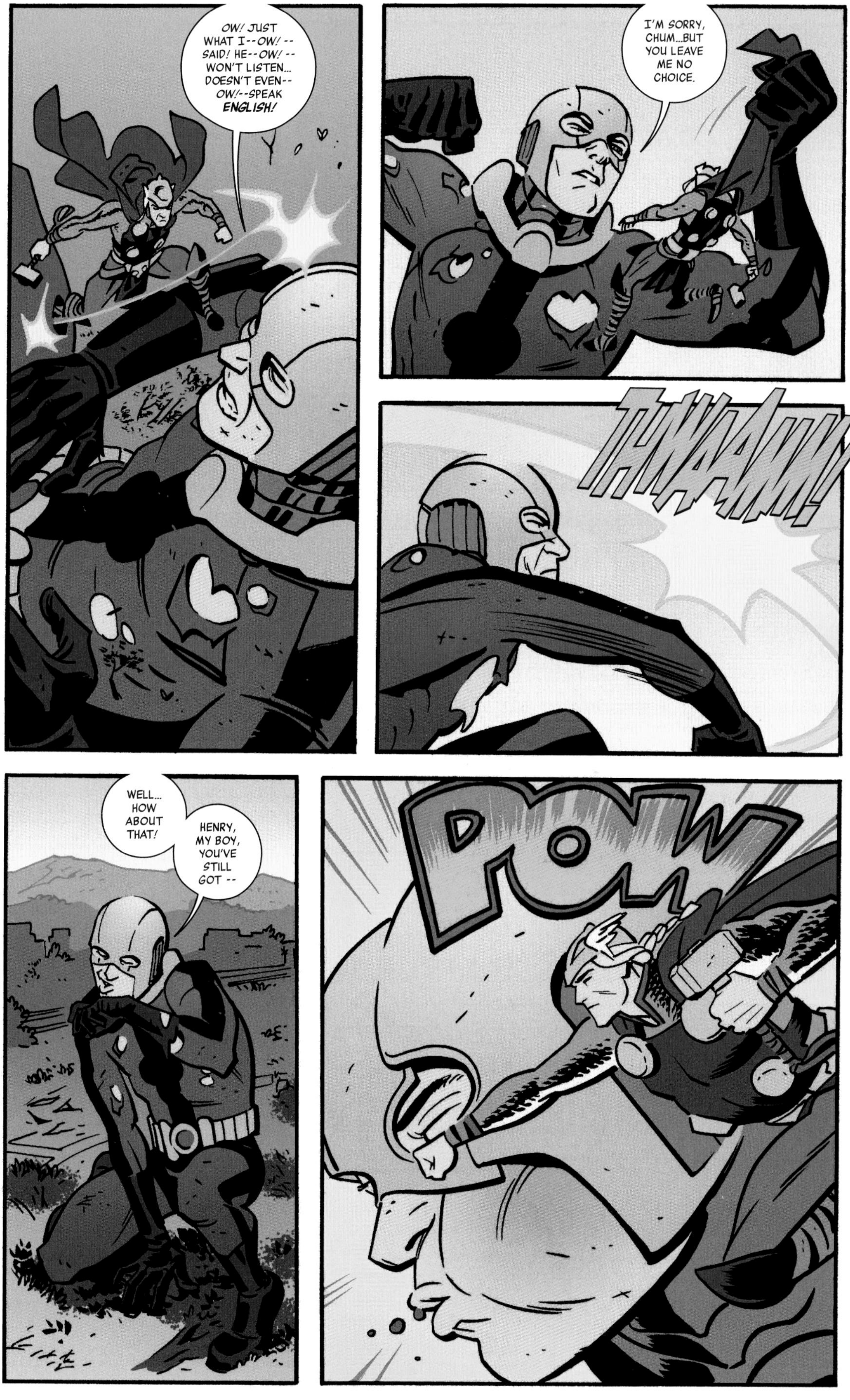
OW! JUST WHAT I--OW! --SAID! HE--OW! --WON'T LISTEN... DOESN'T EVEN--OW!--SPEAK ENGLISH!
I'M SORRY, CHUM...BUT YOU LEAVE ME NO CHOICE.
THWAAMM!
WELL... HOW ABOUT THAT!
HENRY, MY BOY, YOU'VE STILL GOT --
POW

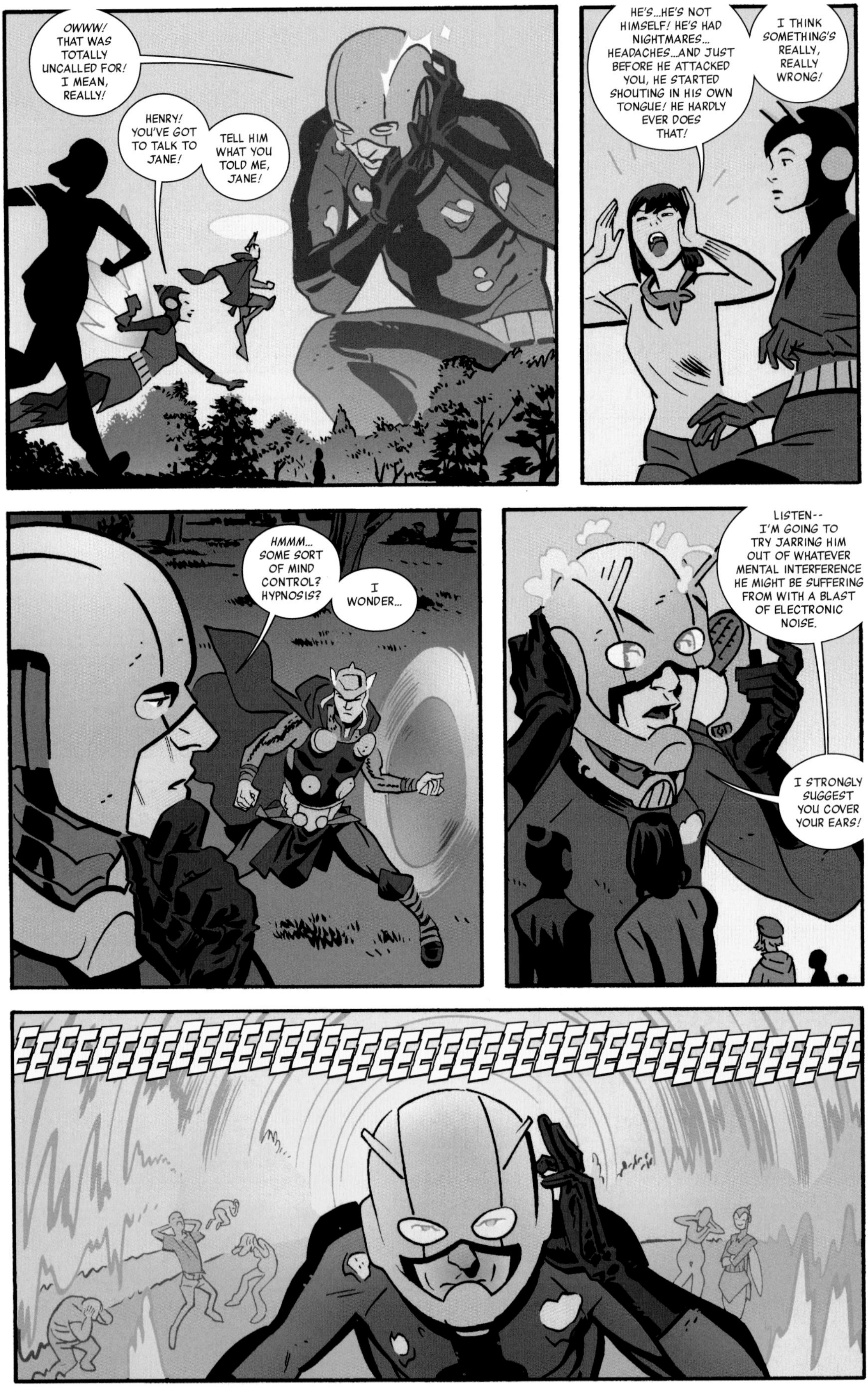
OWWW! THAT WAS TOTALLY UNCALLED FOR! I MEAN, REALLY!
HENRY! YOU'VE GOT TO TALK TO JANE!
TELL HIM WHAT YOU TOLD ME, JANE!
HE'S...HE'S NOT HIMSELF! HE'S HAD NIGHTMARES... HEADACHES...AND JUST BEFORE HE ATTACKED YOU, HE STARTED SHOUTING IN HIS OWN TONGUE! HE HARDLY EVER DOES THAT!
I THINK SOMETHING'S REALLY, REALLY WRONG!
HMMM... SOME SORT OF MIND CONTROL? HYPNOSIS?
I WONDER...
LISTEN-- I'M GOING TO TRY JARRING HIM OUT OF WHATEVER MENTAL INTERFERENCE HE MIGHT BE SUFFERING FROM WITH A BLAST OF ELECTRONIC NOISE.
I STRONGLY SUGGEST YOU COVER YOUR EARS!
EEEEEEEEEEEEEEEEEEEEEEEEEEEEEEEEEEEEEEEE

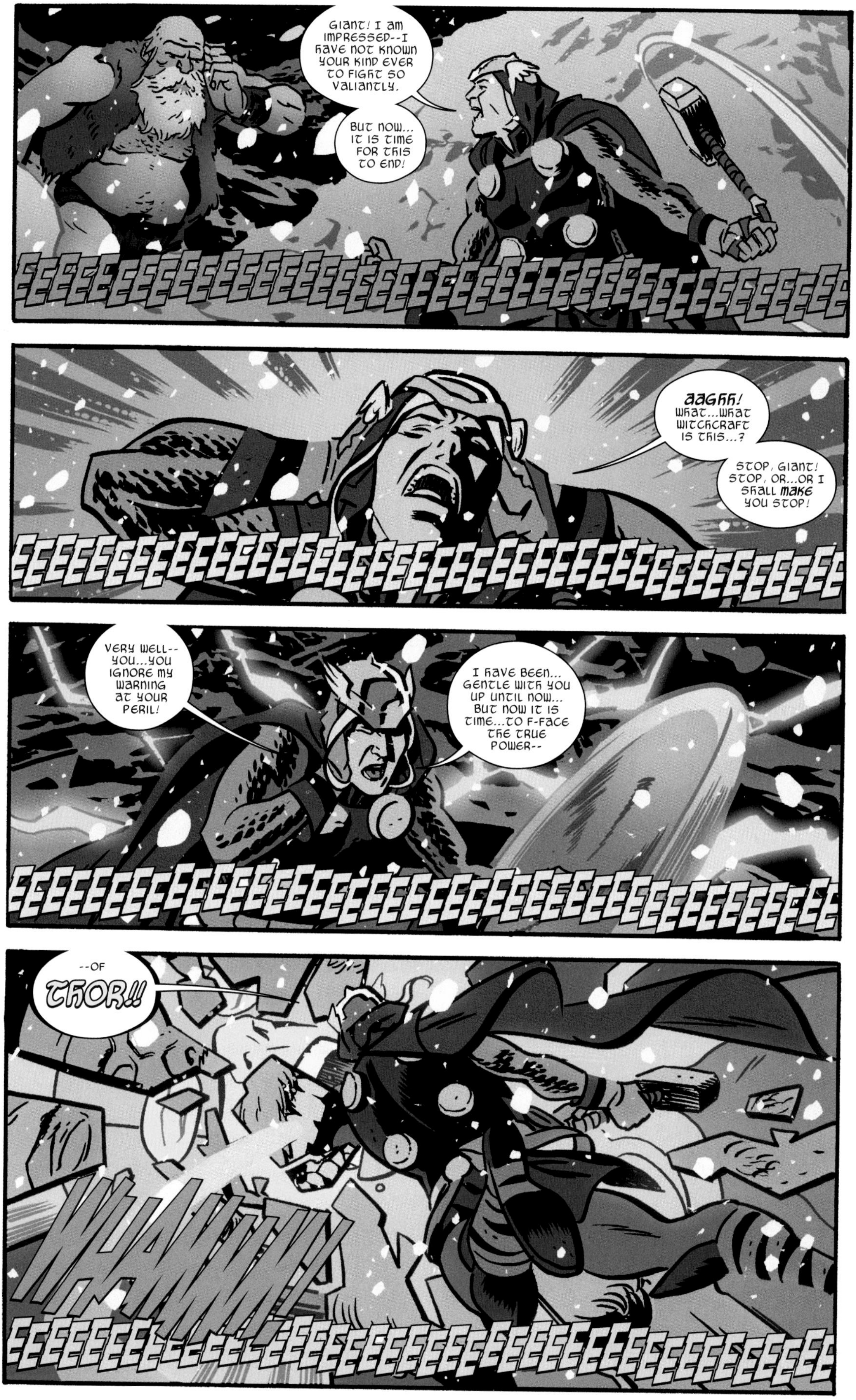
GIANT! I AM IMPRESSED--I HAVE NOT KNOWN YOUR KIND EVER TO FIGHT SO VALIANTLY.
BUT NOW... IT IS TIME FOR THIS TO END!
EEEEEEEEEEEEEEEEEEEEEEEEEEEEEEEEEEEEE
AAGHH! WHAT...WHAT WITCHCRAFT IS THIS...?
STOP, GIANT! STOP, OR...OR I SHALL MAKE YOU STOP!
EEEEEEEEEEEEEEEEEEEEEEEEEEEEEEEEEEEEE
VERY WELL--YOU...YOU IGNORE MY WARNING AT YOUR PERIL!
I HAVE BEEN... GENTLE WITH YOU UP UNTIL NOW... BUT NOW IT IS TIME...TO F-FACE THE TRUE POWER--
EEEEEEEEEEEEEEEEEEEEEEEEEEEEEEEEEEEEE
--OF THOR!!
WHAMM!!
EEEEEEEEEEEEEEEEEEEEEEEEEEEEEEEEEEEEE

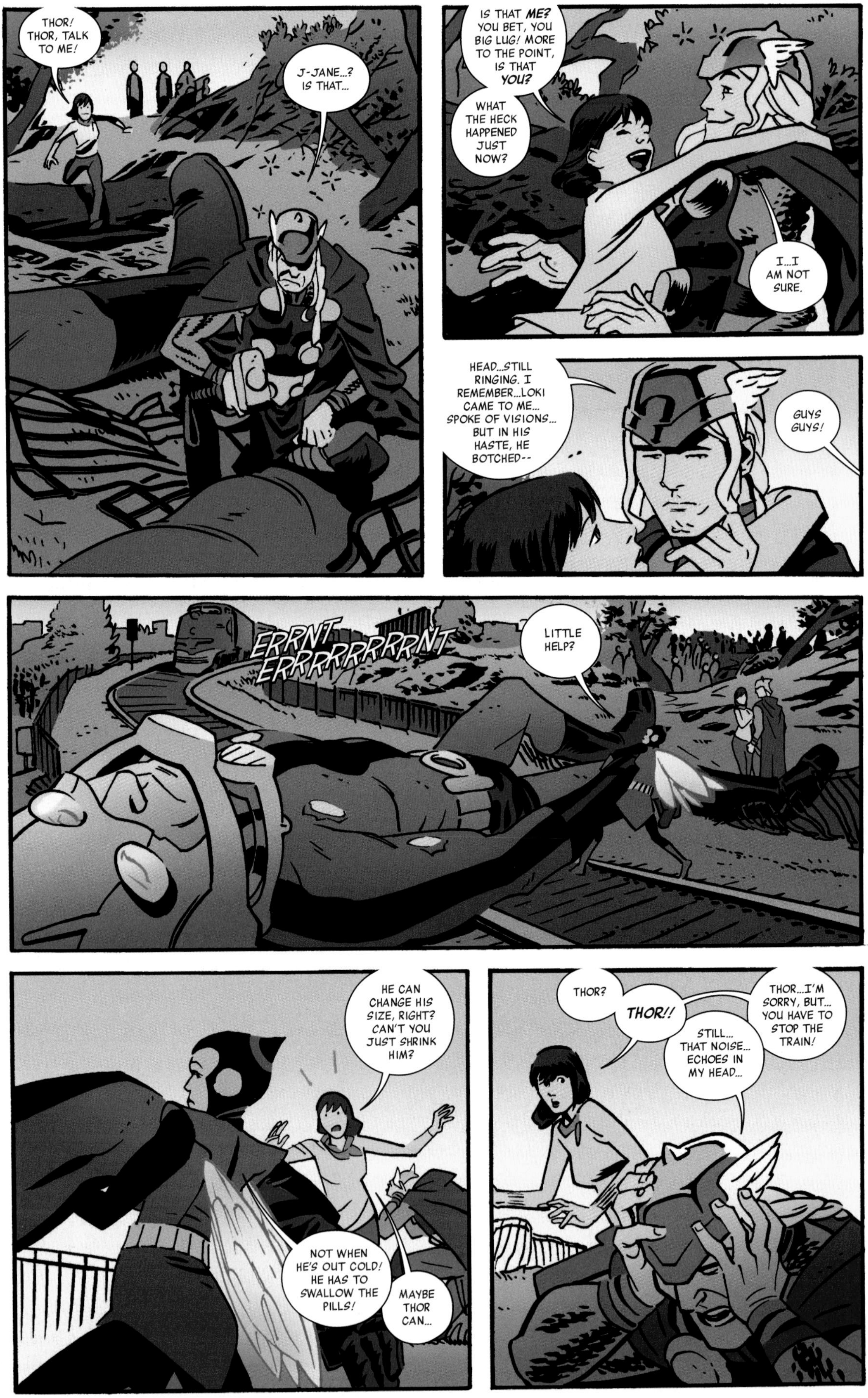
THOR! THOR, TALK TO ME!
J-JANE...? IS THAT...
IS THAT ME? YOU BET, YOU BIG LUG! MORE TO THE POINT, IS THAT YOU?
WHAT THE HECK HAPPENED JUST NOW?
I...I AM NOT SURE.
HEAD...STILL RINGING. I REMEMBER...LOKI CAME TO ME... SPOKE OF VISIONS... BUT IN HIS HASTE, HE BOTCHED--
GUYS GUYS!
ERRNT ERRRRRRRRRNT
LITTLE HELP?
HE CAN CHANGE HIS SIZE, RIGHT? CAN'T YOU JUST SHRINK HIM?
NOT WHEN HE'S OUT COLD! HE HAS TO SWALLOW THE PILLS!
MAYBE THOR CAN...
THOR?
THOR!!
STILL... THAT NOISE... ECHOES IN MY HEAD...
THOR...I'M SORRY, BUT... YOU HAVE TO STOP THE TRAIN!

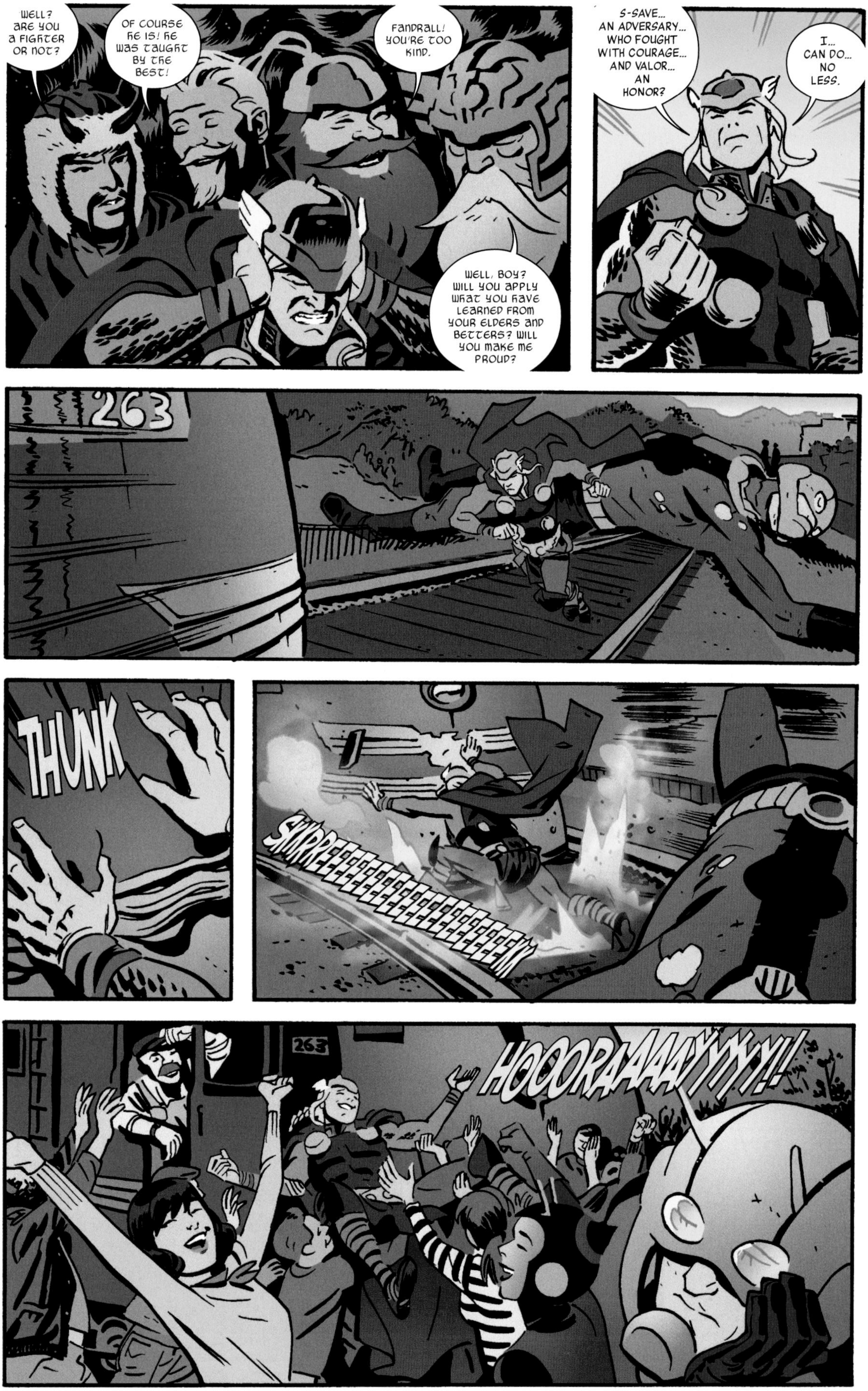
WELL? ARE YOU A FIGHTER OR NOT?
OF COURSE HE IS! HE WAS TAUGHT BY THE BEST!
FANDRALL! YOU'RE TOO KIND.
WELL, BOY? WILL YOU APPLY WHAT YOU HAVE LEARNED FROM YOUR ELDERS AND BETTERS? WILL YOU MAKE ME PROUD?
S-SAVE... AN ADVERSARY... WHO FOUGHT WITH COURAGE... AND VALOR... AN HONOR?
I... CAN DO... NO LESS.
263
THUNK
SKREEEEEEEEEEEEEEEEEEEEEEEEEK
263
HOOORAAAAYYYY!!

LATER!

WELL, THOR, YOU PUT UP ONE DICKENS OF A FIGHT, I'LL GIVE YOU THAT.

YOU OKAY NOW? NO MORE VISIONS?

MY HEAD IS CLEAR ONCE MORE... THANK YOU.

THANK *YOU*-- FOR STOPPING DOCTOR STEPHENS' KILLER. I ONLY WISH IT HAD BEEN ME.

AND IT APPEARS I OWE YOU ONE FOR STOPPING THAT TRAIN. IF YOU EVER NEED ANYTHING...

WHAT...IS THIS?

THOR'S NEW AROUND HERE. THOR, I'LL EXPLAIN LATER.

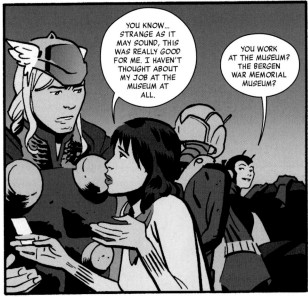

YOU KNOW... STRANGE AS IT MAY SOUND, THIS WAS REALLY GOOD FOR ME. I HAVEN'T THOUGHT ABOUT MY JOB AT THE MUSEUM AT ALL.

YOU WORK AT THE MUSEUM? THE BERGEN WAR MEMORIAL MUSEUM?

UNTIL THIS MORNING.

I'VE BEEN SUSPENDED FOR NOT STOPPING HYDE LAST WEEK.

WHAAAT?! THAT'S OUTRAGEOUS!

TELL ME ABOUT IT.

SO... THAT WAS "SHOPPING"?

SHOPPING? OH, I COMPLETELY FORGOT ABOUT THAT!

DO YOU MIND BEING CONSPICUOUS FOR A FEW MORE DAYS? I DON'T KNOW IF I CAN FACE THAT AGAIN RIGHT NOW...

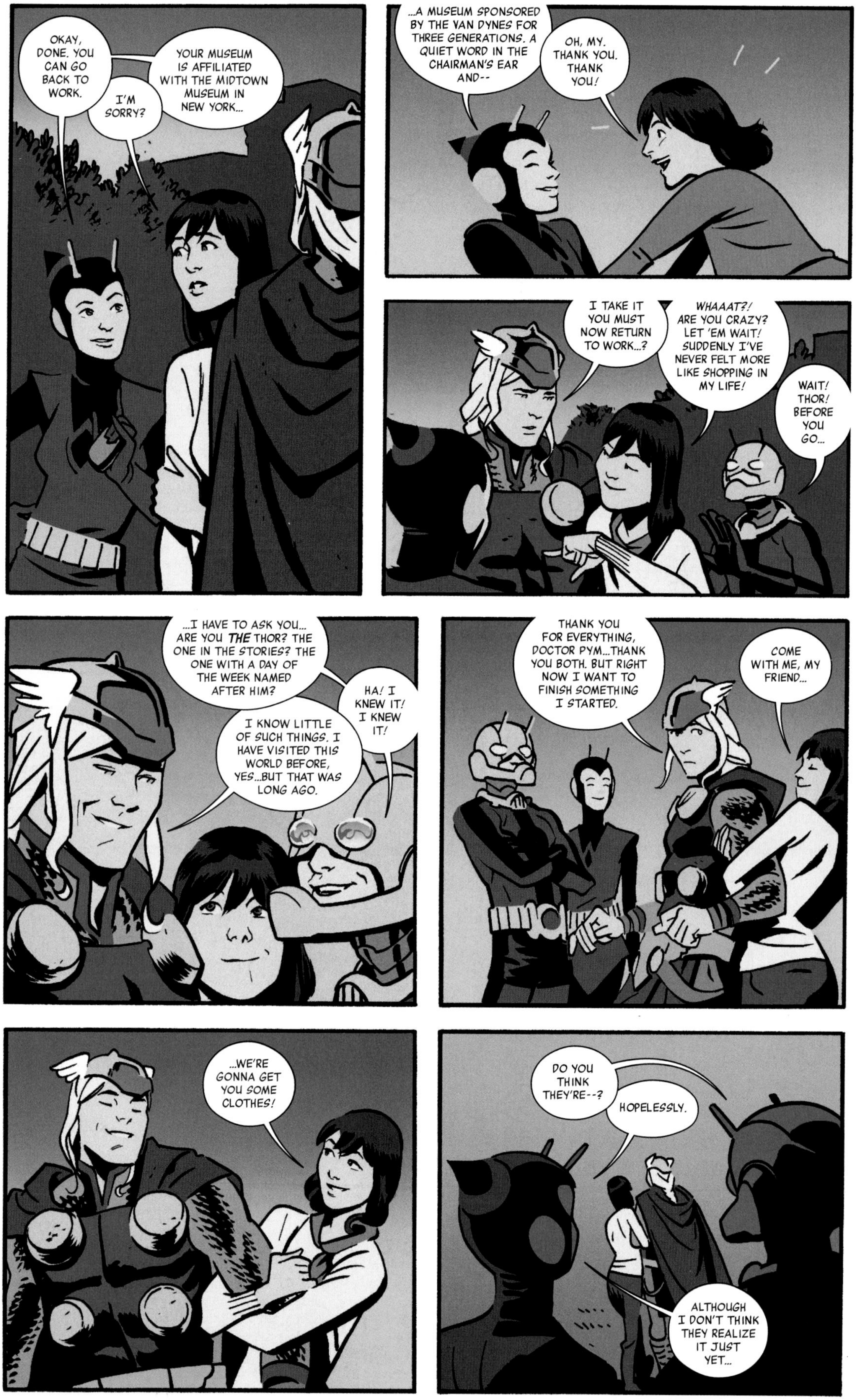
OKAY, DONE. YOU CAN GO BACK TO WORK.
YOUR MUSEUM IS AFFILIATED WITH THE MIDTOWN MUSEUM IN NEW YORK...
I'M SORRY?
...A MUSEUM SPONSORED BY THE VAN DYNES FOR THREE GENERATIONS. A QUIET WORD IN THE CHAIRMAN'S EAR AND--
OH, MY. THANK YOU. THANK YOU!
I TAKE IT YOU MUST NOW RETURN TO WORK...?
WHAAAT?! ARE YOU CRAZY? LET 'EM WAIT! SUDDENLY I'VE NEVER FELT MORE LIKE SHOPPING IN MY LIFE!
WAIT! THOR! BEFORE YOU GO...
...I HAVE TO ASK YOU... ARE YOU THE THOR? THE ONE IN THE STORIES? THE ONE WITH A DAY OF THE WEEK NAMED AFTER HIM?
I KNOW LITTLE OF SUCH THINGS. I HAVE VISITED THIS WORLD BEFORE, YES...BUT THAT WAS LONG AGO.
HA! I KNEW IT! I KNEW IT!
THANK YOU FOR EVERYTHING, DOCTOR PYM...THANK YOU BOTH. BUT RIGHT NOW I WANT TO FINISH SOMETHING I STARTED.
COME WITH ME, MY FRIEND...
...WE'RE GONNA GET YOU SOME CLOTHES!
DO YOU THINK THEY'RE--?
HOPELESSLY.
ALTHOUGH I DON'T THINK THEY REALIZE IT JUST YET...

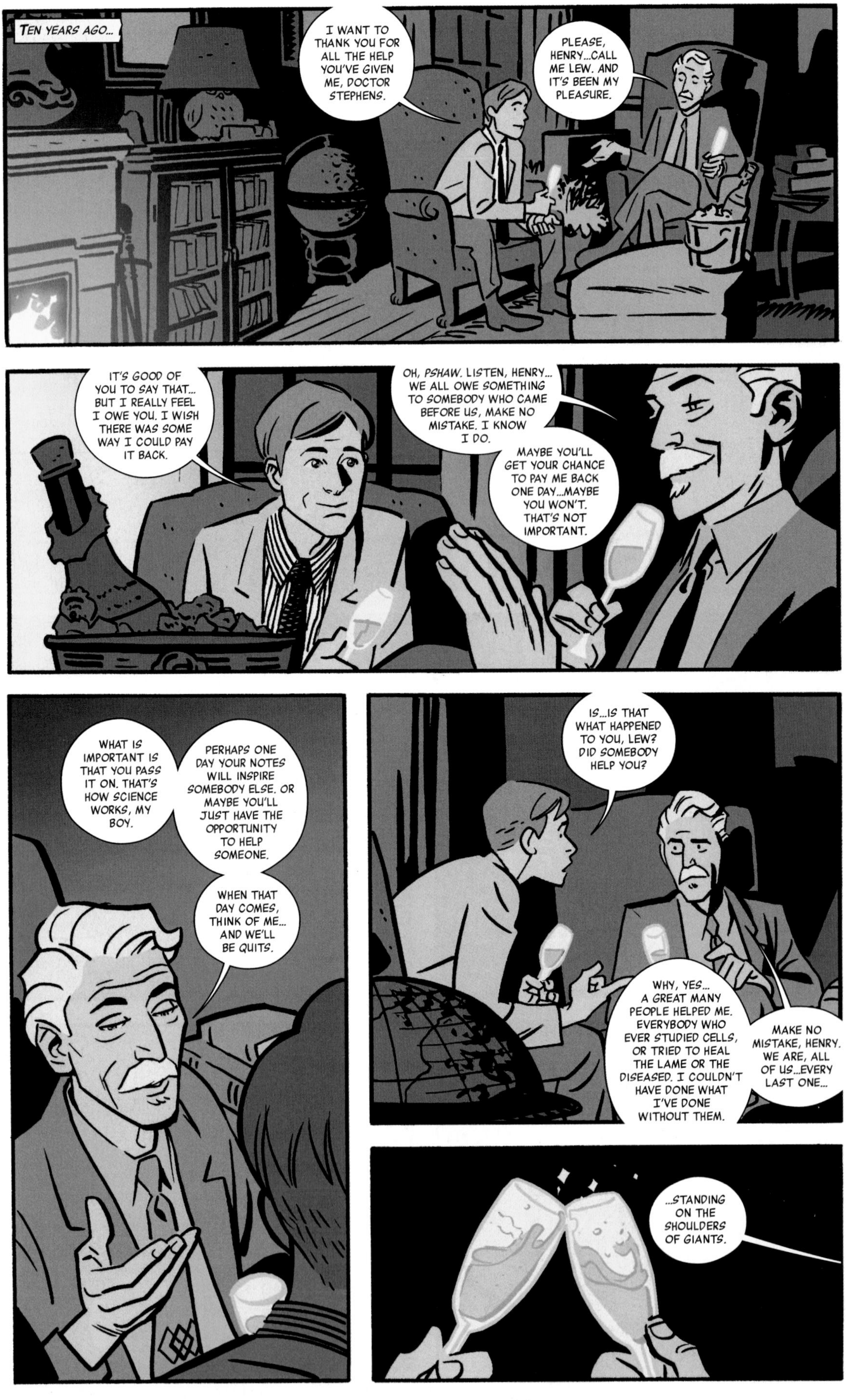
TEN YEARS AGO...
I WANT TO THANK YOU FOR ALL THE HELP YOU'VE GIVEN ME, DOCTOR STEPHENS.
PLEASE, HENRY...CALL ME LEW. AND IT'S BEEN MY PLEASURE.
IT'S GOOD OF YOU TO SAY THAT... BUT I REALLY FEEL I OWE YOU. I WISH THERE WAS SOME WAY I COULD PAY IT BACK.
OH, *PSHAW*. LISTEN, HENRY... WE ALL OWE SOMETHING TO SOMEBODY WHO CAME BEFORE US, MAKE NO MISTAKE. I KNOW I DO.
MAYBE YOU'LL GET YOUR CHANCE TO PAY ME BACK ONE DAY...MAYBE YOU WON'T. THAT'S NOT IMPORTANT.
WHAT IS IMPORTANT IS THAT YOU PASS IT ON. THAT'S HOW SCIENCE WORKS, MY BOY.
PERHAPS ONE DAY YOUR NOTES WILL INSPIRE SOMEBODY ELSE. OR MAYBE YOU'LL JUST HAVE THE OPPORTUNITY TO HELP SOMEONE.
WHEN THAT DAY COMES, THINK OF ME... AND WE'LL BE QUITS.
IS...IS THAT WHAT HAPPENED TO YOU, LEW? DID SOMEBODY HELP YOU?
WHY, YES... A GREAT MANY PEOPLE HELPED ME. EVERYBODY WHO EVER STUDIED CELLS, OR TRIED TO HEAL THE LAME OR THE DISEASED. I COULDN'T HAVE DONE WHAT I'VE DONE WITHOUT THEM.
MAKE NO MISTAKE, HENRY. WE ARE, ALL OF US...EVERY LAST ONE...
...STANDING ON THE SHOULDERS OF GIANTS.

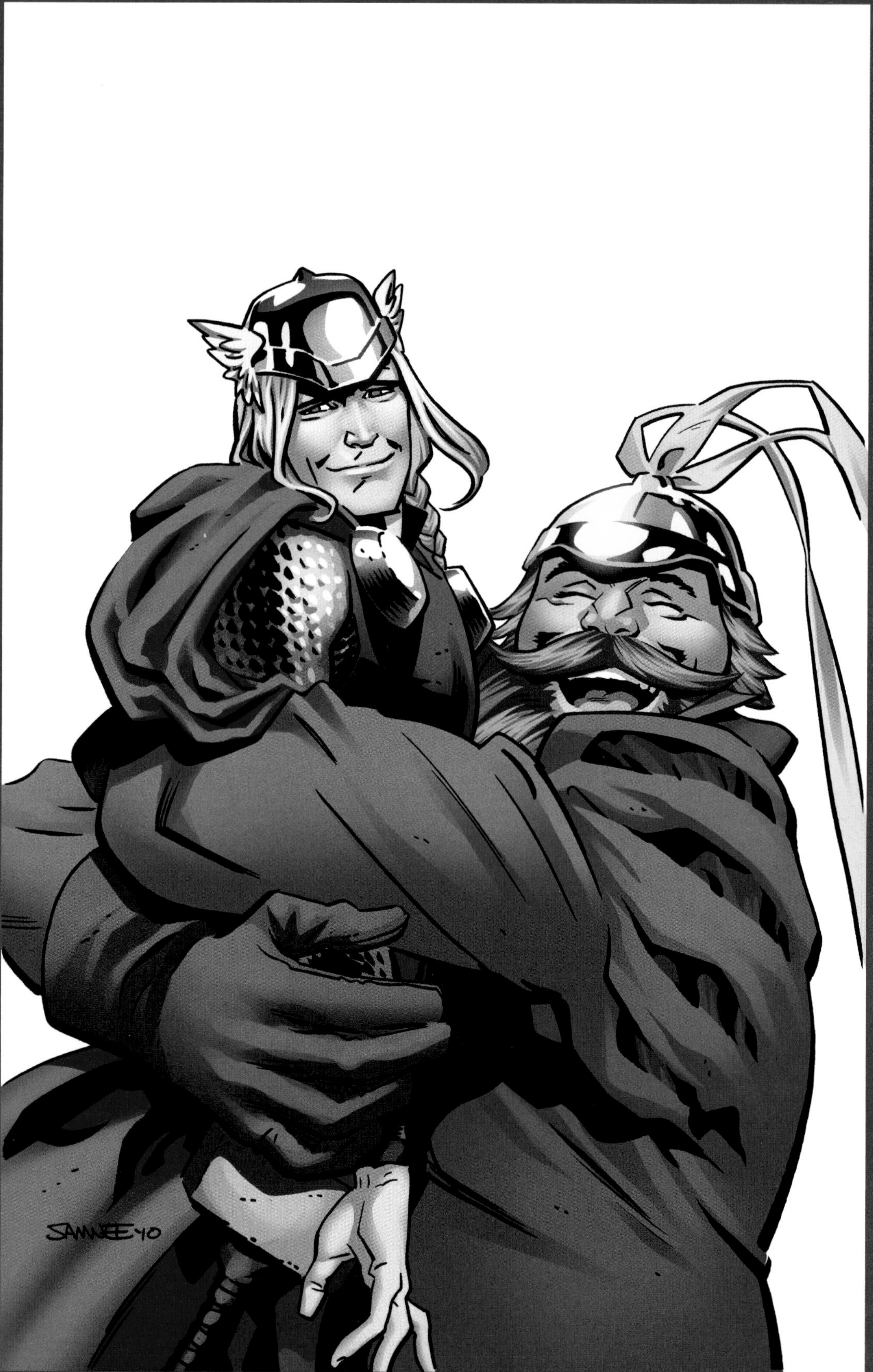

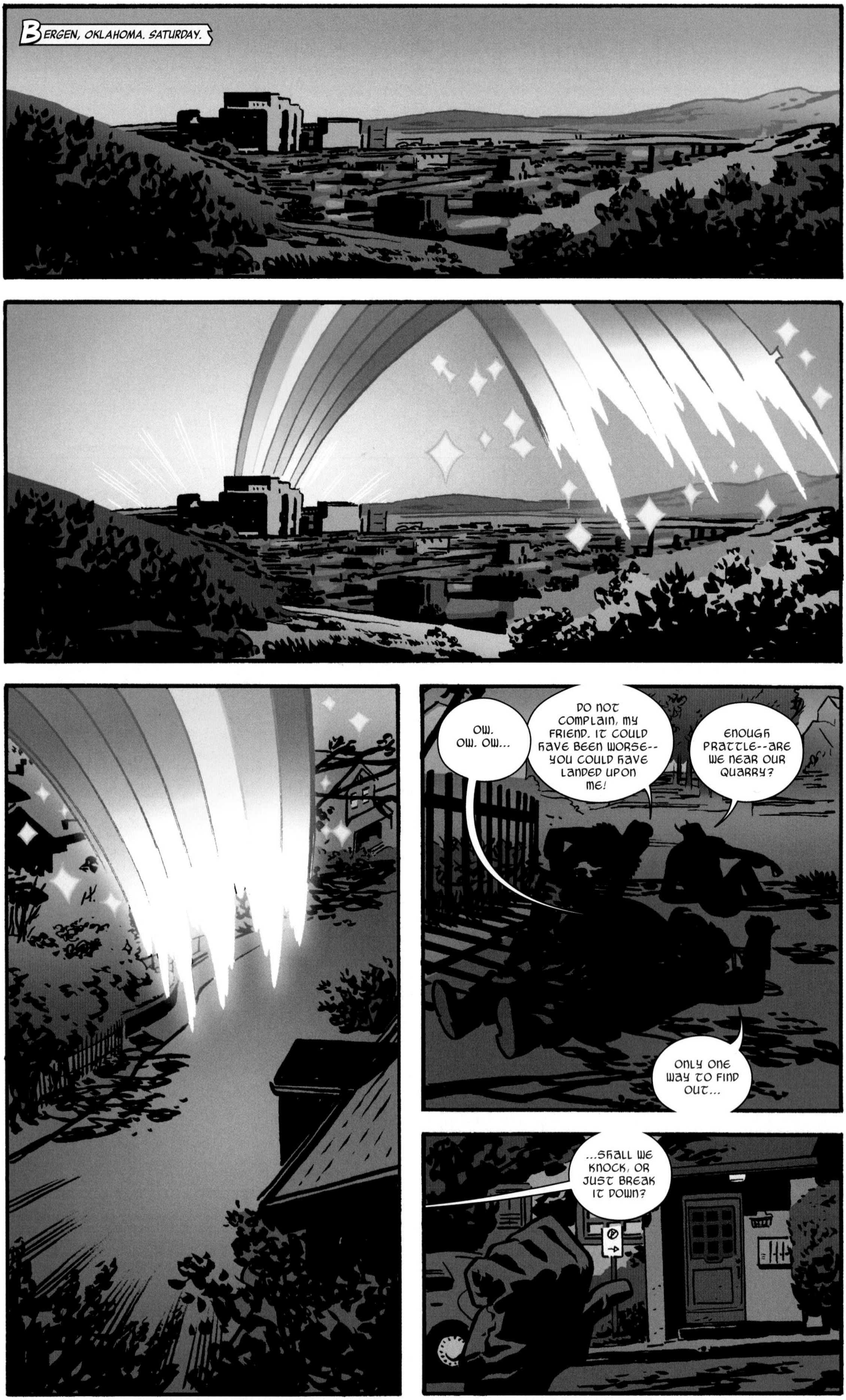
BERGEN, OKLAHOMA. SATURDAY.
OW. OW. OW...
DO NOT COMPLAIN, MY FRIEND. IT COULD HAVE BEEN WORSE--YOU COULD HAVE LANDED UPON ME!
ENOUGH PRATTLE--ARE WE NEAR OUR QUARRY?
ONLY ONE WAY TO FIND OUT...
...SHALL WE KNOCK, OR JUST BREAK IT DOWN?

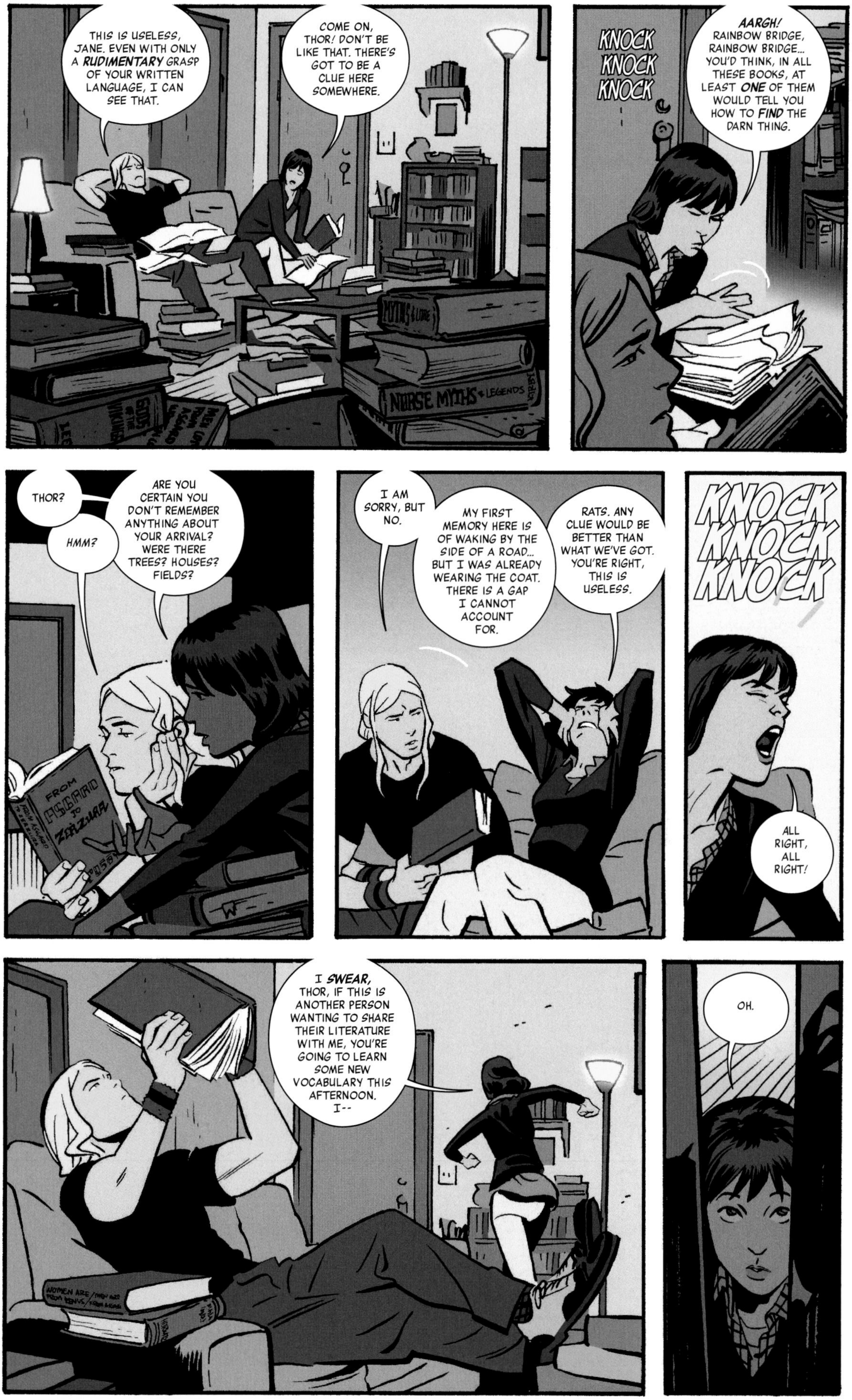
THIS IS USELESS, JANE. EVEN WITH ONLY A RUDIMENTARY GRASP OF YOUR WRITTEN LANGUAGE, I CAN SEE THAT.
COME ON, THOR! DON'T BE LIKE THAT. THERE'S GOT TO BE A CLUE HERE SOMEWHERE.
MYTHS & LORE
NORSE MYTHS & LEGENDS
GODS OF THE VIKINGS
KNOCK KNOCK KNOCK
AARGH! RAINBOW BRIDGE, RAINBOW BRIDGE... YOU'D THINK, IN ALL THESE BOOKS, AT LEAST ONE OF THEM WOULD TELL YOU HOW TO FIND THE DARN THING.
THOR?
HMM?
ARE YOU CERTAIN YOU DON'T REMEMBER ANYTHING ABOUT YOUR ARRIVAL? WERE THERE TREES? HOUSES? FIELDS?
FROM ASGARD TO ZANZIBAR
I AM SORRY, BUT NO.
MY FIRST MEMORY HERE IS OF WAKING BY THE SIDE OF A ROAD... BUT I WAS ALREADY WEARING THE COAT. THERE IS A GAP I CANNOT ACCOUNT FOR.
RATS. ANY CLUE WOULD BE BETTER THAN WHAT WE'VE GOT. YOU'RE RIGHT, THIS IS USELESS.
KNOCK KNOCK KNOCK
ALL RIGHT, ALL RIGHT!
I SWEAR, THOR, IF THIS IS ANOTHER PERSON WANTING TO SHARE THEIR LITERATURE WITH ME, YOU'RE GOING TO LEARN SOME NEW VOCABULARY THIS AFTERNOON. I--
OH.

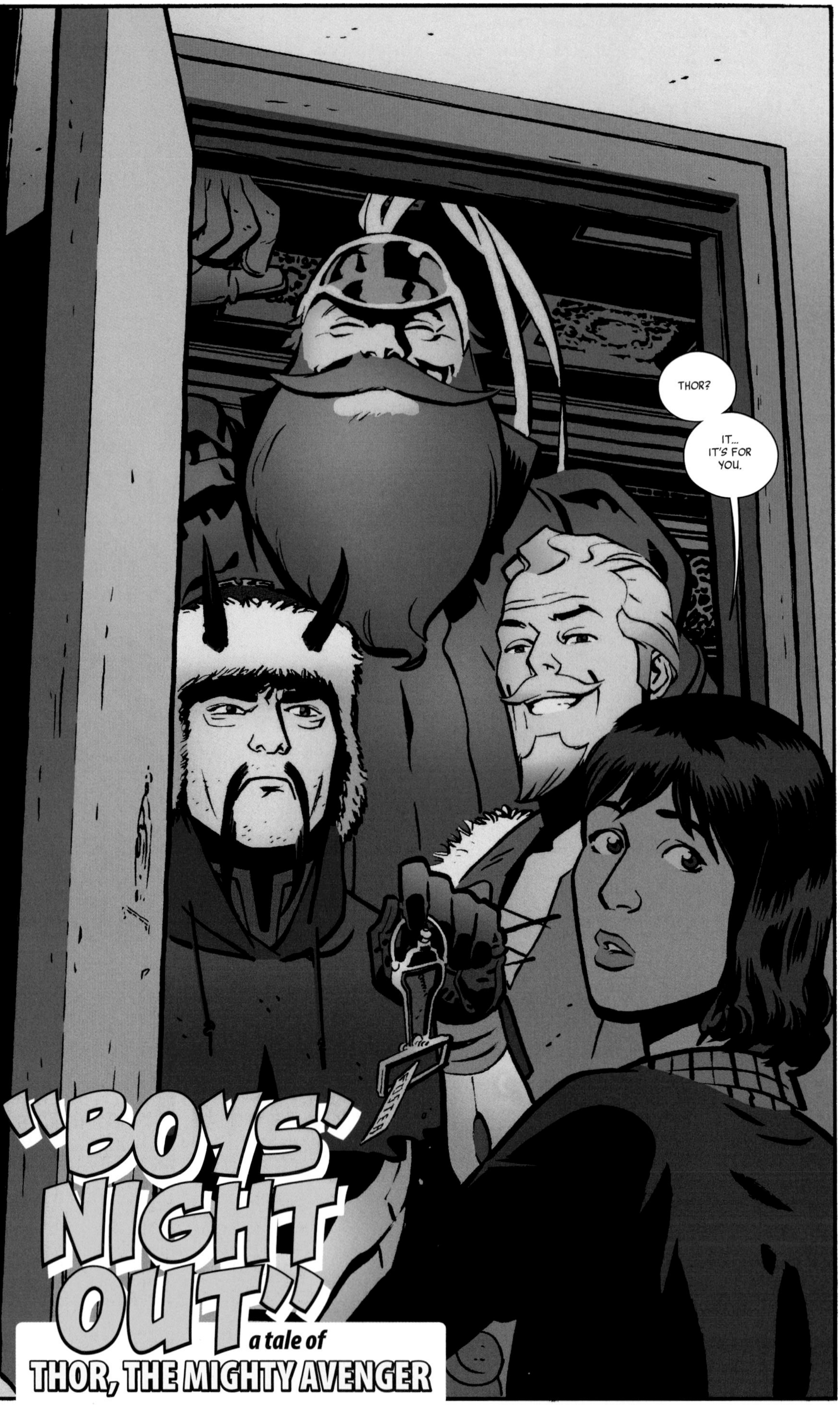
THOR?
IT... IT'S FOR YOU.
"BOYS' NIGHT OUT"
a tale of
THOR, THE MIGHTY AVENGER

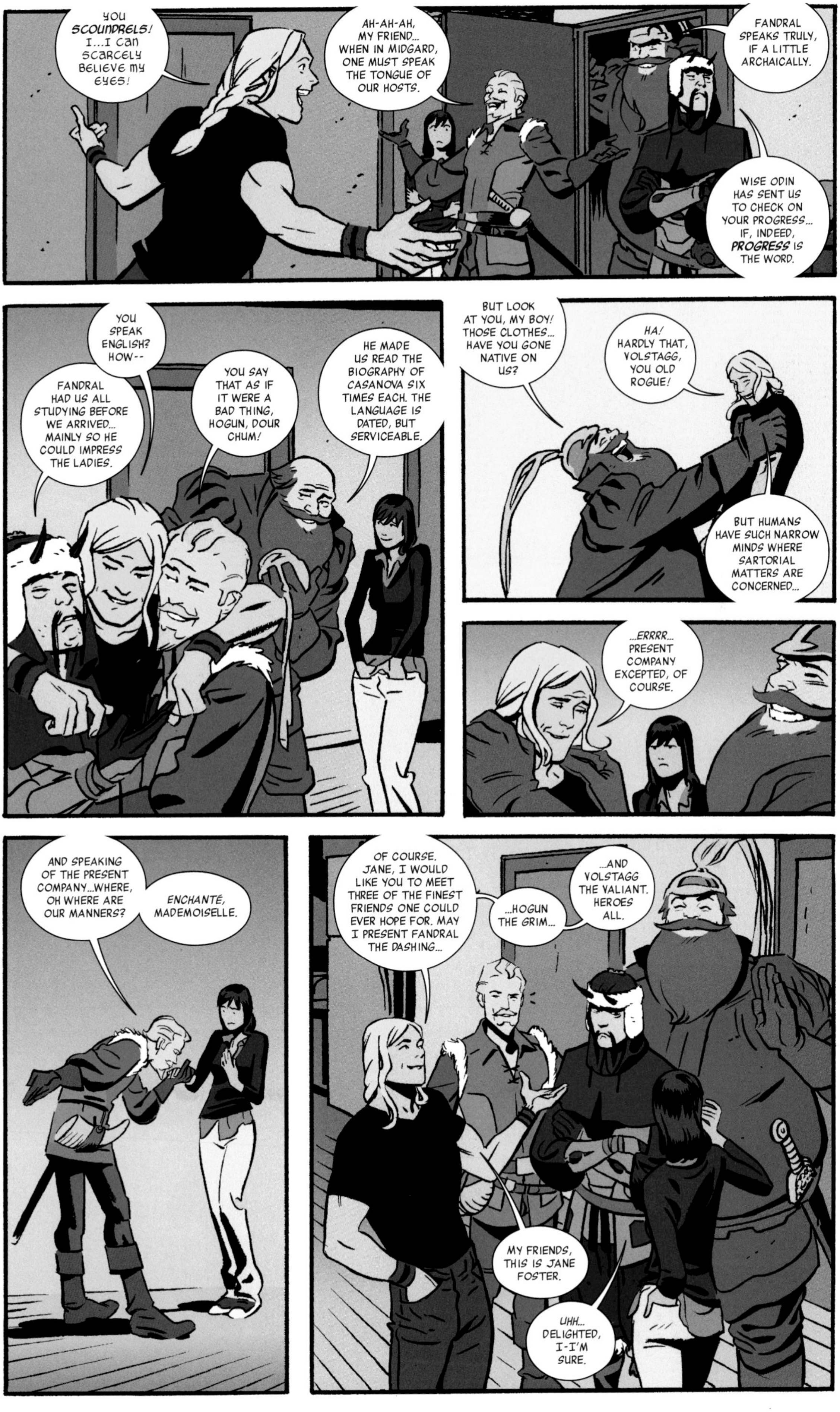

YOU SCOUNDRELS! I...I CAN SCARCELY BELIEVE MY EYES!
AH-AH-AH, MY FRIEND... WHEN IN MIDGARD, ONE MUST SPEAK THE TONGUE OF OUR HOSTS.
FANDRAL SPEAKS TRULY, IF A LITTLE ARCHAICALLY.
WISE ODIN HAS SENT US TO CHECK ON YOUR PROGRESS... IF, INDEED, PROGRESS IS THE WORD.
YOU SPEAK ENGLISH? HOW--
FANDRAL HAD US ALL STUDYING BEFORE WE ARRIVED... MAINLY SO HE COULD IMPRESS THE LADIES.
YOU SAY THAT AS IF IT WERE A BAD THING, HOGUN, DOUR CHUM!
HE MADE US READ THE BIOGRAPHY OF CASANOVA SIX TIMES EACH. THE LANGUAGE IS DATED, BUT SERVICEABLE.
BUT LOOK AT YOU, MY BOY! THOSE CLOTHES... HAVE YOU GONE NATIVE ON US?
HA! HARDLY THAT, VOLSTAGG, YOU OLD ROGUE!
BUT HUMANS HAVE SUCH NARROW MINDS WHERE SARTORIAL MATTERS ARE CONCERNED...
...ERRRR... PRESENT COMPANY EXCEPTED, OF COURSE.
AND SPEAKING OF THE PRESENT COMPANY...WHERE, OH WHERE ARE OUR MANNERS?
ENCHANTÉ, MADEMOISELLE.
OF COURSE. JANE, I WOULD LIKE YOU TO MEET THREE OF THE FINEST FRIENDS ONE COULD EVER HOPE FOR. MAY I PRESENT FANDRAL THE DASHING...
...HOGUN THE GRIM...
...AND VOLSTAGG THE VALIANT. HEROES ALL.
MY FRIENDS, THIS IS JANE FOSTER.
UHH... DELIGHTED, I-I'M SURE.

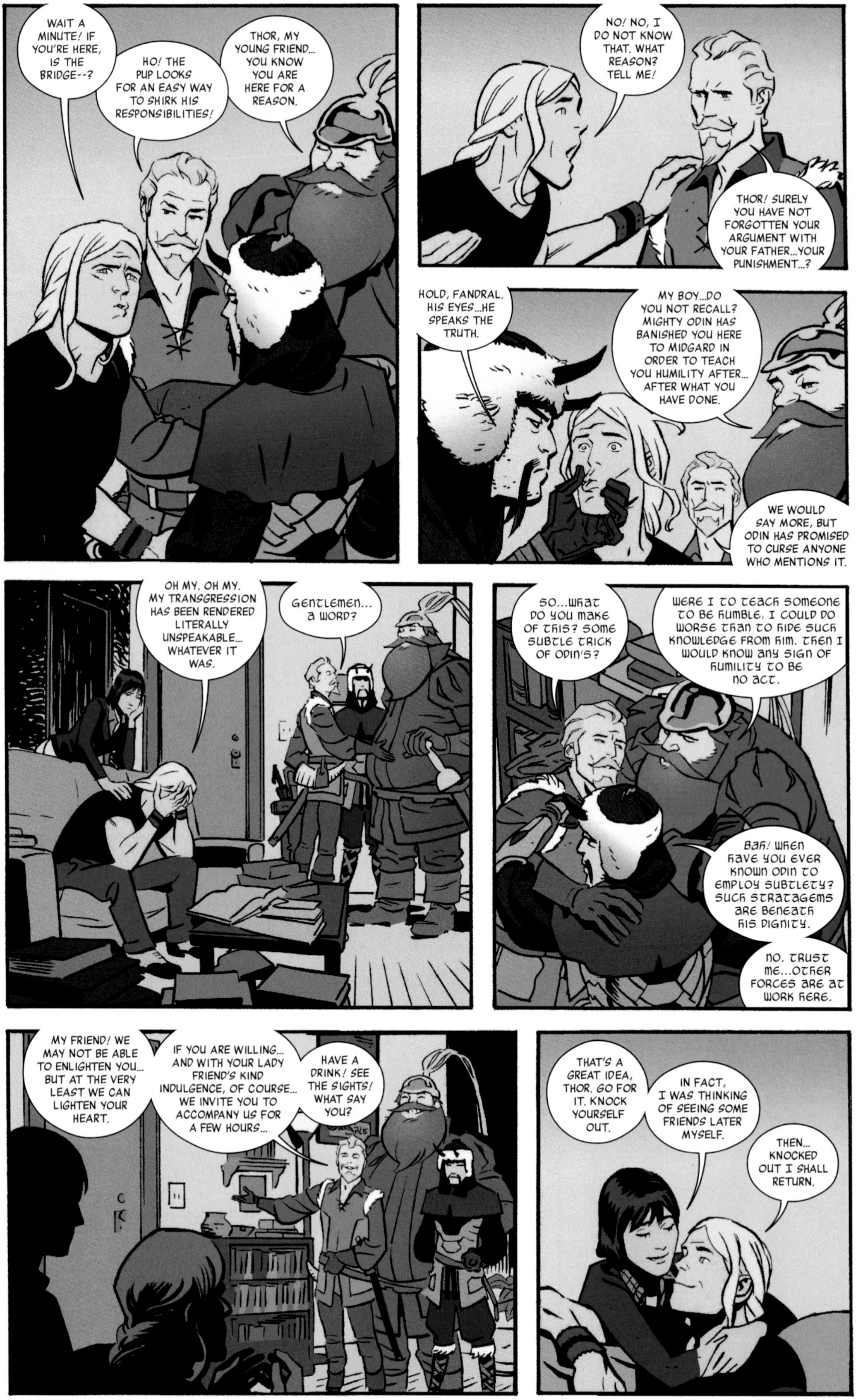
WAIT A MINUTE! IF YOU'RE HERE, IS THE BRIDGE--?
HO! THE PUP LOOKS FOR AN EASY WAY TO SHIRK HIS RESPONSIBILITIES!
THOR, MY YOUNG FRIEND... YOU KNOW YOU ARE HERE FOR A REASON.
NO! NO, I DO NOT KNOW THAT. WHAT REASON? TELL ME!
THOR! SURELY YOU HAVE NOT FORGOTTEN YOUR ARGUMENT WITH YOUR FATHER...YOUR PUNISHMENT...?
HOLD, FANDRAL. HIS EYES...HE SPEAKS THE TRUTH.
MY BOY...DO YOU NOT RECALL? MIGHTY ODIN HAS BANISHED YOU HERE TO MIDGARD IN ORDER TO TEACH YOU HUMILITY AFTER... AFTER WHAT YOU HAVE DONE.
WE WOULD SAY MORE, BUT ODIN HAS PROMISED TO CURSE ANYONE WHO MENTIONS IT.
OH MY. OH MY. MY TRANSGRESSION HAS BEEN RENDERED LITERALLY UNSPEAKABLE... WHATEVER IT WAS.
GENTLEMEN... A WORD?
SO...WHAT DO YOU MAKE OF THIS? SOME SUBTLE TRICK OF ODIN'S?
WERE I TO TEACH SOMEONE TO BE HUMBLE, I COULD DO WORSE THAN TO HIDE SUCH KNOWLEDGE FROM HIM. THEN I WOULD KNOW ANY SIGN OF HUMILITY TO BE NO ACT.
BAH! WHEN HAVE YOU EVER KNOWN ODIN TO EMPLOY SUBTLETY? SUCH STRATAGEMS ARE BENEATH HIS DIGNITY.
NO. TRUST ME...OTHER FORCES ARE AT WORK HERE.
MY FRIEND! WE MAY NOT BE ABLE TO ENLIGHTEN YOU... BUT AT THE VERY LEAST WE CAN LIGHTEN YOUR HEART.
IF YOU ARE WILLING... AND WITH YOUR LADY FRIEND'S KIND INDULGENCE, OF COURSE... WE INVITE YOU TO ACCOMPANY US FOR A FEW HOURS...
HAVE A DRINK! SEE THE SIGHTS! WHAT SAY YOU?
THAT'S A GREAT IDEA, THOR. GO FOR IT. KNOCK YOURSELF OUT.
IN FACT, I WAS THINKING OF SEEING SOME FRIENDS LATER MYSELF.
THEN... KNOCKED OUT I SHALL RETURN.

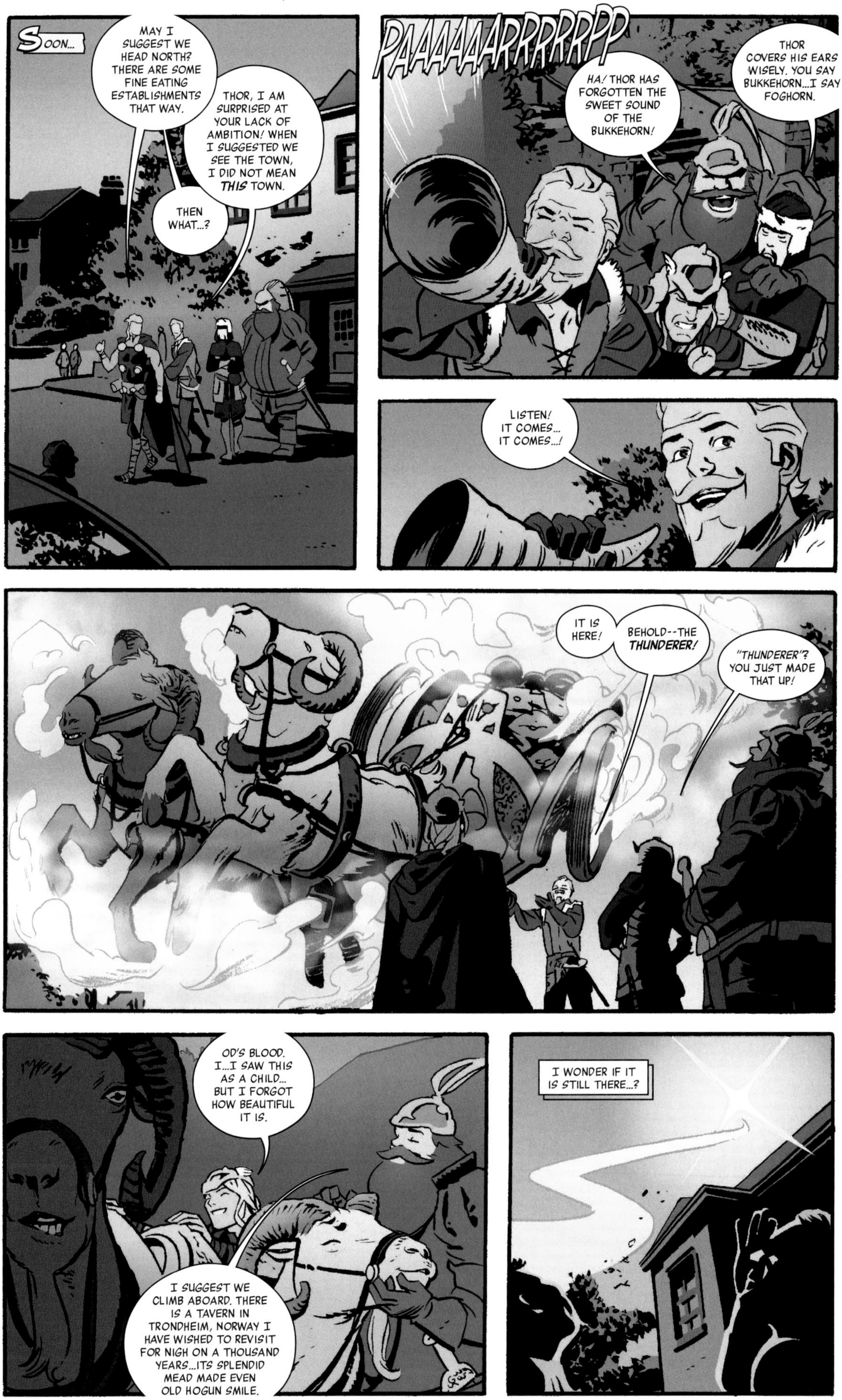

SOON...
MAY I SUGGEST WE HEAD NORTH? THERE ARE SOME FINE EATING ESTABLISHMENTS THAT WAY.
THOR, I AM SURPRISED AT YOUR LACK OF AMBITION! WHEN I SUGGESTED WE SEE THE TOWN, I DID NOT MEAN THIS TOWN.
THEN WHAT...?
PAAAAAARRRRRPP
HA! THOR HAS FORGOTTEN THE SWEET SOUND OF THE BUKKEHORN!
THOR COVERS HIS EARS WISELY. YOU SAY BUKKEHORN...I SAY FOGHORN.
LISTEN! IT COMES... IT COMES...!
IT IS HERE!
BEHOLD--THE THUNDERER!
"THUNDERER"? YOU JUST MADE THAT UP!
OD'S BLOOD. I...I SAW THIS AS A CHILD... BUT I FORGOT HOW BEAUTIFUL IT IS.
I SUGGEST WE CLIMB ABOARD. THERE IS A TAVERN IN TRONDHEIM, NORWAY I HAVE WISHED TO REVISIT FOR NIGH ON A THOUSAND YEARS...ITS SPLENDID MEAD MADE EVEN OLD HOGUN SMILE.
I WONDER IF IT IS STILL THERE...?

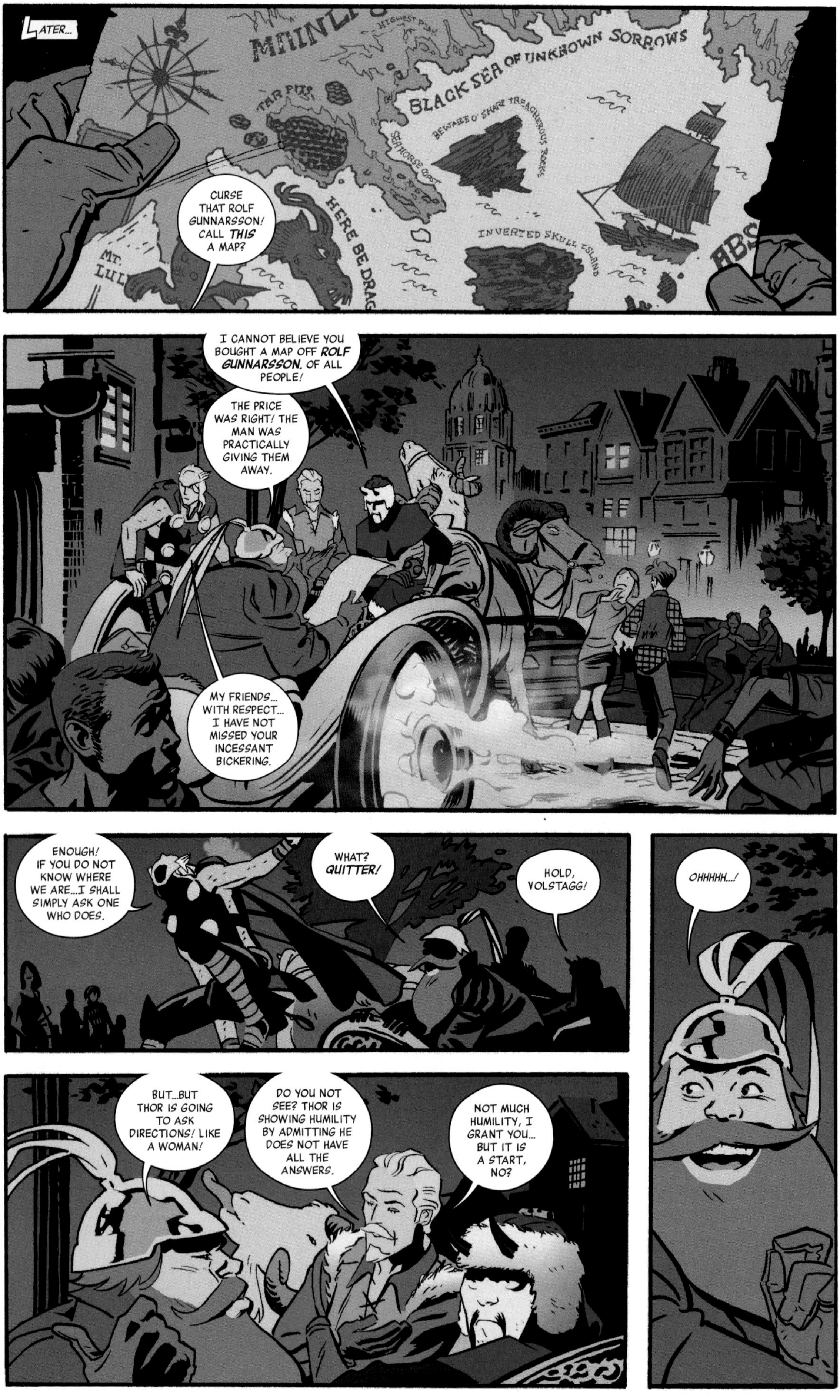
LATER...
HIGHEST PEAK
BLACK SEA OF UNKNOWN SORROWS
TAR PITS
BEWARE O' SHARP TREACHEROUS ROCKS
SEAHORSE COAST
HERE BE DRAG
INVERTED SKULL ISLAND
CURSE THAT ROLF GUNNARSSON! CALL THIS A MAP?
I CANNOT BELIEVE YOU BOUGHT A MAP OFF ROLF GUNNARSSON, OF ALL PEOPLE!
THE PRICE WAS RIGHT! THE MAN WAS PRACTICALLY GIVING THEM AWAY.
MY FRIENDS... WITH RESPECT... I HAVE NOT MISSED YOUR INCESSANT BICKERING.
ENOUGH! IF YOU DO NOT KNOW WHERE WE ARE...I SHALL SIMPLY ASK ONE WHO DOES.
WHAT? QUITTER!
HOLD, VOLSTAGG!
OHHHHH...!
BUT...BUT THOR IS GOING TO ASK DIRECTIONS! LIKE A WOMAN!
DO YOU NOT SEE? THOR IS SHOWING HUMILITY BY ADMITTING HE DOES NOT HAVE ALL THE ANSWERS.
NOT MUCH HUMILITY, I GRANT YOU... BUT IT IS A START, NO?

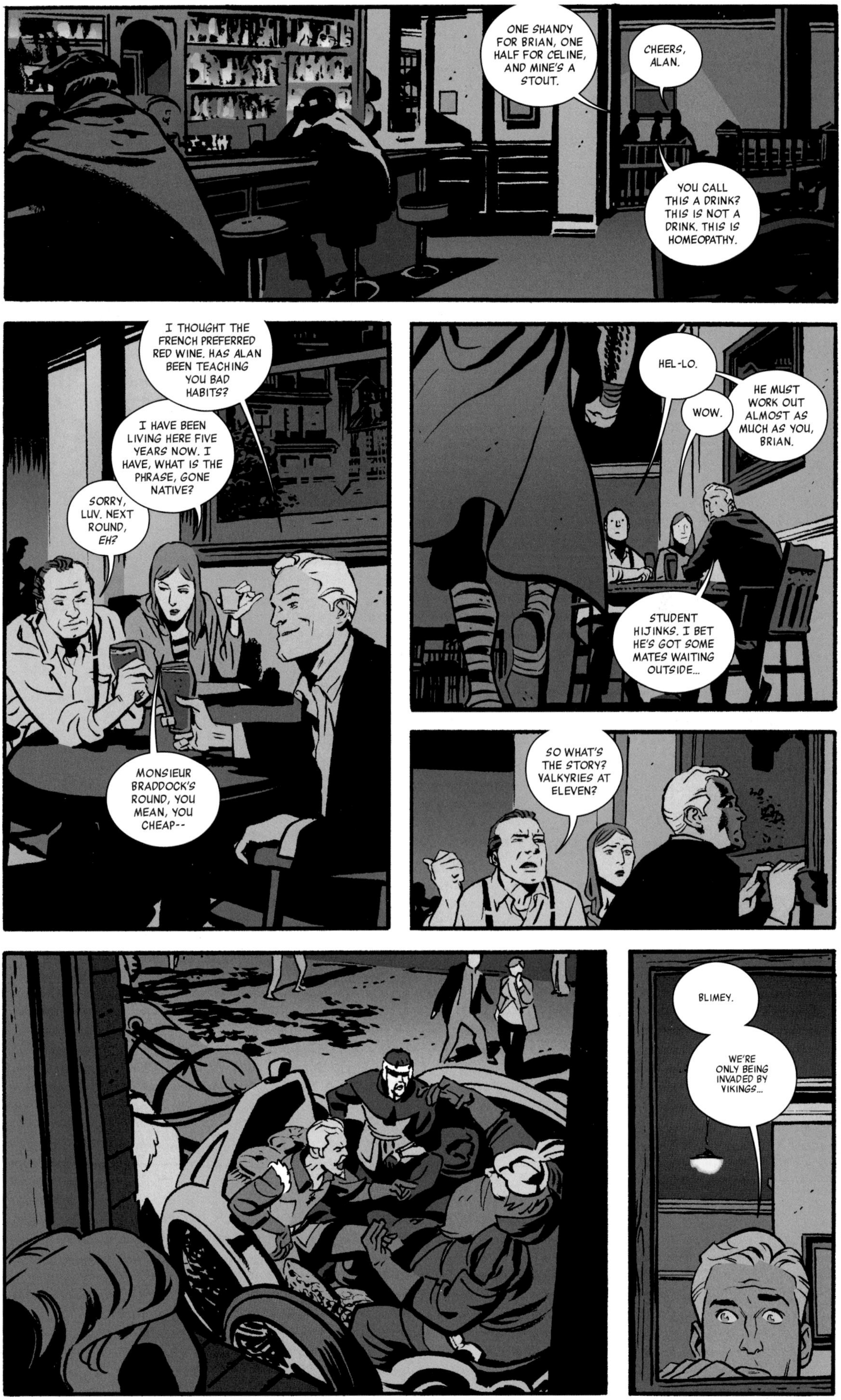
ONE SHANDY FOR BRIAN, ONE HALF FOR CELINE, AND MINE'S A STOUT.
CHEERS, ALAN.
YOU CALL THIS A DRINK? THIS IS NOT A DRINK. THIS IS HOMEOPATHY.
I THOUGHT THE FRENCH PREFERRED RED WINE. HAS ALAN BEEN TEACHING YOU BAD HABITS?
I HAVE BEEN LIVING HERE FIVE YEARS NOW. I HAVE, WHAT IS THE PHRASE, GONE NATIVE?
SORRY, LUV. NEXT ROUND, EH?
MONSIEUR BRADDOCK'S ROUND, YOU MEAN, YOU CHEAP--
HEL-LO.
WOW.
HE MUST WORK OUT ALMOST AS MUCH AS YOU, BRIAN.
STUDENT HIJINKS. I BET HE'S GOT SOME MATES WAITING OUTSIDE...
SO WHAT'S THE STORY? VALKYRIES AT ELEVEN?
BLIMEY.
WE'RE ONLY BEING INVADED BY VIKINGS...

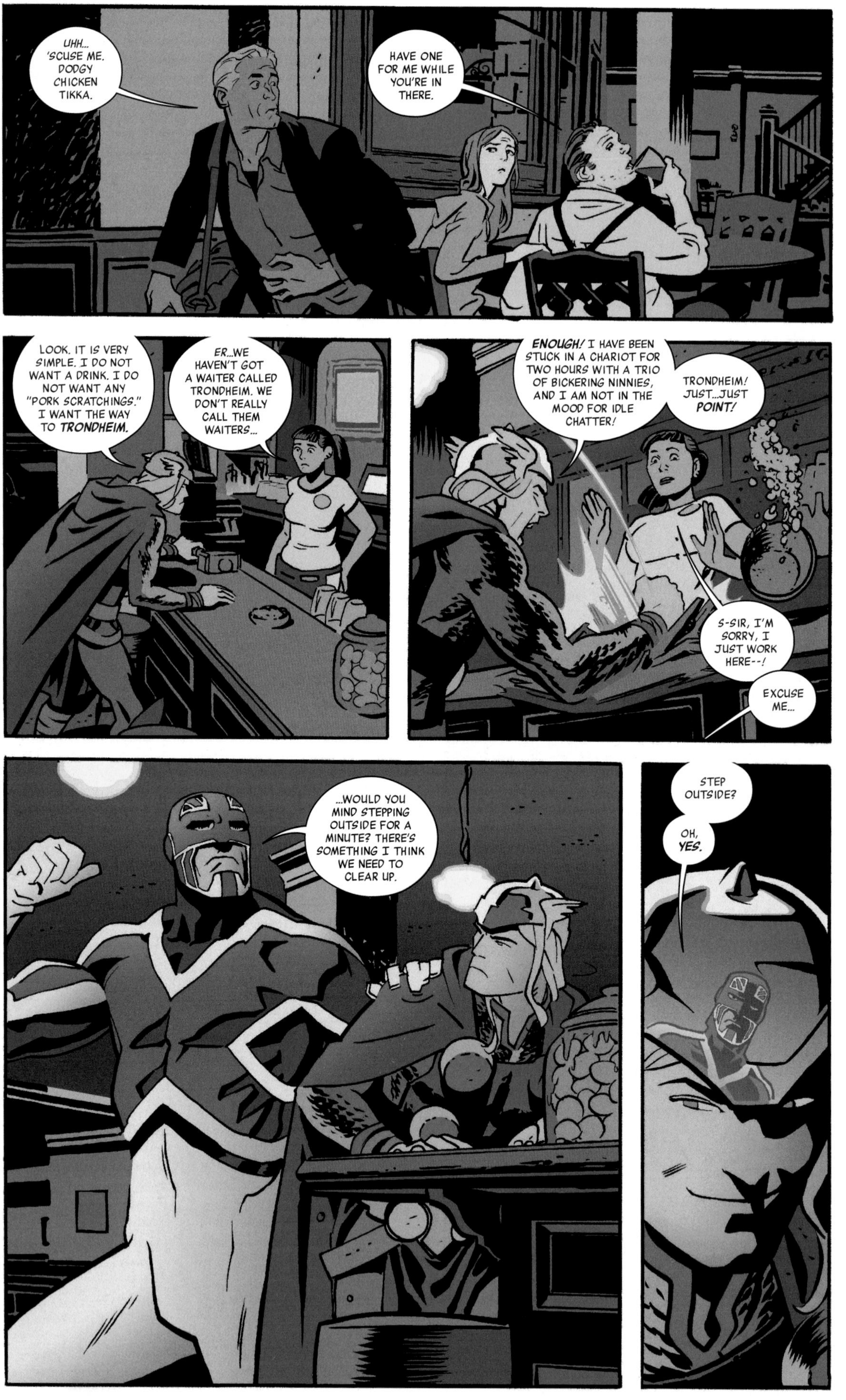
UHH... 'SCUSE ME. DODGY CHICKEN TIKKA.
HAVE ONE FOR ME WHILE YOU'RE IN THERE.
LOOK. IT IS VERY SIMPLE. I DO NOT WANT A DRINK. I DO NOT WANT ANY "PORK SCRATCHINGS." I WANT THE WAY TO TRONDHEIM.
ER...WE HAVEN'T GOT A WAITER CALLED TRONDHEIM. WE DON'T REALLY CALL THEM WAITERS...
ENOUGH! I HAVE BEEN STUCK IN A CHARIOT FOR TWO HOURS WITH A TRIO OF BICKERING NINNIES, AND I AM NOT IN THE MOOD FOR IDLE CHATTER!
TRONDHEIM! JUST...JUST POINT!
S-SIR, I'M SORRY, I JUST WORK HERE--!
EXCUSE ME...
...WOULD YOU MIND STEPPING OUTSIDE FOR A MINUTE? THERE'S SOMETHING I THINK WE NEED TO CLEAR UP.
STEP OUTSIDE?
OH, YES.

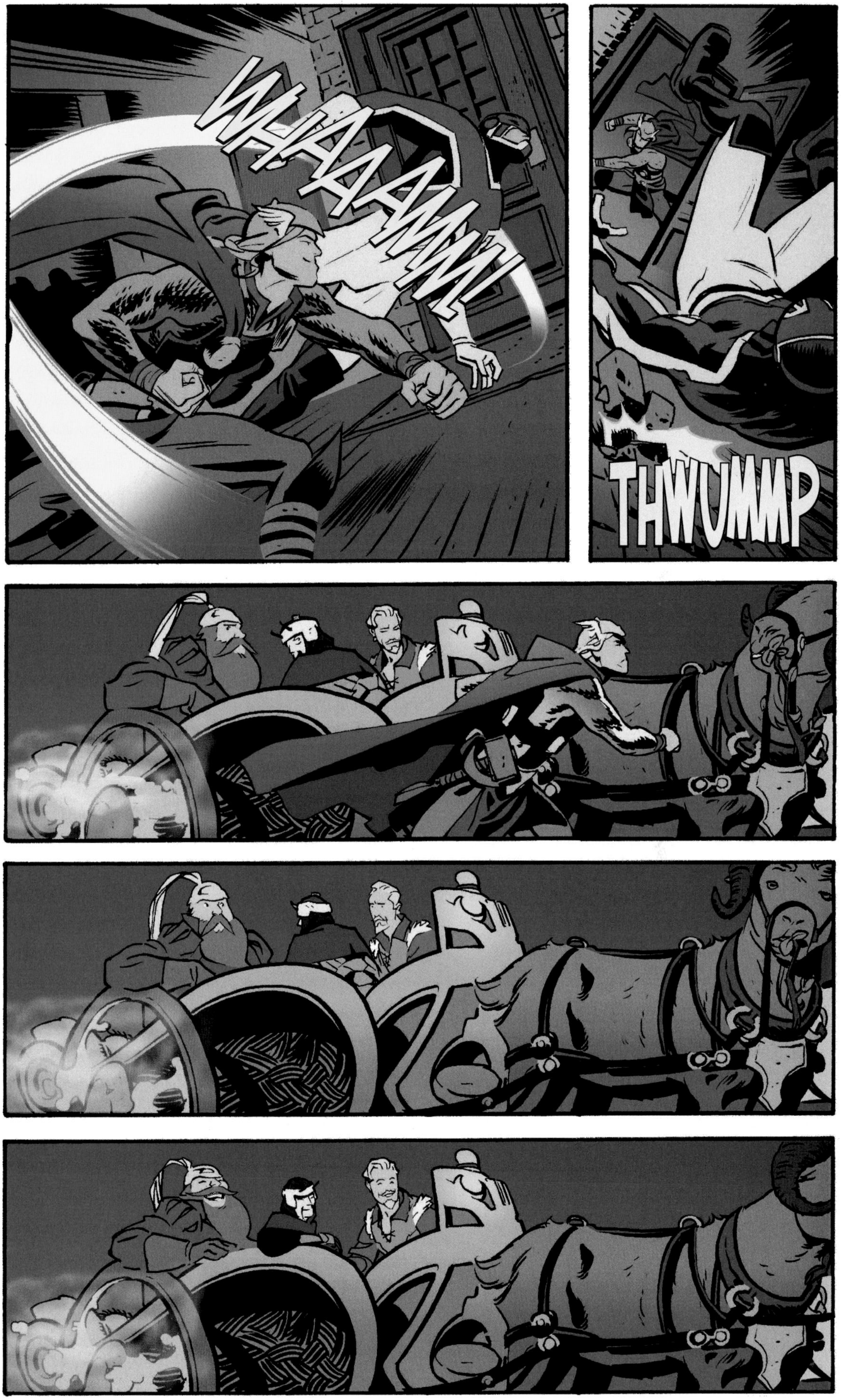
WHAAAMM!
THWUMMP

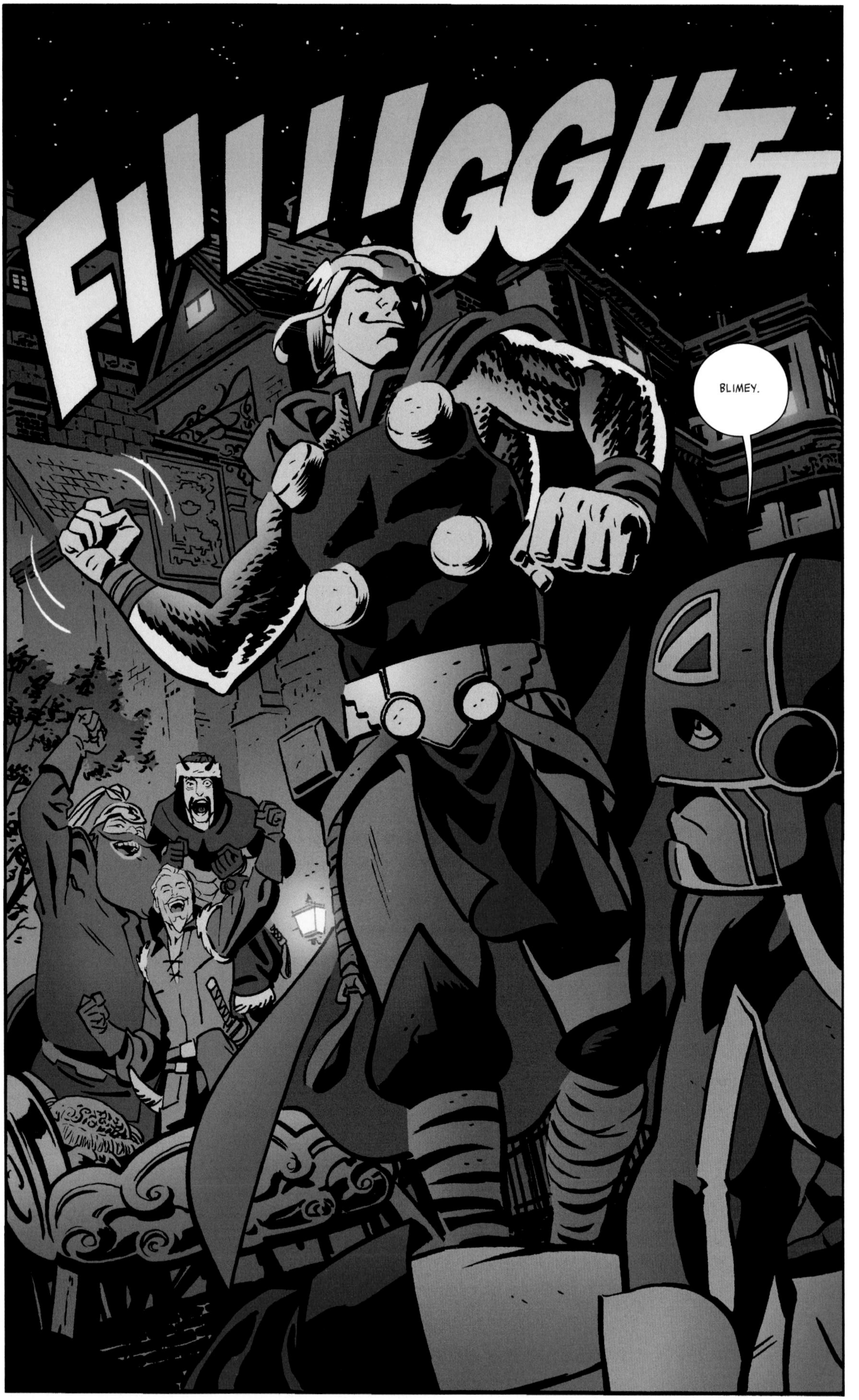
FIIIIIGGHHTT
BLIMEY.

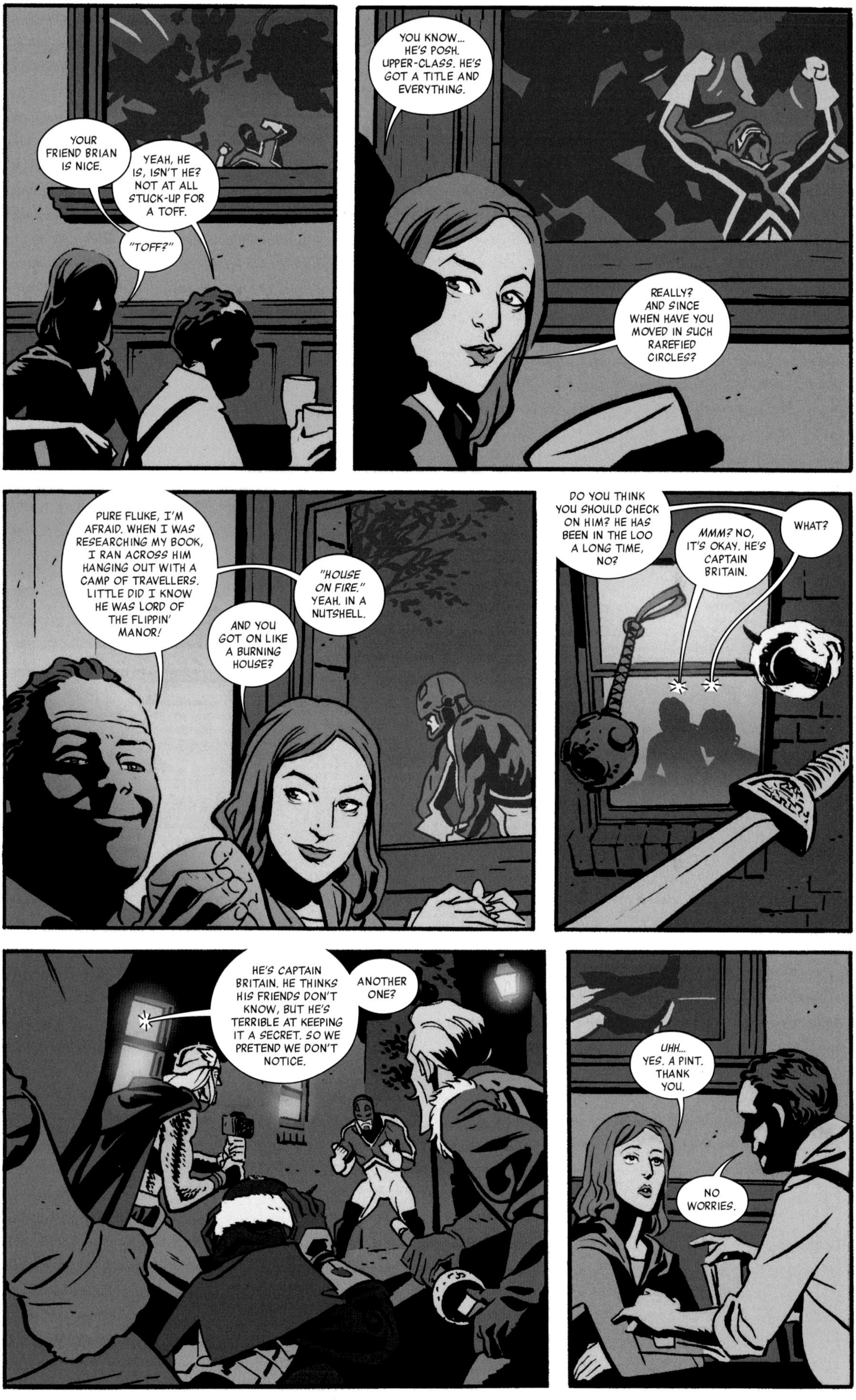
YOUR FRIEND BRIAN IS NICE.
YEAH, HE IS, ISN'T HE? NOT AT ALL STUCK-UP FOR A TOFF.
"TOFF?"
YOU KNOW... HE'S POSH. UPPER-CLASS. HE'S GOT A TITLE AND EVERYTHING.
REALLY? AND SINCE WHEN HAVE YOU MOVED IN SUCH RAREFIED CIRCLES?
PURE FLUKE, I'M AFRAID. WHEN I WAS RESEARCHING MY BOOK, I RAN ACROSS HIM HANGING OUT WITH A CAMP OF TRAVELLERS. LITTLE DID I KNOW HE WAS LORD OF THE FLIPPIN' MANOR!
AND YOU GOT ON LIKE A BURNING HOUSE?
"HOUSE ON FIRE." YEAH. IN A NUTSHELL.
DO YOU THINK YOU SHOULD CHECK ON HIM? HE HAS BEEN IN THE LOO A LONG TIME, NO?
MMM? NO, IT'S OKAY. HE'S CAPTAIN BRITAIN.
WHAT?
HE'S CAPTAIN BRITAIN. HE THINKS HIS FRIENDS DON'T KNOW, BUT HE'S TERRIBLE AT KEEPING IT A SECRET. SO WE PRETEND WE DON'T NOTICE.
ANOTHER ONE?
UHH... YES. A PINT. THANK YOU.
NO WORRIES.

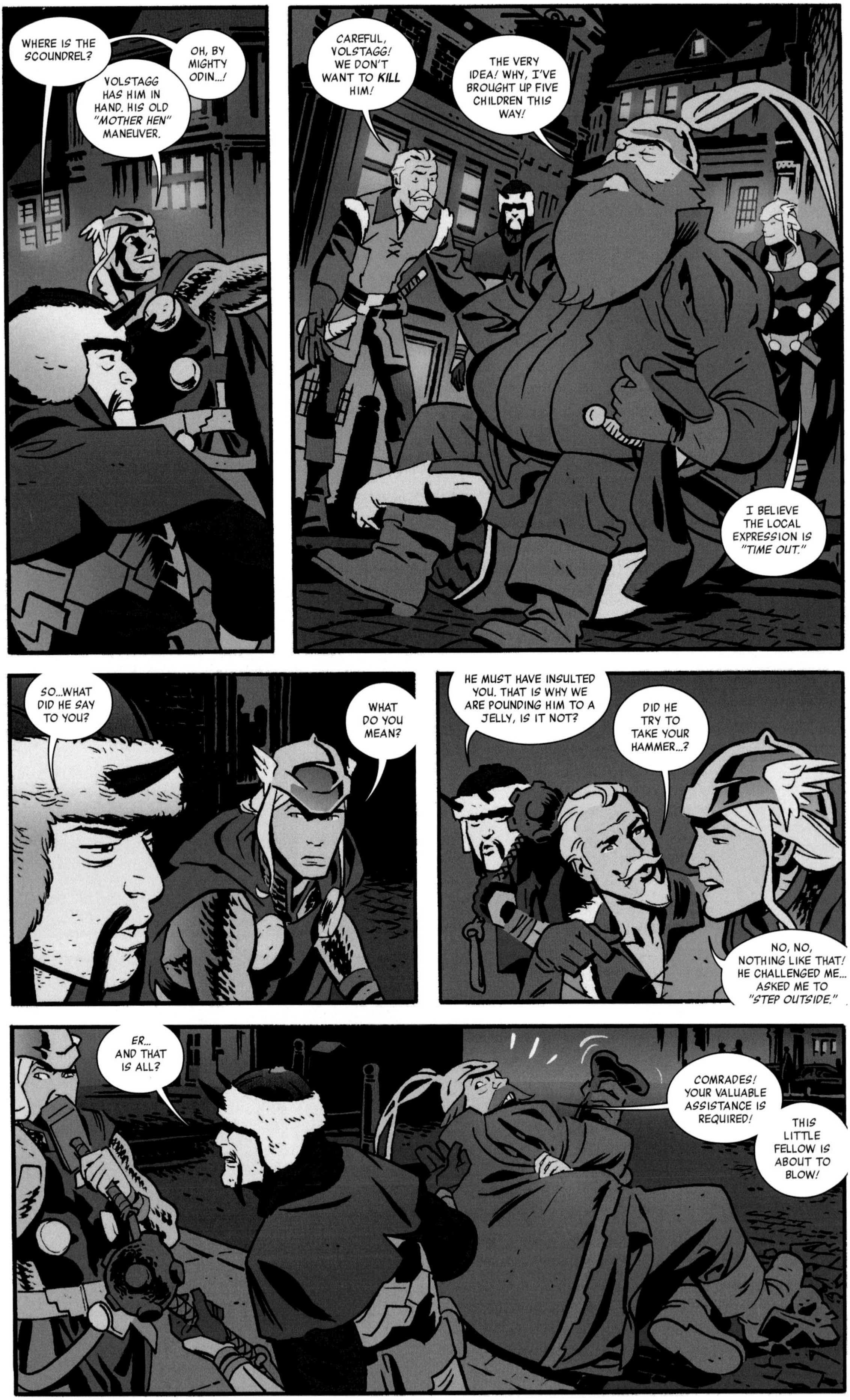
WHERE IS THE SCOUNDREL?
OH, BY MIGHTY ODIN...!
VOLSTAGG HAS HIM IN HAND. HIS OLD "MOTHER HEN" MANEUVER.
CAREFUL, VOLSTAGG! WE DON'T WANT TO KILL HIM!
THE VERY IDEA! WHY, I'VE BROUGHT UP FIVE CHILDREN THIS WAY!
I BELIEVE THE LOCAL EXPRESSION IS "TIME OUT."
SO...WHAT DID HE SAY TO YOU?
WHAT DO YOU MEAN?
HE MUST HAVE INSULTED YOU. THAT IS WHY WE ARE POUNDING HIM TO A JELLY, IS IT NOT?
DID HE TRY TO TAKE YOUR HAMMER...?
NO, NO, NOTHING LIKE THAT! HE CHALLENGED ME... ASKED ME TO "STEP OUTSIDE."
ER... AND THAT IS ALL?
COMRADES! YOUR VALUABLE ASSISTANCE IS REQUIRED!
THIS LITTLE FELLOW IS ABOUT TO BLOW!

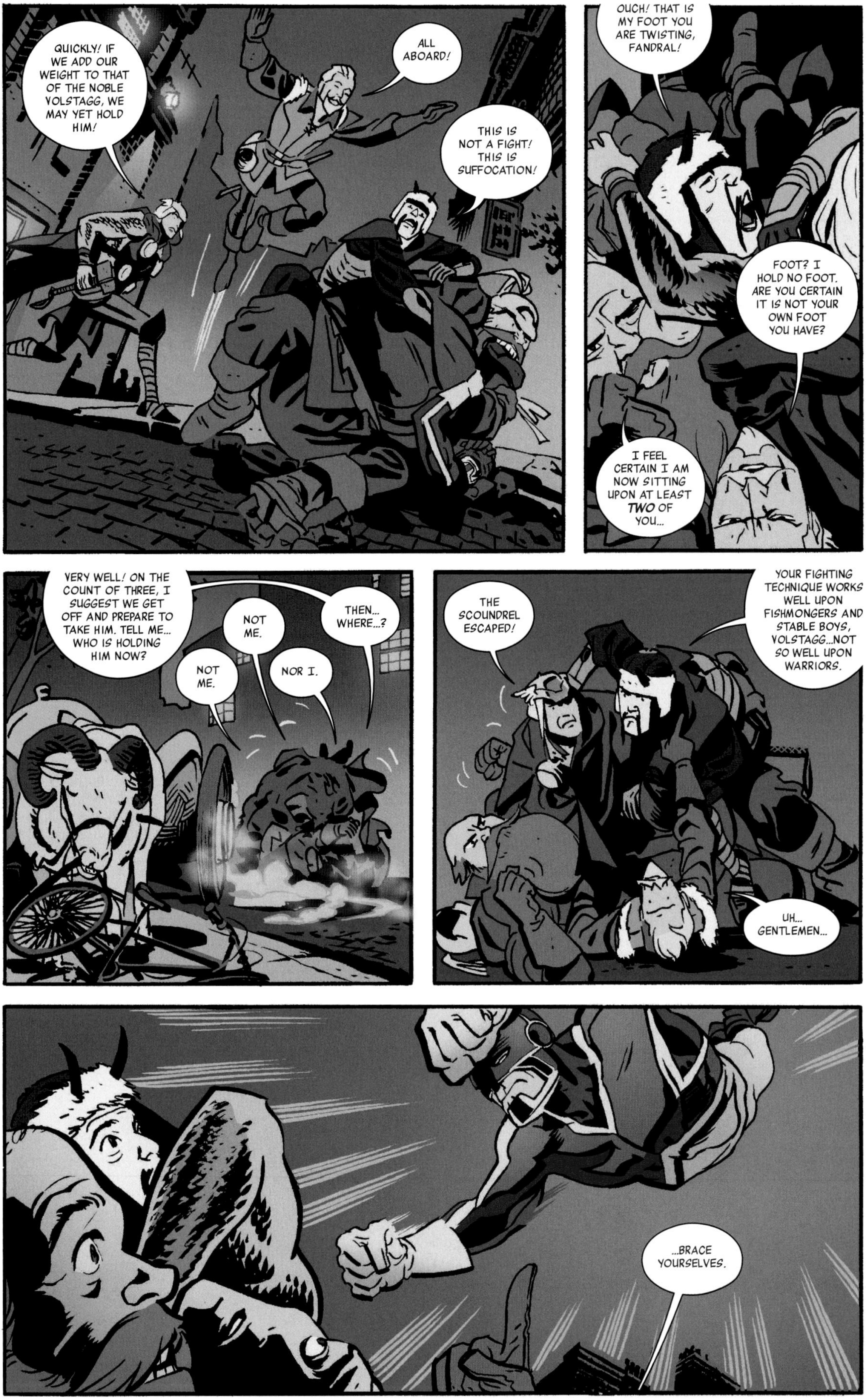
QUICKLY! IF WE ADD OUR WEIGHT TO THAT OF THE NOBLE VOLSTAGG, WE MAY YET HOLD HIM!
ALL ABOARD!
THIS IS NOT A FIGHT! THIS IS SUFFOCATION!
OUCH! THAT IS MY FOOT YOU ARE TWISTING, FANDRAL!
FOOT? I HOLD NO FOOT. ARE YOU CERTAIN IT IS NOT YOUR OWN FOOT YOU HAVE?
I FEEL CERTAIN I AM NOW SITTING UPON AT LEAST TWO OF YOU...
VERY WELL! ON THE COUNT OF THREE, I SUGGEST WE GET OFF AND PREPARE TO TAKE HIM. TELL ME... WHO IS HOLDING HIM NOW?
NOT ME.
NOT ME.
NOR I.
THEN... WHERE...?
THE SCOUNDREL ESCAPED!
YOUR FIGHTING TECHNIQUE WORKS WELL UPON FISHMONGERS AND STABLE BOYS, VOLSTAGG...NOT SO WELL UPON WARRIORS.
UH... GENTLEMEN...
...BRACE YOURSELVES.

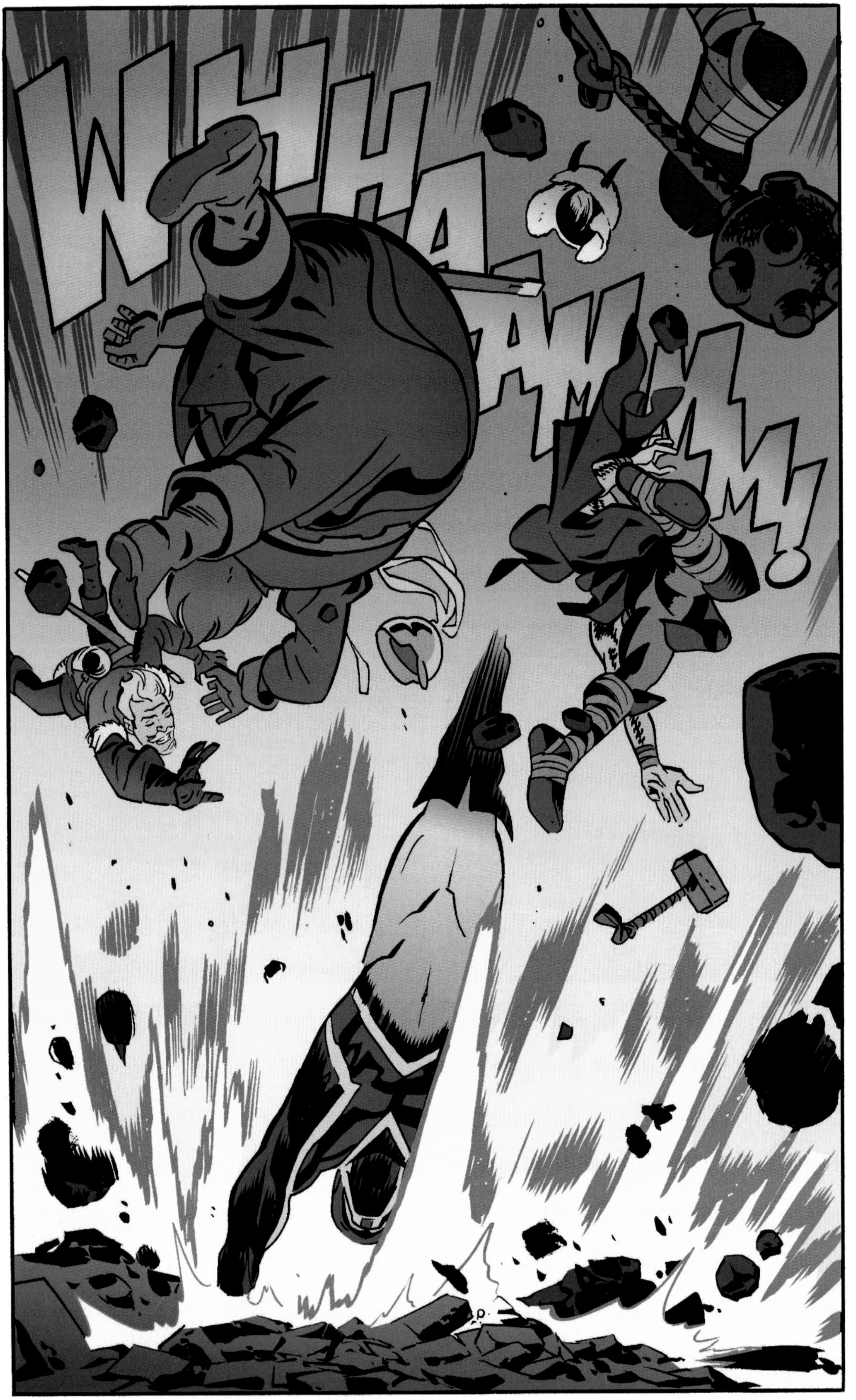
WHHAAMMM!

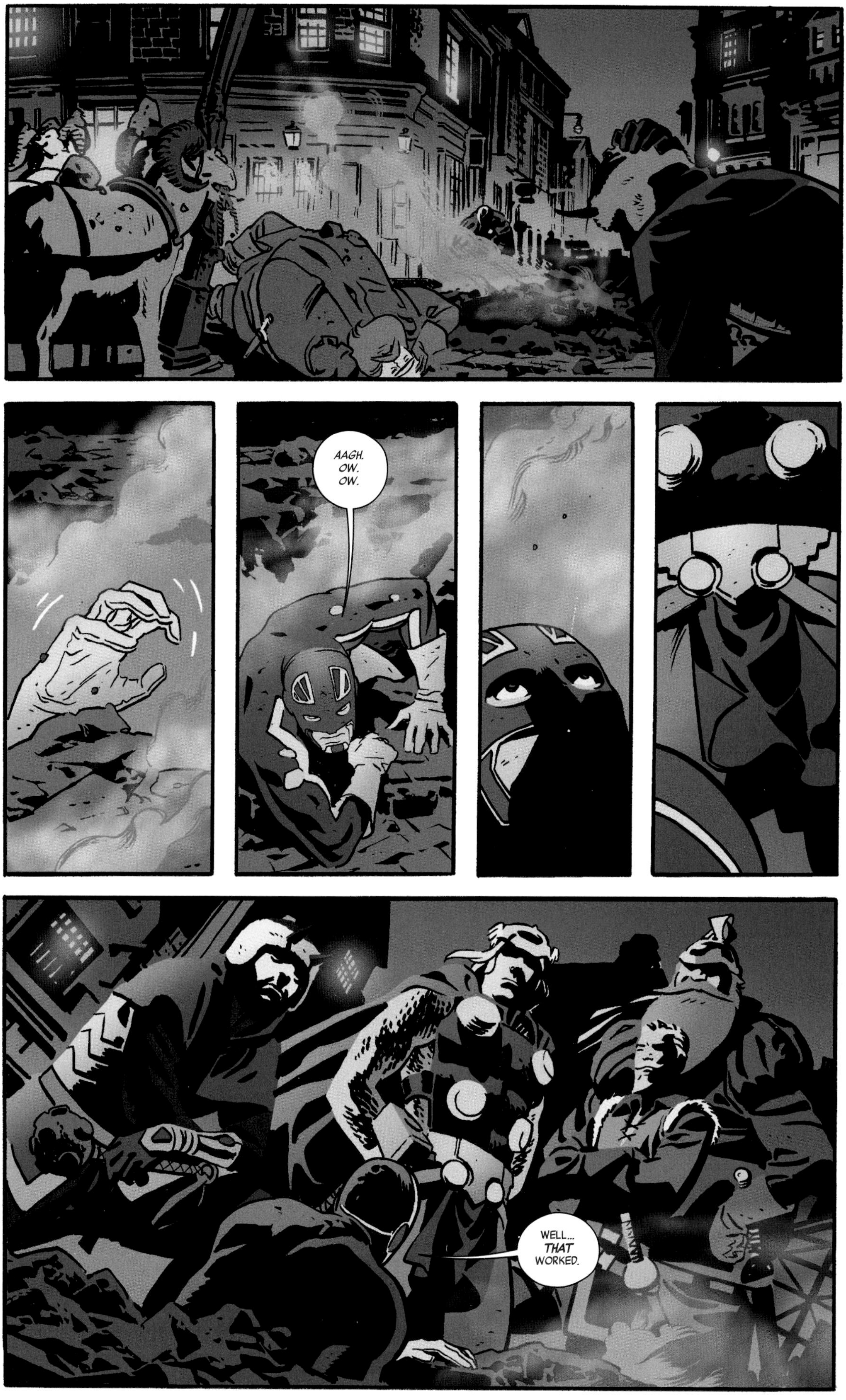
AAGH. OW. OW.
WELL... THAT WORKED.

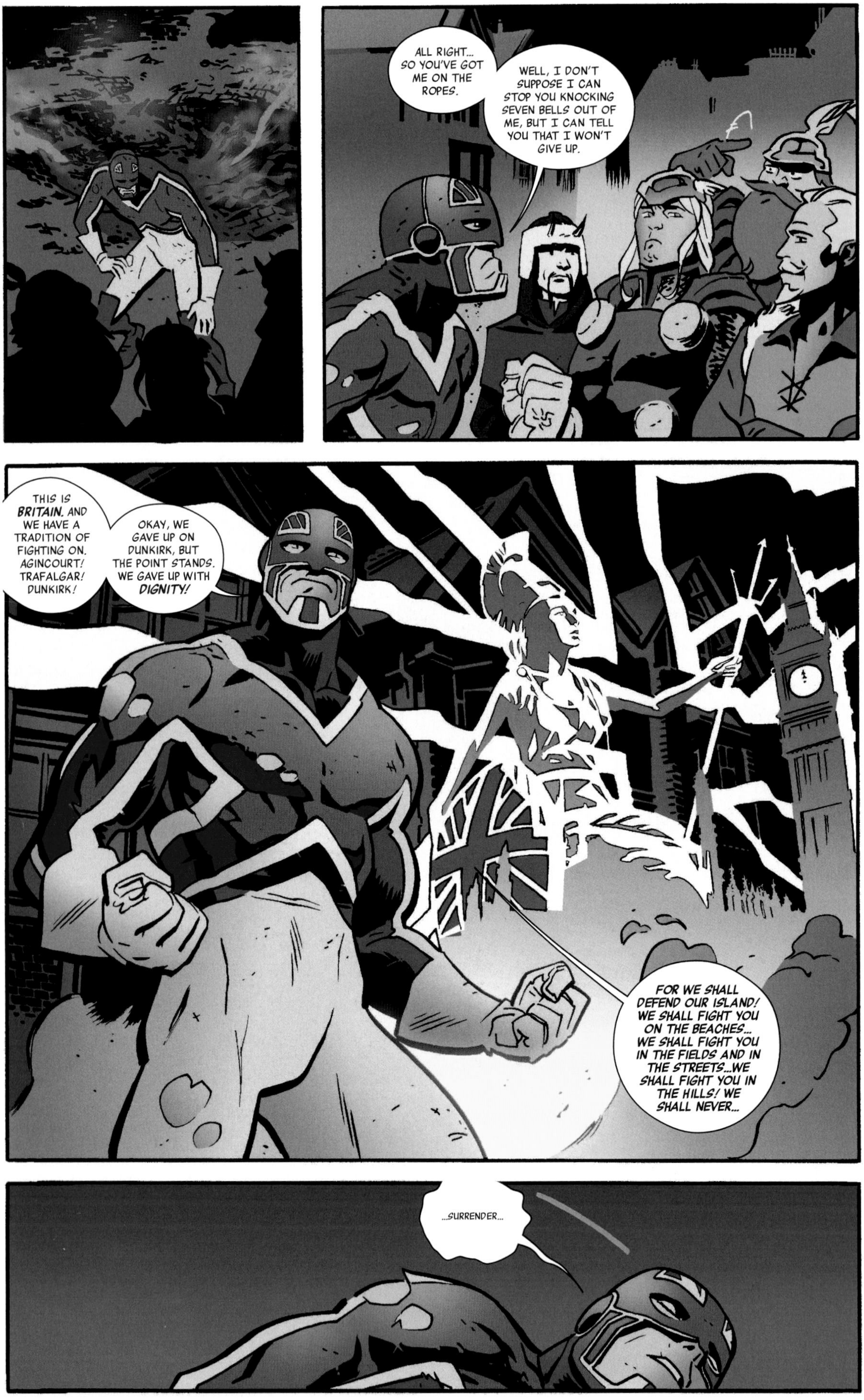
ALL RIGHT... SO YOU'VE GOT ME ON THE ROPES.
WELL, I DON'T SUPPOSE I CAN STOP YOU KNOCKING SEVEN BELLS OUT OF ME, BUT I CAN TELL YOU THAT I WON'T GIVE UP.
THIS IS **BRITAIN.** AND WE HAVE A TRADITION OF FIGHTING ON. AGINCOURT! TRAFALGAR! DUNKIRK!
OKAY, WE GAVE UP ON DUNKIRK, BUT THE POINT STANDS. WE GAVE UP WITH ***DIGNITY!***
FOR WE SHALL DEFEND OUR ISLAND! WE SHALL FIGHT YOU ON THE BEACHES... WE SHALL FIGHT YOU IN THE FIELDS AND IN THE STREETS...WE SHALL FIGHT YOU IN THE HILLS! WE SHALL NEVER...
...SURRENDER...

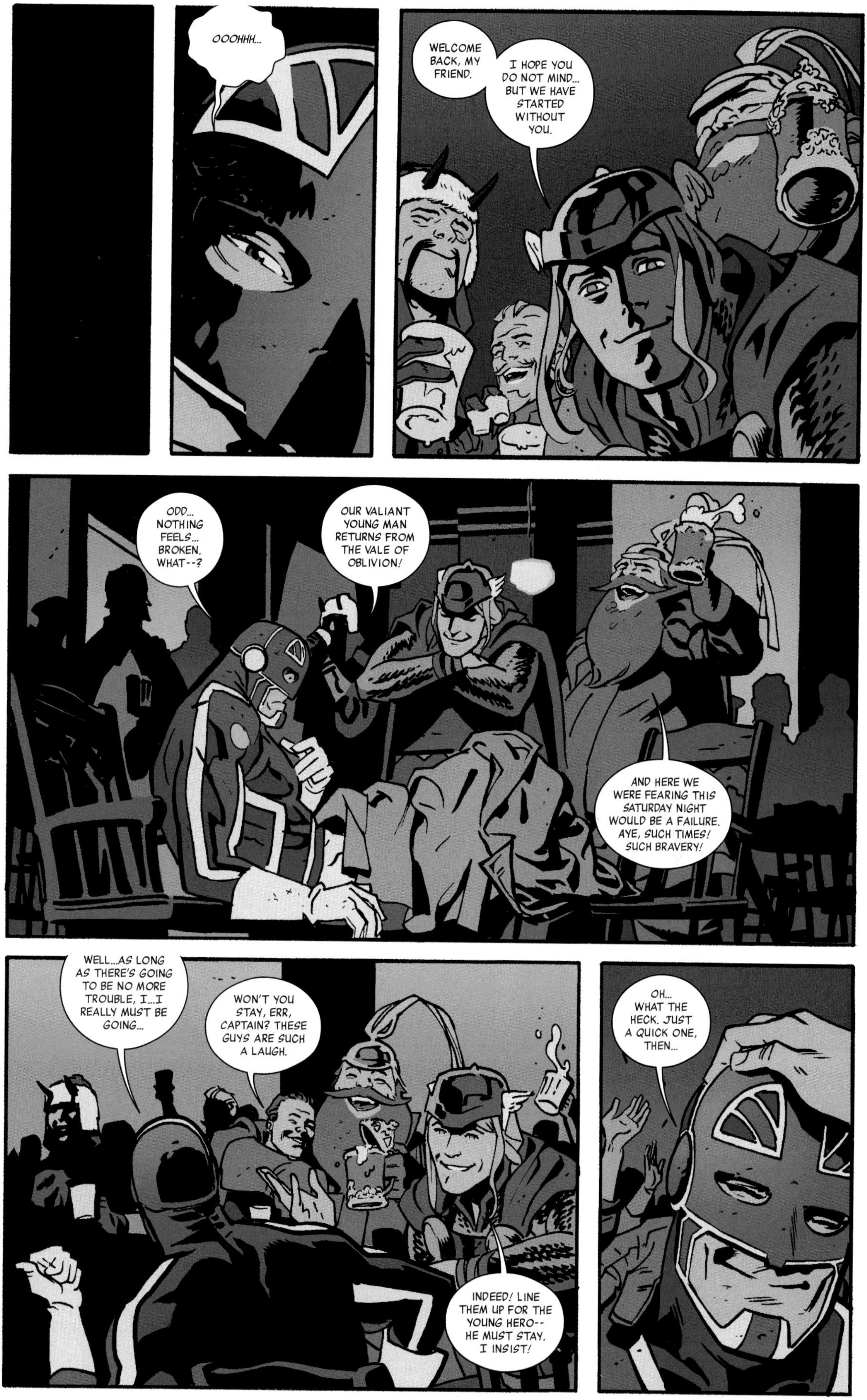
OOOHHH...
WELCOME BACK, MY FRIEND.
I HOPE YOU DO NOT MIND... BUT WE HAVE STARTED WITHOUT YOU.
ODD... NOTHING FEELS... BROKEN. WHAT--?
OUR VALIANT YOUNG MAN RETURNS FROM THE VALE OF OBLIVION!
AND HERE WE WERE FEARING THIS SATURDAY NIGHT WOULD BE A FAILURE. AYE, SUCH TIMES! SUCH BRAVERY!
WELL...AS LONG AS THERE'S GOING TO BE NO MORE TROUBLE, I...I REALLY MUST BE GOING...
WON'T YOU STAY, ERR, CAPTAIN? THESE GUYS ARE SUCH A LAUGH.
INDEED! LINE THEM UP FOR THE YOUNG HERO-- HE MUST STAY. I INSIST!
OH... WHAT THE HECK. JUST A QUICK ONE, THEN...

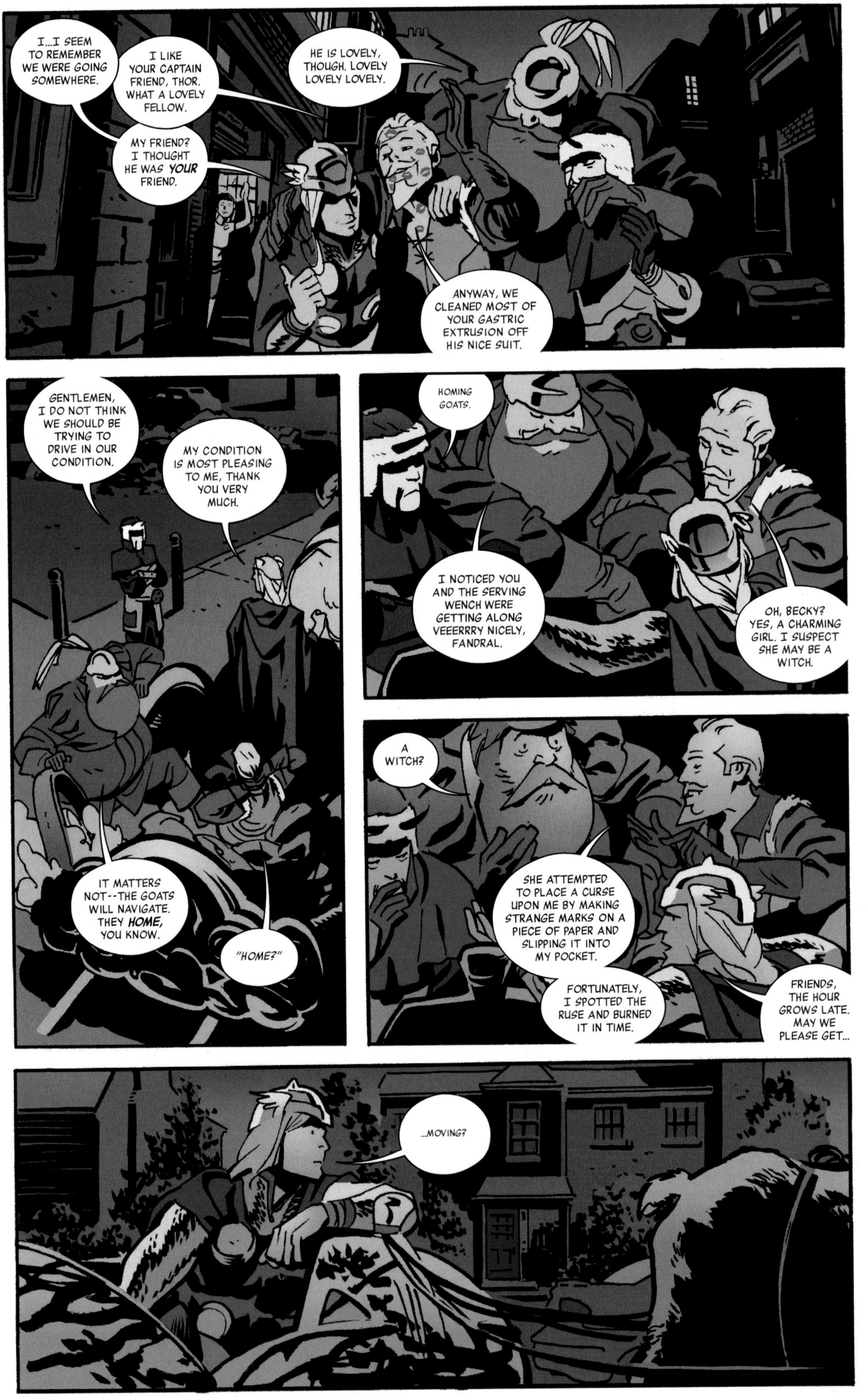
I...I SEEM TO REMEMBER WE WERE GOING SOMEWHERE.
I LIKE YOUR CAPTAIN FRIEND, THOR. WHAT A LOVELY FELLOW.
MY FRIEND? I THOUGHT HE WAS YOUR FRIEND.
HE IS LOVELY, THOUGH. LOVELY LOVELY LOVELY.
ANYWAY, WE CLEANED MOST OF YOUR GASTRIC EXTRUSION OFF HIS NICE SUIT.
GENTLEMEN, I DO NOT THINK WE SHOULD BE TRYING TO DRIVE IN OUR CONDITION.
MY CONDITION IS MOST PLEASING TO ME, THANK YOU VERY MUCH.
IT MATTERS NOT--THE GOATS WILL NAVIGATE. THEY HOME, YOU KNOW.
"HOME?"
HOMING GOATS.
I NOTICED YOU AND THE SERVING WENCH WERE GETTING ALONG VEEERRRY NICELY, FANDRAL.
OH, BECKY? YES, A CHARMING GIRL. I SUSPECT SHE MAY BE A WITCH.
A WITCH?
SHE ATTEMPTED TO PLACE A CURSE UPON ME BY MAKING STRANGE MARKS ON A PIECE OF PAPER AND SLIPPING IT INTO MY POCKET.
FORTUNATELY, I SPOTTED THE RUSE AND BURNED IT IN TIME.
FRIENDS, THE HOUR GROWS LATE. MAY WE PLEASE GET...
...MOVING?

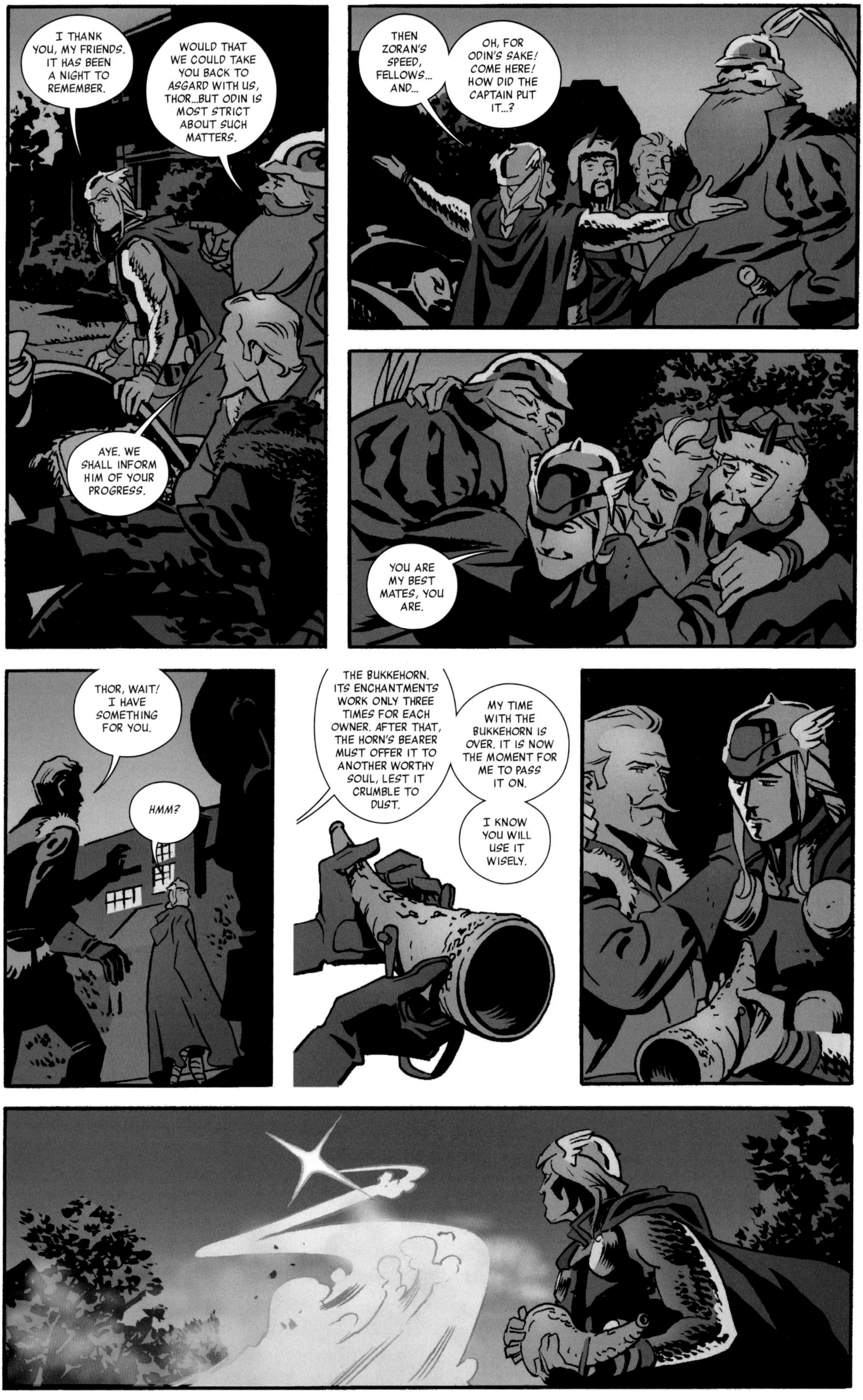
I THANK YOU, MY FRIENDS. IT HAS BEEN A NIGHT TO REMEMBER.
WOULD THAT WE COULD TAKE YOU BACK TO ASGARD WITH US, THOR...BUT ODIN IS MOST STRICT ABOUT SUCH MATTERS.
AYE. WE SHALL INFORM HIM OF YOUR PROGRESS.
THEN ZORAN'S SPEED, FELLOWS... AND...
OH, FOR ODIN'S SAKE! COME HERE! HOW DID THE CAPTAIN PUT IT...?
YOU ARE MY BEST MATES, YOU ARE.
THOR, WAIT! I HAVE SOMETHING FOR YOU.
HMM?
THE BUKKEHORN. ITS ENCHANTMENTS WORK ONLY THREE TIMES FOR EACH OWNER. AFTER THAT, THE HORN'S BEARER MUST OFFER IT TO ANOTHER WORTHY SOUL, LEST IT CRUMBLE TO DUST.
MY TIME WITH THE BUKKEHORN IS OVER. IT IS NOW THE MOMENT FOR ME TO PASS IT ON.
I KNOW YOU WILL USE IT WISELY.

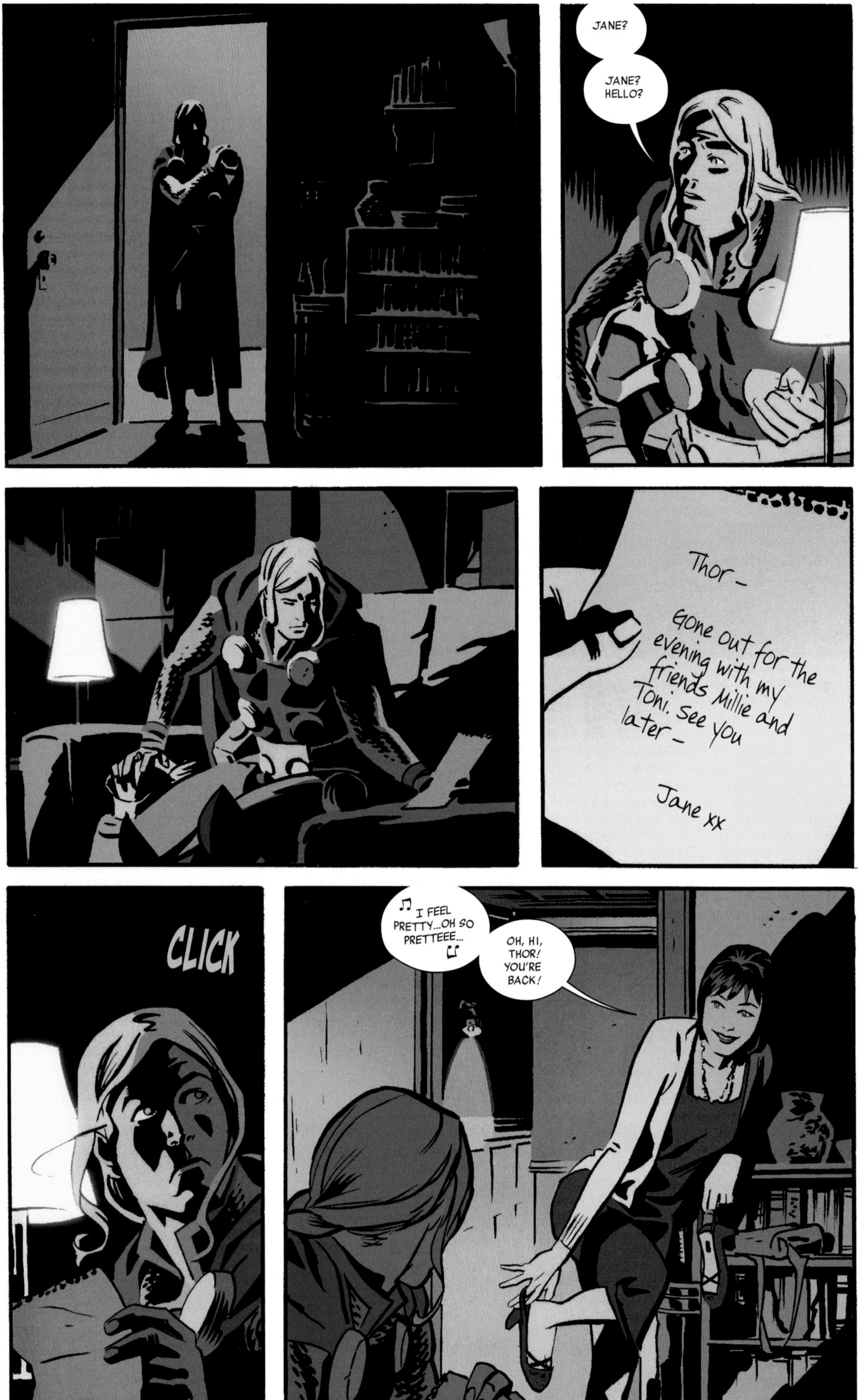
JANE?
JANE? HELLO?
Thor –
Gone out for the evening with my friends Millie and Toni. See you later –
Jane xx
CLICK
♫ I FEEL PRETTY...OH SO PRETTEEE... ♫
OH, HI, THOR! YOU'RE BACK!

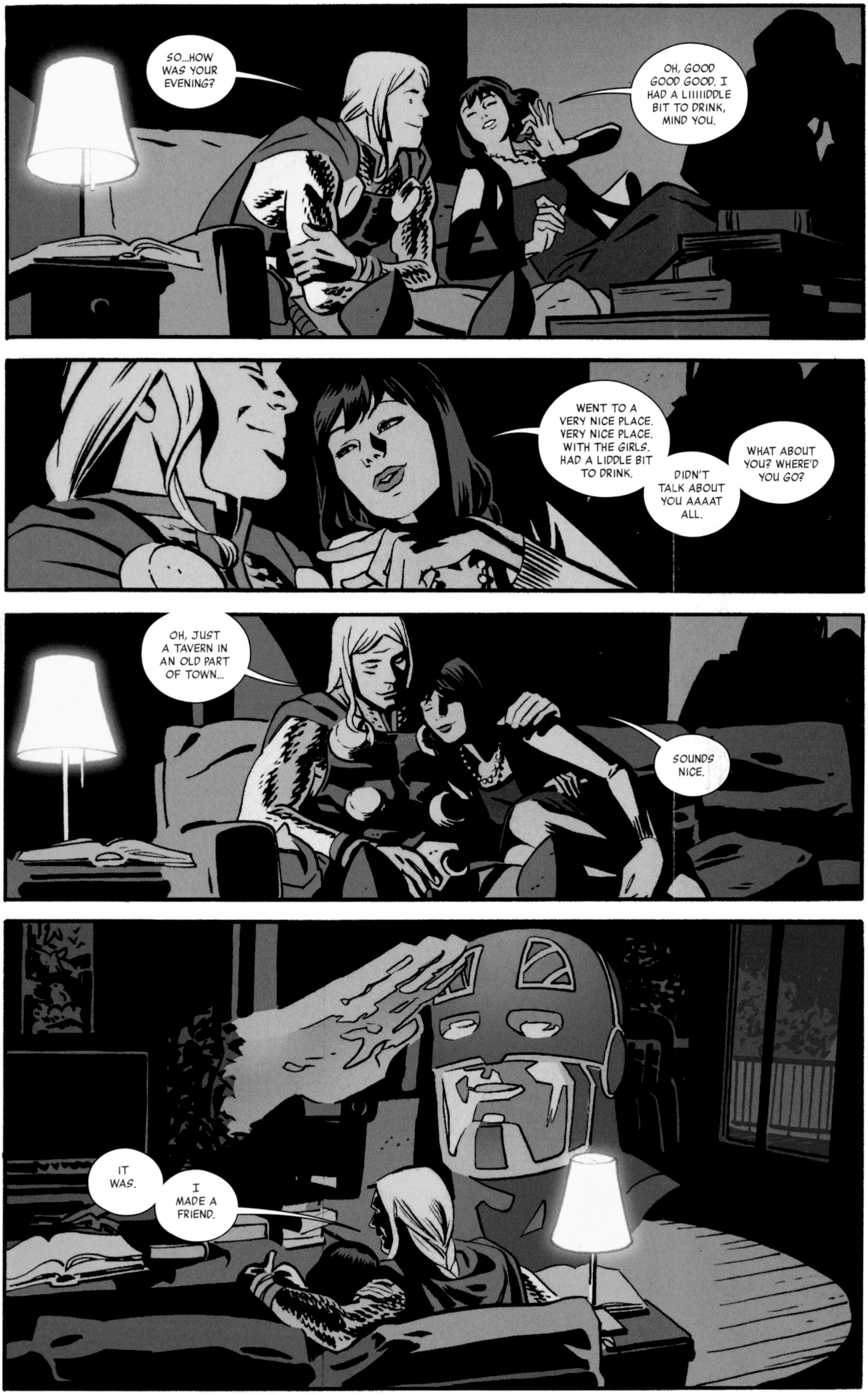
SO...HOW WAS YOUR EVENING?
OH, GOOD GOOD GOOD. I HAD A LIIIIIDDLE BIT TO DRINK, MIND YOU.
WENT TO A VERY NICE PLACE. VERY NICE PLACE. WITH THE GIRLS. HAD A LIDDLE BIT TO DRINK.
DIDN'T TALK ABOUT YOU AAAAT ALL.
WHAT ABOUT YOU? WHERE'D YOU GO?
OH, JUST A TAVERN IN AN OLD PART OF TOWN...
SOUNDS NICE.
IT WAS.
I MADE A FRIEND.

THOR THE MIGHTY AVENGER #5

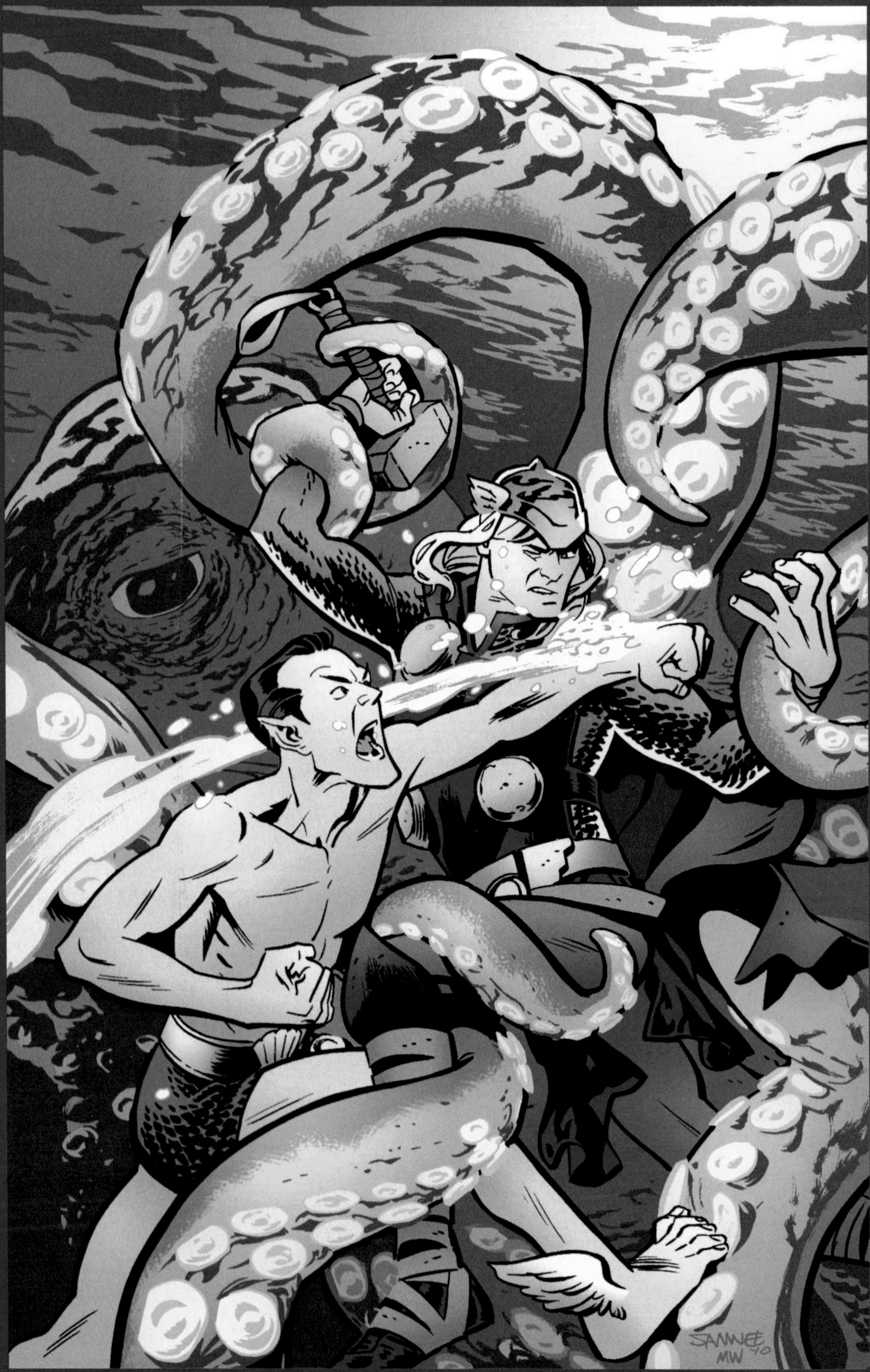
SAMNEE '10
MW

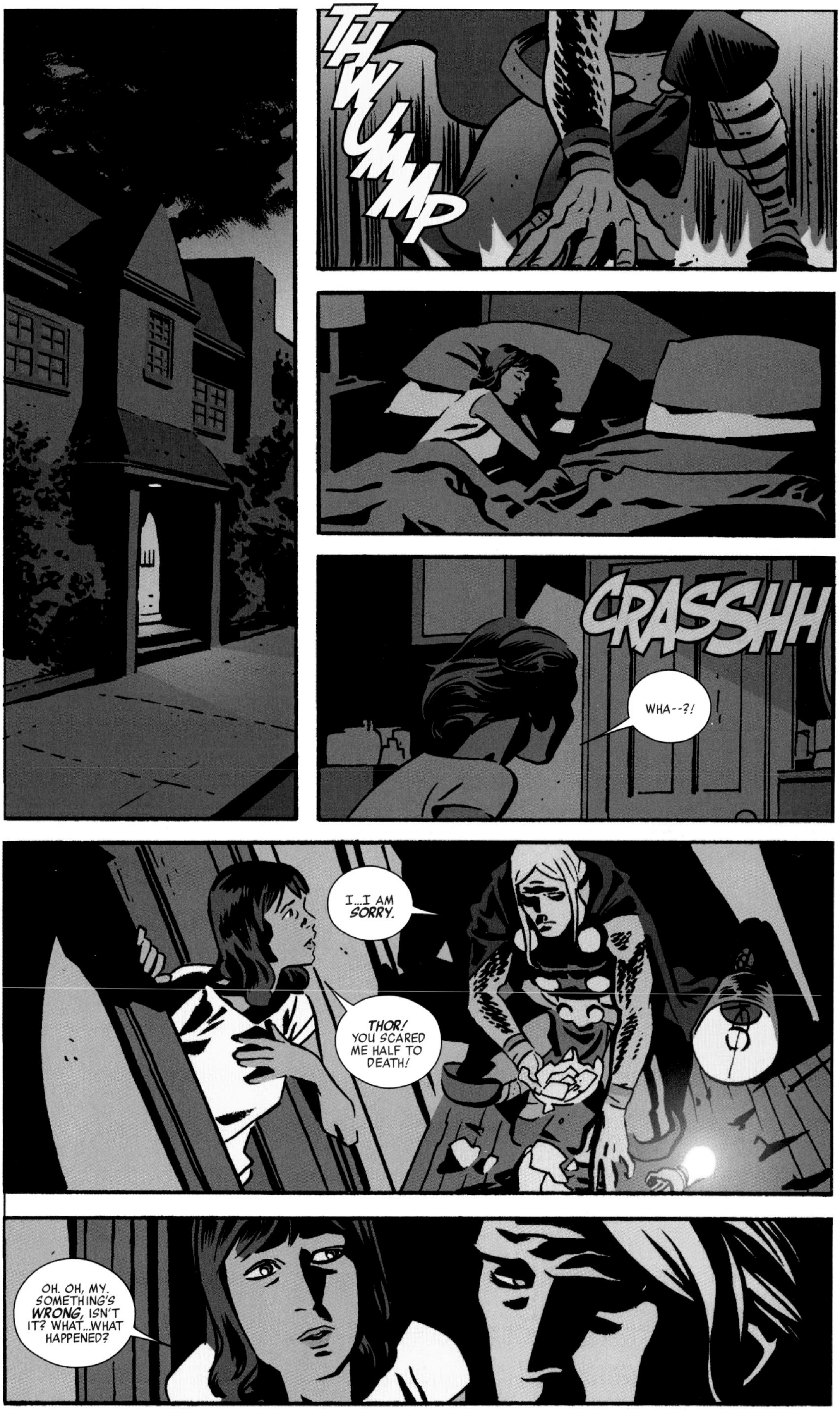
THWUMMP
CRASSHH
WHA--?!
I...I AM SORRY.
THOR! YOU SCARED ME HALF TO DEATH!
OH. OH, MY. SOMETHING'S WRONG, ISN'T IT? WHAT...WHAT HAPPENED?

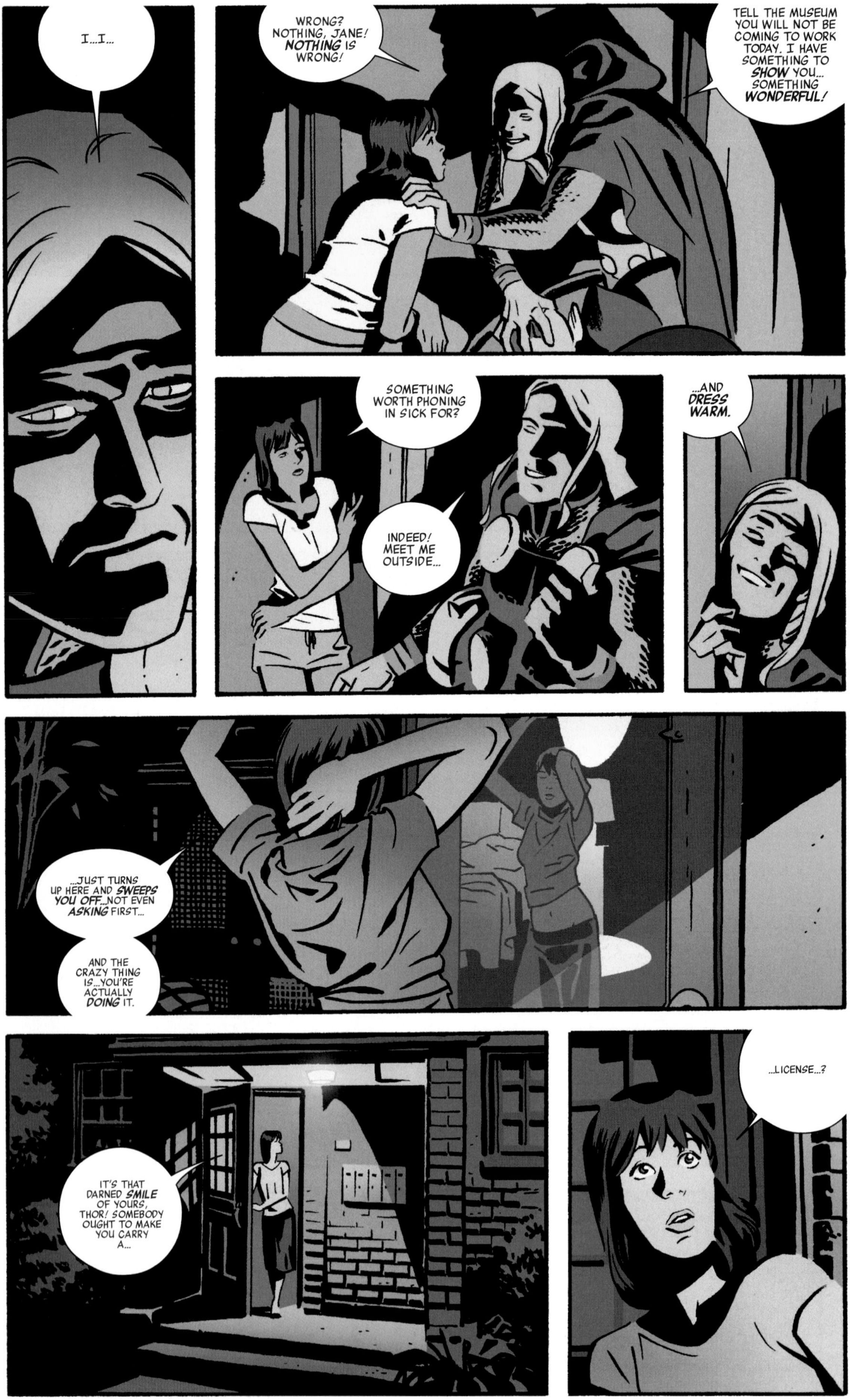
I...I...
WRONG? NOTHING, JANE! NOTHING IS WRONG!
TELL THE MUSEUM YOU WILL NOT BE COMING TO WORK TODAY. I HAVE SOMETHING TO SHOW YOU... SOMETHING WONDERFUL!
SOMETHING WORTH PHONING IN SICK FOR?
INDEED! MEET ME OUTSIDE...
...AND DRESS WARM.
...JUST TURNS UP HERE AND SWEEPS YOU OFF...NOT EVEN ASKING FIRST...
AND THE CRAZY THING IS...YOU'RE ACTUALLY DOING IT.
IT'S THAT DARNED SMILE OF YOURS, THOR! SOMEBODY OUGHT TO MAKE YOU CARRY A...
...LICENSE...?

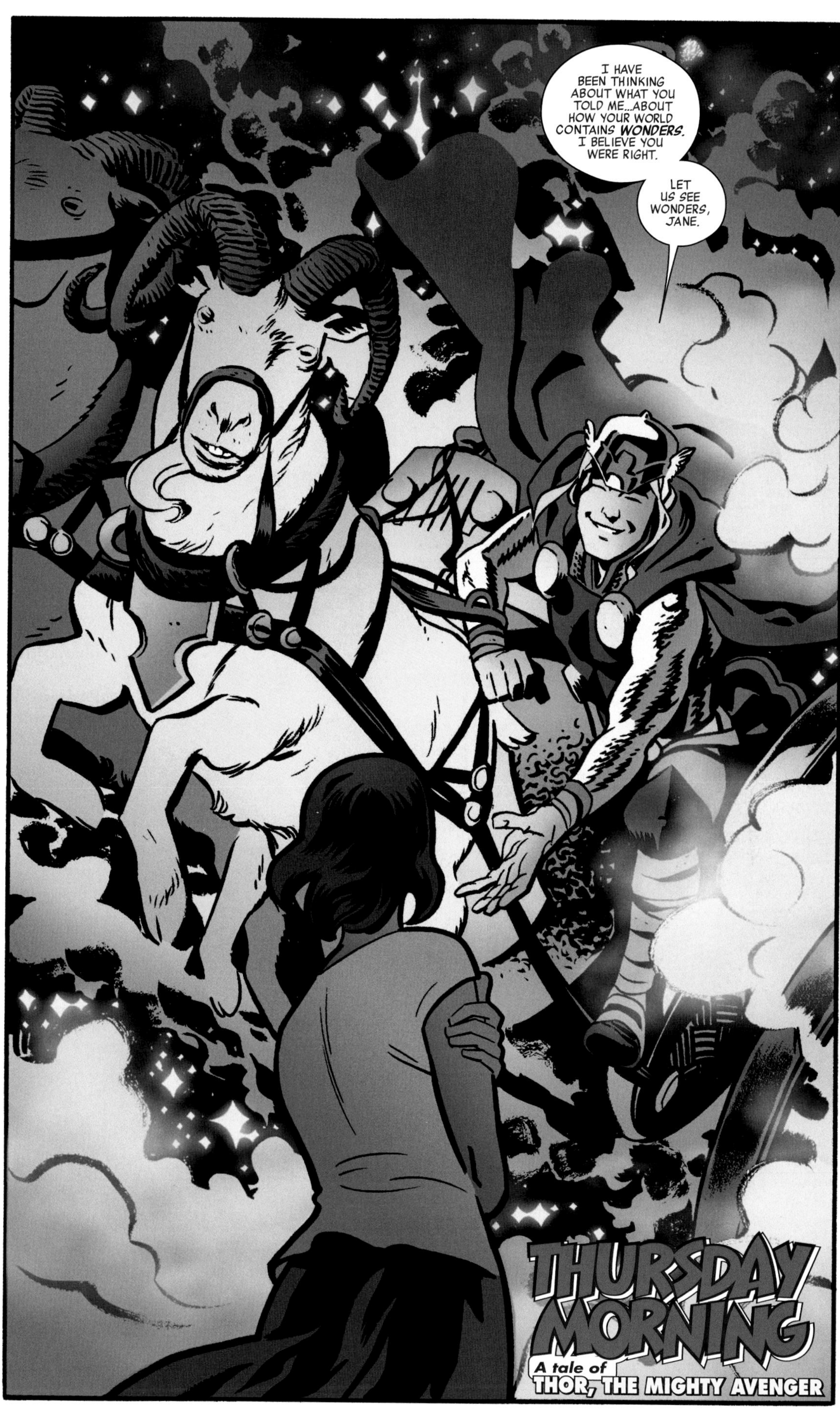
I HAVE BEEN THINKING ABOUT WHAT YOU TOLD ME...ABOUT HOW YOUR WORLD CONTAINS WONDERS. I BELIEVE YOU WERE RIGHT.
LET US SEE WONDERS, JANE.
THURSDAY MORNING
A tale of
THOR, THE MIGHTY AVENGER

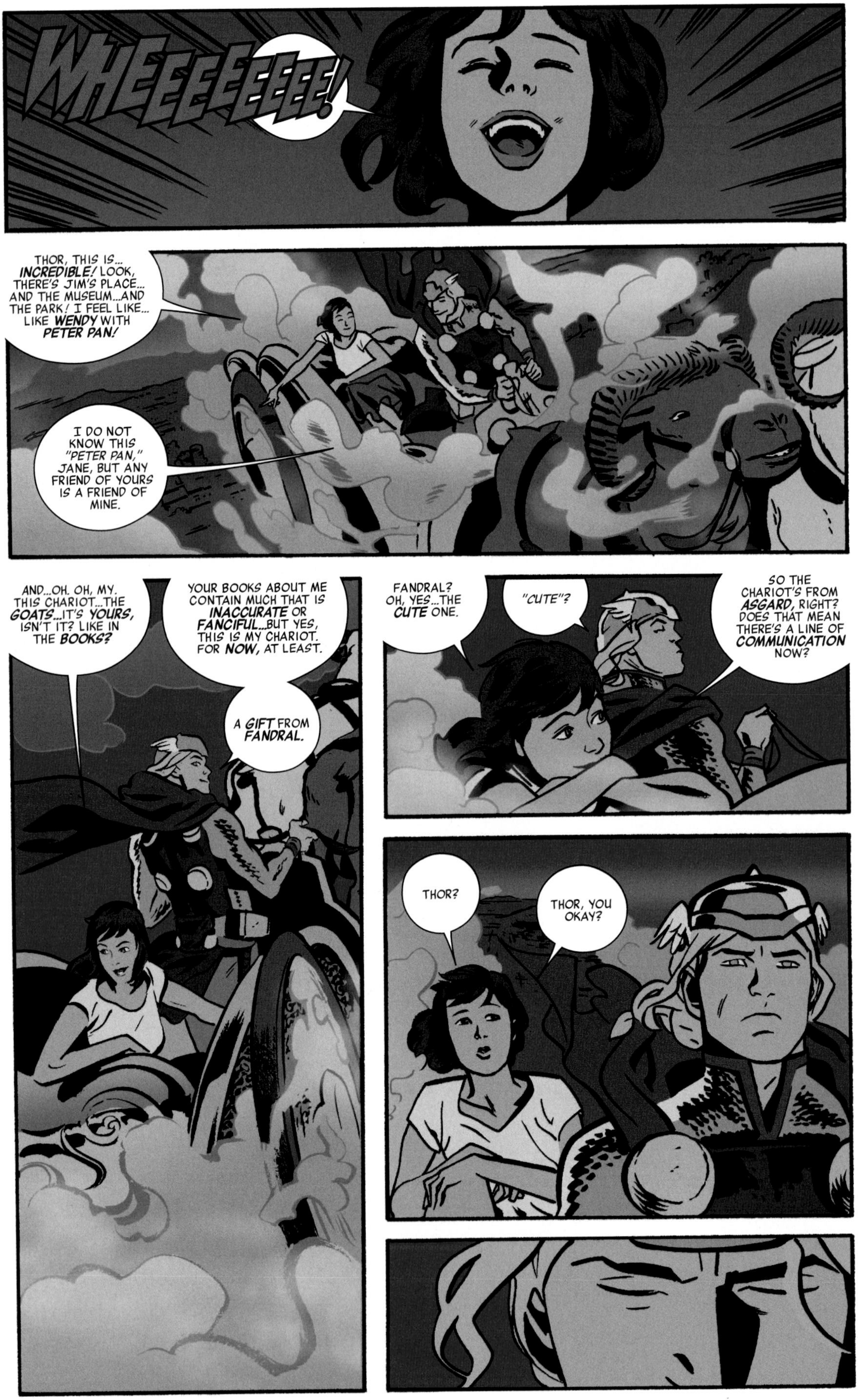
WHEEEEEEEE!
THOR, THIS IS... INCREDIBLE! LOOK, THERE'S JIM'S PLACE... AND THE MUSEUM...AND THE PARK! I FEEL LIKE... LIKE WENDY WITH PETER PAN!
I DO NOT KNOW THIS "PETER PAN," JANE, BUT ANY FRIEND OF YOURS IS A FRIEND OF MINE.
AND...OH. OH, MY. THIS CHARIOT...THE GOATS...IT'S YOURS, ISN'T IT? LIKE IN THE BOOKS?
YOUR BOOKS ABOUT ME CONTAIN MUCH THAT IS INACCURATE OR FANCIFUL...BUT YES, THIS IS MY CHARIOT. FOR NOW, AT LEAST.
A GIFT FROM FANDRAL.
FANDRAL? OH, YES...THE CUTE ONE.
"CUTE"?
SO THE CHARIOT'S FROM ASGARD, RIGHT? DOES THAT MEAN THERE'S A LINE OF COMMUNICATION NOW?
THOR?
THOR, YOU OKAY?

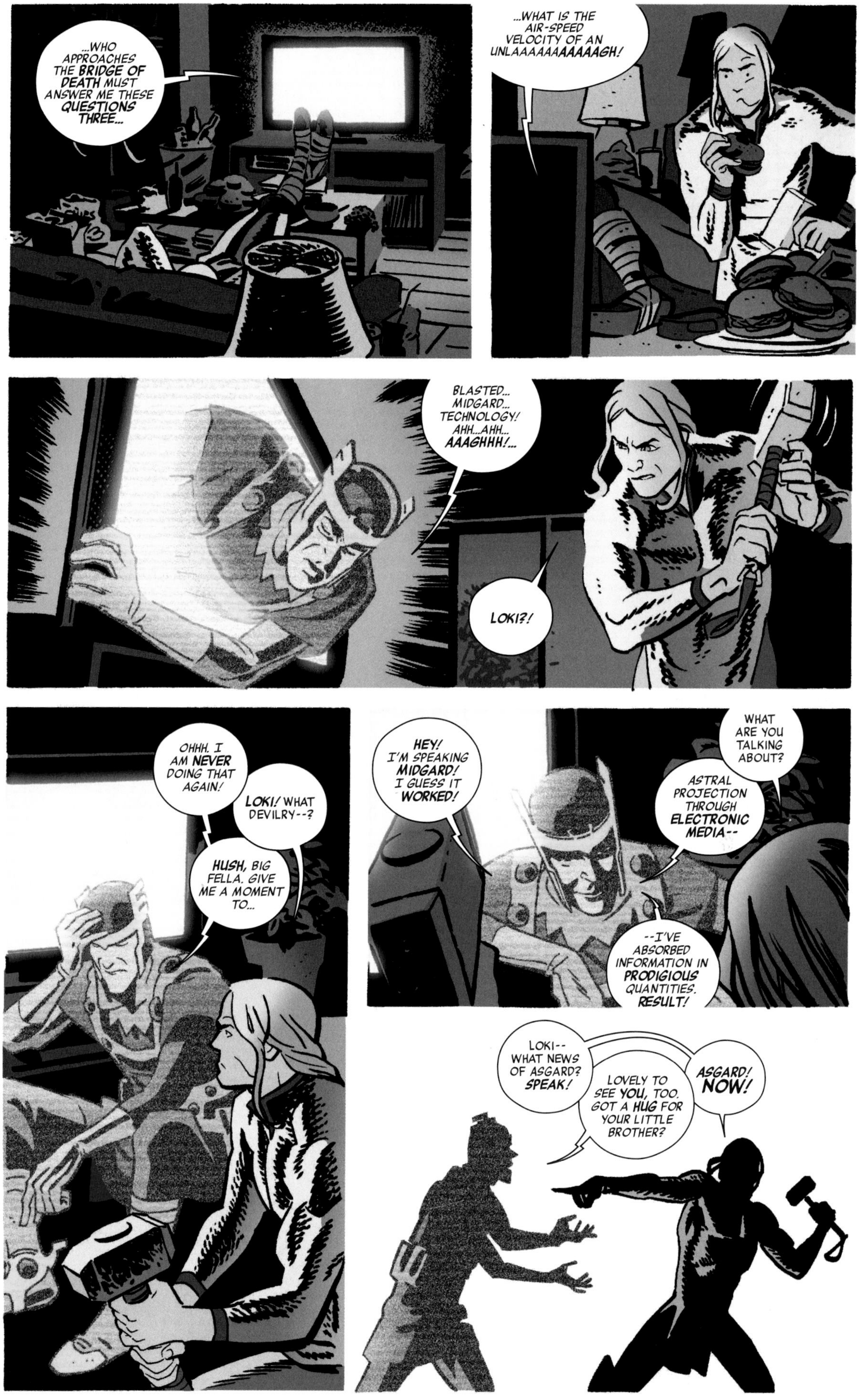
...WHO APPROACHES THE BRIDGE OF DEATH MUST ANSWER ME THESE QUESTIONS THREE...
...WHAT IS THE AIR-SPEED VELOCITY OF AN UNLAAAAAAAAAAAAGH!
BLASTED... MIDGARD... TECHNOLOGY! AHH...AHH... AAAGHHH!...
LOKI?!
OHHH. I AM NEVER DOING THAT AGAIN!
LOKI! WHAT DEVILRY--?
HUSH, BIG FELLA. GIVE ME A MOMENT TO...
HEY! I'M SPEAKING MIDGARD! I GUESS IT WORKED!
WHAT ARE YOU TALKING ABOUT?
ASTRAL PROJECTION THROUGH ELECTRONIC MEDIA--
--I'VE ABSORBED INFORMATION IN PRODIGIOUS QUANTITIES. RESULT!
LOKI-- WHAT NEWS OF ASGARD? SPEAK!
LOVELY TO SEE YOU, TOO. GOT A HUG FOR YOUR LITTLE BROTHER?
ASGARD! NOW!

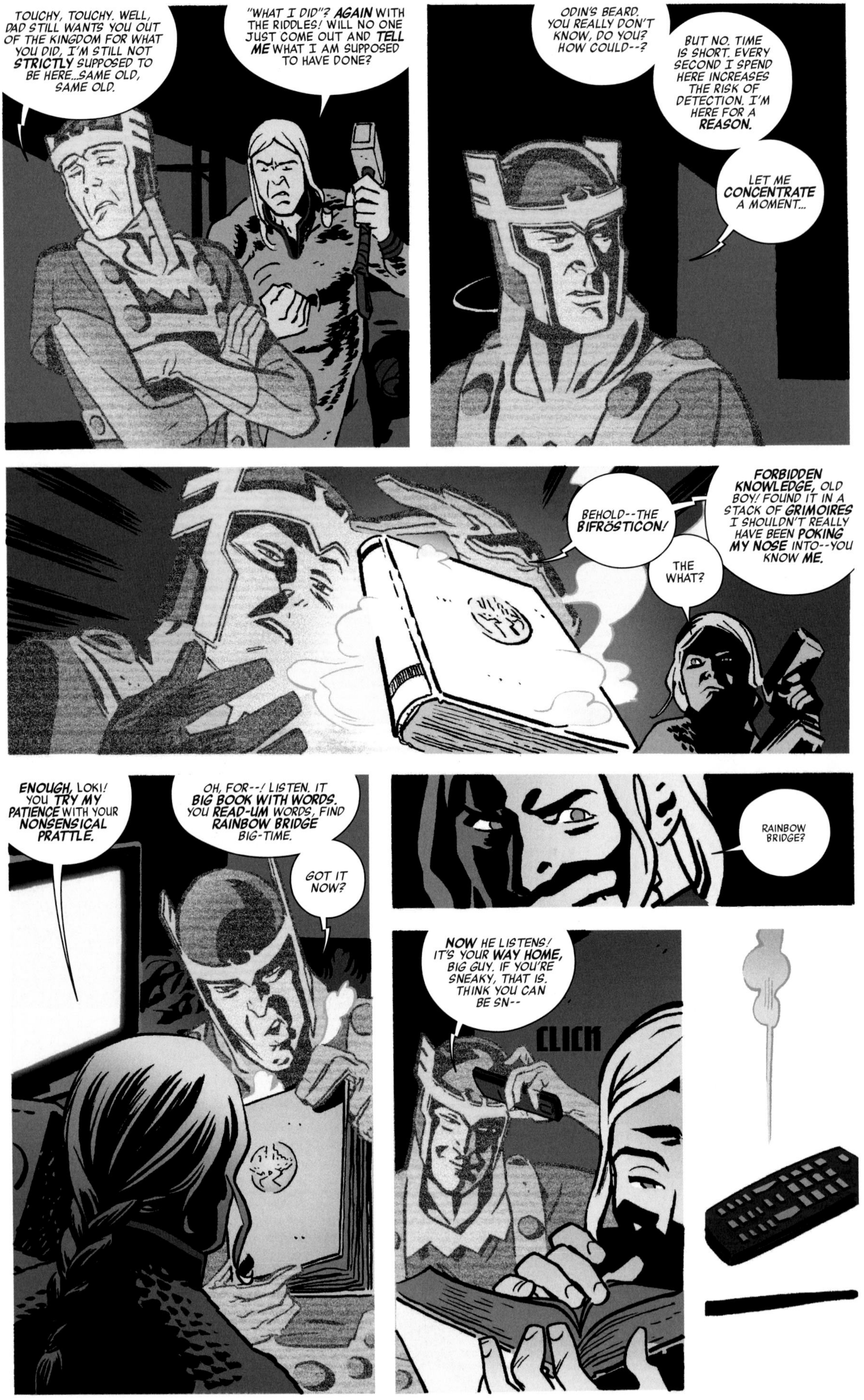
TOUCHY, TOUCHY. WELL, DAD STILL WANTS YOU OUT OF THE KINGDOM FOR WHAT YOU DID, I'M STILL NOT STRICTLY SUPPOSED TO BE HERE...SAME OLD, SAME OLD.
"WHAT I DID"? AGAIN WITH THE RIDDLES! WILL NO ONE JUST COME OUT AND TELL ME WHAT I AM SUPPOSED TO HAVE DONE?
ODIN'S BEARD. YOU REALLY DON'T KNOW, DO YOU? HOW COULD--?
BUT NO. TIME IS SHORT. EVERY SECOND I SPEND HERE INCREASES THE RISK OF DETECTION. I'M HERE FOR A REASON.
LET ME CONCENTRATE A MOMENT...
BEHOLD--THE BIFRÖSTICON!
FORBIDDEN KNOWLEDGE, OLD BOY! FOUND IT IN A STACK OF GRIMOIRES I SHOULDN'T REALLY HAVE BEEN POKING MY NOSE INTO--YOU KNOW ME.
THE WHAT?
ENOUGH, LOKI! YOU TRY MY PATIENCE WITH YOUR NONSENSICAL PRATTLE.
OH, FOR--! LISTEN. IT BIG BOOK WITH WORDS. YOU READ-UM WORDS, FIND RAINBOW BRIDGE BIG-TIME.
GOT IT NOW?
RAINBOW BRIDGE?
NOW HE LISTENS! IT'S YOUR WAY HOME, BIG GUY. IF YOU'RE SNEAKY, THAT IS. THINK YOU CAN BE SN--
CLICK

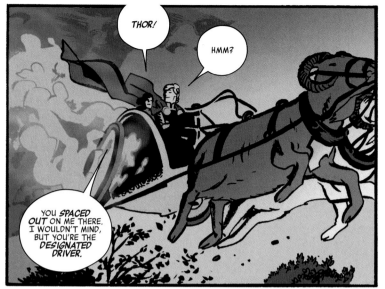

THOR!

HMM?

YOU *SPACED OUT* ON ME THERE. I WOULDN'T MIND, BUT YOU'RE THE *DESIGNATED DRIVER*.

I APOLOGIZE. I PROMISED YOU *WONDERS*, DID I NOT?

THEN LET US BEGIN...

...HERE!

OH!

IN *ASGARD* WE HAVE A TREE CALLED *YGGDRASIL*. IT IS SAID TO CONTAIN *ENTIRE WORLDS*.

THESE SEQUOIAS CONTAIN *ECHOES* OF THAT GREAT TREE. I CANNOT SHOW YOU YGGDRASIL...

...AND YET I AM CONFIDENT THAT THESE *EARTHLY* TREES WILL NOT *DISAPPOINT*.

THEY'RE...THEY'RE *MAGNIFICENT*.

YES, THEY ARE. ONE OF THE BIGGEST LIVING ORGANISMS ON EARTH.

WOULD YOU LIKE TO SEE A *BIGGER* ONE?

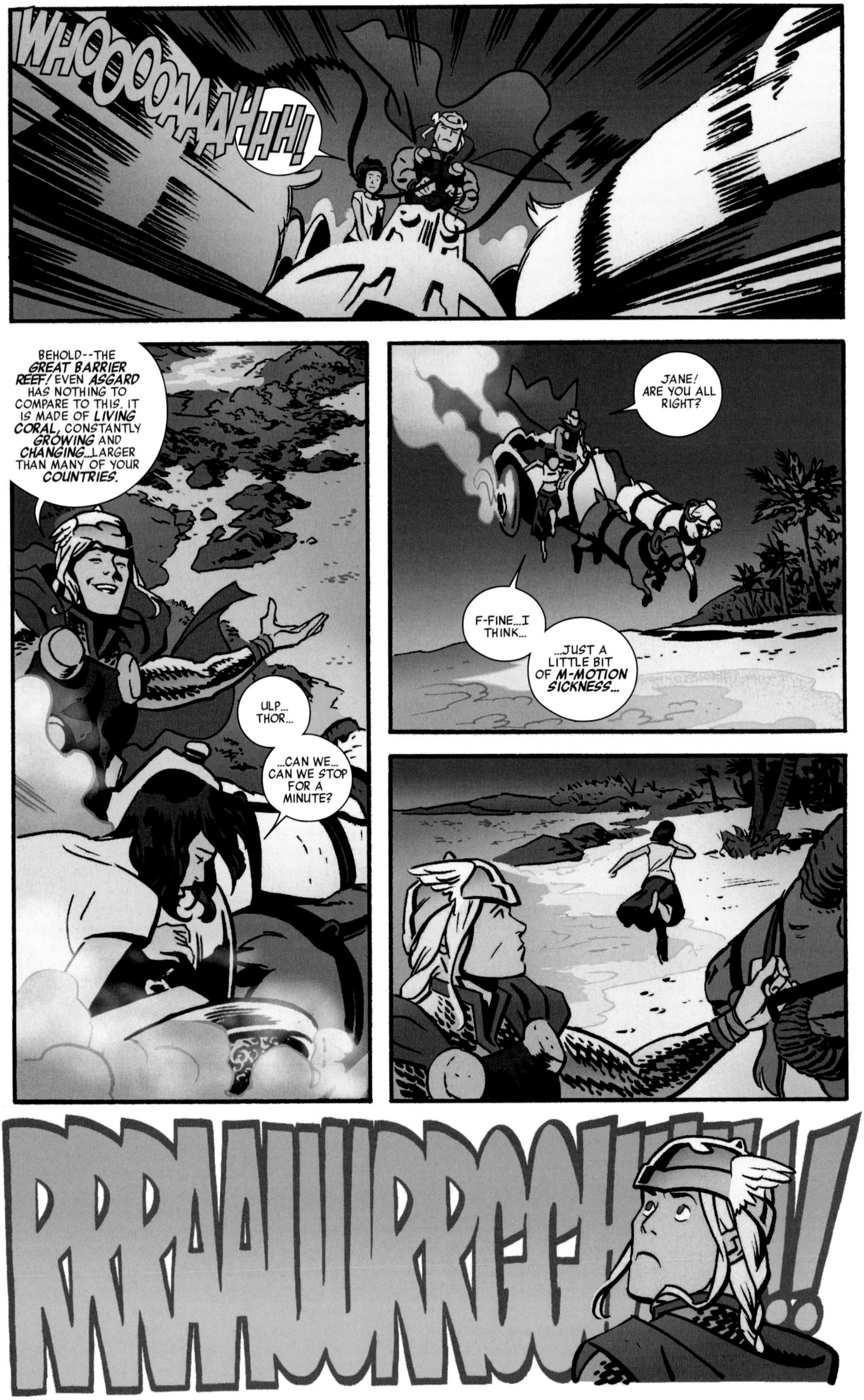
WHOOOOAAAHHH!
BEHOLD--THE GREAT BARRIER REEF! EVEN ASGARD HAS NOTHING TO COMPARE TO THIS. IT IS MADE OF LIVING CORAL, CONSTANTLY GROWING AND CHANGING...LARGER THAN MANY OF YOUR COUNTRIES.
ULP... THOR...
...CAN WE... CAN WE STOP FOR A MINUTE?
JANE! ARE YOU ALL RIGHT?
F-FINE...I THINK...
...JUST A LITTLE BIT OF M-MOTION SICKNESS...
RRRAAUURRGGHH!!

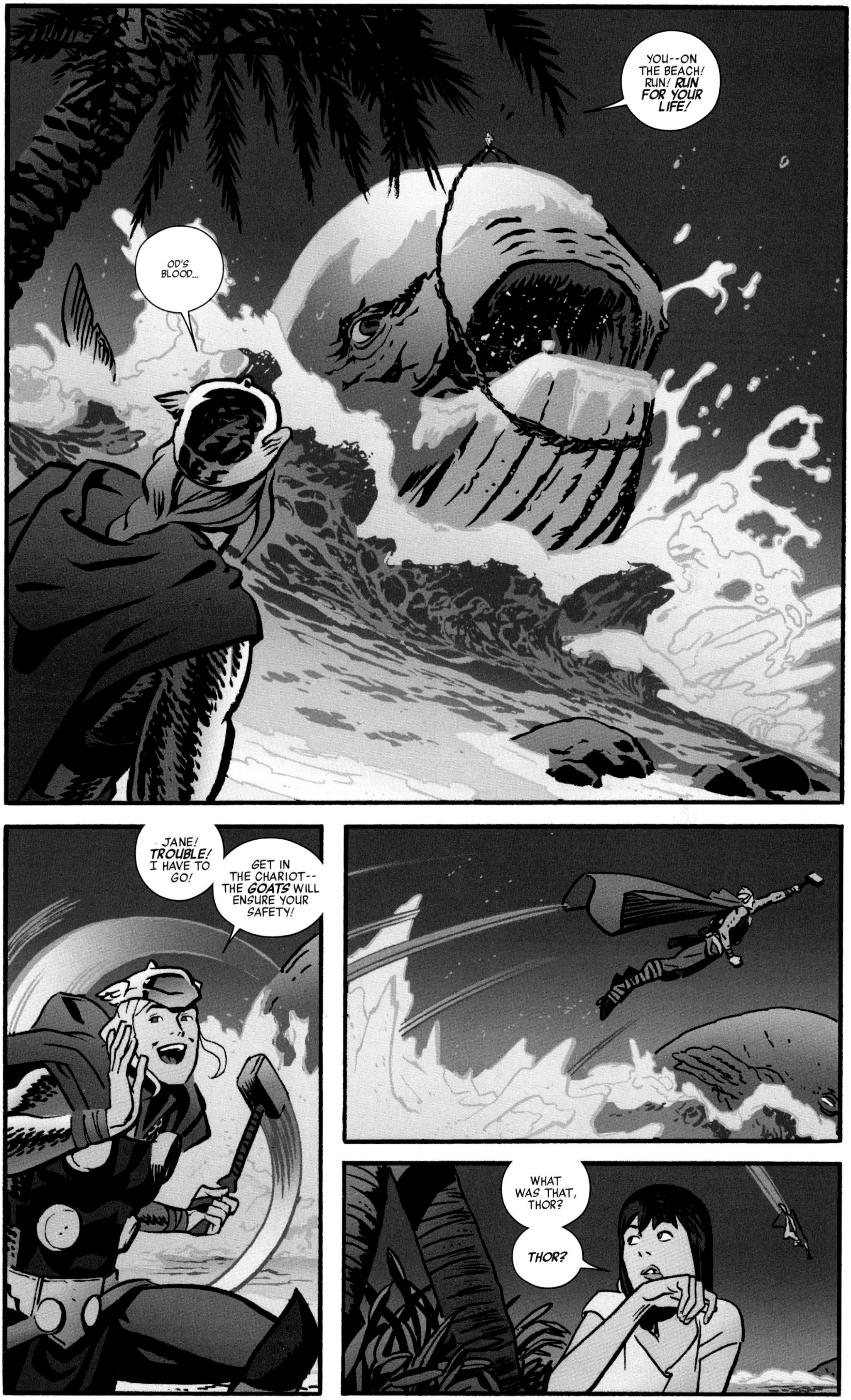
YOU--ON THE BEACH! RUN! **RUN FOR YOUR LIFE!**
OD'S BLOOD...
JANE! **TROUBLE!** I HAVE TO GO!
GET IN THE CHARIOT--THE **GOATS** WILL ENSURE YOUR SAFETY!
WHAT WAS THAT, THOR?
THOR?

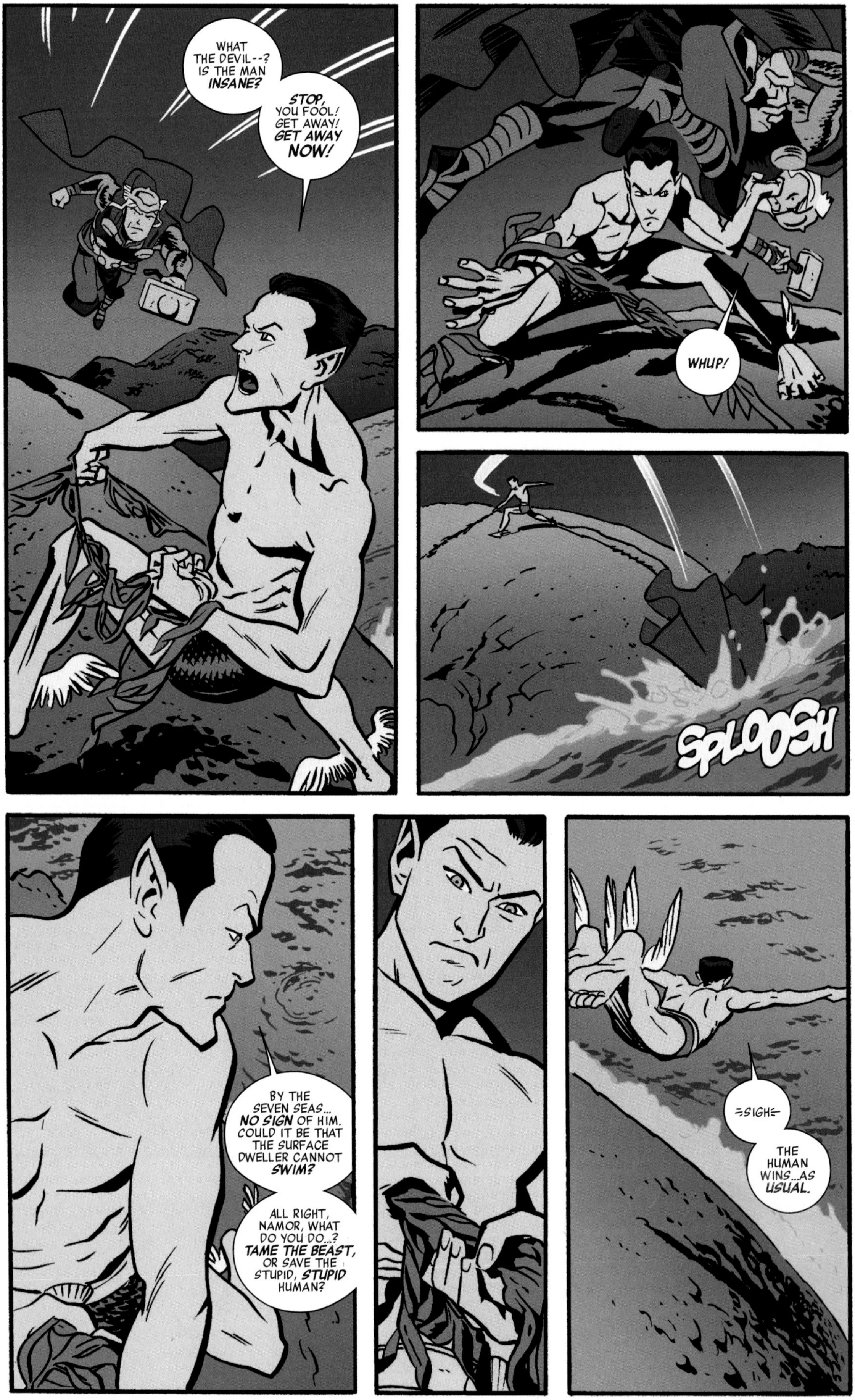
WHAT THE DEVIL--? IS THE MAN INSANE?
STOP, YOU FOOL! GET AWAY! GET AWAY NOW!
WHUP!
SPLOOSH
BY THE SEVEN SEAS... NO SIGN OF HIM. COULD IT BE THAT THE SURFACE DWELLER CANNOT SWIM?
ALL RIGHT, NAMOR, WHAT DO YOU DO...? TAME THE BEAST, OR SAVE THE STUPID, STUPID HUMAN?
=SIGH=
THE HUMAN WINS...AS USUAL.

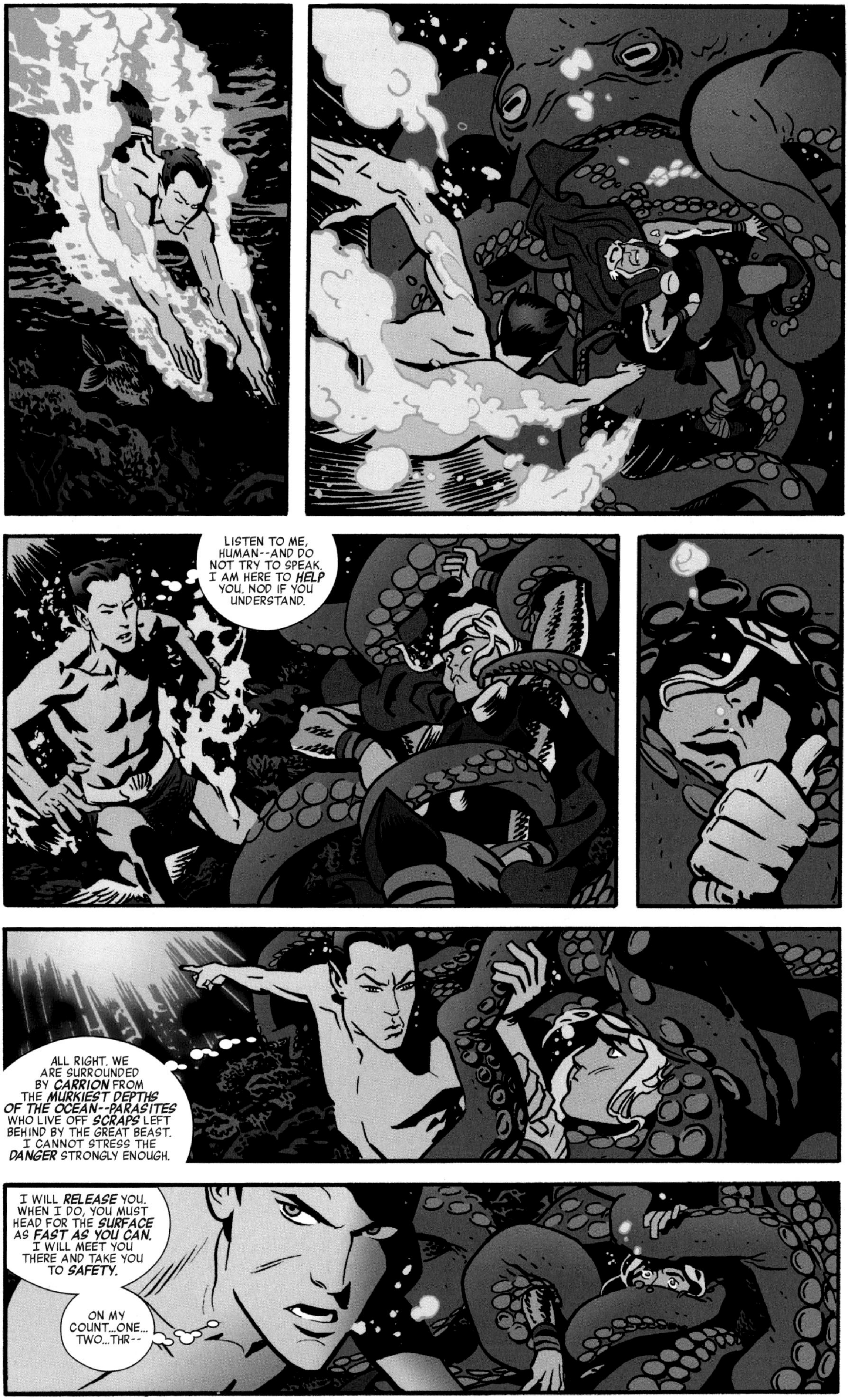
LISTEN TO ME, HUMAN--AND DO NOT TRY TO SPEAK. I AM HERE TO HELP YOU. NOD IF YOU UNDERSTAND.
ALL RIGHT. WE ARE SURROUNDED BY CARRION FROM THE MURKIEST DEPTHS OF THE OCEAN--PARASITES WHO LIVE OFF SCRAPS LEFT BEHIND BY THE GREAT BEAST. I CANNOT STRESS THE DANGER STRONGLY ENOUGH.
I WILL RELEASE YOU. WHEN I DO, YOU MUST HEAD FOR THE SURFACE AS FAST AS YOU CAN. I WILL MEET YOU THERE AND TAKE YOU TO SAFETY.
ON MY COUNT...ONE... TWO...THR--

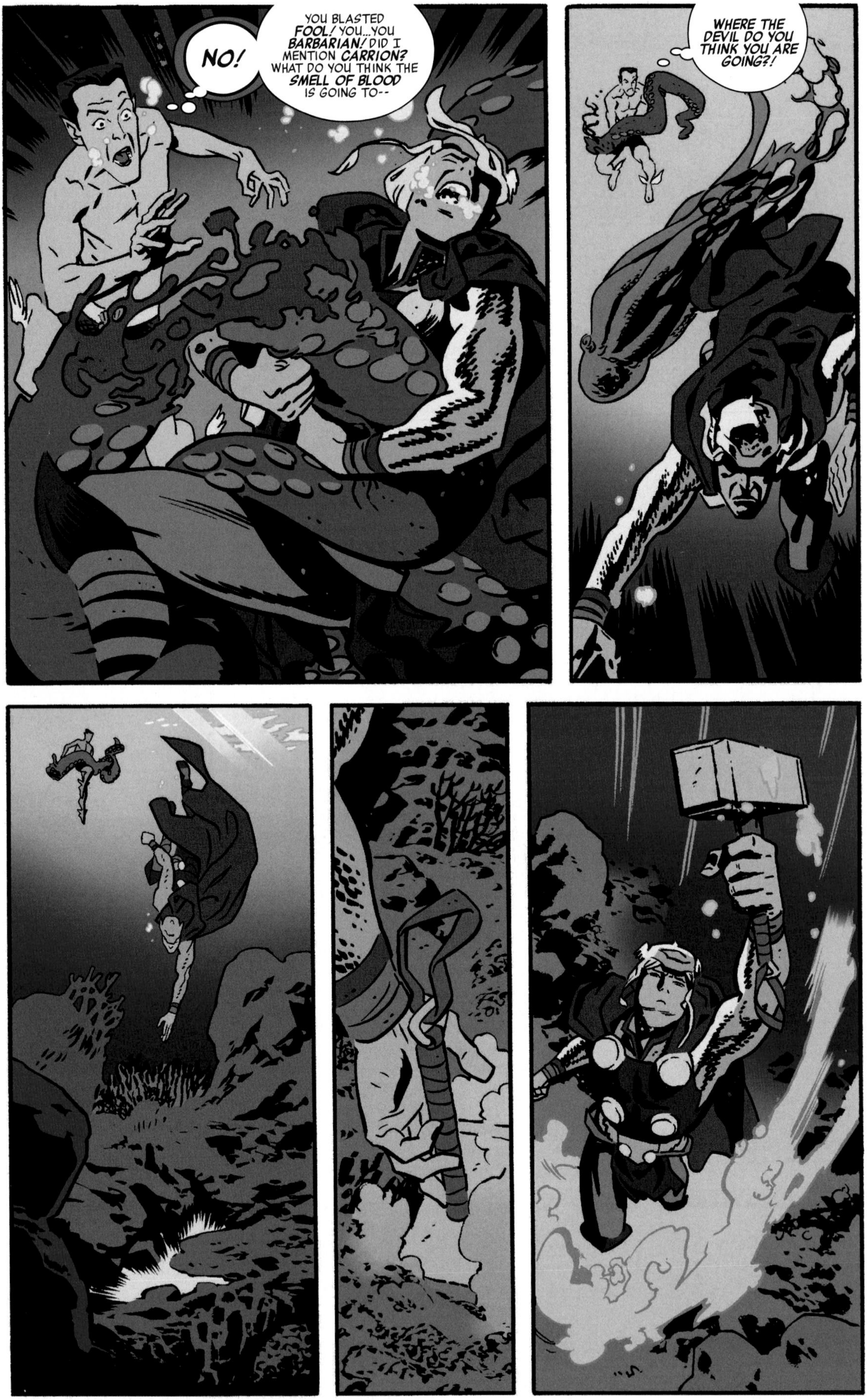
NO!
YOU BLASTED FOOL! YOU...YOU BARBARIAN! DID I MENTION CARRION? WHAT DO YOU THINK THE SMELL OF BLOOD IS GOING TO--
WHERE THE DEVIL DO YOU THINK YOU ARE GOING?!

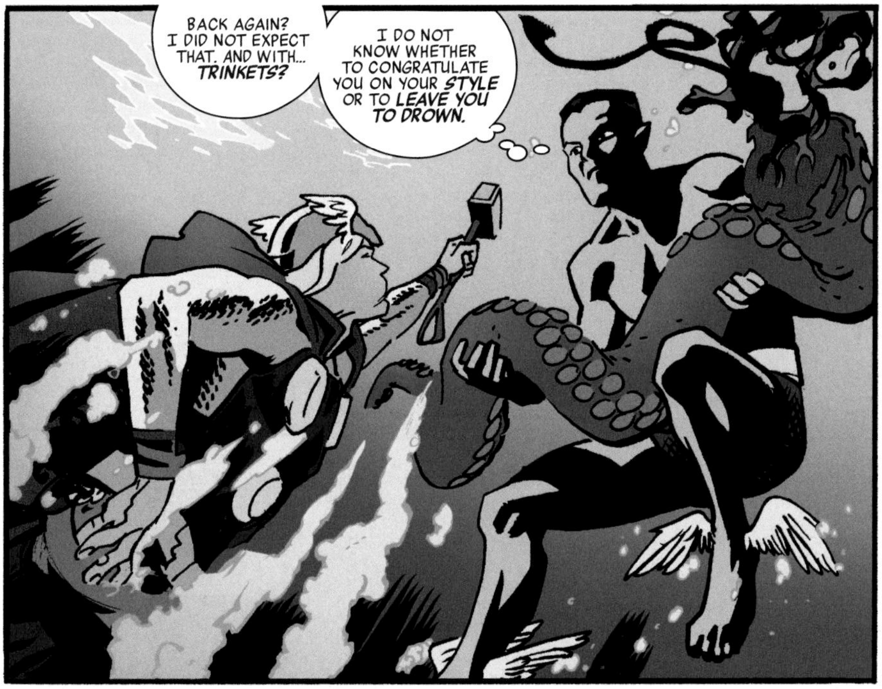
BACK AGAIN? I DID NOT EXPECT THAT. AND WITH... TRINKETS?
I DO NOT KNOW WHETHER TO CONGRATULATE YOU ON YOUR STYLE OR TO LEAVE YOU TO DROWN.

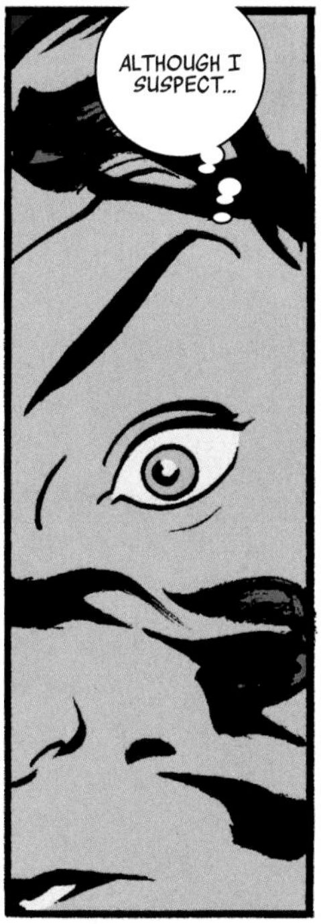
ALTHOUGH I SUSPECT...

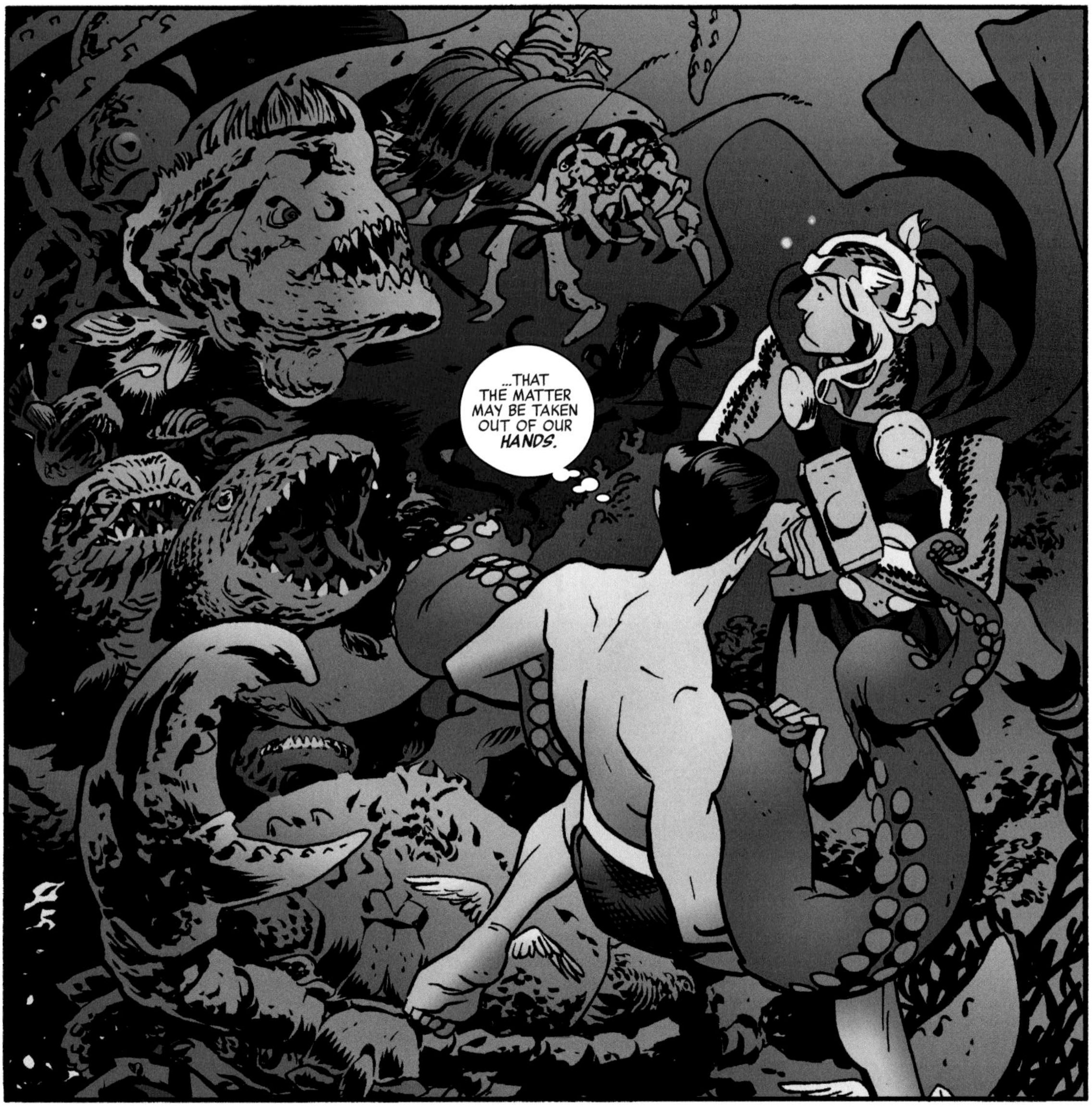
...THAT THE MATTER MAY BE TAKEN OUT OF OUR HANDS.

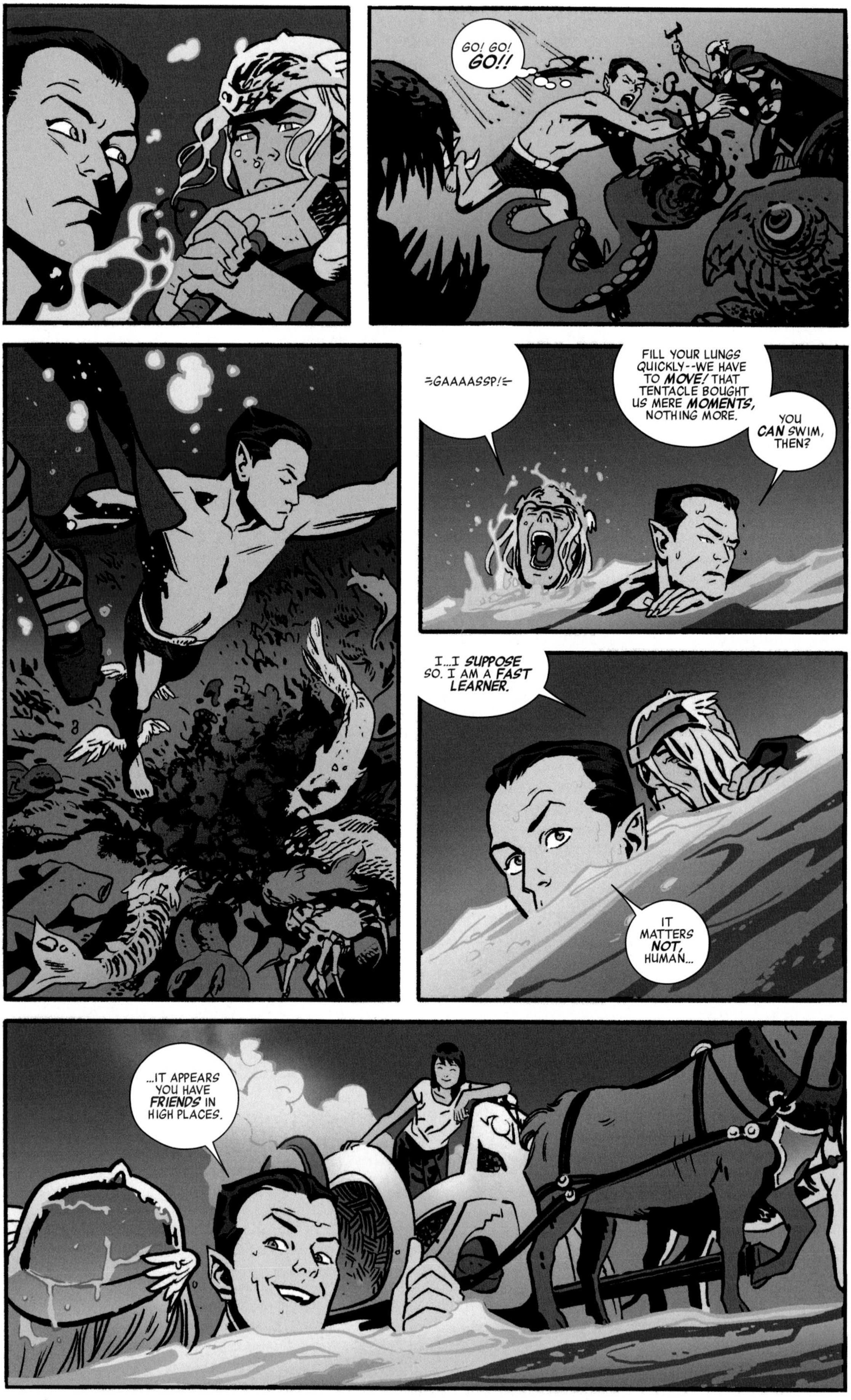
GO! GO! GO!!
=GAAAAASSP!=
FILL YOUR LUNGS QUICKLY--WE HAVE TO MOVE! THAT TENTACLE BOUGHT US MERE MOMENTS, NOTHING MORE.
YOU CAN SWIM, THEN?
I...I SUPPOSE SO. I AM A FAST LEARNER.
IT MATTERS NOT, HUMAN...
...IT APPEARS YOU HAVE FRIENDS IN HIGH PLACES.

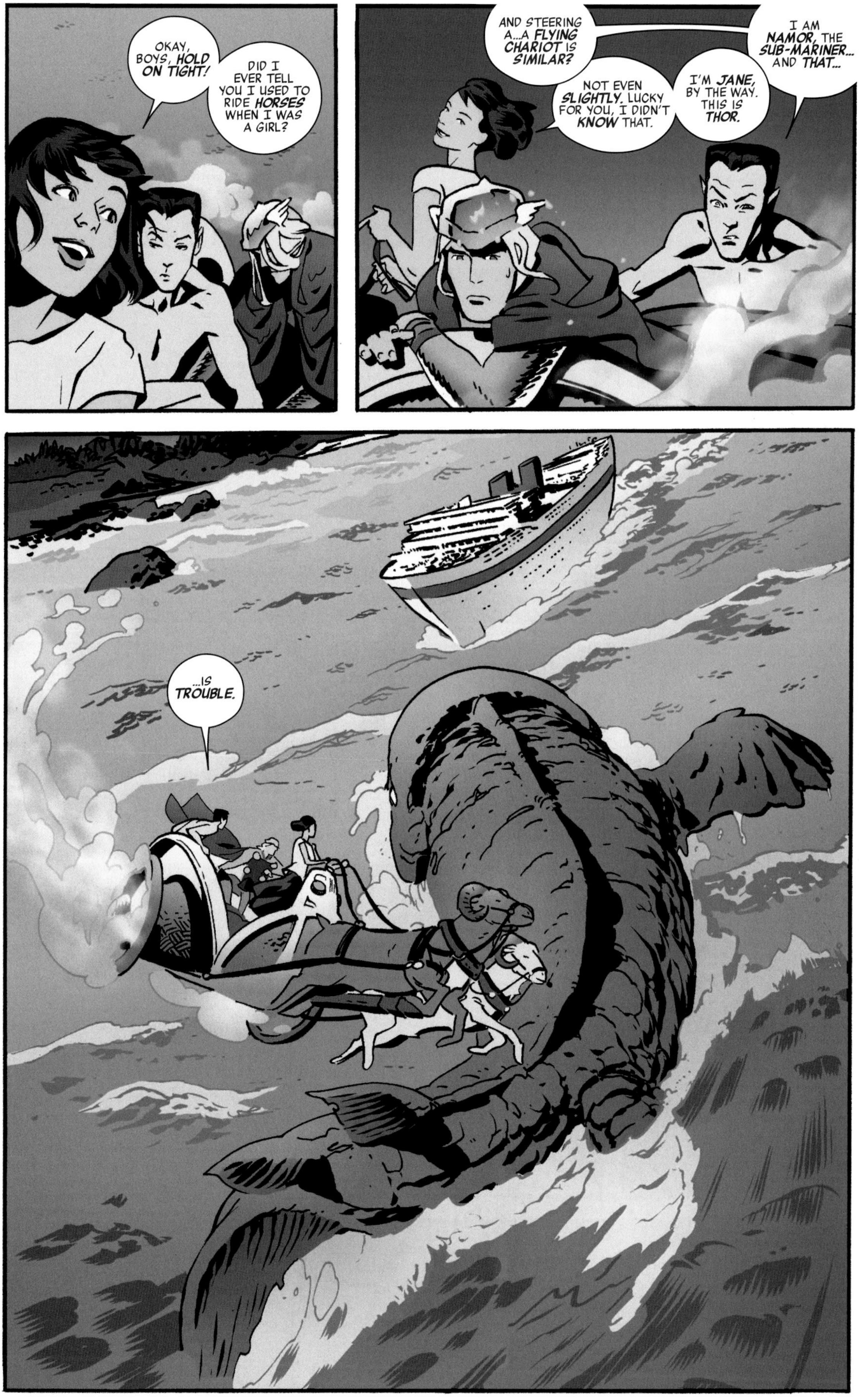
OKAY, BOYS, HOLD ON TIGHT!
DID I EVER TELL YOU I USED TO RIDE HORSES WHEN I WAS A GIRL?
AND STEERING A...A FLYING CHARIOT IS SIMILAR?
NOT EVEN SLIGHTLY. LUCKY FOR YOU, I DIDN'T KNOW THAT.
I'M JANE, BY THE WAY. THIS IS THOR.
I AM NAMOR, THE SUB-MARINER... AND THAT...
...IS TROUBLE.

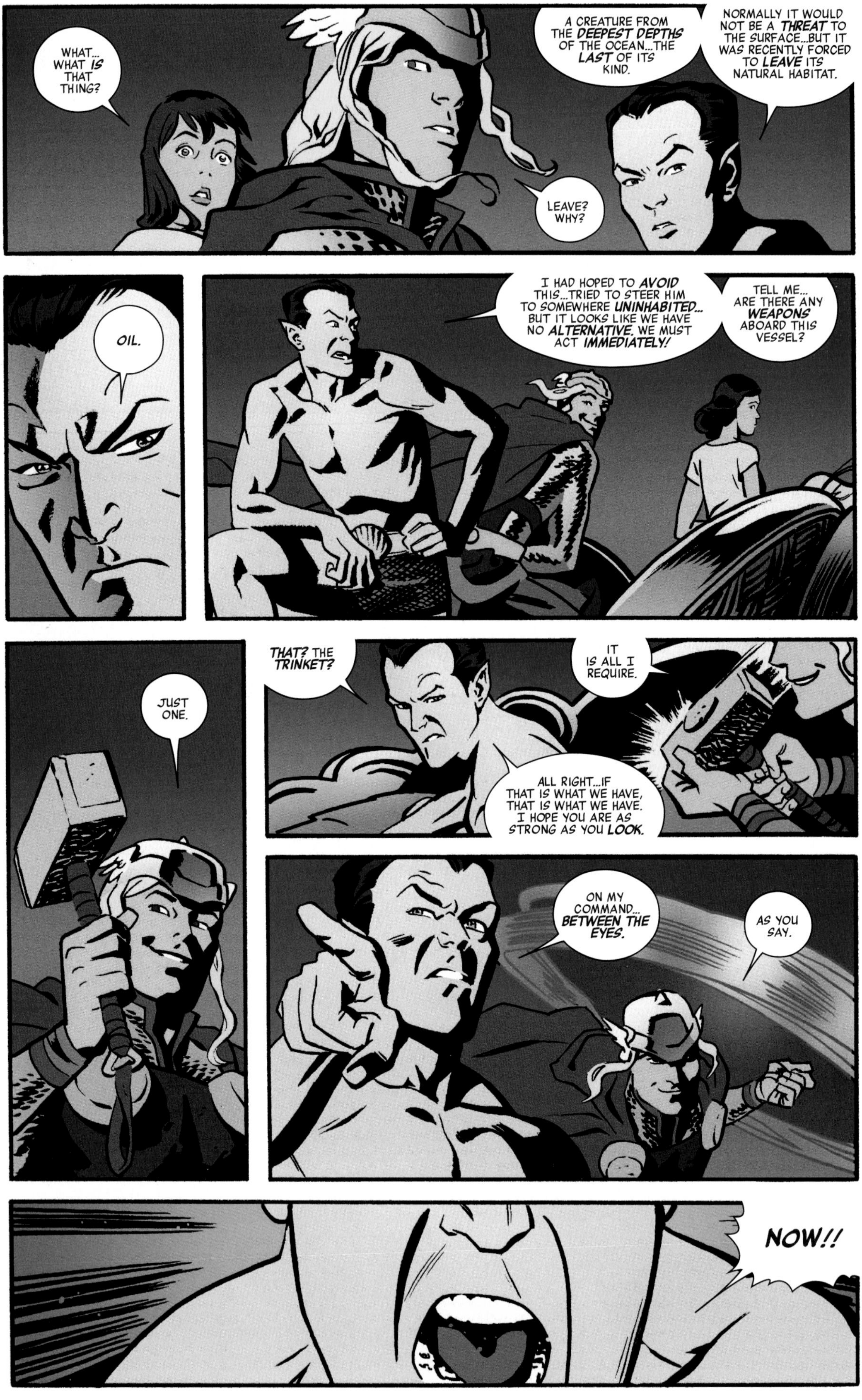
WHAT... WHAT IS THAT THING?
A CREATURE FROM THE DEEPEST DEPTHS OF THE OCEAN...THE LAST OF ITS KIND.
NORMALLY IT WOULD NOT BE A THREAT TO THE SURFACE...BUT IT WAS RECENTLY FORCED TO LEAVE ITS NATURAL HABITAT.
LEAVE? WHY?
OIL.
I HAD HOPED TO AVOID THIS...TRIED TO STEER HIM TO SOMEWHERE UNINHABITED... BUT IT LOOKS LIKE WE HAVE NO ALTERNATIVE. WE MUST ACT IMMEDIATELY!
TELL ME... ARE THERE ANY WEAPONS ABOARD THIS VESSEL?
JUST ONE.
THAT? THE TRINKET?
IT IS ALL I REQUIRE.
ALL RIGHT...IF THAT IS WHAT WE HAVE, THAT IS WHAT WE HAVE. I HOPE YOU ARE AS STRONG AS YOU LOOK.
ON MY COMMAND... BETWEEN THE EYES.
AS YOU SAY.
NOW!!

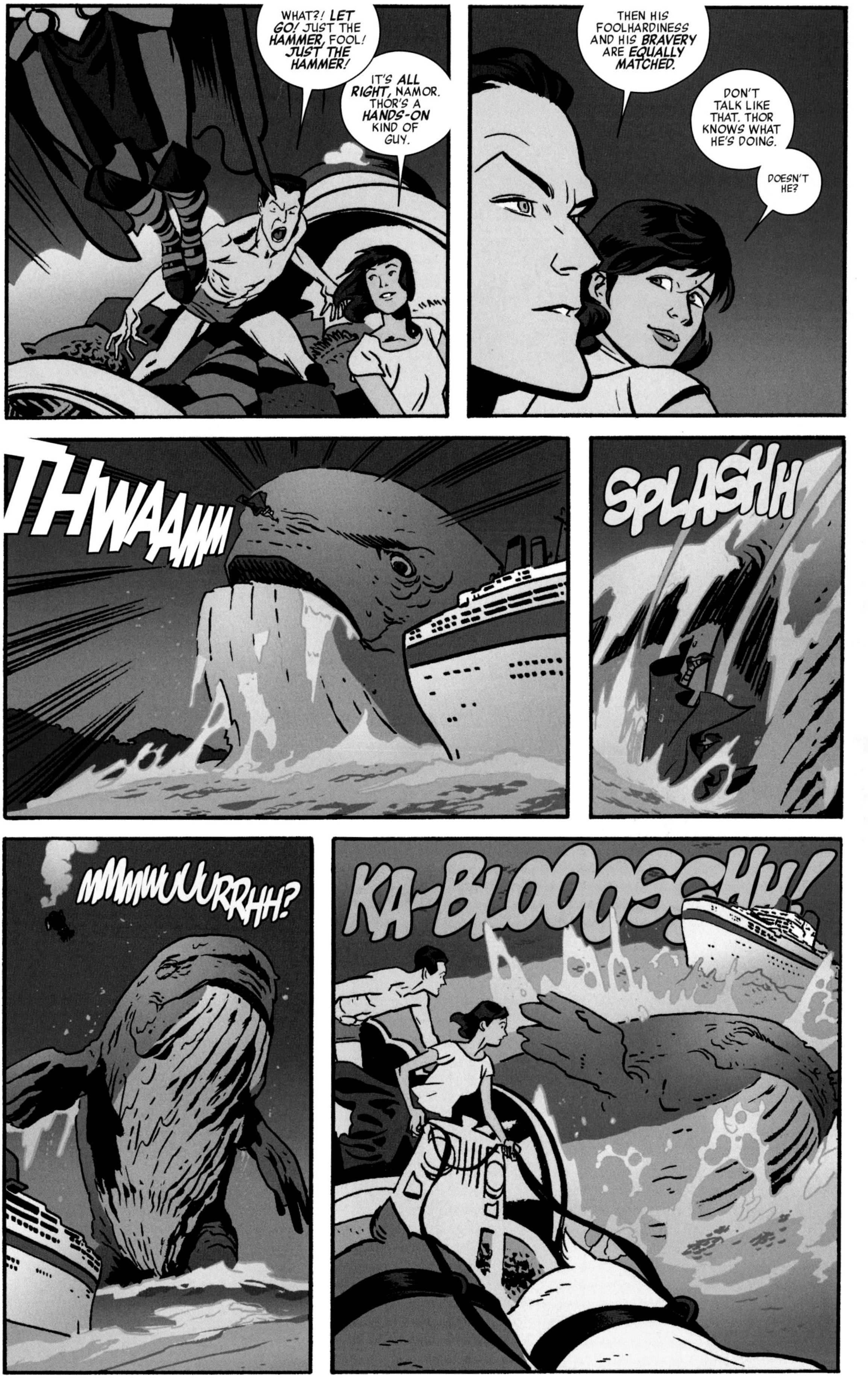
WHAT?! LET GO! JUST THE HAMMER, FOOL! JUST THE HAMMER!
IT'S ALL RIGHT, NAMOR. THOR'S A HANDS-ON KIND OF GUY.
THEN HIS FOOLHARDINESS AND HIS BRAVERY ARE EQUALLY MATCHED.
DON'T TALK LIKE THAT. THOR KNOWS WHAT HE'S DOING.
DOESN'T HE?
THWAAMM
SPLASHH
MMMWUURRHH?
KA-BLOOOSCHH!

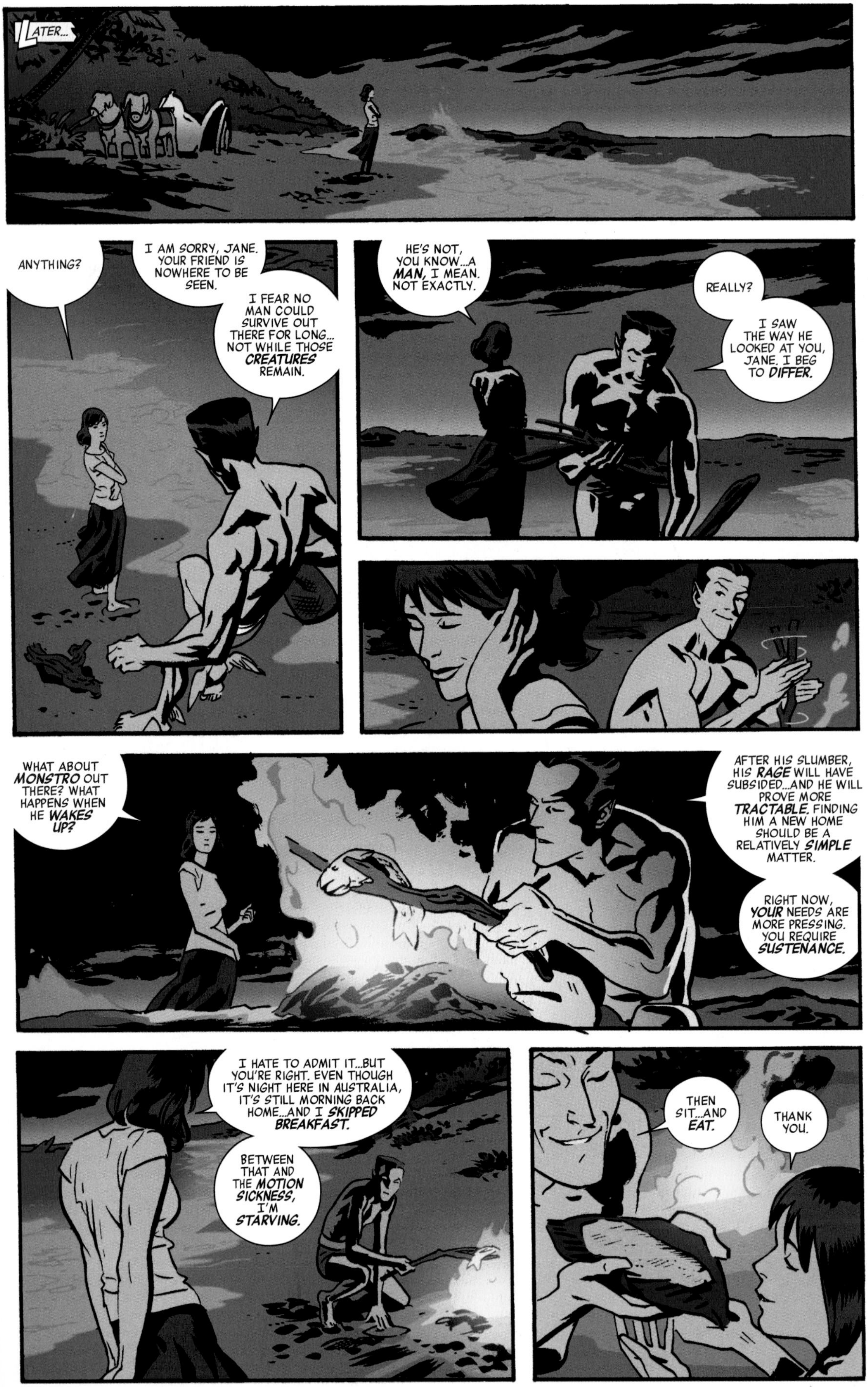
LATER...
ANYTHING?
I AM SORRY, JANE. YOUR FRIEND IS NOWHERE TO BE SEEN.
I FEAR NO MAN COULD SURVIVE OUT THERE FOR LONG... NOT WHILE THOSE CREATURES REMAIN.
HE'S NOT, YOU KNOW...A MAN, I MEAN. NOT EXACTLY.
REALLY?
I SAW THE WAY HE LOOKED AT YOU, JANE. I BEG TO DIFFER.
WHAT ABOUT MONSTRO OUT THERE? WHAT HAPPENS WHEN HE WAKES UP?
AFTER HIS SLUMBER, HIS RAGE WILL HAVE SUBSIDED...AND HE WILL PROVE MORE TRACTABLE. FINDING HIM A NEW HOME SHOULD BE A RELATIVELY SIMPLE MATTER.
RIGHT NOW, YOUR NEEDS ARE MORE PRESSING. YOU REQUIRE SUSTENANCE.
I HATE TO ADMIT IT...BUT YOU'RE RIGHT. EVEN THOUGH IT'S NIGHT HERE IN AUSTRALIA, IT'S STILL MORNING BACK HOME...AND I SKIPPED BREAKFAST.
BETWEEN THAT AND THE MOTION SICKNESS, I'M STARVING.
THEN SIT...AND EAT.
THANK YOU.

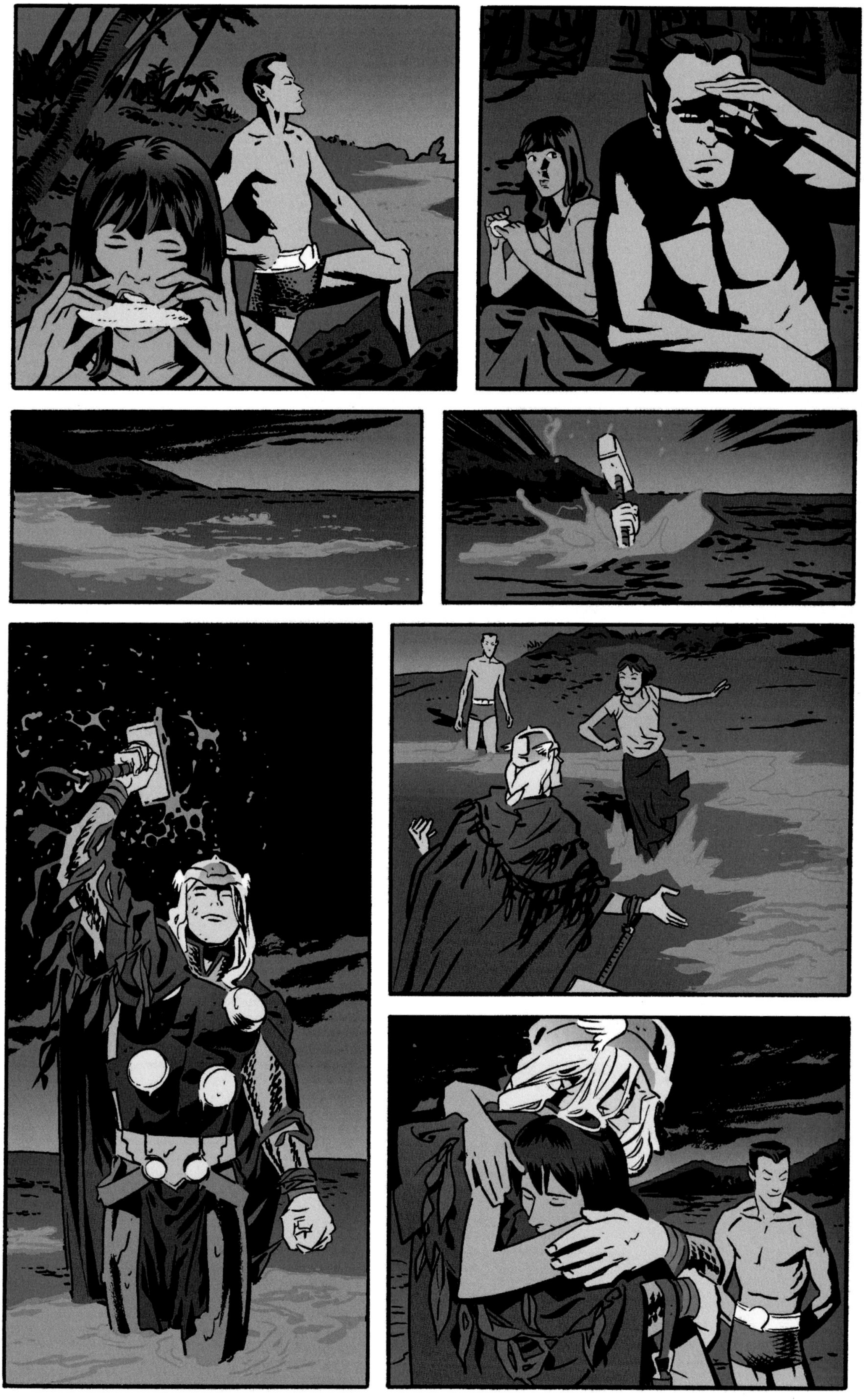

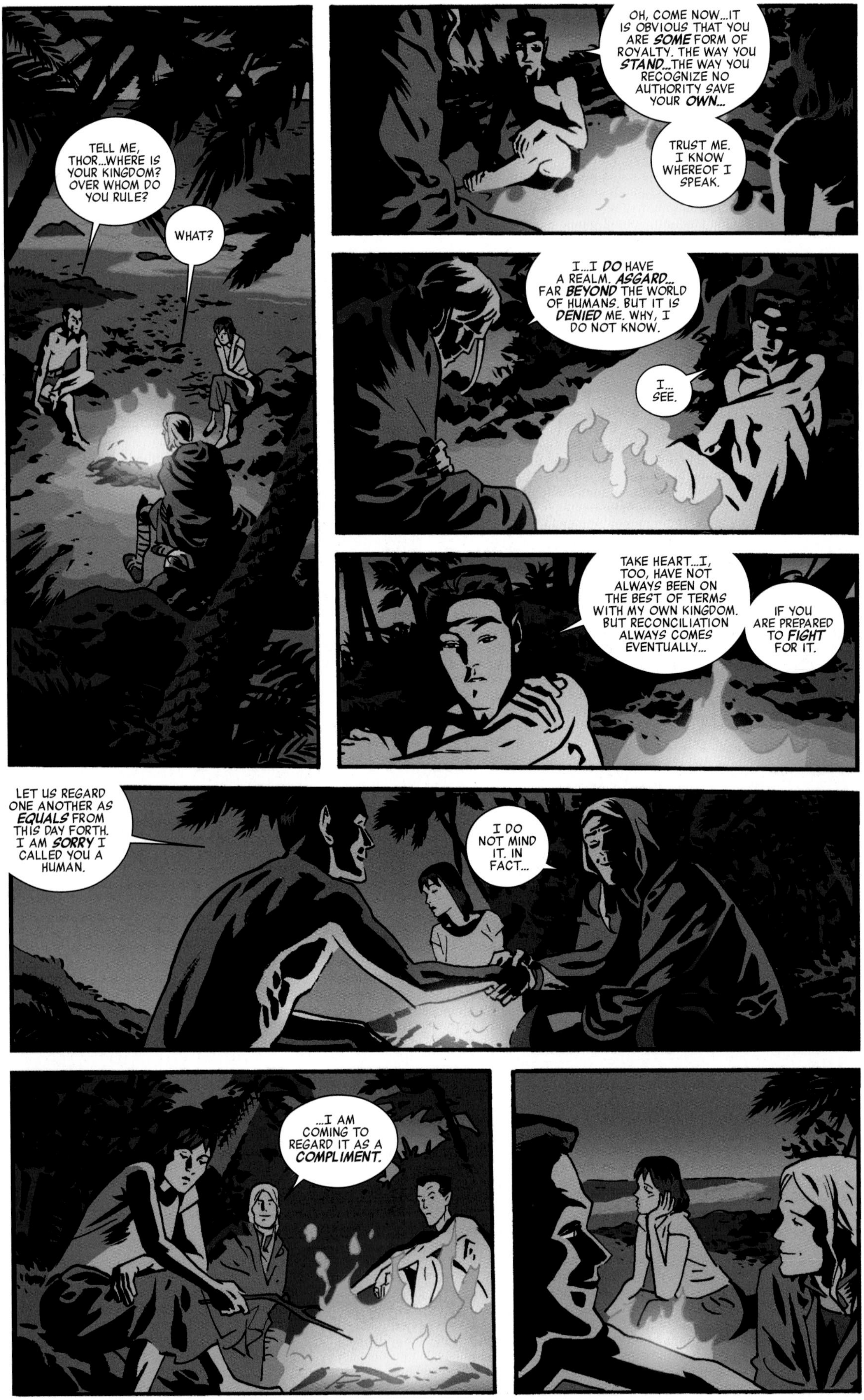
TELL ME, THOR...WHERE IS YOUR KINGDOM? OVER WHOM DO YOU RULE?
WHAT?
OH, COME NOW...IT IS OBVIOUS THAT YOU ARE SOME FORM OF ROYALTY. THE WAY YOU STAND...THE WAY YOU RECOGNIZE NO AUTHORITY SAVE YOUR OWN...
TRUST ME. I KNOW WHEREOF I SPEAK.
I...I DO HAVE A REALM. ASGARD... FAR BEYOND THE WORLD OF HUMANS. BUT IT IS DENIED ME. WHY, I DO NOT KNOW.
I... SEE.
TAKE HEART...I, TOO, HAVE NOT ALWAYS BEEN ON THE BEST OF TERMS WITH MY OWN KINGDOM. BUT RECONCILIATION ALWAYS COMES EVENTUALLY...
IF YOU ARE PREPARED TO FIGHT FOR IT.
LET US REGARD ONE ANOTHER AS EQUALS FROM THIS DAY FORTH. I AM SORRY I CALLED YOU A HUMAN.
I DO NOT MIND IT. IN FACT...
...I AM COMING TO REGARD IT AS A COMPLIMENT.

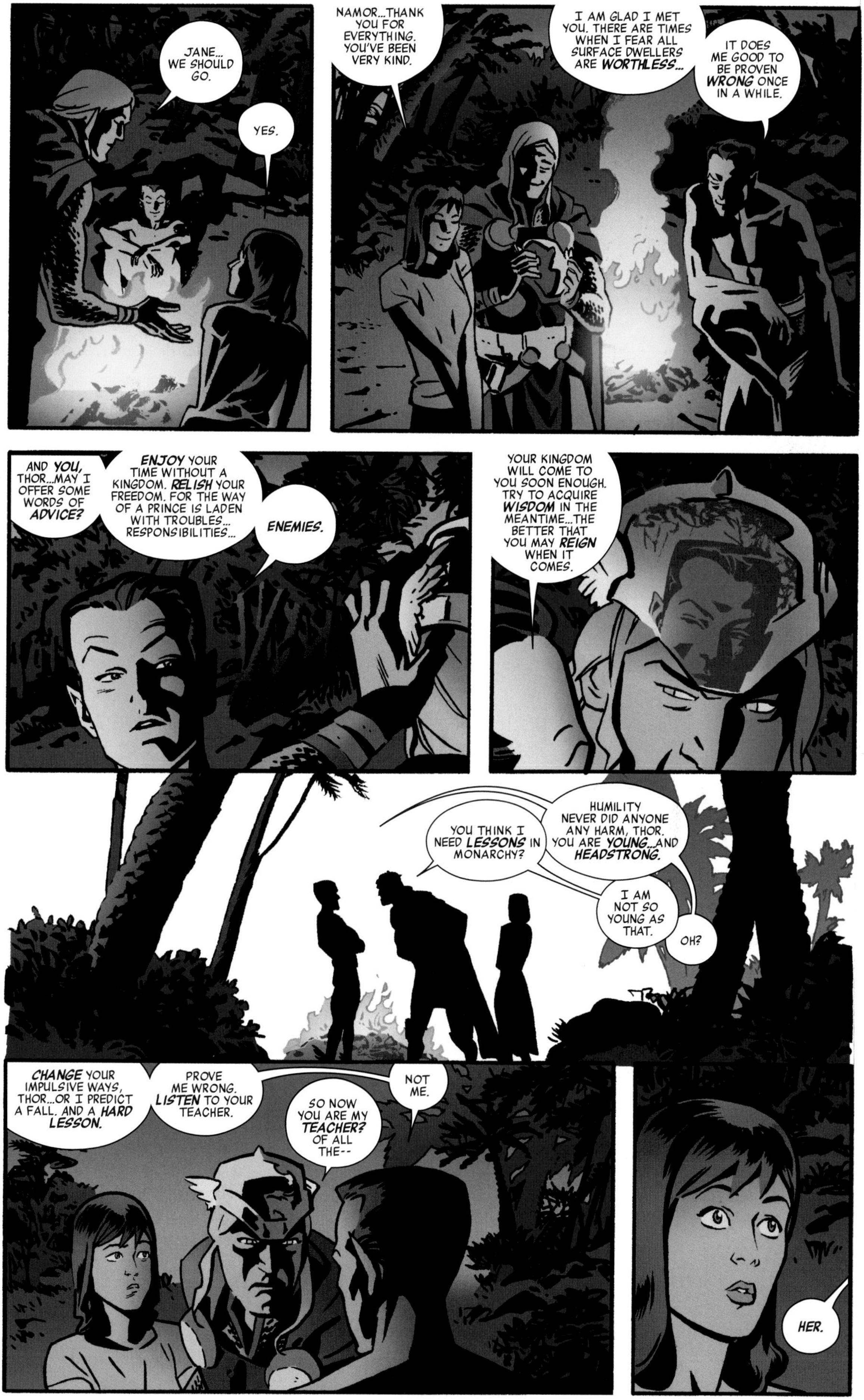
JANE... WE SHOULD GO.
YES.
NAMOR...THANK YOU FOR EVERYTHING. YOU'VE BEEN VERY KIND.
I AM GLAD I MET YOU. THERE ARE TIMES WHEN I FEAR ALL SURFACE DWELLERS ARE WORTHLESS...
IT DOES ME GOOD TO BE PROVEN WRONG ONCE IN A WHILE.
AND YOU, THOR...MAY I OFFER SOME WORDS OF ADVICE?
ENJOY YOUR TIME WITHOUT A KINGDOM. RELISH YOUR FREEDOM. FOR THE WAY OF A PRINCE IS LADEN WITH TROUBLES... RESPONSIBILITIES...
ENEMIES.
YOUR KINGDOM WILL COME TO YOU SOON ENOUGH. TRY TO ACQUIRE WISDOM IN THE MEANTIME...THE BETTER THAT YOU MAY REIGN WHEN IT COMES.
HUMILITY NEVER DID ANYONE ANY HARM, THOR. YOU ARE YOUNG...AND HEADSTRONG.
YOU THINK I NEED LESSONS IN MONARCHY?
I AM NOT SO YOUNG AS THAT.
OH?
CHANGE YOUR IMPULSIVE WAYS, THOR...OR I PREDICT A FALL. AND A HARD LESSON.
PROVE ME WRONG. LISTEN TO YOUR TEACHER.
SO NOW YOU ARE MY TEACHER? OF ALL THE--
NOT ME.
HER.

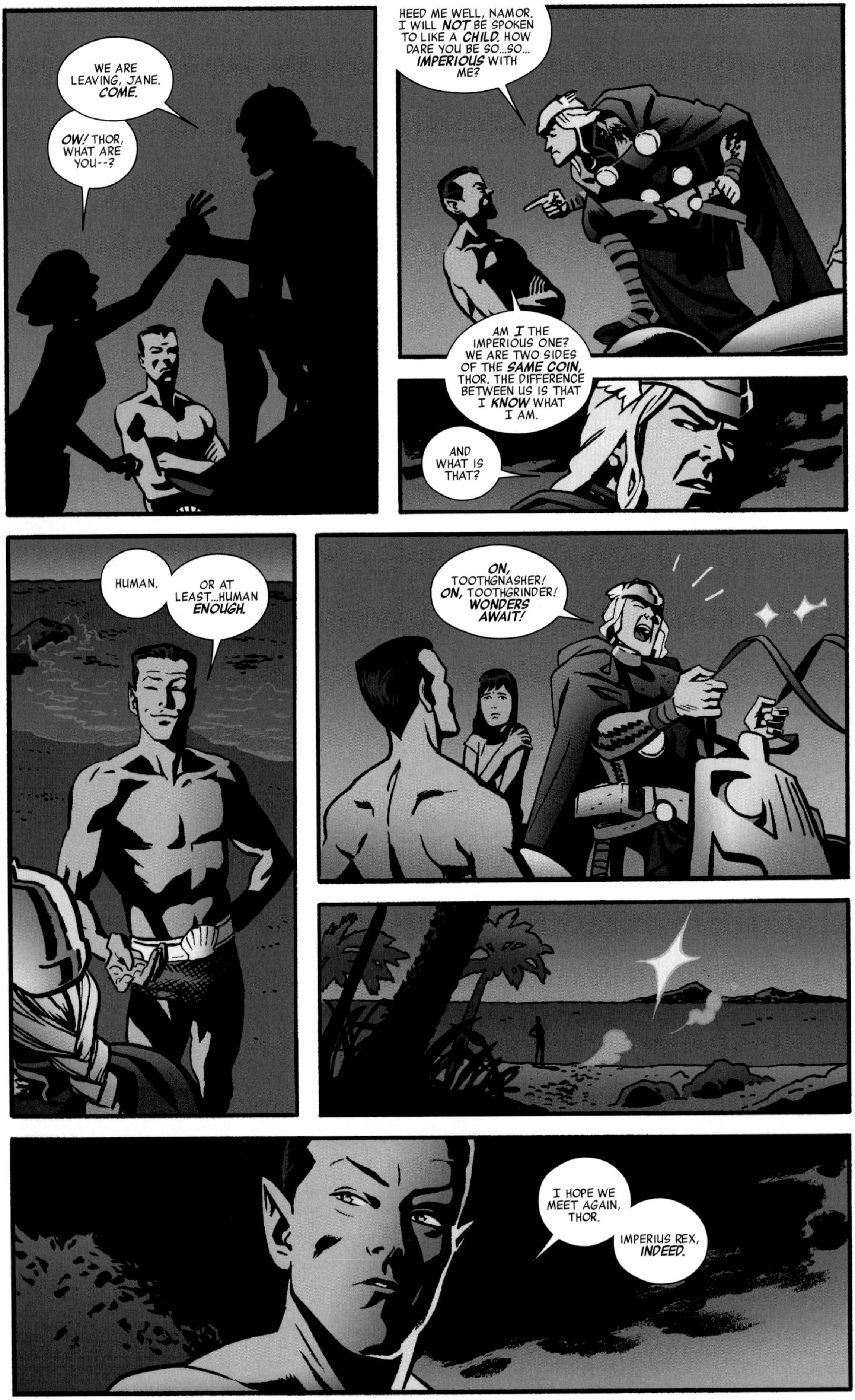
WE ARE LEAVING, JANE. COME.
OW! THOR, WHAT ARE YOU--?
HEED ME WELL, NAMOR. I WILL NOT BE SPOKEN TO LIKE A CHILD. HOW DARE YOU BE SO...SO... IMPERIOUS WITH ME?
AM I THE IMPERIOUS ONE? WE ARE TWO SIDES OF THE SAME COIN, THOR. THE DIFFERENCE BETWEEN US IS THAT I KNOW WHAT I AM.
AND WHAT IS THAT?
HUMAN.
OR AT LEAST...HUMAN ENOUGH.
ON, TOOTHGNASHER! ON, TOOTHGRINDER! WONDERS AWAIT!
I HOPE WE MEET AGAIN, THOR.
IMPERIUS REX, INDEED.

THOR THE MIGHTY AVENGER #6

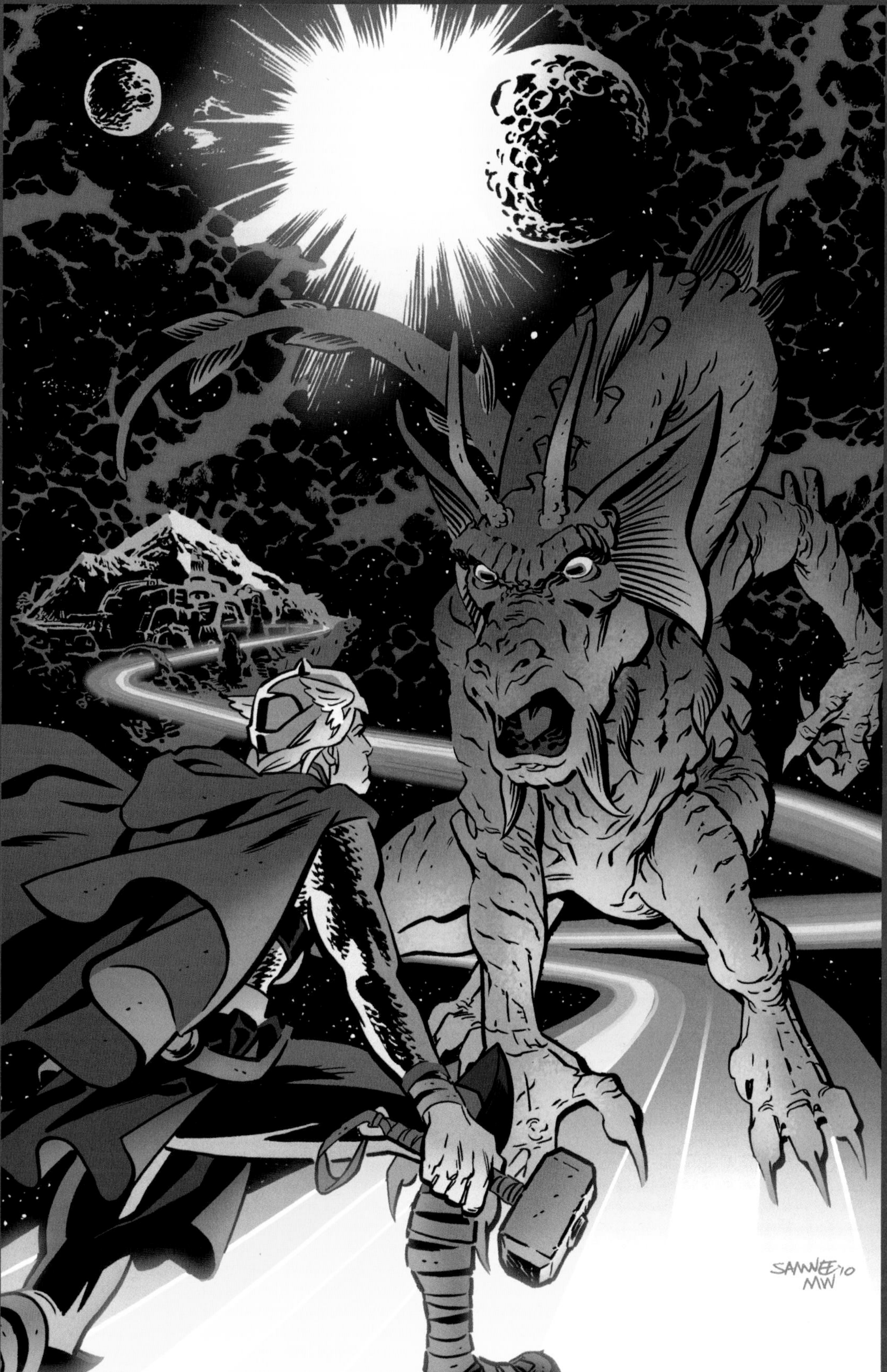
SAMNEE '10
MW

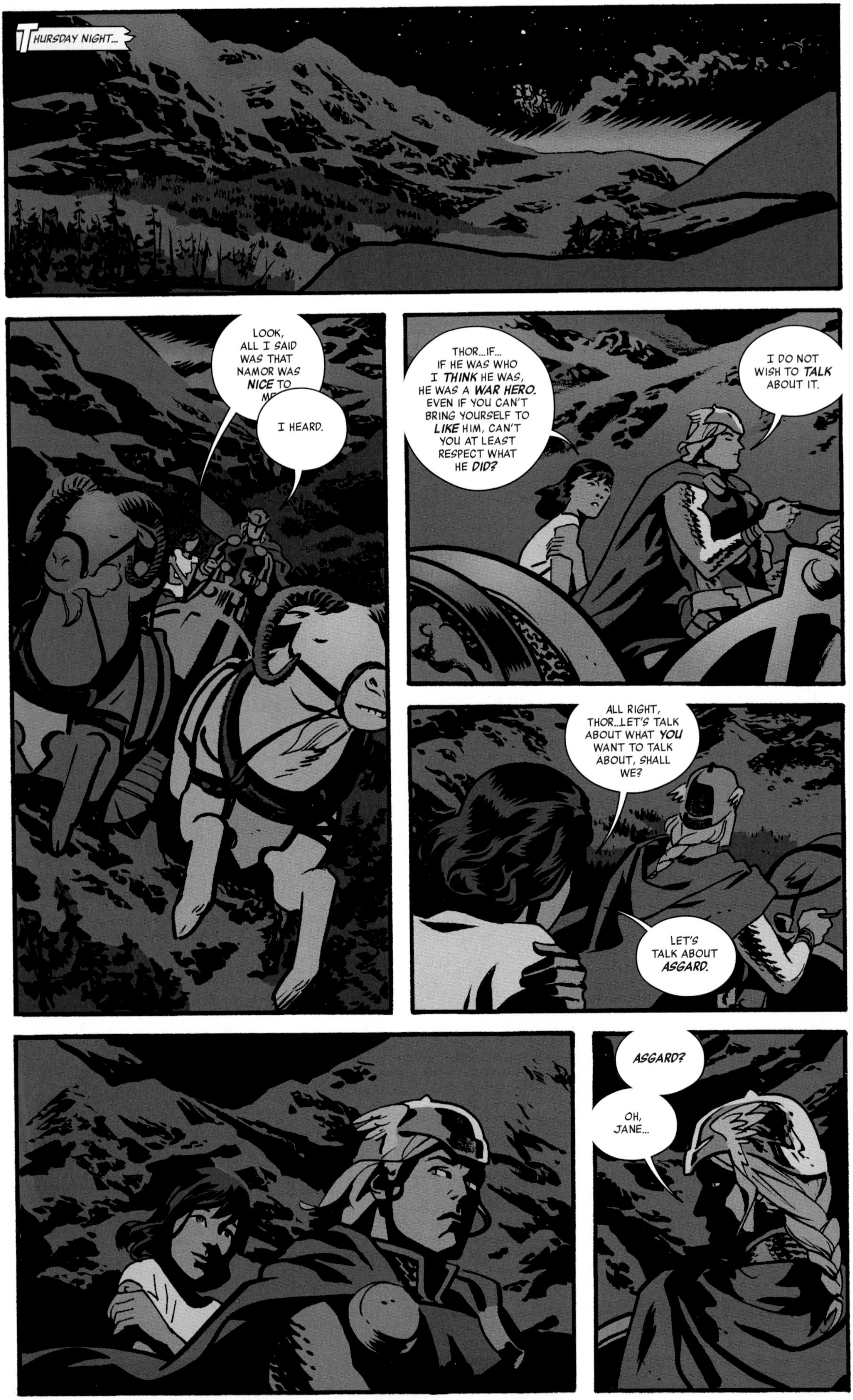
THURSDAY NIGHT...
LOOK, ALL I SAID WAS THAT NAMOR WAS NICE TO
I HEARD.
THOR...IF... IF HE WAS WHO I THINK HE WAS, HE WAS A WAR HERO. EVEN IF YOU CAN'T BRING YOURSELF TO LIKE HIM, CAN'T YOU AT LEAST RESPECT WHAT HE DID?
I DO NOT WISH TO TALK ABOUT IT.
ALL RIGHT, THOR...LET'S TALK ABOUT WHAT YOU WANT TO TALK ABOUT, SHALL WE?
LET'S TALK ABOUT ASGARD.
ASGARD?
OH, JANE...

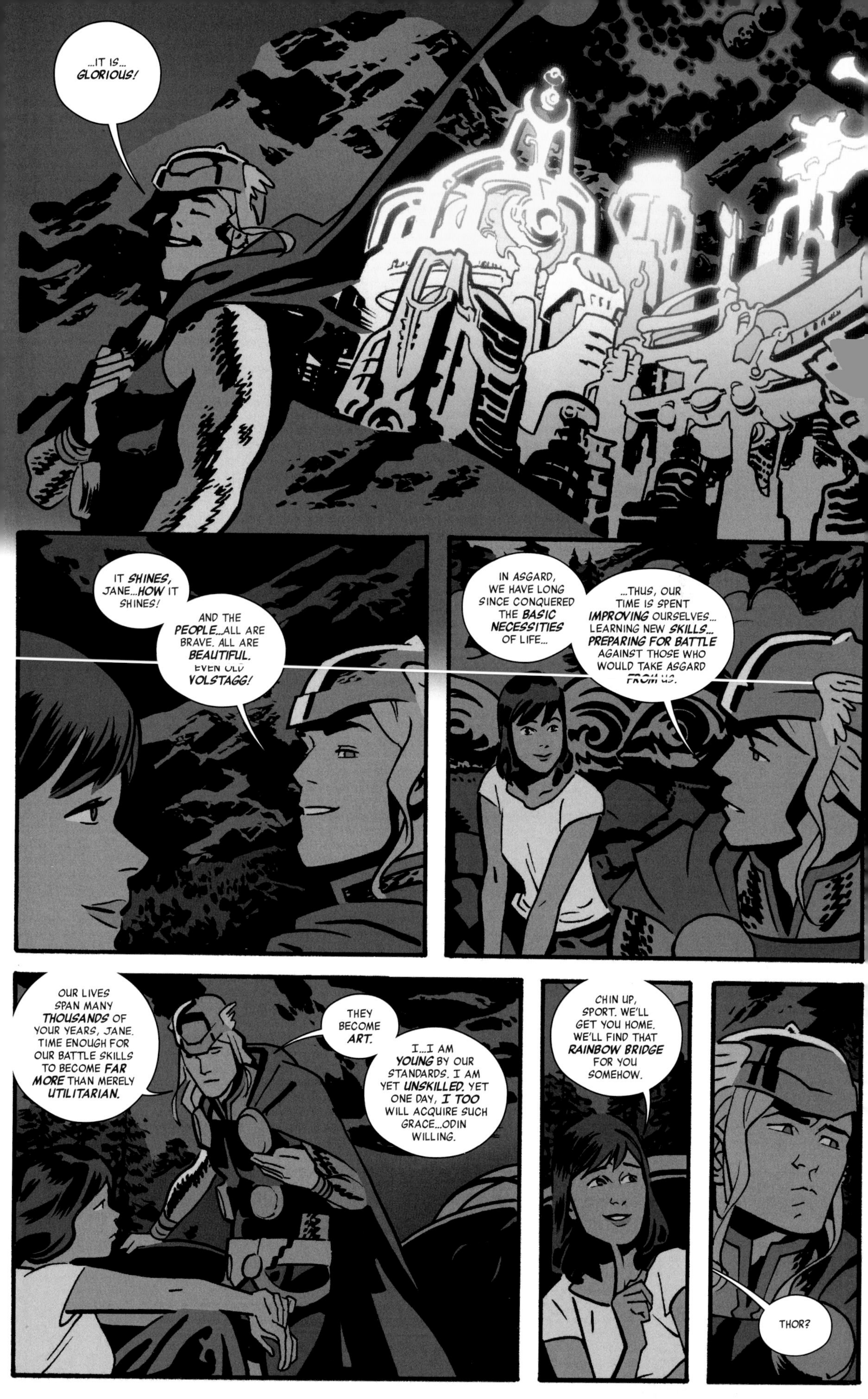
...IT IS... GLORIOUS!
IT SHINES, JANE...HOW IT SHINES!
AND THE PEOPLE...ALL ARE BRAVE. ALL ARE BEAUTIFUL. EVEN OLD VOLSTAGG!
IN ASGARD, WE HAVE LONG SINCE CONQUERED THE BASIC NECESSITIES OF LIFE...
...THUS, OUR TIME IS SPENT IMPROVING OURSELVES... LEARNING NEW SKILLS... PREPARING FOR BATTLE AGAINST THOSE WHO WOULD TAKE ASGARD FROM US.
OUR LIVES SPAN MANY THOUSANDS OF YOUR YEARS, JANE. TIME ENOUGH FOR OUR BATTLE SKILLS TO BECOME FAR MORE THAN MERELY UTILITARIAN.
THEY BECOME ART.
I...I AM YOUNG BY OUR STANDARDS. I AM YET UNSKILLED. YET ONE DAY, I TOO WILL ACQUIRE SUCH GRACE...ODIN WILLING.
CHIN UP, SPORT. WE'LL GET YOU HOME. WE'LL FIND THAT RAINBOW BRIDGE FOR YOU SOMEHOW.
THOR?

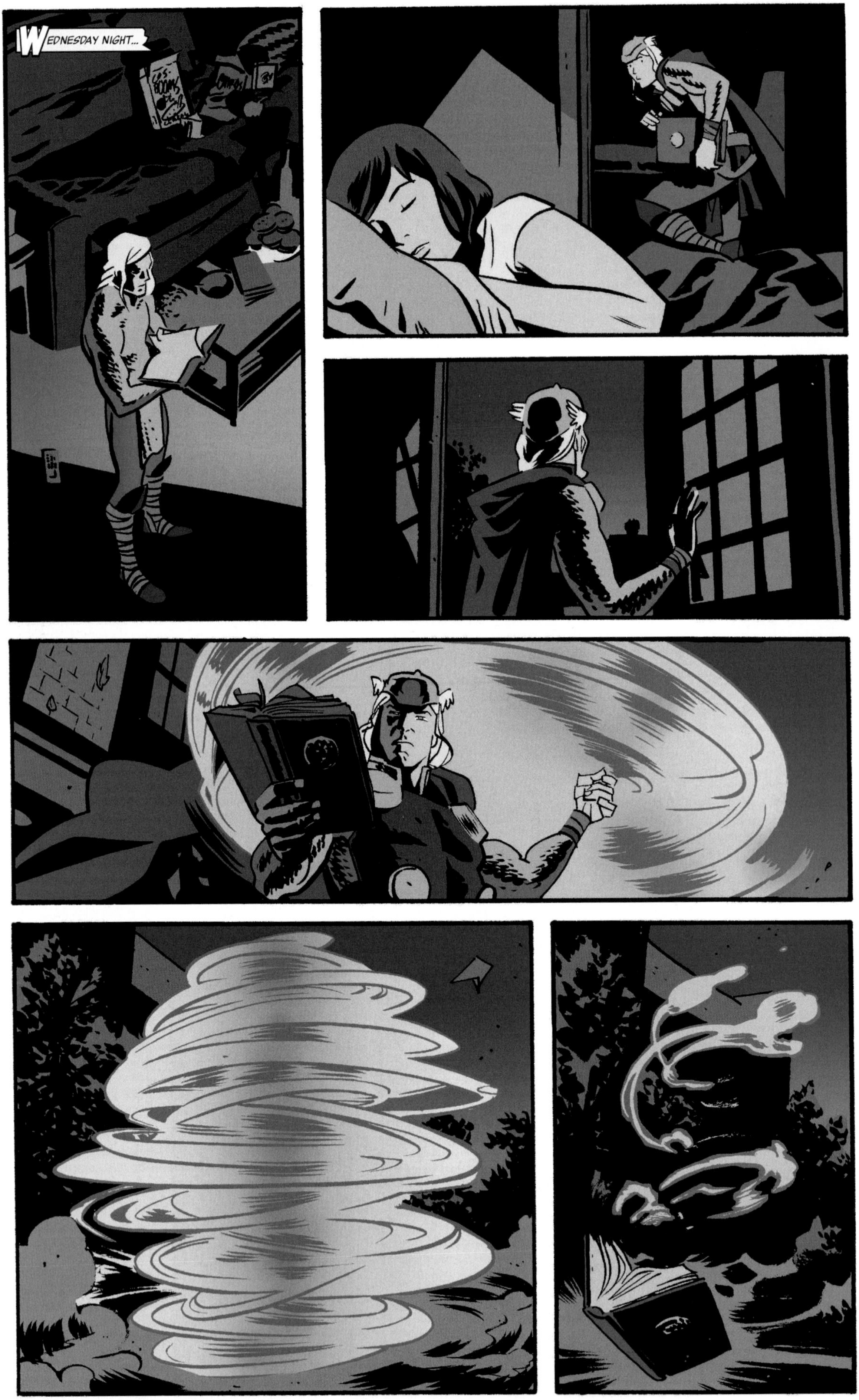
WEDNESDAY NIGHT...

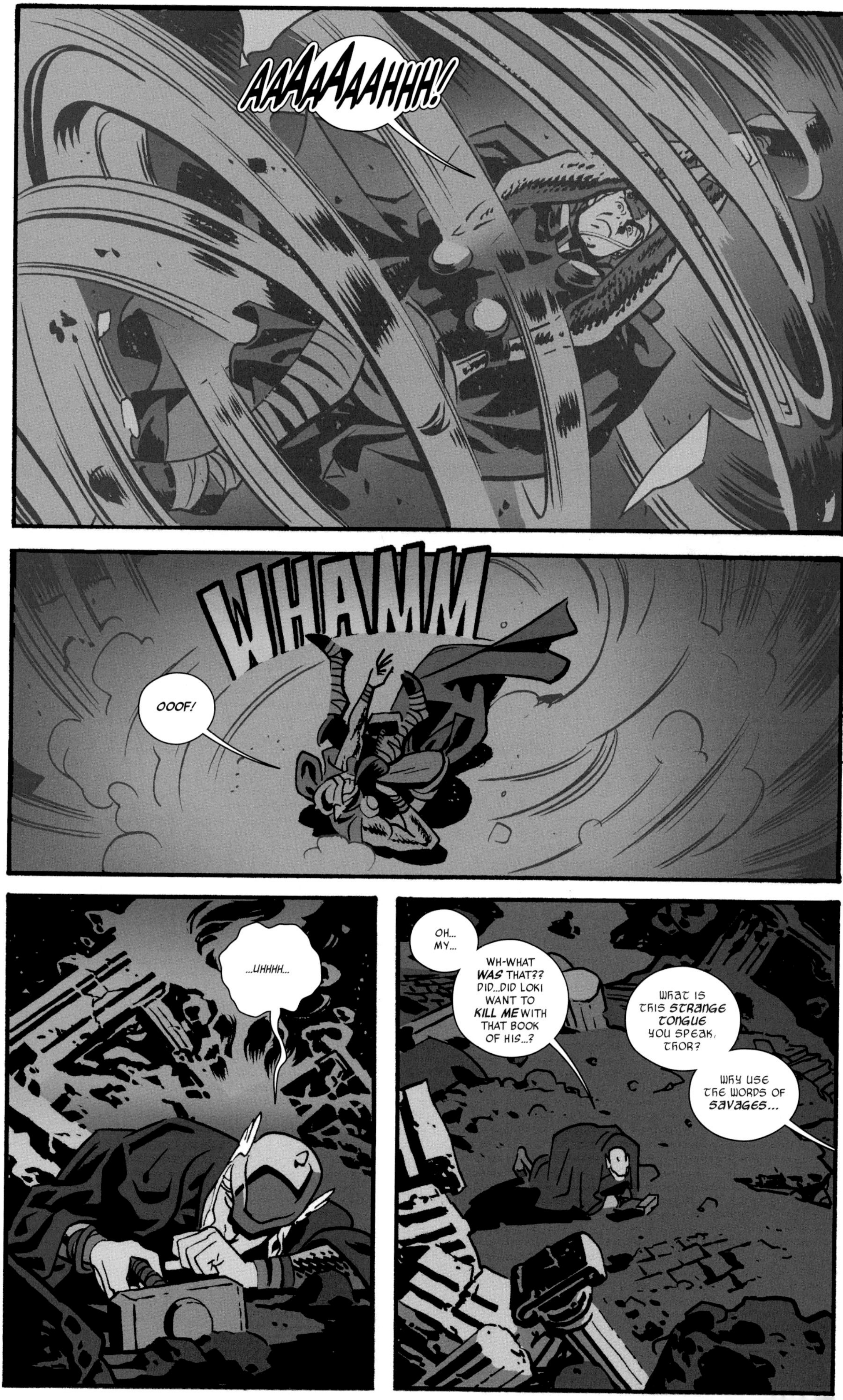
AAAAAAAHHH!
WHAMM
OOOF!
...UHHHH...
OH... MY...
WH-WHAT WAS THAT?? DID...DID LOKI WANT TO KILL ME WITH THAT BOOK OF HIS...?
WHAT IS THIS STRANGE TONGUE YOU SPEAK, THOR?
WHY USE THE WORDS OF SAVAGES...

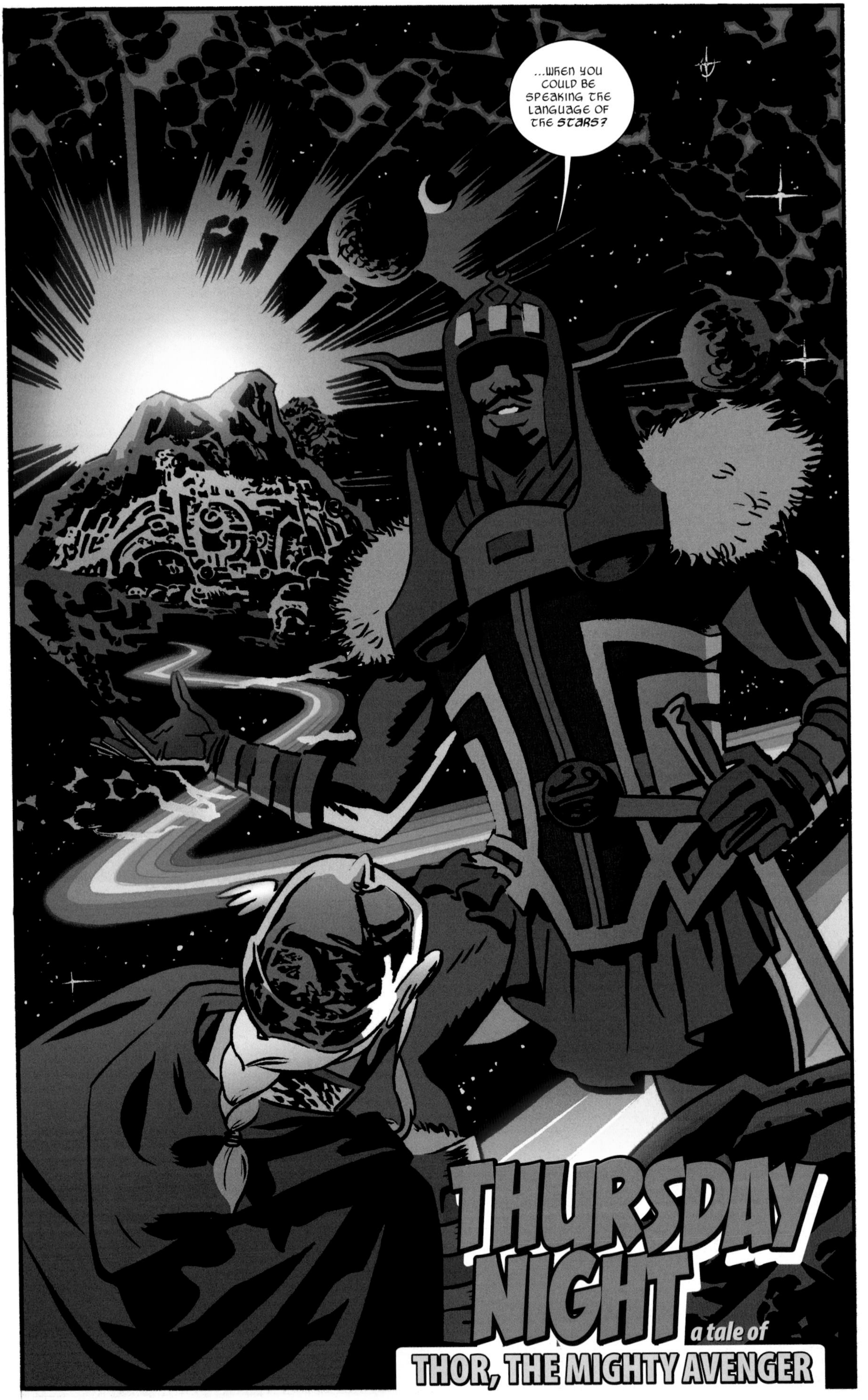
...WHEN YOU COULD BE SPEAKING THE LANGUAGE OF THE STARS?
THURSDAY NIGHT
a tale of
THOR, THE MIGHTY AVENGER

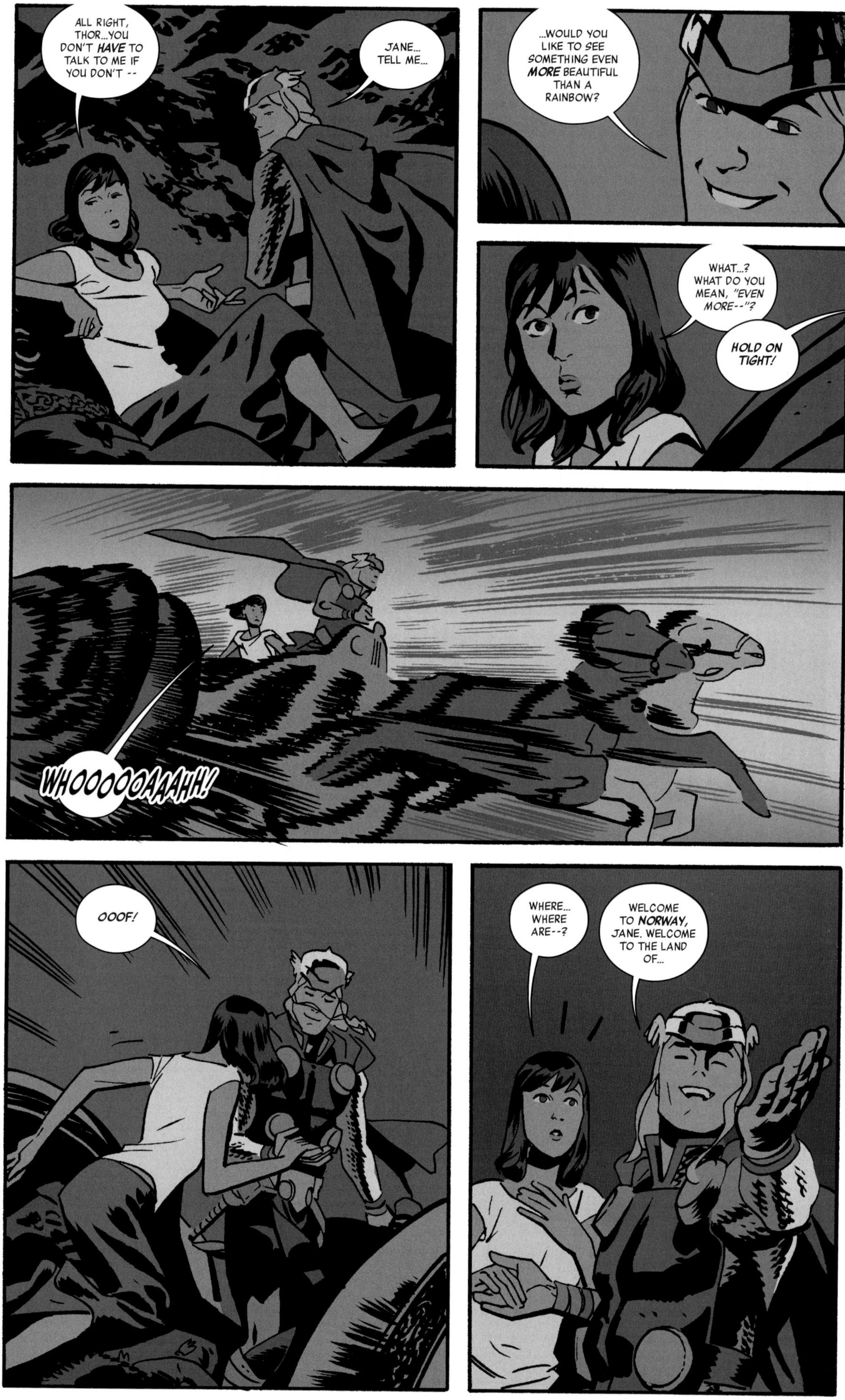
ALL RIGHT, THOR...YOU DON'T HAVE TO TALK TO ME IF YOU DON'T --
JANE... TELL ME...
...WOULD YOU LIKE TO SEE SOMETHING EVEN MORE BEAUTIFUL THAN A RAINBOW?
WHAT...? WHAT DO YOU MEAN, "EVEN MORE--"?
HOLD ON TIGHT!
WHOOOOOAAAHH!
OOOF!
WHERE... WHERE ARE--?
WELCOME TO NORWAY, JANE. WELCOME TO THE LAND OF...

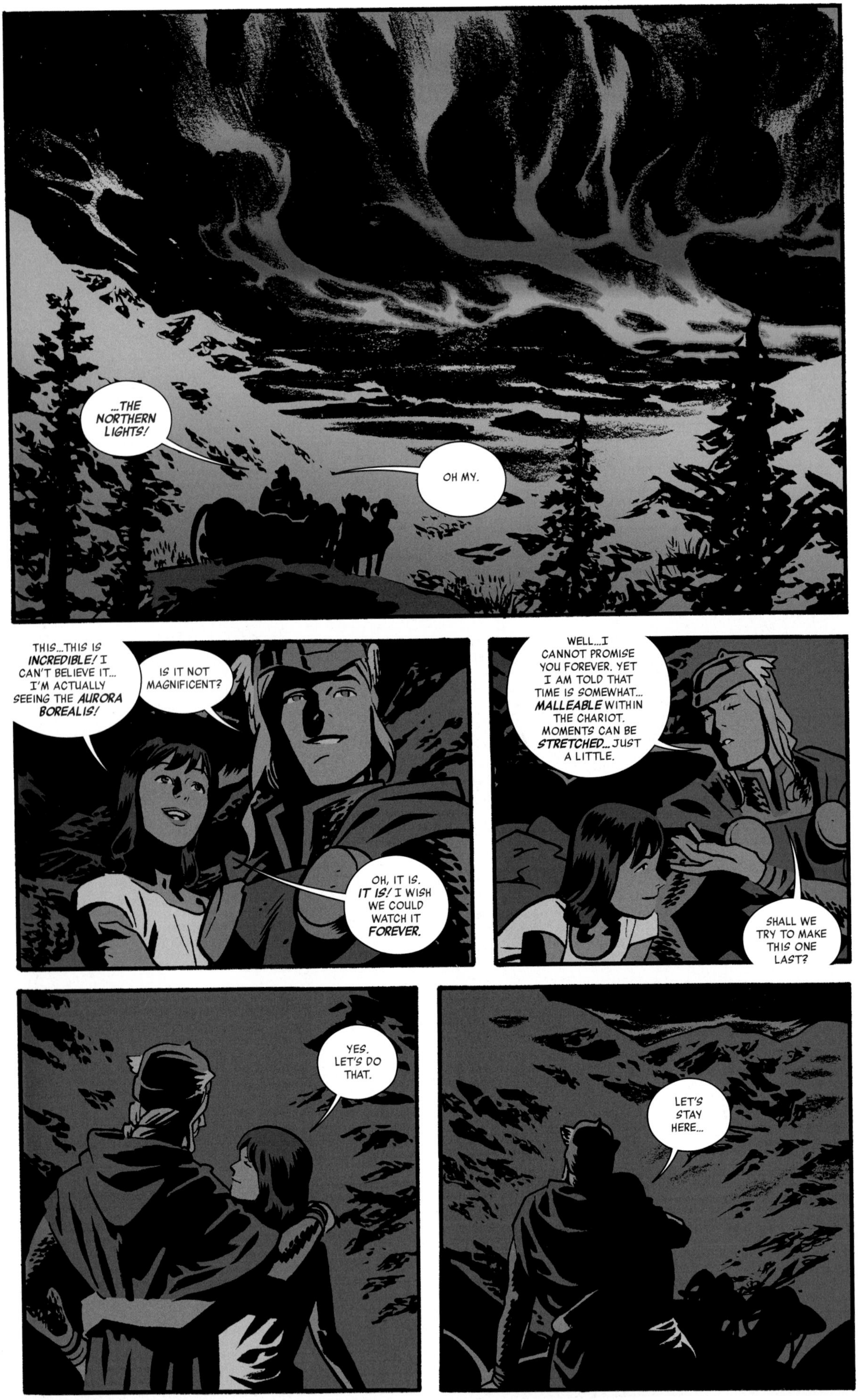
...THE NORTHERN LIGHTS!
OH MY.
THIS...THIS IS INCREDIBLE! I CAN'T BELIEVE IT... I'M ACTUALLY SEEING THE AURORA BOREALIS!
IS IT NOT MAGNIFICENT?
OH, IT IS. IT IS! I WISH WE COULD WATCH IT FOREVER.
WELL...I CANNOT PROMISE YOU FOREVER. YET I AM TOLD THAT TIME IS SOMEWHAT... MALLEABLE WITHIN THE CHARIOT. MOMENTS CAN BE STRETCHED... JUST A LITTLE.
SHALL WE TRY TO MAKE THIS ONE LAST?
YES. LET'S DO THAT.
LET'S STAY HERE...

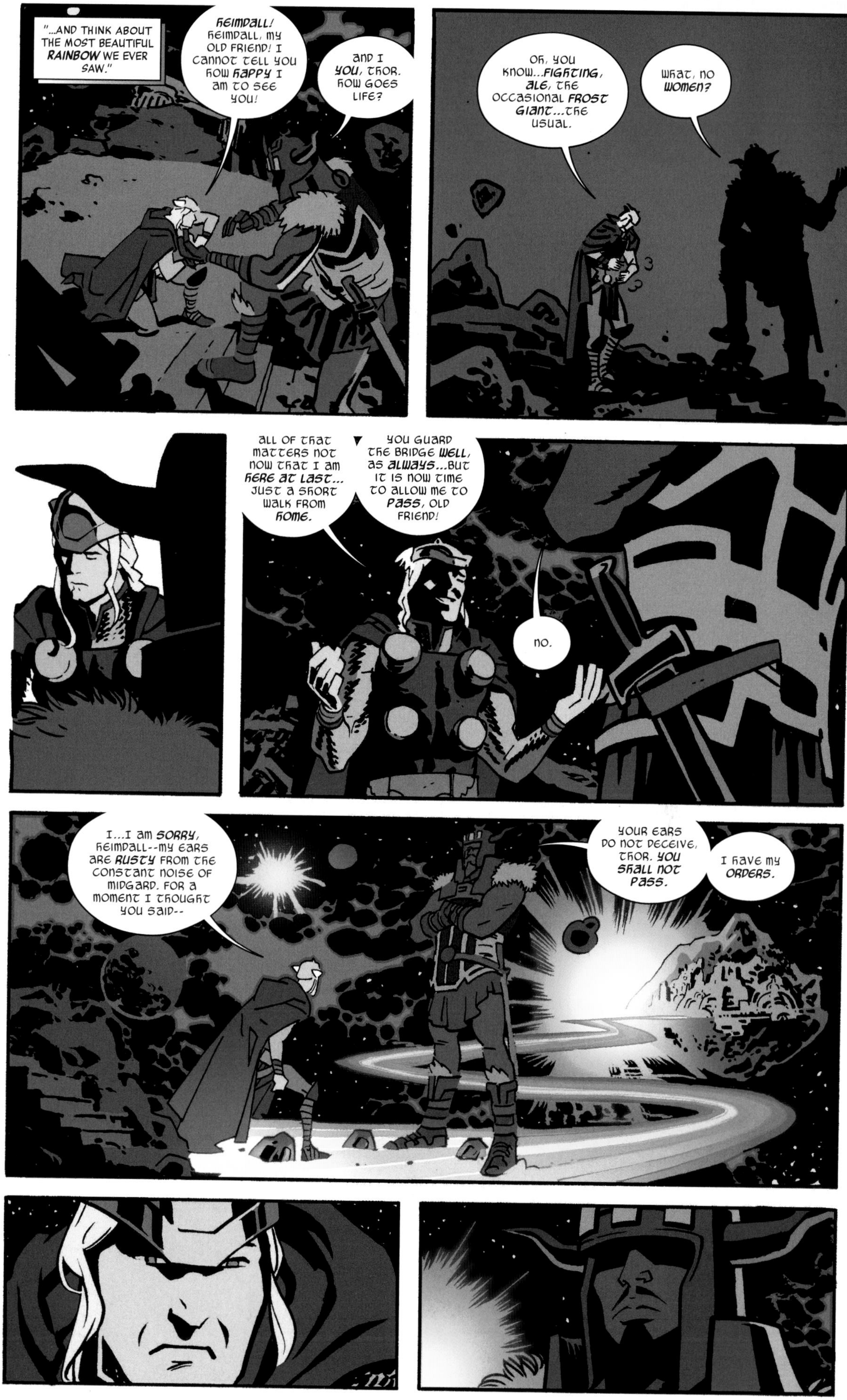
"...AND THINK ABOUT THE MOST BEAUTIFUL RAINBOW WE EVER SAW."
HEIMDALL! HEIMDALL, MY OLD FRIEND! I CANNOT TELL YOU HOW HAPPY I AM TO SEE YOU!
AND I YOU, THOR. HOW GOES LIFE?
OH, YOU KNOW...FIGHTING, ALE, THE OCCASIONAL FROST GIANT...THE USUAL.
WHAT, NO WOMEN?
ALL OF THAT MATTERS NOT NOW THAT I AM HERE AT LAST... JUST A SHORT WALK FROM HOME.
YOU GUARD THE BRIDGE WELL, AS ALWAYS...BUT IT IS NOW TIME TO ALLOW ME TO PASS, OLD FRIEND!
NO.
I...I AM SORRY, HEIMDALL--MY EARS ARE RUSTY FROM THE CONSTANT NOISE OF MIDGARD. FOR A MOMENT I THOUGHT YOU SAID--
YOUR EARS DO NOT DECEIVE, THOR. YOU SHALL NOT PASS.
I HAVE MY ORDERS.

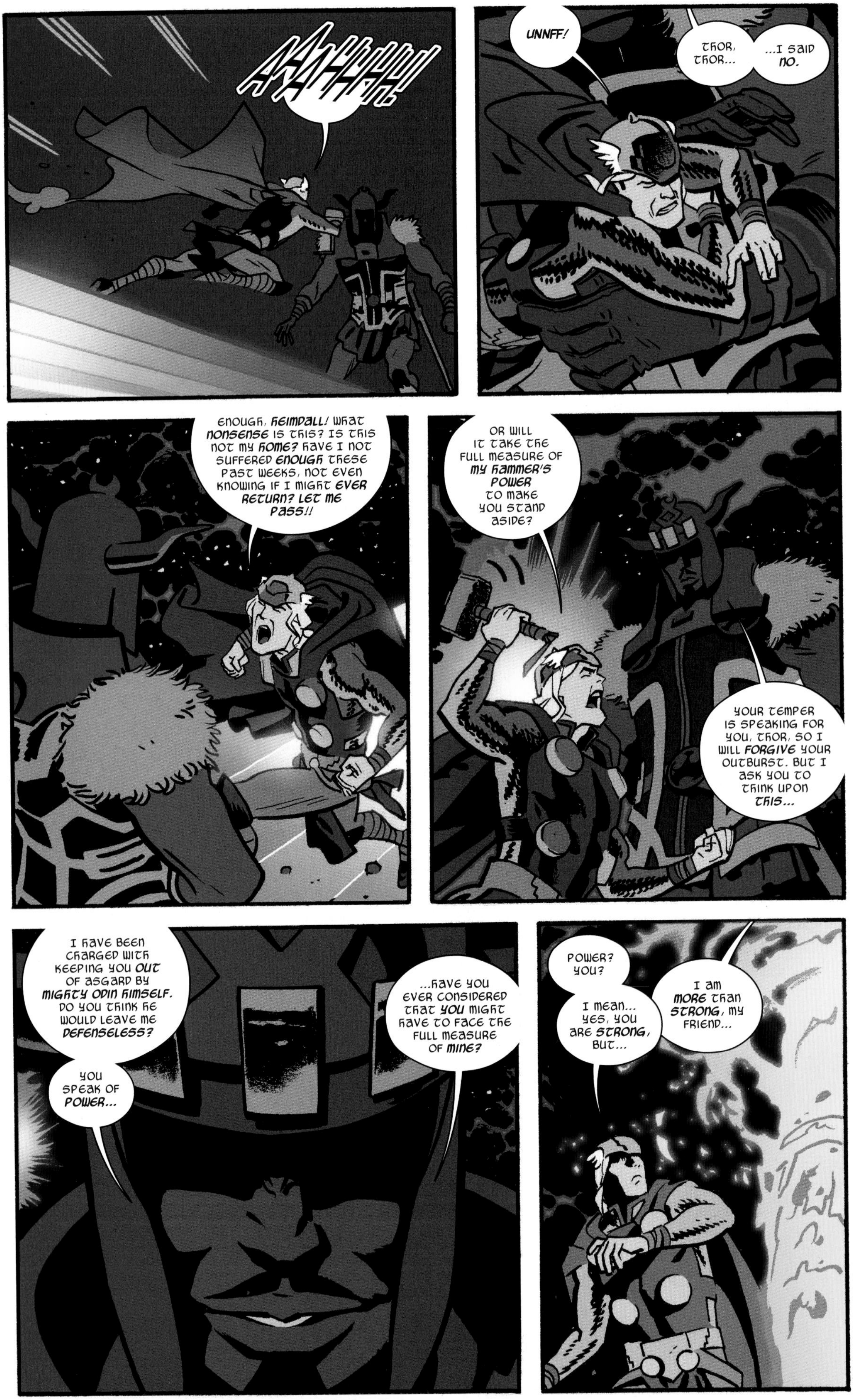
AAAHHH!
UNNFF!
THOR, THOR...
...I SAID NO.
ENOUGH, HEIMDALL! WHAT NONSENSE IS THIS? IS THIS NOT MY HOME? HAVE I NOT SUFFERED ENOUGH THESE PAST WEEKS, NOT EVEN KNOWING IF I MIGHT EVER RETURN? LET ME PASS!!
OR WILL IT TAKE THE FULL MEASURE OF MY HAMMER'S POWER TO MAKE YOU STAND ASIDE?
YOUR TEMPER IS SPEAKING FOR YOU, THOR, SO I WILL FORGIVE YOUR OUTBURST. BUT I ASK YOU TO THINK UPON THIS...
I HAVE BEEN CHARGED WITH KEEPING YOU OUT OF ASGARD BY MIGHTY ODIN HIMSELF. DO YOU THINK HE WOULD LEAVE ME DEFENSELESS?
YOU SPEAK OF POWER...
...HAVE YOU EVER CONSIDERED THAT YOU MIGHT HAVE TO FACE THE FULL MEASURE OF MINE?
POWER? YOU?
I MEAN... YES, YOU ARE STRONG, BUT...
I AM MORE THAN STRONG, MY FRIEND...

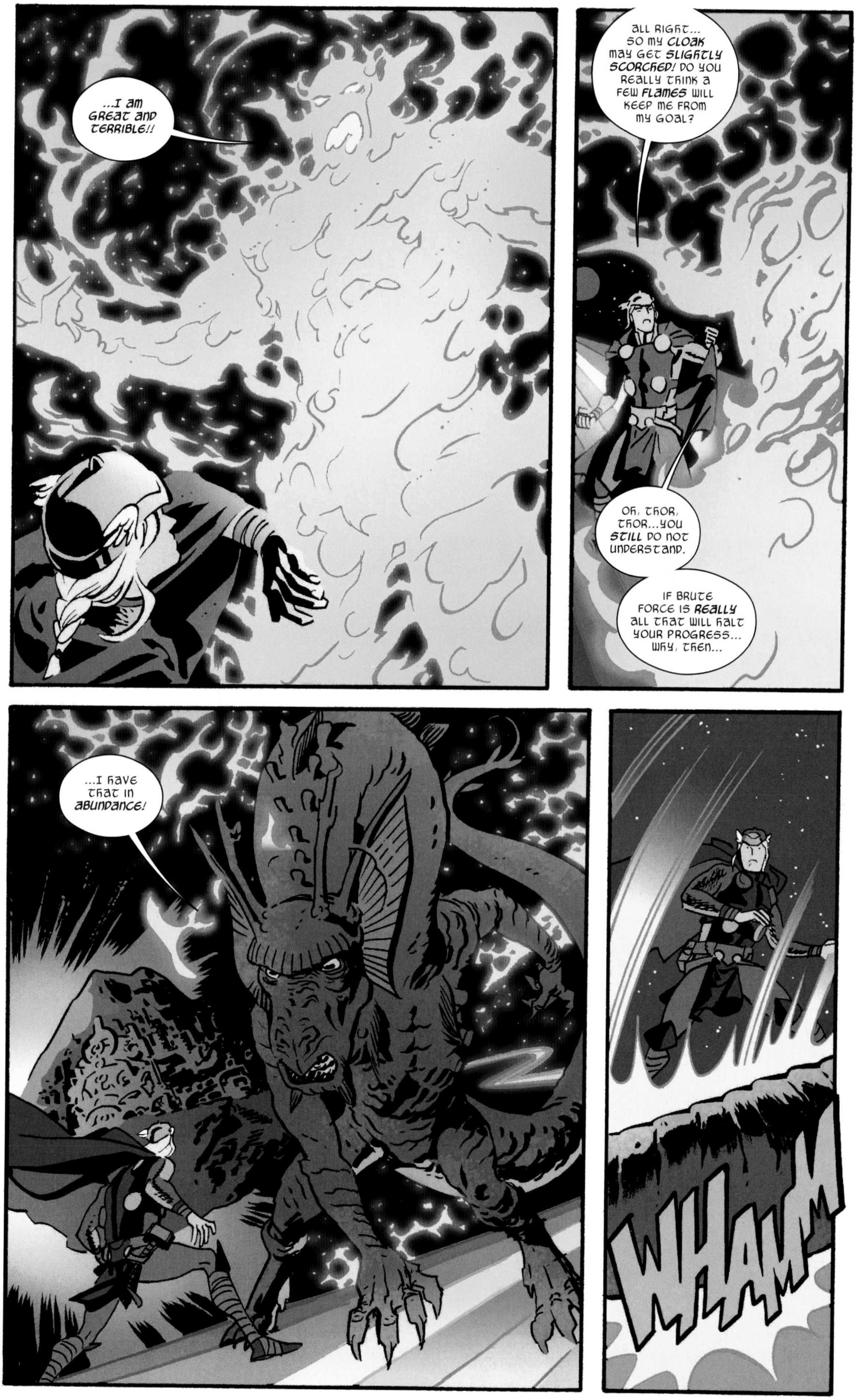

...I AM GREAT AND TERRIBLE!!
ALL RIGHT... SO MY CLOAK MAY GET SLIGHTLY SCORCHED! DO YOU REALLY THINK A FEW FLAMES WILL KEEP ME FROM MY GOAL?
OH, THOR, THOR...YOU STILL DO NOT UNDERSTAND.
IF BRUTE FORCE IS REALLY ALL THAT WILL HALT YOUR PROGRESS... WHY, THEN...
...I HAVE THAT IN ABUNDANCE!
WHAM

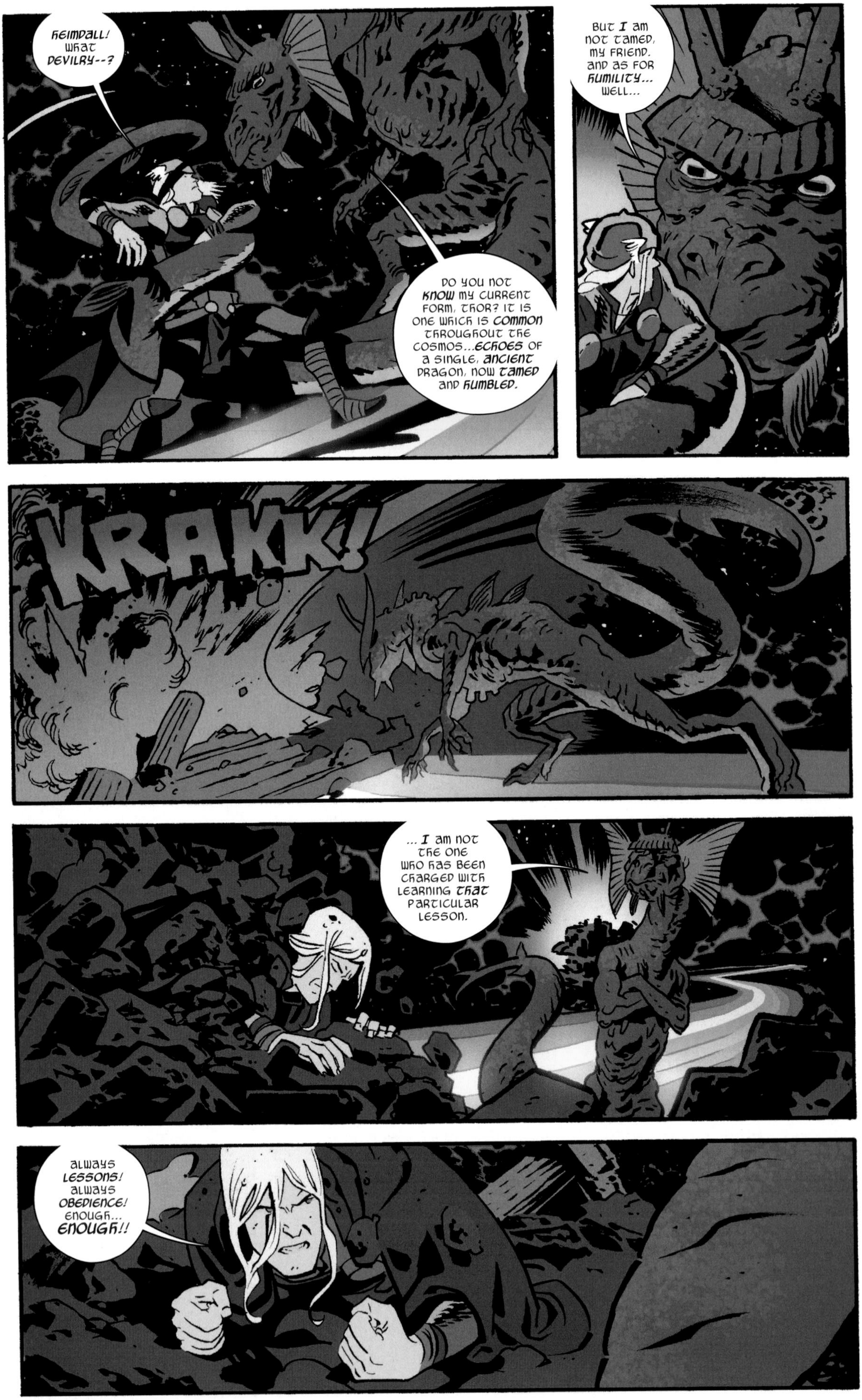
HEIMDALL! WHAT DEVILRY--?
DO YOU NOT KNOW MY CURRENT FORM, THOR? IT IS ONE WHICH IS COMMON THROUGHOUT THE COSMOS...ECHOES OF A SINGLE, ANCIENT DRAGON, NOW TAMED AND HUMBLED.
BUT I AM NOT TAMED, MY FRIEND. AND AS FOR HUMILITY... WELL...
KRAKK!
...I AM NOT THE ONE WHO HAS BEEN CHARGED WITH LEARNING THAT PARTICULAR LESSON.
ALWAYS LESSONS! ALWAYS OBEDIENCE! ENOUGH... ENOUGH!!

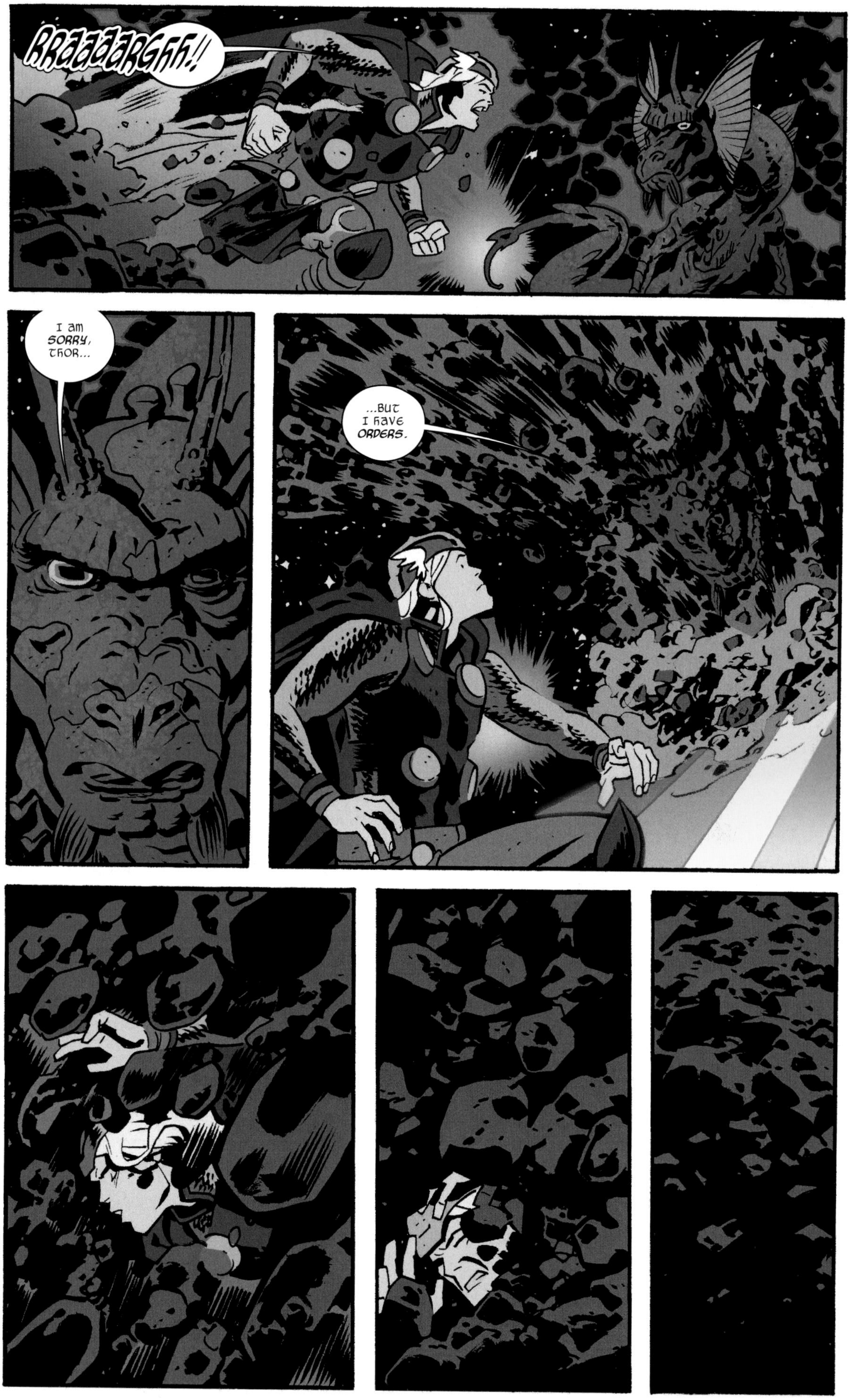
BRAAAARGHH!!
I AM SORRY, THOR...
...BUT I HAVE ORDERS.

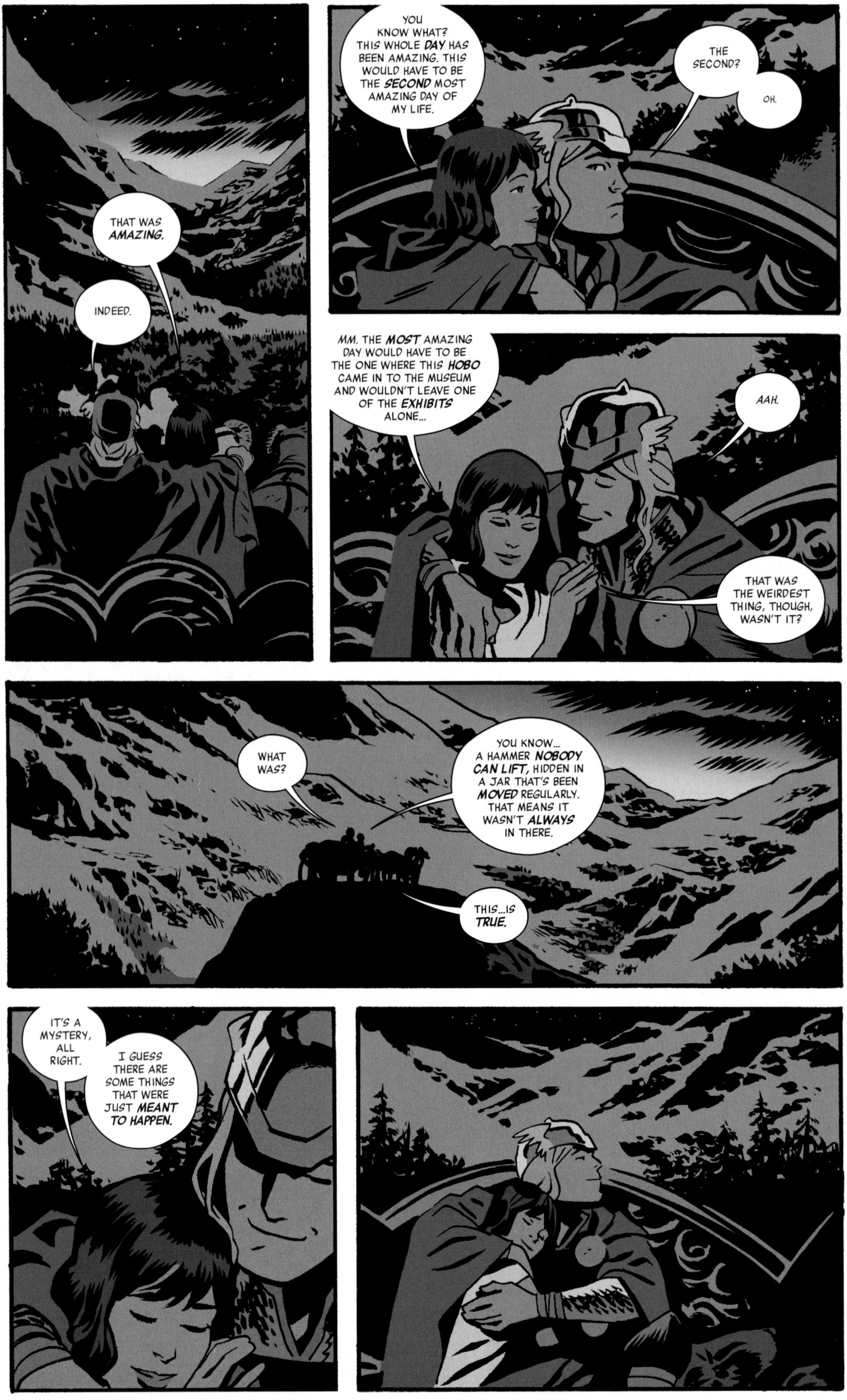
THAT WAS AMAZING.
INDEED.
YOU KNOW WHAT? THIS WHOLE DAY HAS BEEN AMAZING. THIS WOULD HAVE TO BE THE SECOND MOST AMAZING DAY OF MY LIFE.
THE SECOND?
OH.
MM. THE MOST AMAZING DAY WOULD HAVE TO BE THE ONE WHERE THIS HOBO CAME IN TO THE MUSEUM AND WOULDN'T LEAVE ONE OF THE EXHIBITS ALONE...
AAH.
THAT WAS THE WEIRDEST THING, THOUGH, WASN'T IT?
WHAT WAS?
YOU KNOW... A HAMMER NOBODY CAN LIFT, HIDDEN IN A JAR THAT'S BEEN MOVED REGULARLY. THAT MEANS IT WASN'T ALWAYS IN THERE.
THIS...IS TRUE.
IT'S A MYSTERY, ALL RIGHT.
I GUESS THERE ARE SOME THINGS THAT WERE JUST MEANT TO HAPPEN.

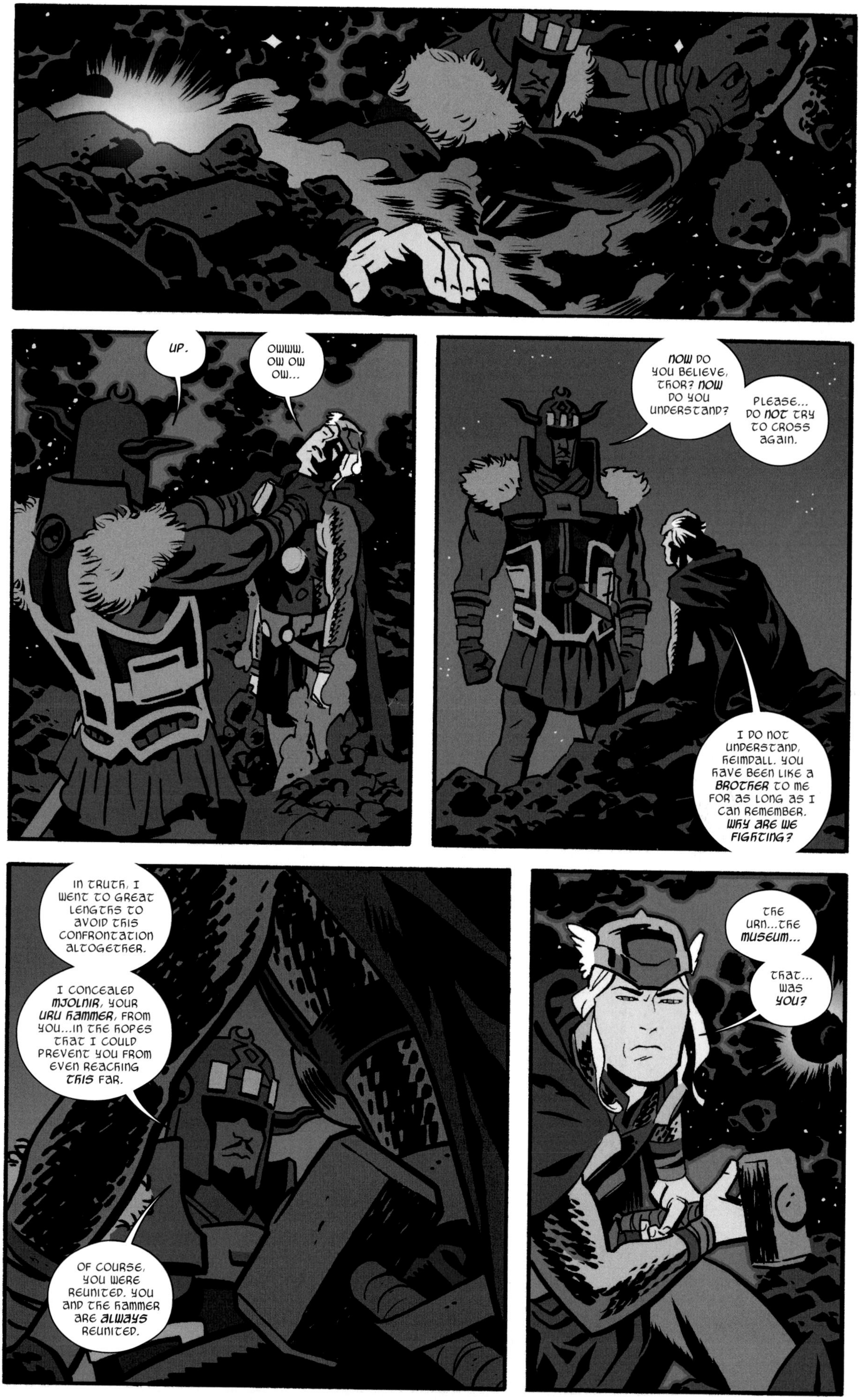
UP.
OWWW. OW OW OW...
NOW DO YOU BELIEVE, THOR? NOW DO YOU UNDERSTAND?
PLEASE... DO NOT TRY TO CROSS AGAIN.
I DO NOT UNDERSTAND, HEIMDALL. YOU HAVE BEEN LIKE A BROTHER TO ME FOR AS LONG AS I CAN REMEMBER. WHY ARE WE FIGHTING?
IN TRUTH, I WENT TO GREAT LENGTHS TO AVOID THIS CONFRONTATION ALTOGETHER.
I CONCEALED MJOLNIR, YOUR URU HAMMER, FROM YOU...IN THE HOPES THAT I COULD PREVENT YOU FROM EVEN REACHING THIS FAR.
OF COURSE, YOU WERE REUNITED. YOU AND THE HAMMER ARE ALWAYS REUNITED.
THE URN...THE MUSEUM...
THAT... WAS YOU?

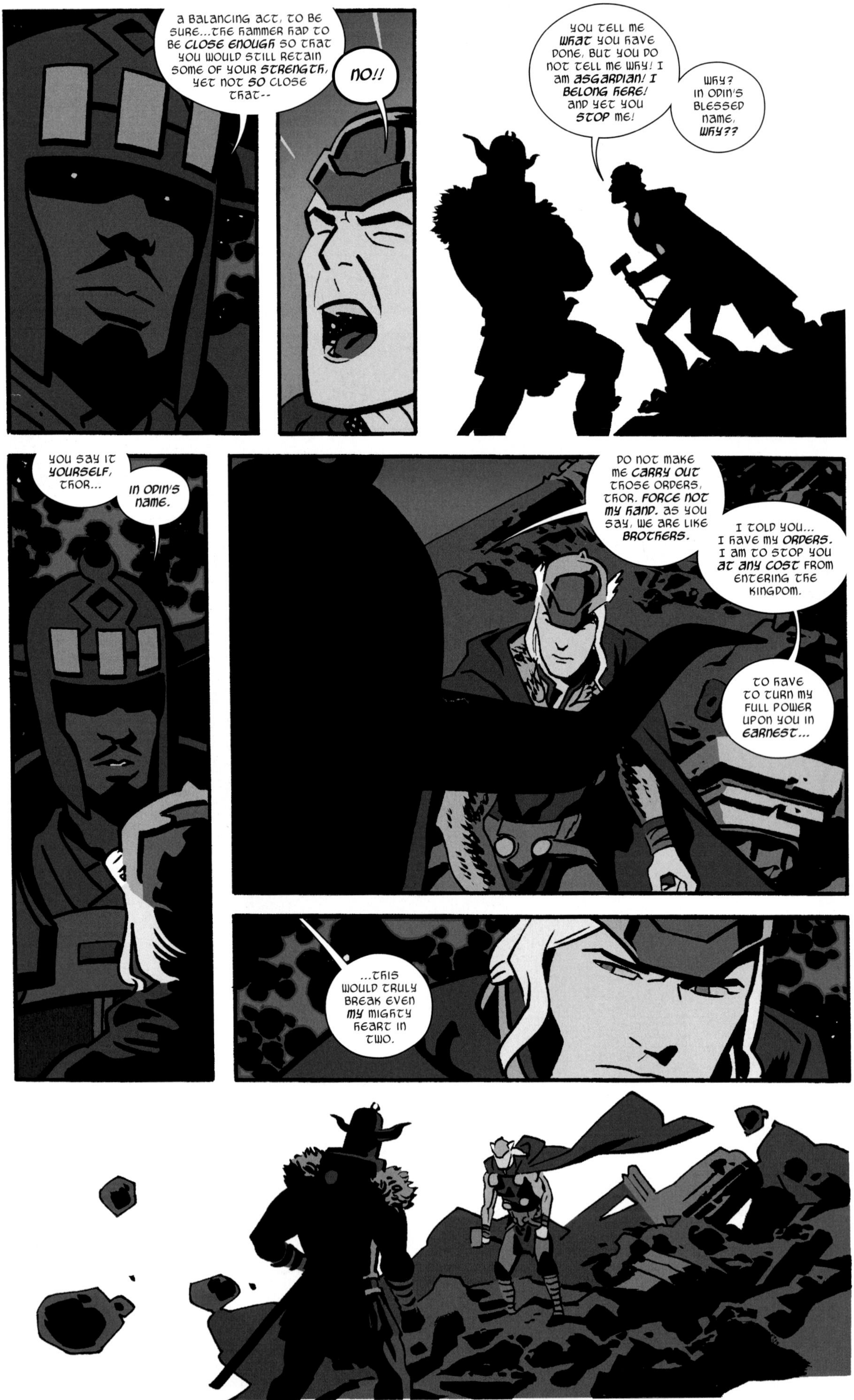
A BALANCING ACT, TO BE SURE...THE HAMMER HAD TO BE CLOSE ENOUGH SO THAT YOU WOULD STILL RETAIN SOME OF YOUR STRENGTH, YET NOT SO CLOSE THAT--
NO!!
YOU TELL ME WHAT YOU HAVE DONE, BUT YOU DO NOT TELL ME WHY! I AM ASGARDIAN! I BELONG HERE! AND YET YOU STOP ME!
WHY? IN ODIN'S BLESSED NAME, WHY??
YOU SAY IT YOURSELF, THOR...
IN ODIN'S NAME.
I TOLD YOU... I HAVE MY ORDERS. I AM TO STOP YOU AT ANY COST FROM ENTERING THE KINGDOM.
DO NOT MAKE ME CARRY OUT THOSE ORDERS, THOR. FORCE NOT MY HAND. AS YOU SAY, WE ARE LIKE BROTHERS.
TO HAVE TO TURN MY FULL POWER UPON YOU IN EARNEST...
...THIS WOULD TRULY BREAK EVEN MY MIGHTY HEART IN TWO.

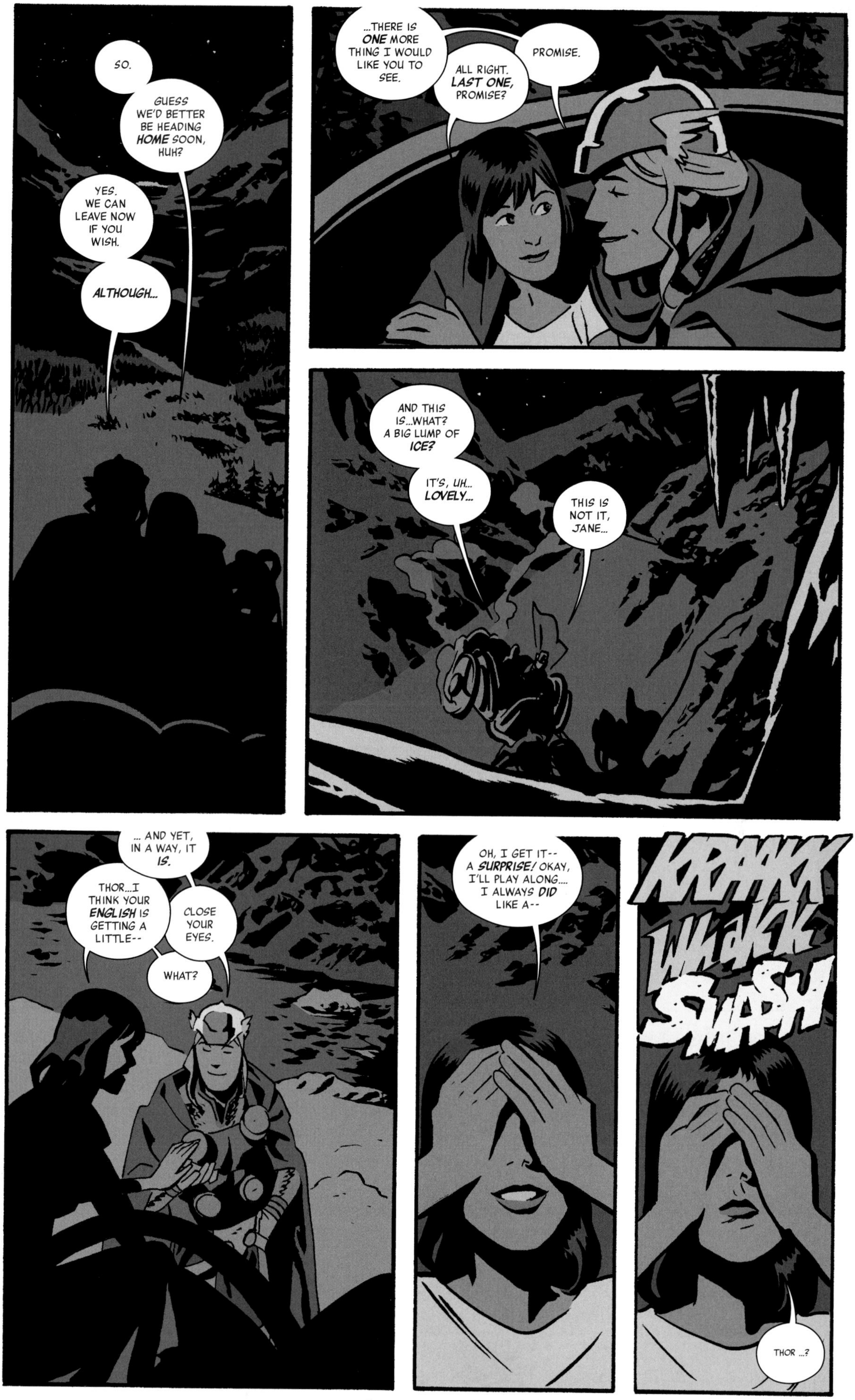
SO.
GUESS WE'D BETTER BE HEADING HOME SOON, HUH?
YES. WE CAN LEAVE NOW IF YOU WISH.
ALTHOUGH...
...THERE IS ONE MORE THING I WOULD LIKE YOU TO SEE.
ALL RIGHT. LAST ONE, PROMISE?
PROMISE.
AND THIS IS...WHAT? A BIG LUMP OF ICE?
IT'S, UH... LOVELY...
THIS IS NOT IT, JANE...
... AND YET, IN A WAY, IT IS.
THOR...I THINK YOUR ENGLISH IS GETTING A LITTLE--
CLOSE YOUR EYES.
WHAT?
OH, I GET IT-- A SURPRISE! OKAY, I'LL PLAY ALONG.... I ALWAYS DID LIKE A--
KRAAKK
WHAKK
SMASH
THOR ...?

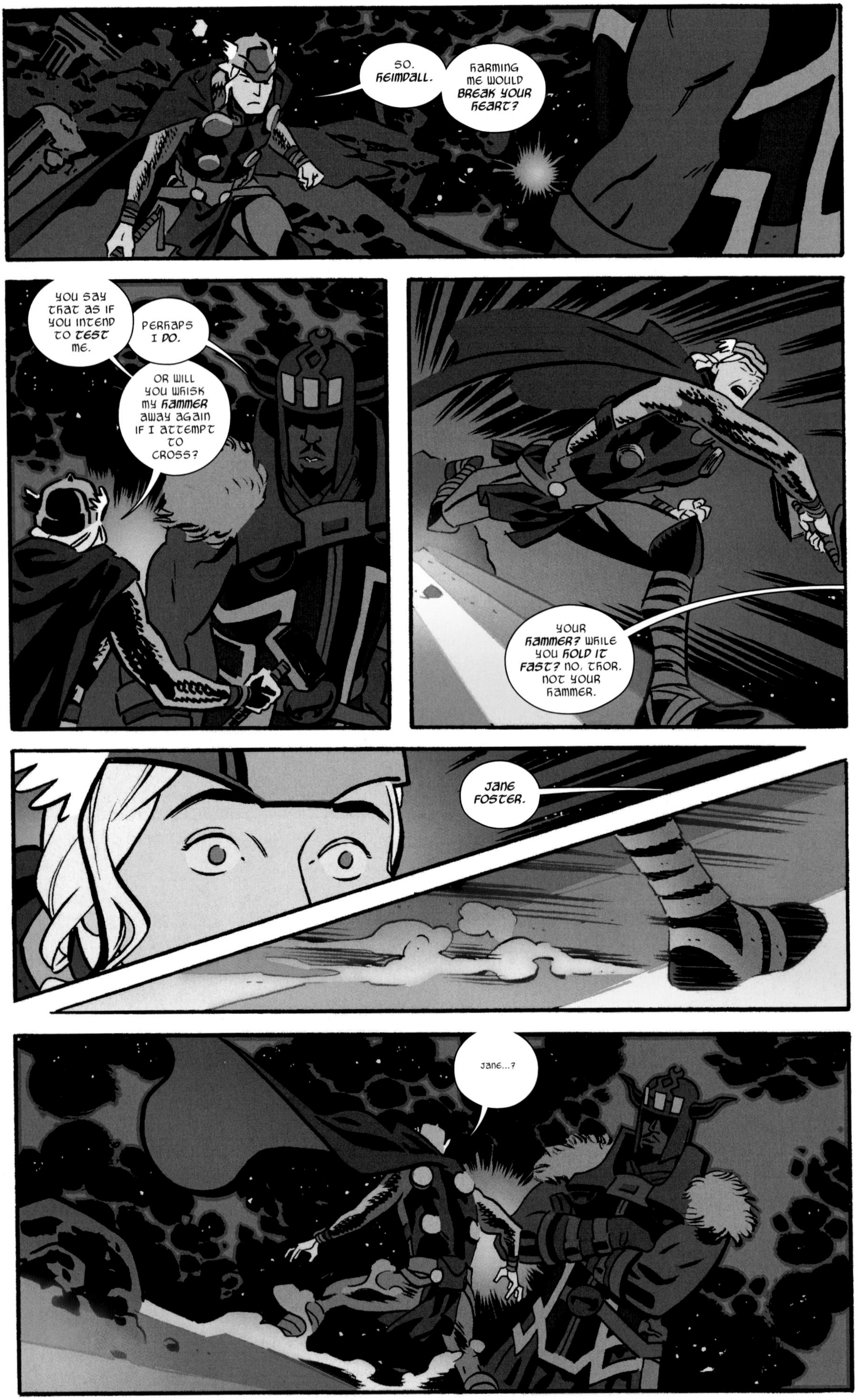
SO. HEIMDALL.
HARMING ME WOULD BREAK YOUR HEART?
YOU SAY THAT AS IF YOU INTEND TO TEST ME.
PERHAPS I DO.
OR WILL YOU WHISK MY HAMMER AWAY AGAIN IF I ATTEMPT TO CROSS?
YOUR HAMMER? WHILE YOU HOLD IT FAST? NO, THOR. NOT YOUR HAMMER.
JANE FOSTER.
JANE...?

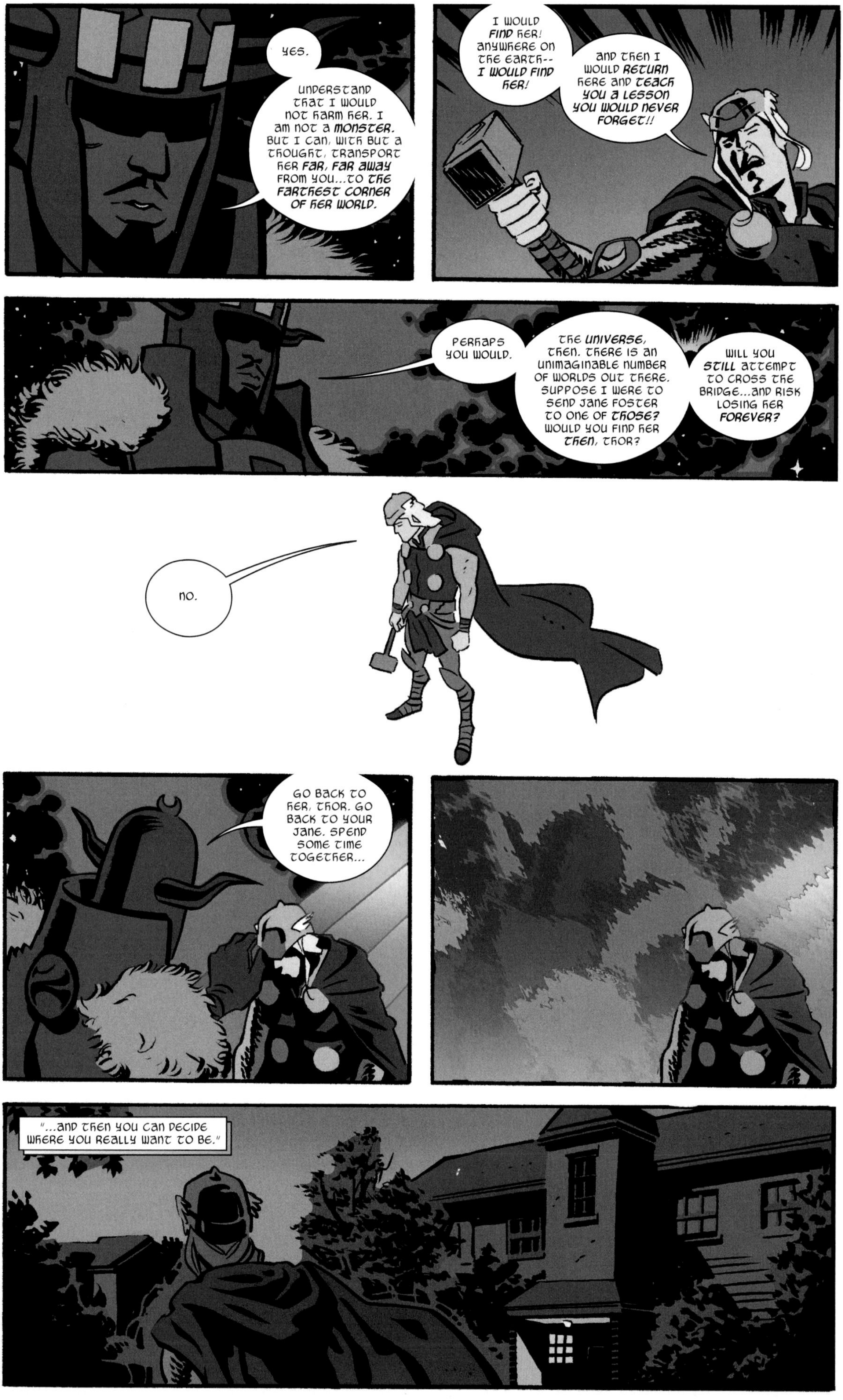
YES.
UNDERSTAND THAT I WOULD NOT HARM HER. I AM NOT A MONSTER. BUT I CAN, WITH BUT A THOUGHT, TRANSPORT HER FAR, FAR AWAY FROM YOU...TO THE FARTHEST CORNER OF HER WORLD.
I WOULD FIND HER! ANYWHERE ON THE EARTH-- I WOULD FIND HER!
AND THEN I WOULD RETURN HERE AND TEACH YOU A LESSON YOU WOULD NEVER FORGET!!
PERHAPS YOU WOULD.
THE UNIVERSE, THEN. THERE IS AN UNIMAGINABLE NUMBER OF WORLDS OUT THERE. SUPPOSE I WERE TO SEND JANE FOSTER TO ONE OF THOSE? WOULD YOU FIND HER THEN, THOR?
WILL YOU STILL ATTEMPT TO CROSS THE BRIDGE...AND RISK LOSING HER FOREVER?
NO.
GO BACK TO HER, THOR. GO BACK TO YOUR JANE. SPEND SOME TIME TOGETHER...
"...AND THEN YOU CAN DECIDE WHERE YOU REALLY WANT TO BE."

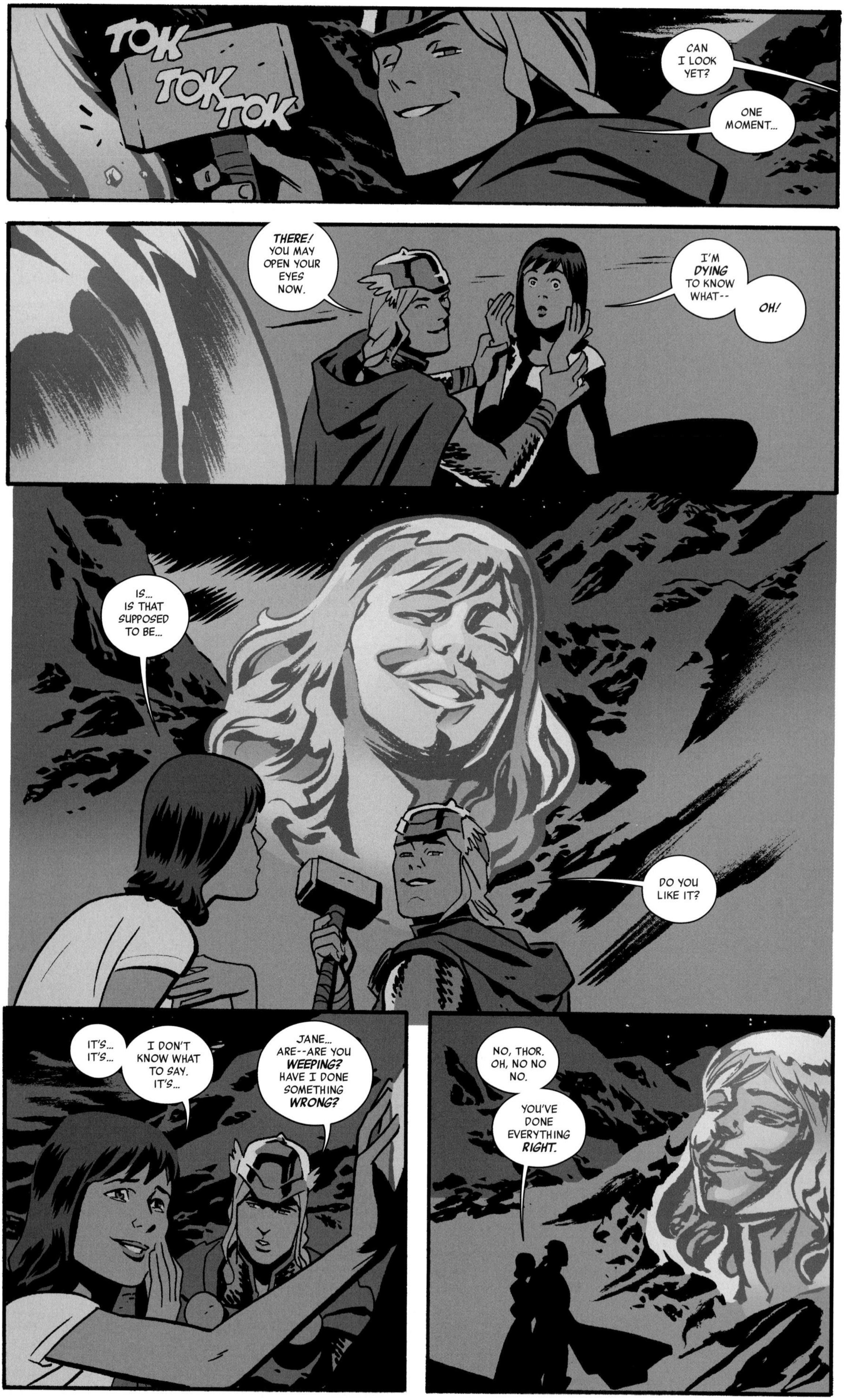

TOK
TOK TOK
CAN I LOOK YET?
ONE MOMENT...
THERE! YOU MAY OPEN YOUR EYES NOW.
I'M DYING TO KNOW WHAT--
OH!
IS... IS THAT SUPPOSED TO BE...
DO YOU LIKE IT?
IT'S... IT'S...
I DON'T KNOW WHAT TO SAY. IT'S...
JANE... ARE--ARE YOU WEEPING? HAVE I DONE SOMETHING WRONG?
NO, THOR. OH, NO NO NO.
YOU'VE DONE EVERYTHING RIGHT.

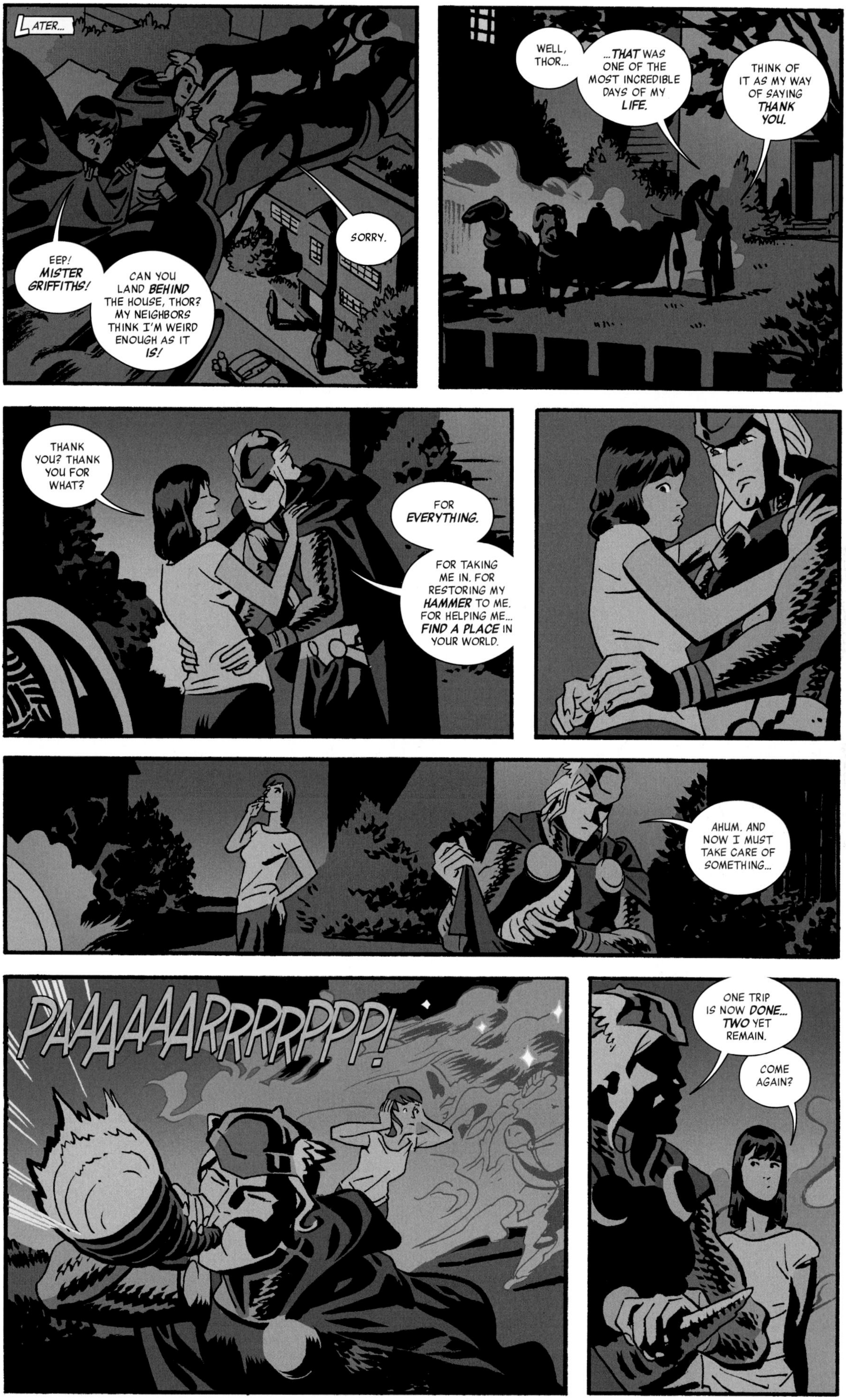
LATER...
EEP! MISTER GRIFFITHS!
CAN YOU LAND BEHIND THE HOUSE, THOR? MY NEIGHBORS THINK I'M WEIRD ENOUGH AS IT IS!
SORRY.
WELL, THOR...
...THAT WAS ONE OF THE MOST INCREDIBLE DAYS OF MY LIFE.
THINK OF IT AS MY WAY OF SAYING THANK YOU.
THANK YOU? THANK YOU FOR WHAT?
FOR EVERYTHING.
FOR TAKING ME IN. FOR RESTORING MY HAMMER TO ME. FOR HELPING ME... FIND A PLACE IN YOUR WORLD.
AHUM. AND NOW I MUST TAKE CARE OF SOMETHING...
PAAAAAARRRRRPPPP!
ONE TRIP IS NOW DONE... TWO YET REMAIN.
COME AGAIN?

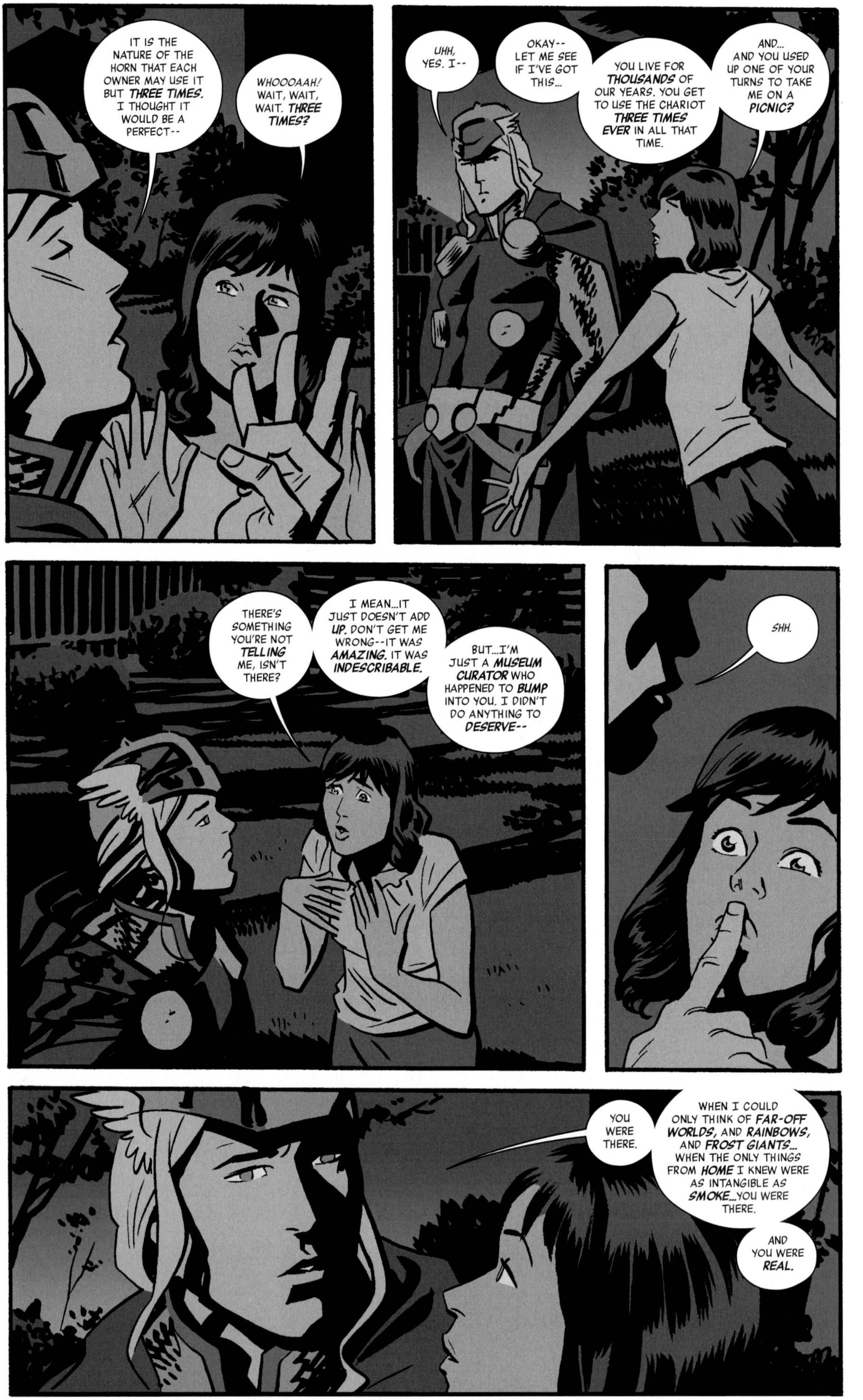
IT IS THE NATURE OF THE HORN THAT EACH OWNER MAY USE IT BUT THREE TIMES. I THOUGHT IT WOULD BE A PERFECT--
WHOOOAAH! WAIT, WAIT, WAIT. THREE TIMES?
UHH, YES. I--
OKAY-- LET ME SEE IF I'VE GOT THIS...
YOU LIVE FOR THOUSANDS OF OUR YEARS. YOU GET TO USE THE CHARIOT THREE TIMES EVER IN ALL THAT TIME.
AND... AND YOU USED UP ONE OF YOUR TURNS TO TAKE ME ON A PICNIC?
THERE'S SOMETHING YOU'RE NOT TELLING ME, ISN'T THERE?
I MEAN...IT JUST DOESN'T ADD UP. DON'T GET ME WRONG--IT WAS AMAZING. IT WAS INDESCRIBABLE.
BUT...I'M JUST A MUSEUM CURATOR WHO HAPPENED TO BUMP INTO YOU. I DIDN'T DO ANYTHING TO DESERVE--
SHH.
WHEN I COULD ONLY THINK OF FAR-OFF WORLDS, AND RAINBOWS, AND FROST GIANTS... WHEN THE ONLY THINGS FROM HOME I KNEW WERE AS INTANGIBLE AS SMOKE...YOU WERE THERE.
YOU WERE THERE.
AND YOU WERE REAL.

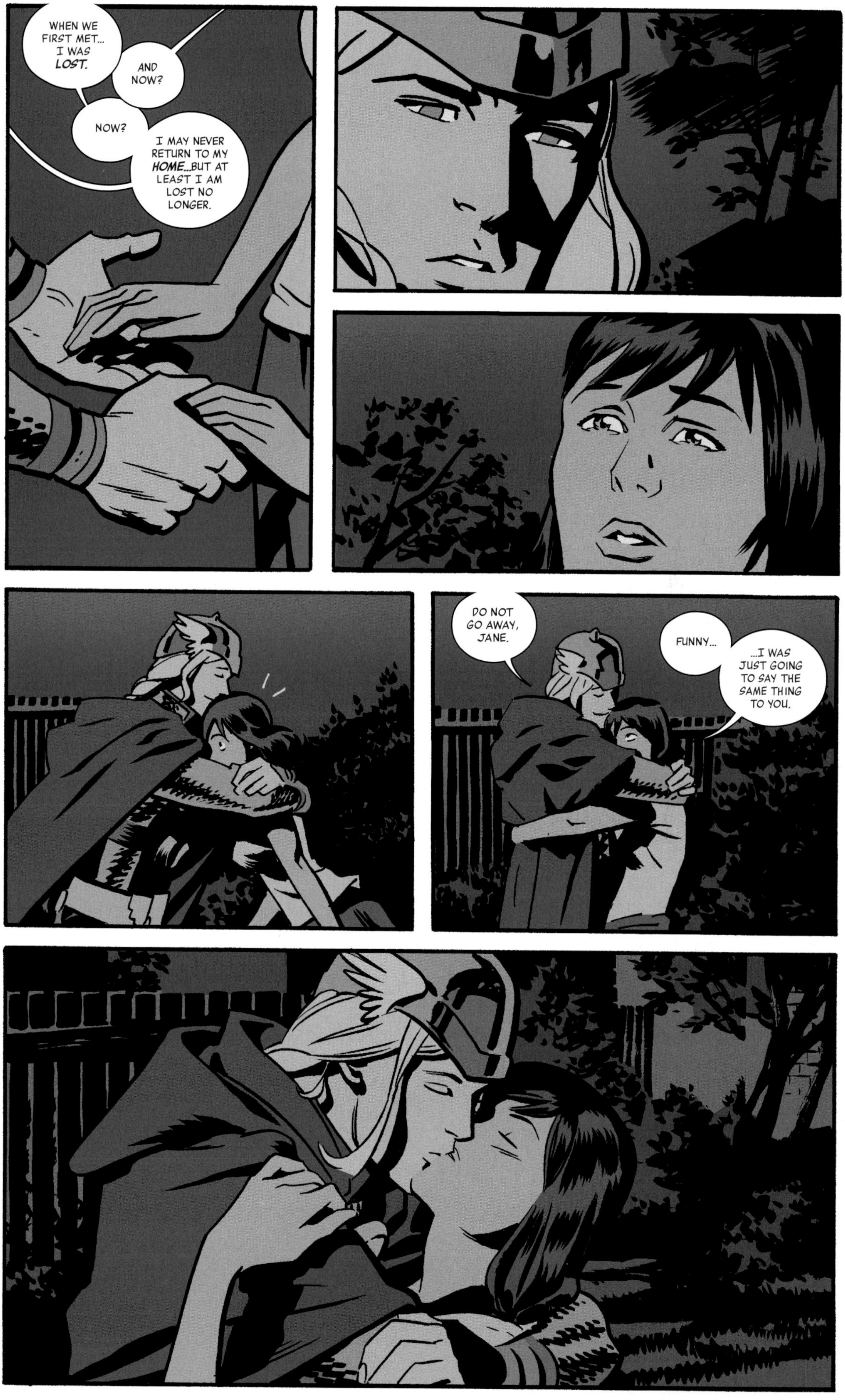
WHEN WE FIRST MET... I WAS LOST.
AND NOW?
NOW?
I MAY NEVER RETURN TO MY HOME...BUT AT LEAST I AM LOST NO LONGER.
DO NOT GO AWAY, JANE.
FUNNY...
...I WAS JUST GOING TO SAY THE SAME THING TO YOU.

THOR THE MIGHTY AVENGER #7

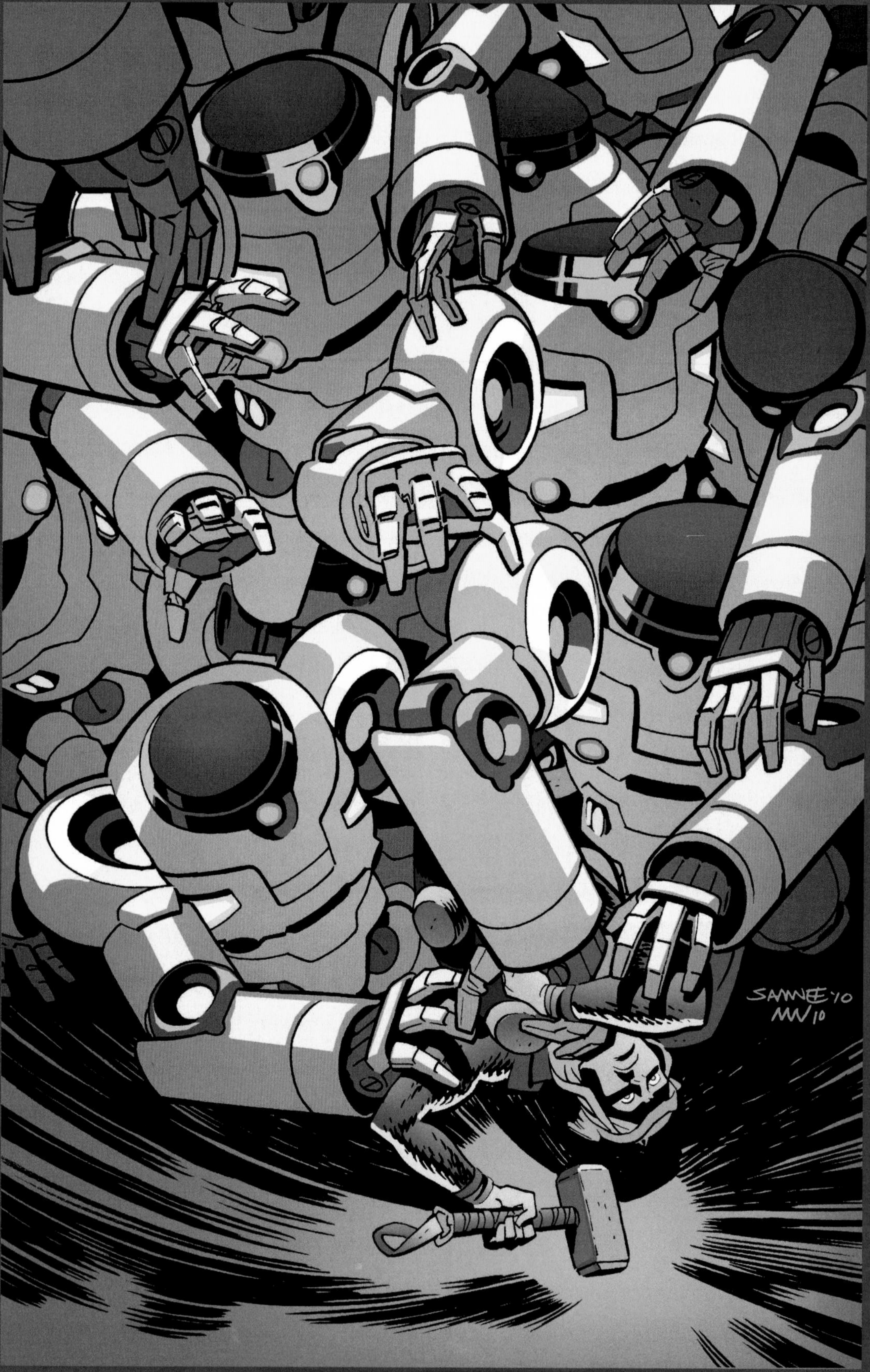
SAMNEE '10
MW 10

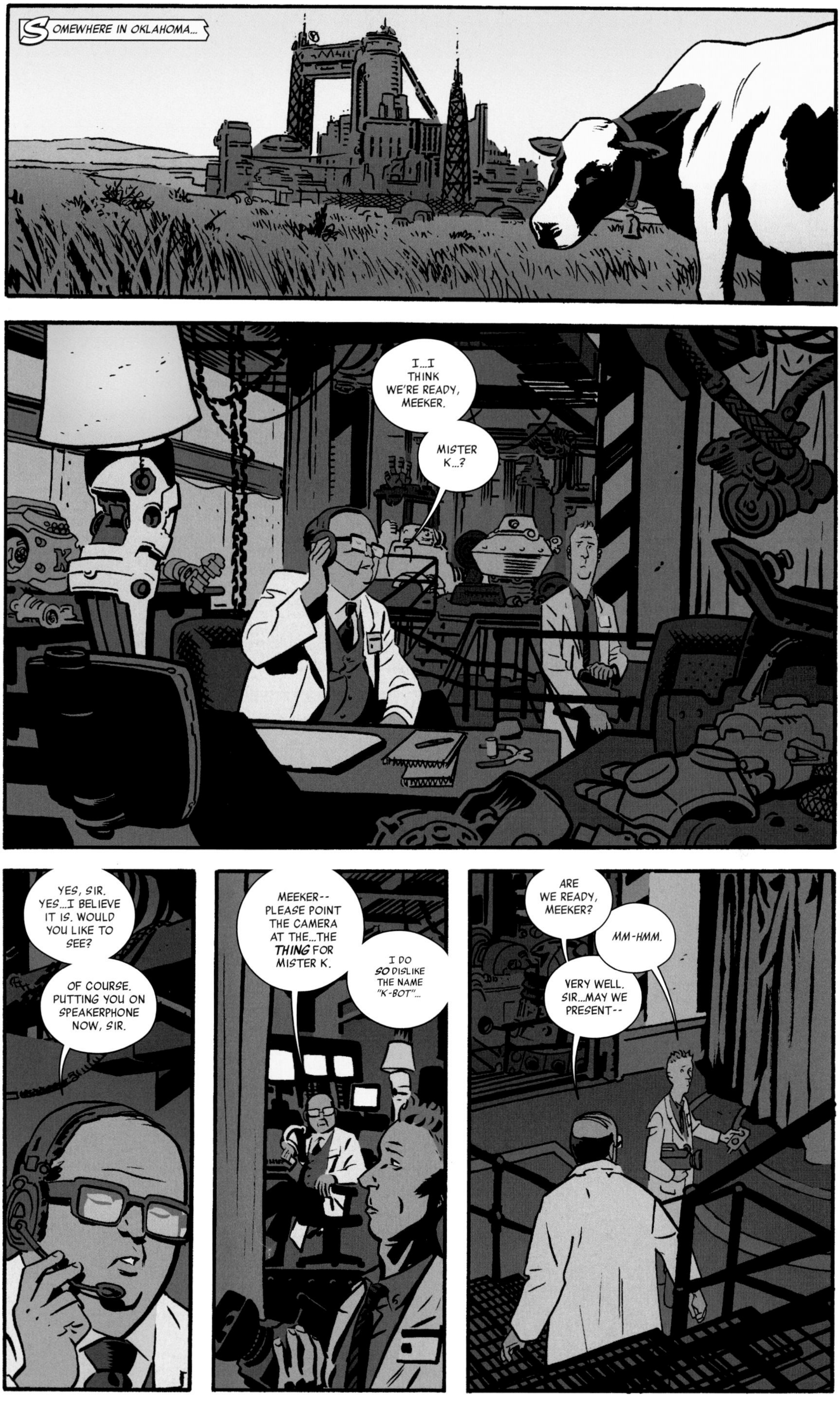
SOMEWHERE IN OKLAHOMA...
I...I THINK WE'RE READY, MEEKER.
MISTER K...?
YES, SIR. YES...I BELIEVE IT IS. WOULD YOU LIKE TO SEE?
OF COURSE. PUTTING YOU ON SPEAKERPHONE NOW, SIR.
MEEKER--PLEASE POINT THE CAMERA AT THE...THE THING FOR MISTER K.
I DO SO DISLIKE THE NAME "K-BOT"...
ARE WE READY, MEEKER?
MM-HMM.
VERY WELL. SIR...MAY WE PRESENT--

--THE K-BOT 3000!

IT HAS ALL THE SPECIFICATIONS YOU REQUESTED, SIR-- IT CAN DO EVERYTHING THE *PREVIOUS* K-BOTS COULD DO, AND *MORE* BESIDES.

AND, OF COURSE...IT'S MORE THAN *TWICE THE SIZE* OF THE OTHERS.

EXCELLENT WORK, DOCTOR HALLIWELL. YOU AND DOCTOR MEEKER HAVE BOUGHT YOURSELVES THREE MORE MONTHS.

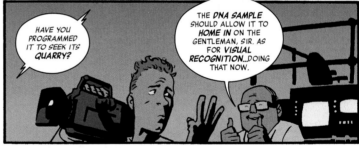

HAVE YOU PROGRAMMED IT TO SEEK ITS *QUARRY?*

THE *DNA SAMPLE* SHOULD ALLOW IT TO *HOME IN* ON THE GENTLEMAN, SIR. AS FOR *VISUAL RECOGNITION*...DOING THAT NOW.

ALTHOUGH WHAT YOU INTEND TO DO WITH THAT *BUM* YOU HAD IN HERE A WHILE BACK...MUCH LESS WHY YOU NEED A *K-BOT* TO BRING HIM IN...

TAKKATATAKKATATAK TAK TAK

...IS *QUITE* BEYOND ME.

TIK!

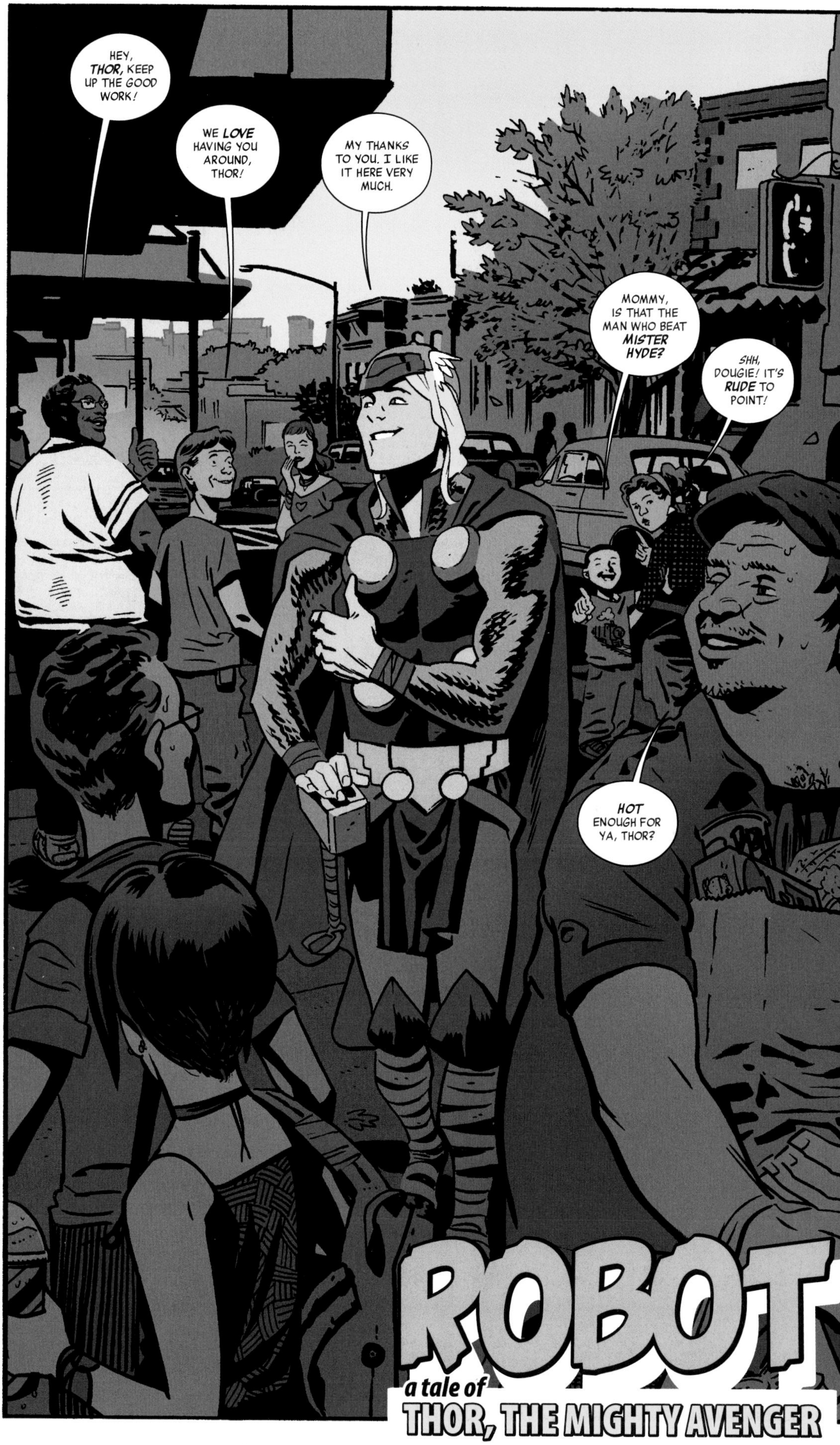
HEY, THOR, KEEP UP THE GOOD WORK!
WE LOVE HAVING YOU AROUND, THOR!
MY THANKS TO YOU. I LIKE IT HERE VERY MUCH.
MOMMY, IS THAT THE MAN WHO BEAT MISTER HYDE?
SHH, DOUGIE! IT'S RUDE TO POINT!
HOT ENOUGH FOR YA, THOR?
ROBOT
a tale of
THOR, THE MIGHTY AVENGER

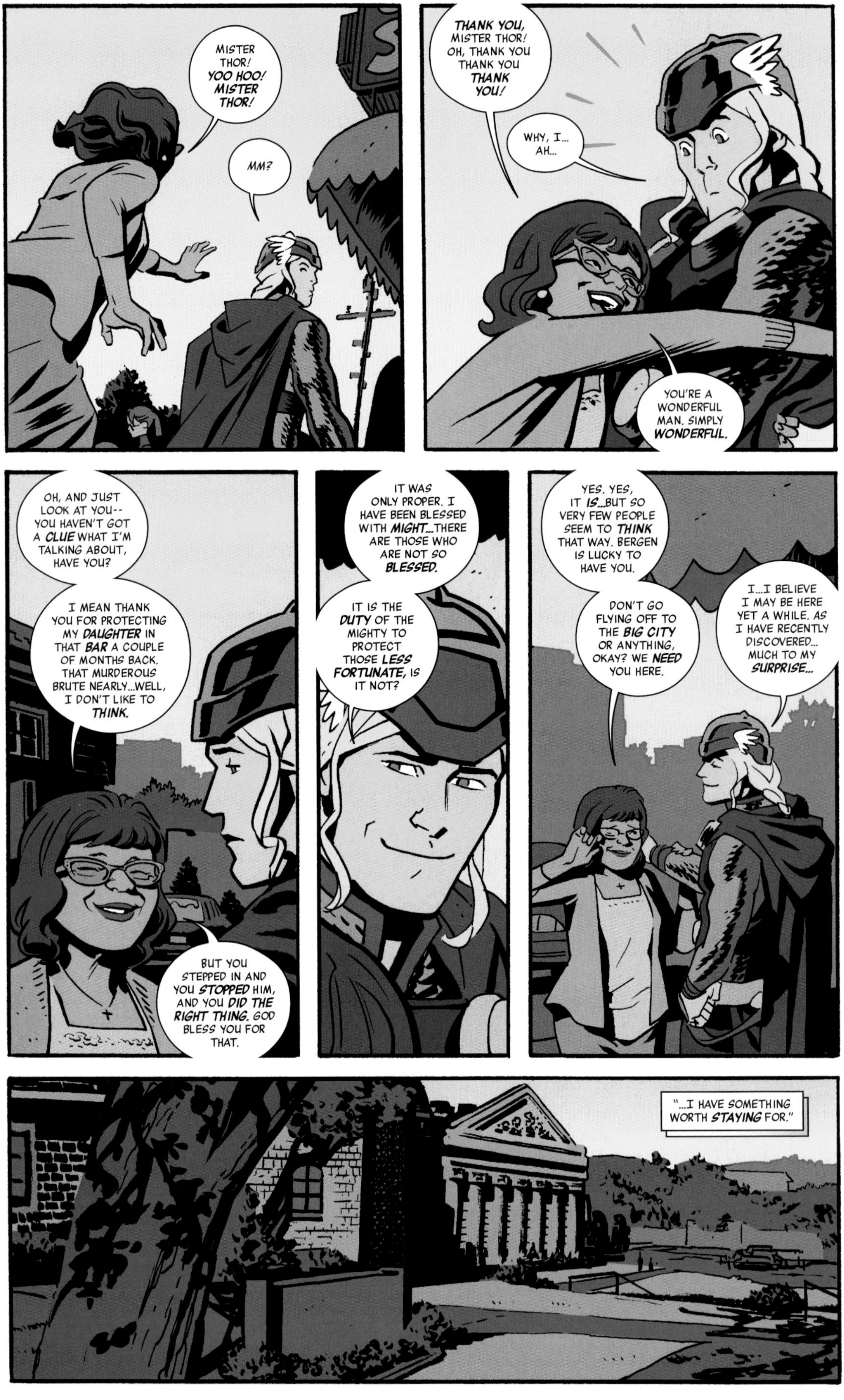
MISTER THOR! YOO HOO! MISTER THOR!
MM?
THANK YOU, MISTER THOR! OH, THANK YOU THANK YOU THANK YOU!
WHY, I... AH...
YOU'RE A WONDERFUL MAN. SIMPLY WONDERFUL.
OH, AND JUST LOOK AT YOU--YOU HAVEN'T GOT A CLUE WHAT I'M TALKING ABOUT, HAVE YOU?
I MEAN THANK YOU FOR PROTECTING MY DAUGHTER IN THAT BAR A COUPLE OF MONTHS BACK. THAT MURDEROUS BRUTE NEARLY...WELL, I DON'T LIKE TO THINK.
BUT YOU STEPPED IN AND YOU STOPPED HIM, AND YOU DID THE RIGHT THING. GOD BLESS YOU FOR THAT.
IT WAS ONLY PROPER. I HAVE BEEN BLESSED WITH MIGHT...THERE ARE THOSE WHO ARE NOT SO BLESSED.
IT IS THE DUTY OF THE MIGHTY TO PROTECT THOSE LESS FORTUNATE, IS IT NOT?
YES. YES, IT IS...BUT SO VERY FEW PEOPLE SEEM TO THINK THAT WAY. BERGEN IS LUCKY TO HAVE YOU.
DON'T GO FLYING OFF TO THE BIG CITY OR ANYTHING, OKAY? WE NEED YOU HERE.
I...I BELIEVE I MAY BE HERE YET A WHILE. AS I HAVE RECENTLY DISCOVERED... MUCH TO MY SURPRISE...
"...I HAVE SOMETHING WORTH STAYING FOR."

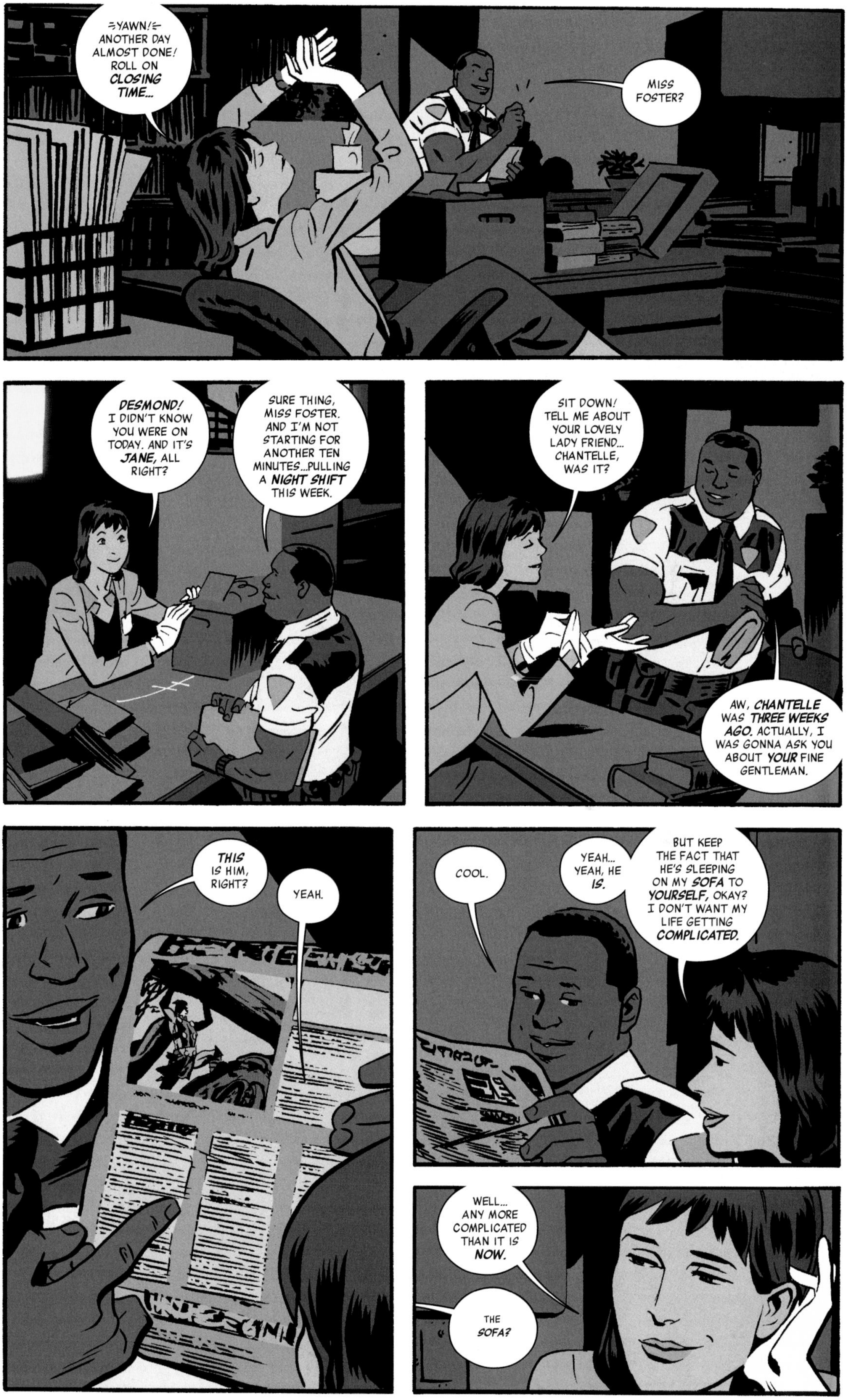

=YAWN!= ANOTHER DAY ALMOST DONE! ROLL ON CLOSING TIME...
MISS FOSTER?
DESMOND! I DIDN'T KNOW YOU WERE ON TODAY. AND IT'S JANE, ALL RIGHT?
SURE THING, MISS FOSTER. AND I'M NOT STARTING FOR ANOTHER TEN MINUTES...PULLING A NIGHT SHIFT THIS WEEK.
SIT DOWN! TELL ME ABOUT YOUR LOVELY LADY FRIEND... CHANTELLE, WAS IT?
AW, CHANTELLE WAS THREE WEEKS AGO. ACTUALLY, I WAS GONNA ASK YOU ABOUT YOUR FINE GENTLEMAN.
THIS IS HIM, RIGHT?
YEAH.
COOL.
YEAH... YEAH, HE IS.
BUT KEEP THE FACT THAT HE'S SLEEPING ON MY SOFA TO YOURSELF, OKAY? I DON'T WANT MY LIFE GETTING COMPLICATED.
WELL... ANY MORE COMPLICATED THAN IT IS NOW.
THE SOFA?

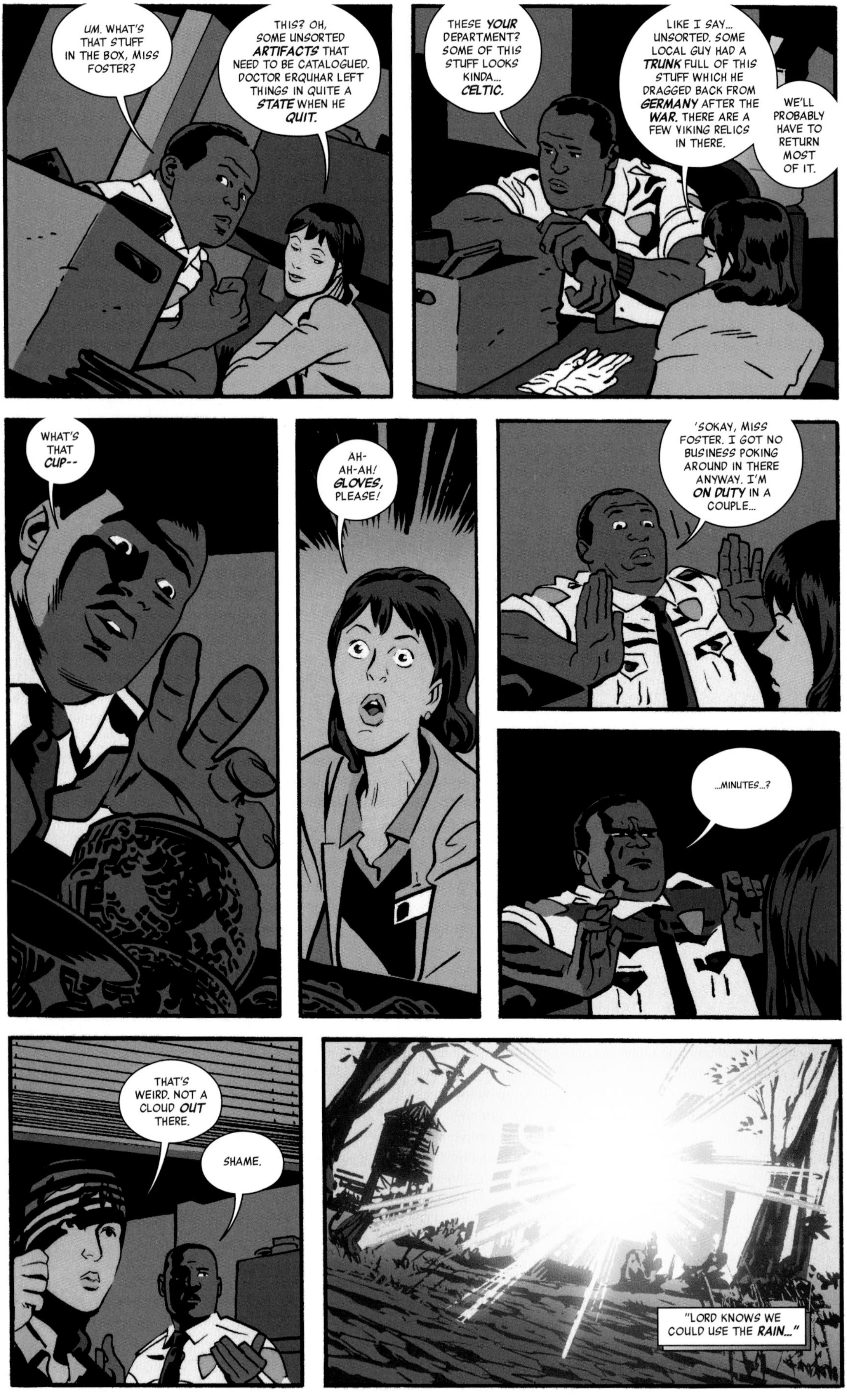
UM. WHAT'S THAT STUFF IN THE BOX, MISS FOSTER?
THIS? OH, SOME UNSORTED ARTIFACTS THAT NEED TO BE CATALOGUED. DOCTOR ERQUHAR LEFT THINGS IN QUITE A STATE WHEN HE QUIT.
THESE YOUR DEPARTMENT? SOME OF THIS STUFF LOOKS KINDA... CELTIC.
LIKE I SAY... UNSORTED. SOME LOCAL GUY HAD A TRUNK FULL OF THIS STUFF WHICH HE DRAGGED BACK FROM GERMANY AFTER THE WAR. THERE ARE A FEW VIKING RELICS IN THERE.
WE'LL PROBABLY HAVE TO RETURN MOST OF IT.
WHAT'S THAT CUP--
AH-AH-AH! GLOVES, PLEASE!
'SOKAY, MISS FOSTER. I GOT NO BUSINESS POKING AROUND IN THERE ANYWAY. I'M ON DUTY IN A COUPLE...
...MINUTES...?
THAT'S WEIRD. NOT A CLOUD OUT THERE.
SHAME.
"LORD KNOWS WE COULD USE THE RAIN..."

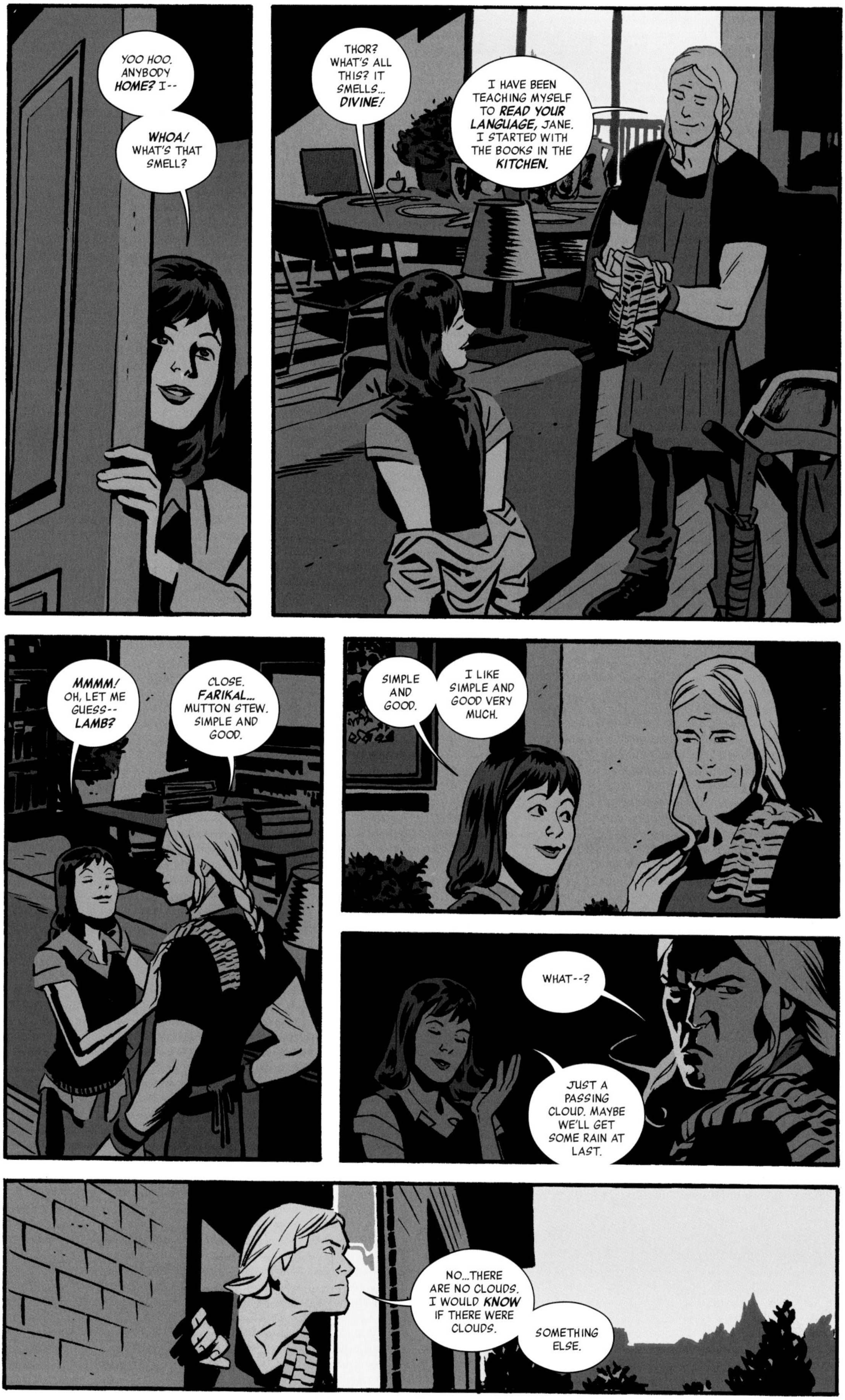
YOO HOO. ANYBODY HOME? I--
WHOA! WHAT'S THAT SMELL?
THOR? WHAT'S ALL THIS? IT SMELLS... DIVINE!
I HAVE BEEN TEACHING MYSELF TO READ YOUR LANGUAGE, JANE. I STARTED WITH THE BOOKS IN THE KITCHEN.
MMMM! OH, LET ME GUESS-- LAMB?
CLOSE. FARIKAL... MUTTON STEW. SIMPLE AND GOOD.
SIMPLE AND GOOD.
I LIKE SIMPLE AND GOOD VERY MUCH.
WHAT--?
JUST A PASSING CLOUD. MAYBE WE'LL GET SOME RAIN AT LAST.
NO...THERE ARE NO CLOUDS. I WOULD KNOW IF THERE WERE CLOUDS.
SOMETHING ELSE.

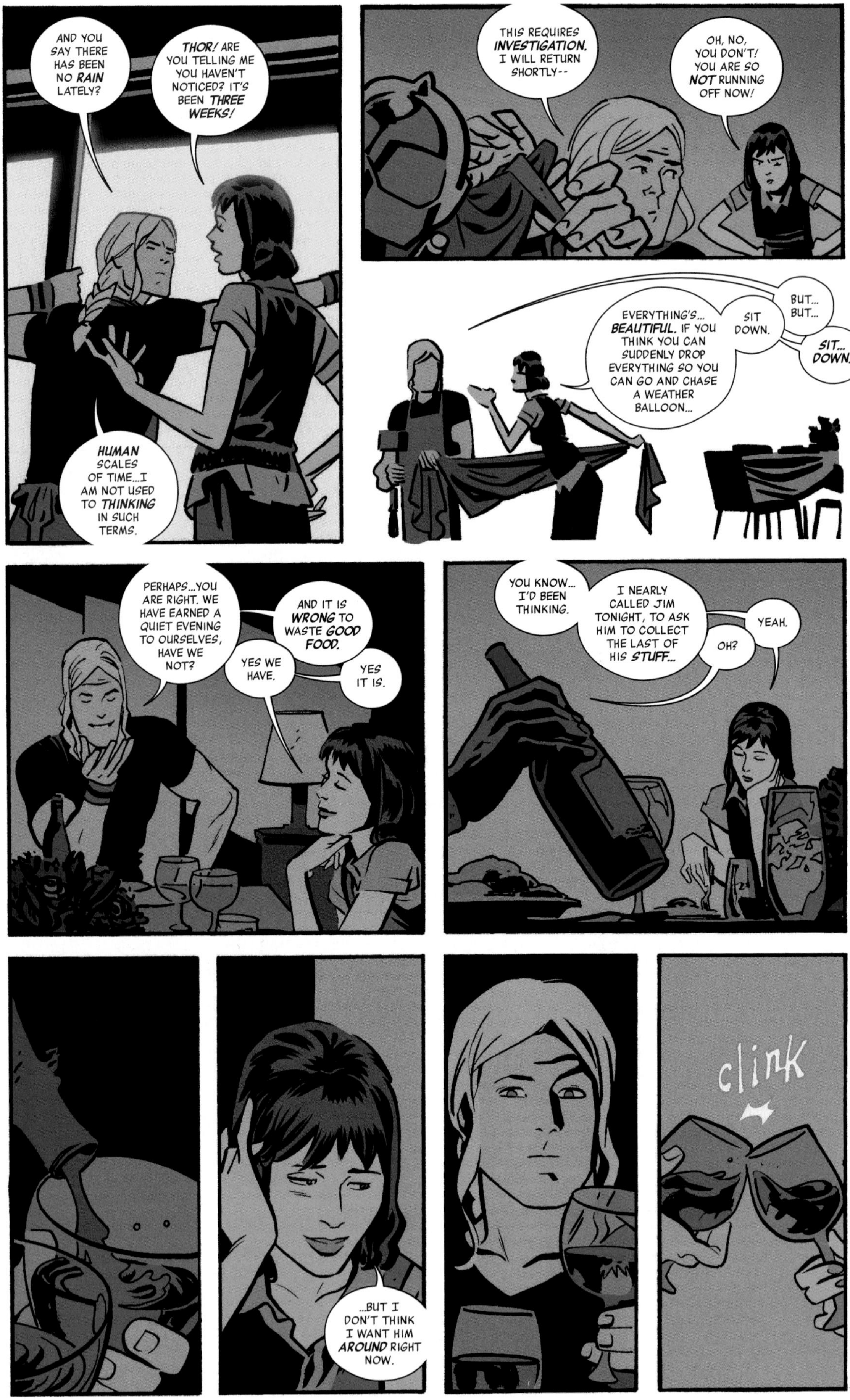
AND YOU SAY THERE HAS BEEN NO RAIN LATELY?
THOR! ARE YOU TELLING ME YOU HAVEN'T NOTICED? IT'S BEEN THREE WEEKS!
HUMAN SCALES OF TIME...I AM NOT USED TO THINKING IN SUCH TERMS.
THIS REQUIRES INVESTIGATION. I WILL RETURN SHORTLY--
OH, NO, YOU DON'T! YOU ARE SO NOT RUNNING OFF NOW!
EVERYTHING'S... BEAUTIFUL. IF YOU THINK YOU CAN SUDDENLY DROP EVERYTHING SO YOU CAN GO AND CHASE A WEATHER BALLOON...
SIT DOWN.
BUT... BUT...
SIT... DOWN.
PERHAPS...YOU ARE RIGHT. WE HAVE EARNED A QUIET EVENING TO OURSELVES, HAVE WE NOT?
YES WE HAVE.
AND IT IS WRONG TO WASTE GOOD FOOD.
YES IT IS.
YOU KNOW... I'D BEEN THINKING.
I NEARLY CALLED JIM TONIGHT, TO ASK HIM TO COLLECT THE LAST OF HIS STUFF...
OH?
YEAH.
...BUT I DON'T THINK I WANT HIM AROUND RIGHT NOW.
clink

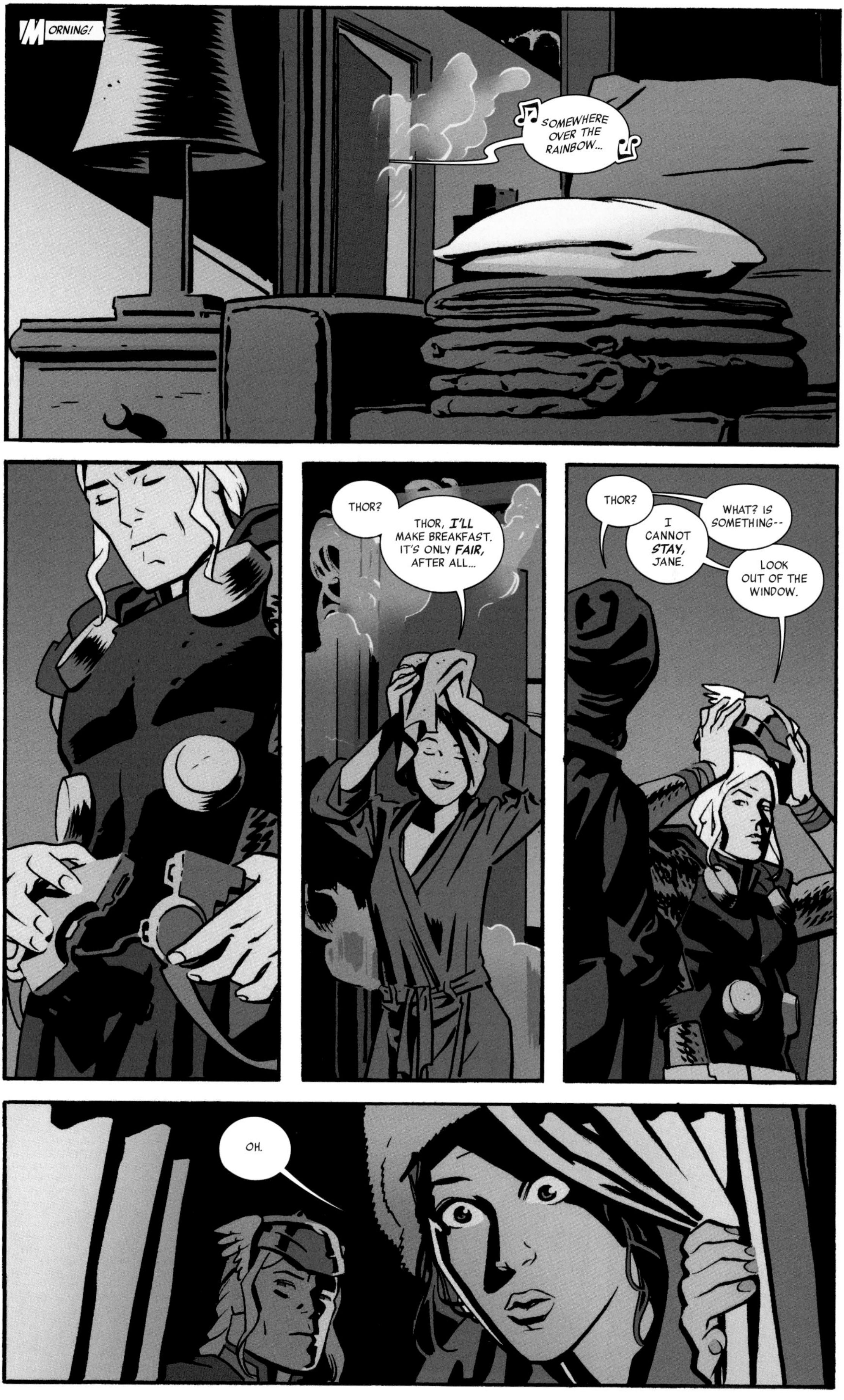
MORNING!
SOMEWHERE OVER THE RAINBOW...
THOR?
THOR, I'LL MAKE BREAKFAST. IT'S ONLY FAIR, AFTER ALL...
THOR?
WHAT? IS SOMETHING--
I CANNOT STAY, JANE.
LOOK OUT OF THE WINDOW.
OH.

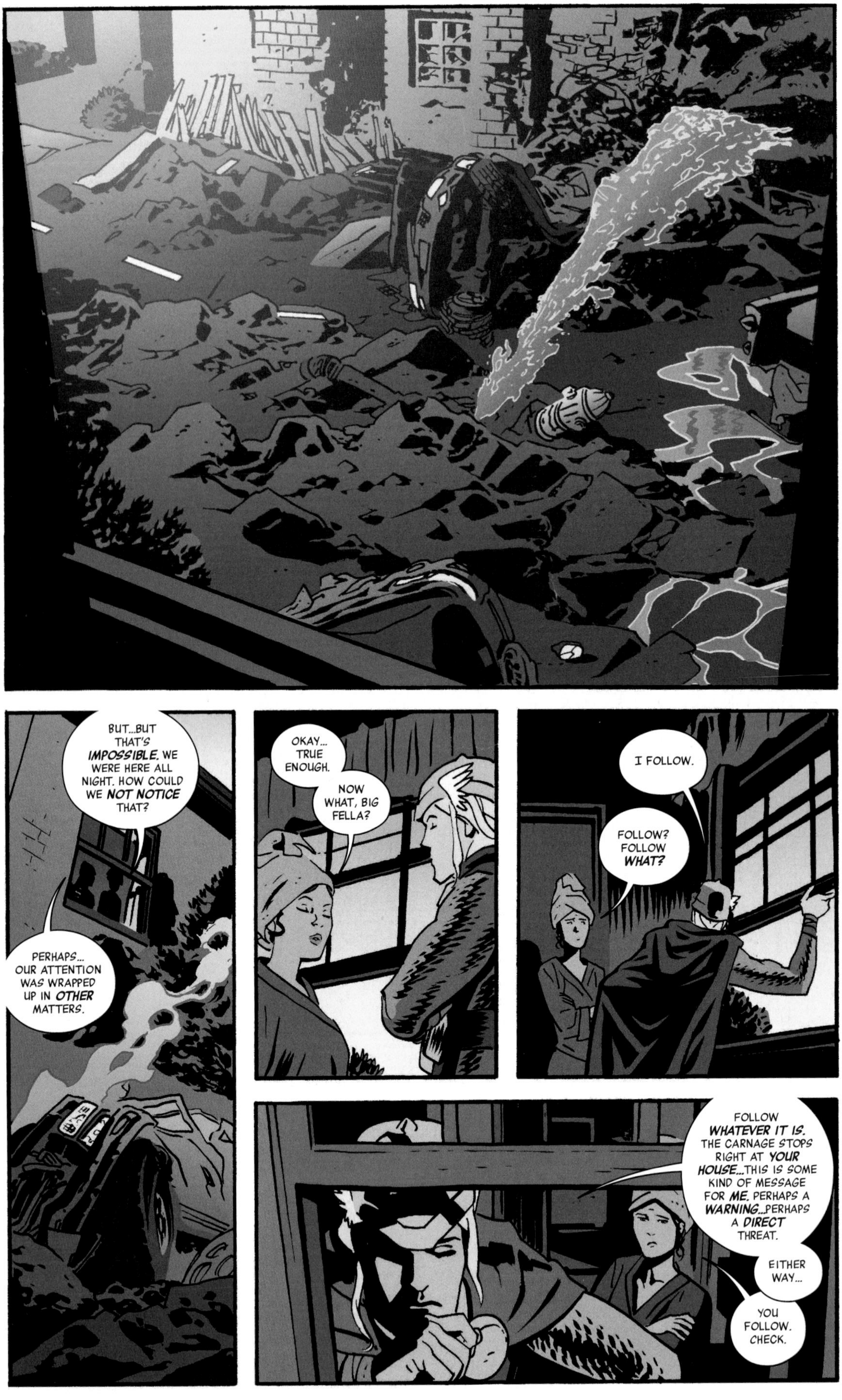
BUT...BUT THAT'S IMPOSSIBLE. WE WERE HERE ALL NIGHT. HOW COULD WE NOT NOTICE THAT?
PERHAPS... OUR ATTENTION WAS WRAPPED UP IN OTHER MATTERS.
OKAY... TRUE ENOUGH.
NOW WHAT, BIG FELLA?
I FOLLOW.
FOLLOW? FOLLOW WHAT?
FOLLOW WHATEVER IT IS. THE CARNAGE STOPS RIGHT AT YOUR HOUSE...THIS IS SOME KIND OF MESSAGE FOR ME. PERHAPS A WARNING...PERHAPS A DIRECT THREAT.
EITHER WAY...
YOU FOLLOW. CHECK.

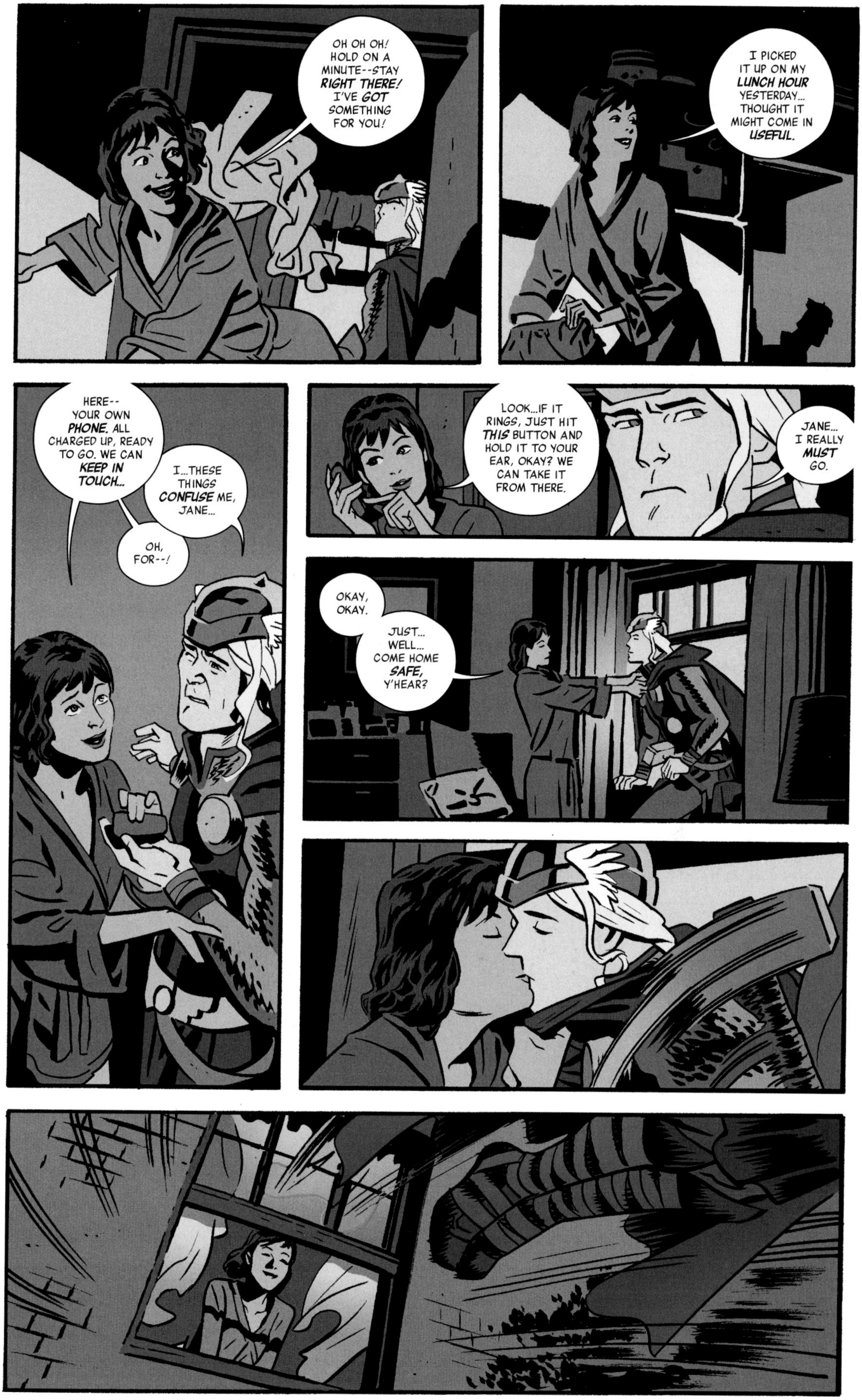
OH OH OH! HOLD ON A MINUTE--STAY RIGHT THERE! I'VE GOT SOMETHING FOR YOU!
I PICKED IT UP ON MY LUNCH HOUR YESTERDAY... THOUGHT IT MIGHT COME IN USEFUL.
HERE-- YOUR OWN PHONE. ALL CHARGED UP, READY TO GO. WE CAN KEEP IN TOUCH...
I...THESE THINGS CONFUSE ME, JANE...
OH, FOR--!
LOOK...IF IT RINGS, JUST HIT THIS BUTTON AND HOLD IT TO YOUR EAR, OKAY? WE CAN TAKE IT FROM THERE.
JANE... I REALLY MUST GO.
OKAY, OKAY.
JUST... WELL... COME HOME SAFE, Y'HEAR?

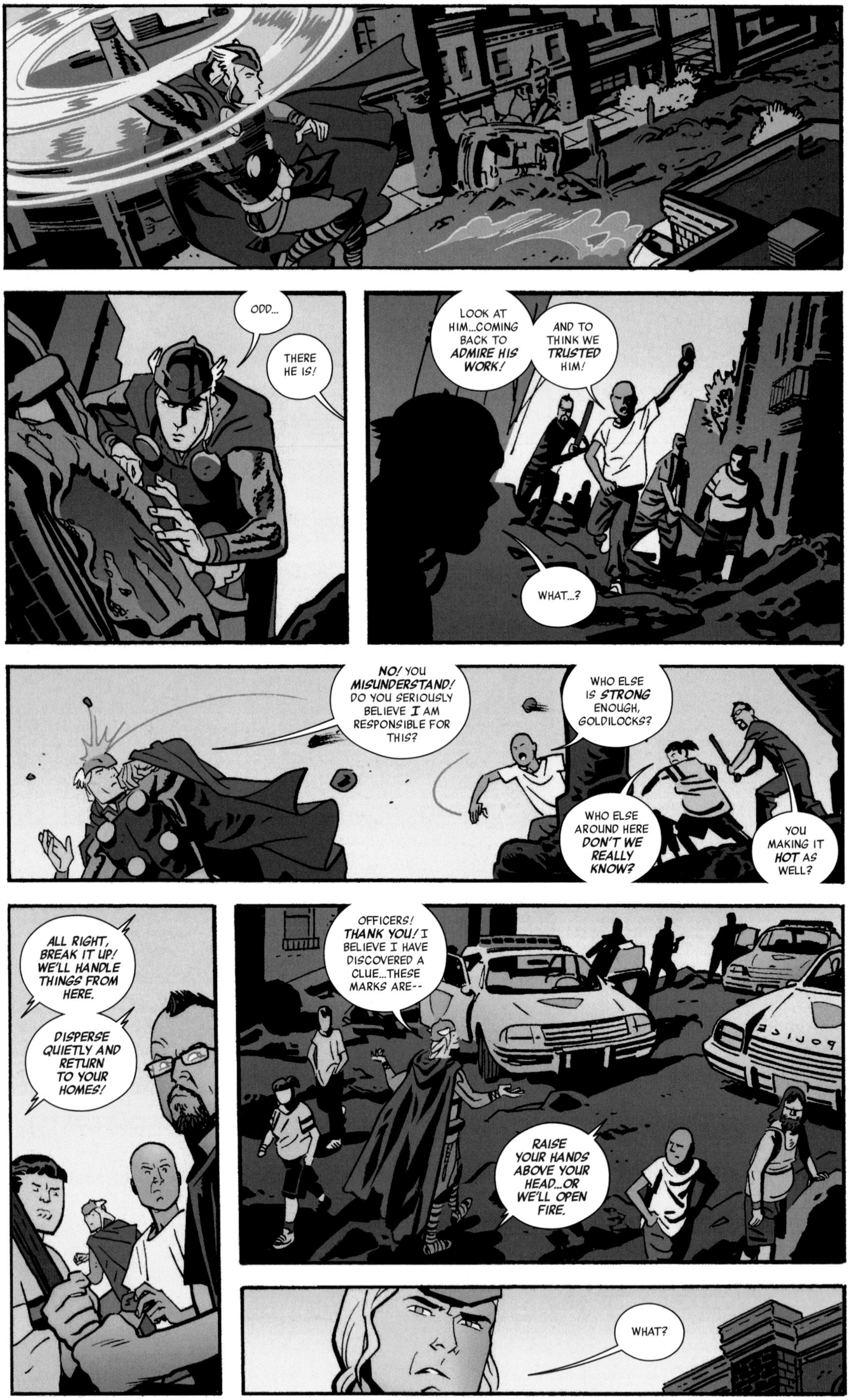
ODD...
THERE HE IS!
LOOK AT HIM...COMING BACK TO ADMIRE HIS WORK!
AND TO THINK WE TRUSTED HIM!
WHAT...?
NO! YOU MISUNDERSTAND! DO YOU SERIOUSLY BELIEVE I AM RESPONSIBLE FOR THIS?
WHO ELSE IS STRONG ENOUGH, GOLDILOCKS?
WHO ELSE AROUND HERE DON'T WE REALLY KNOW?
YOU MAKING IT HOT AS WELL?
ALL RIGHT, BREAK IT UP! WE'LL HANDLE THINGS FROM HERE.
DISPERSE QUIETLY AND RETURN TO YOUR HOMES!
OFFICERS! THANK YOU! I BELIEVE I HAVE DISCOVERED A CLUE...THESE MARKS ARE--
RAISE YOUR HANDS ABOVE YOUR HEAD...OR WE'LL OPEN FIRE.
WHAT?

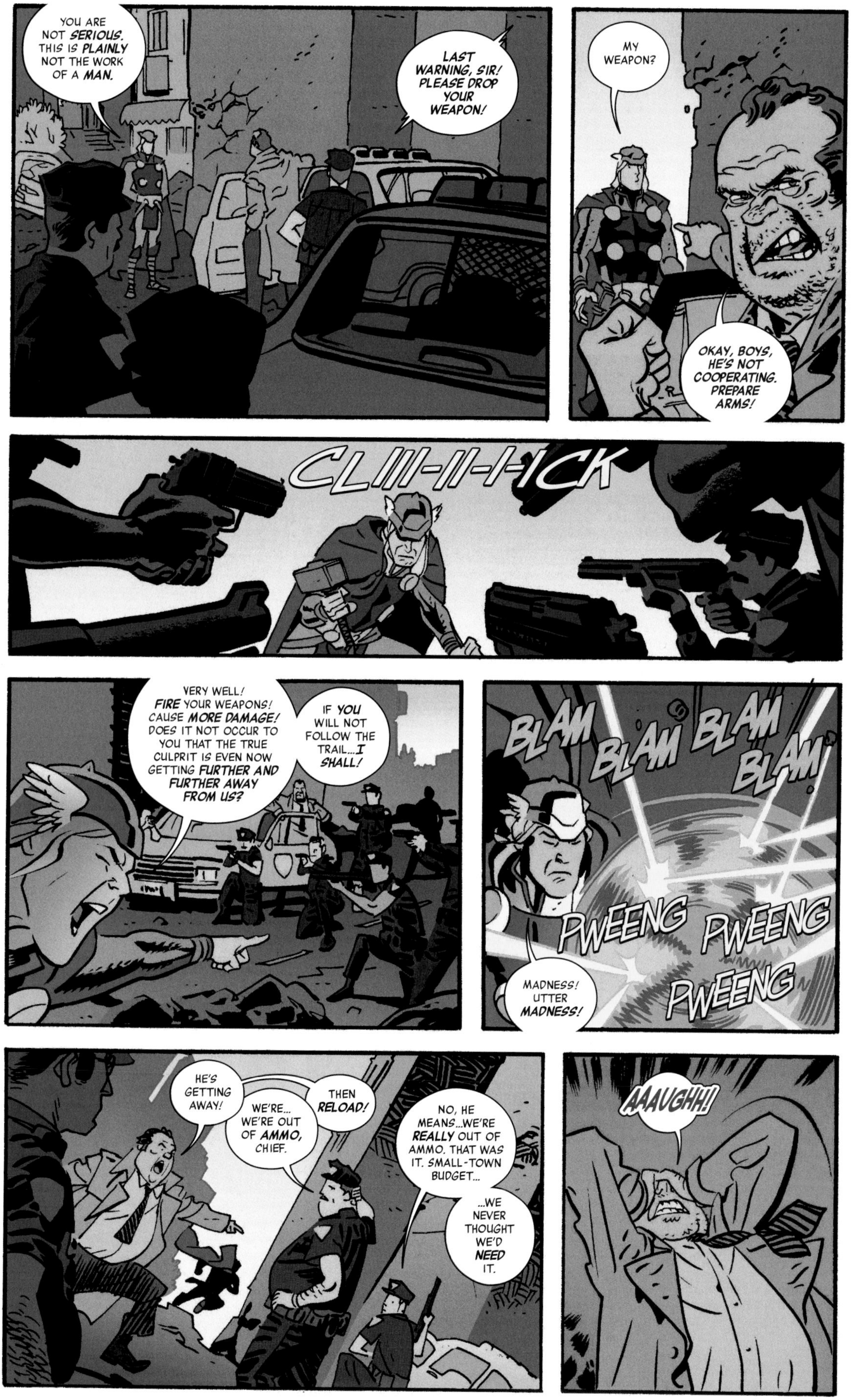
YOU ARE NOT SERIOUS. THIS IS PLAINLY NOT THE WORK OF A MAN.
LAST WARNING, SIR! PLEASE DROP YOUR WEAPON!
MY WEAPON?
OKAY, BOYS, HE'S NOT COOPERATING. PREPARE ARMS!
CLIII-II-I-ICK
VERY WELL! FIRE YOUR WEAPONS! CAUSE MORE DAMAGE! DOES IT NOT OCCUR TO YOU THAT THE TRUE CULPRIT IS EVEN NOW GETTING FURTHER AND FURTHER AWAY FROM US?
IF YOU WILL NOT FOLLOW THE TRAIL...I SHALL!
BLAM BLAM BLAM BLAM
PWEENG PWEENG PWEENG
MADNESS! UTTER MADNESS!
HE'S GETTING AWAY!
THEN RELOAD!
WE'RE... WE'RE OUT OF AMMO, CHIEF.
NO, HE MEANS...WE'RE REALLY OUT OF AMMO. THAT WAS IT. SMALL-TOWN BUDGET...
...WE NEVER THOUGHT WE'D NEED IT.
AAAUGHH!

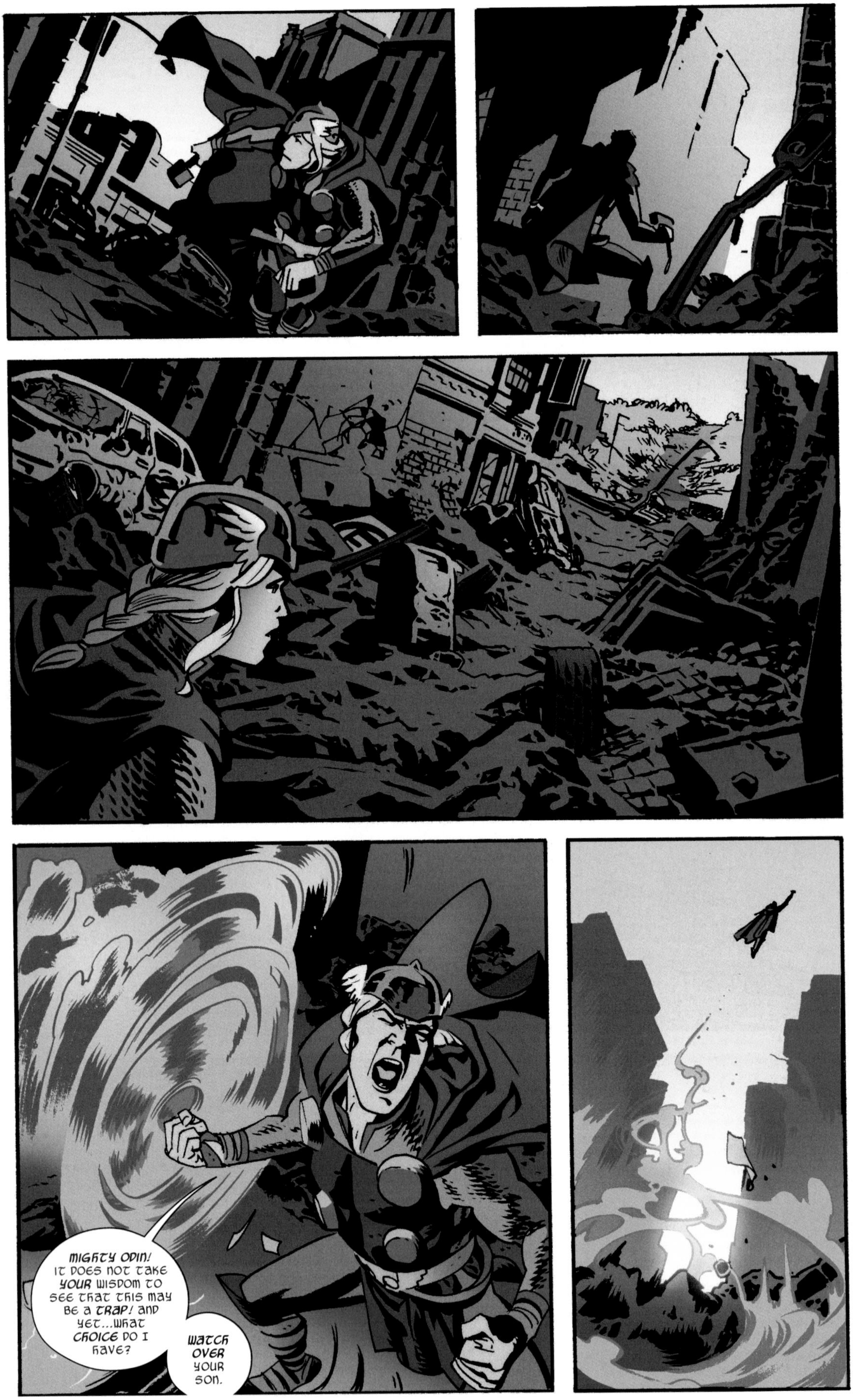

MIGHTY ODIN! IT DOES NOT TAKE YOUR WISDOM TO SEE THAT THIS MAY BE A TRAP! AND YET...WHAT CHOICE DO I HAVE?
WATCH OVER YOUR SON.

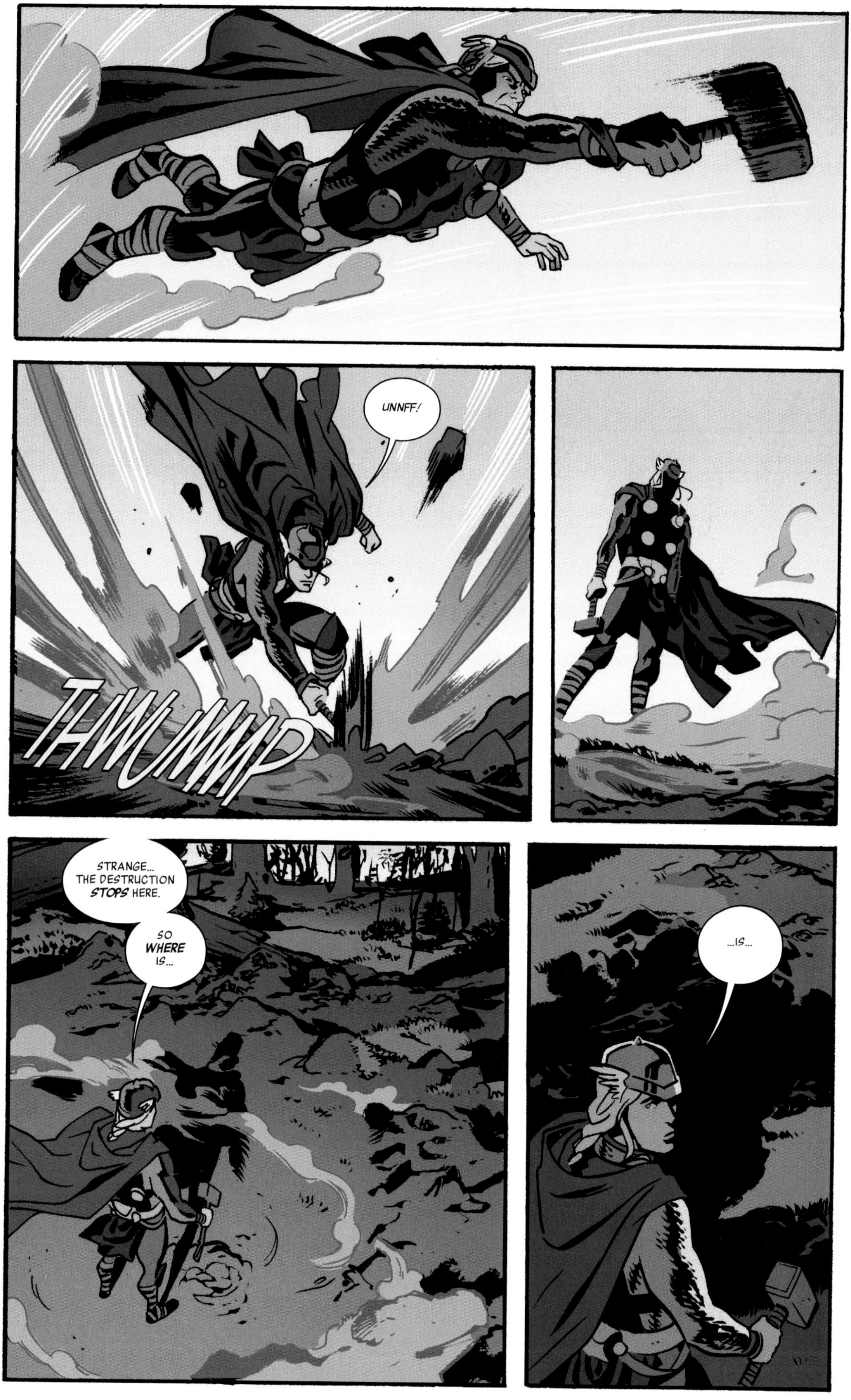
UNNFF!
THWUMMP
STRANGE... THE DESTRUCTION STOPS HERE.
SO WHERE IS...
...IS...

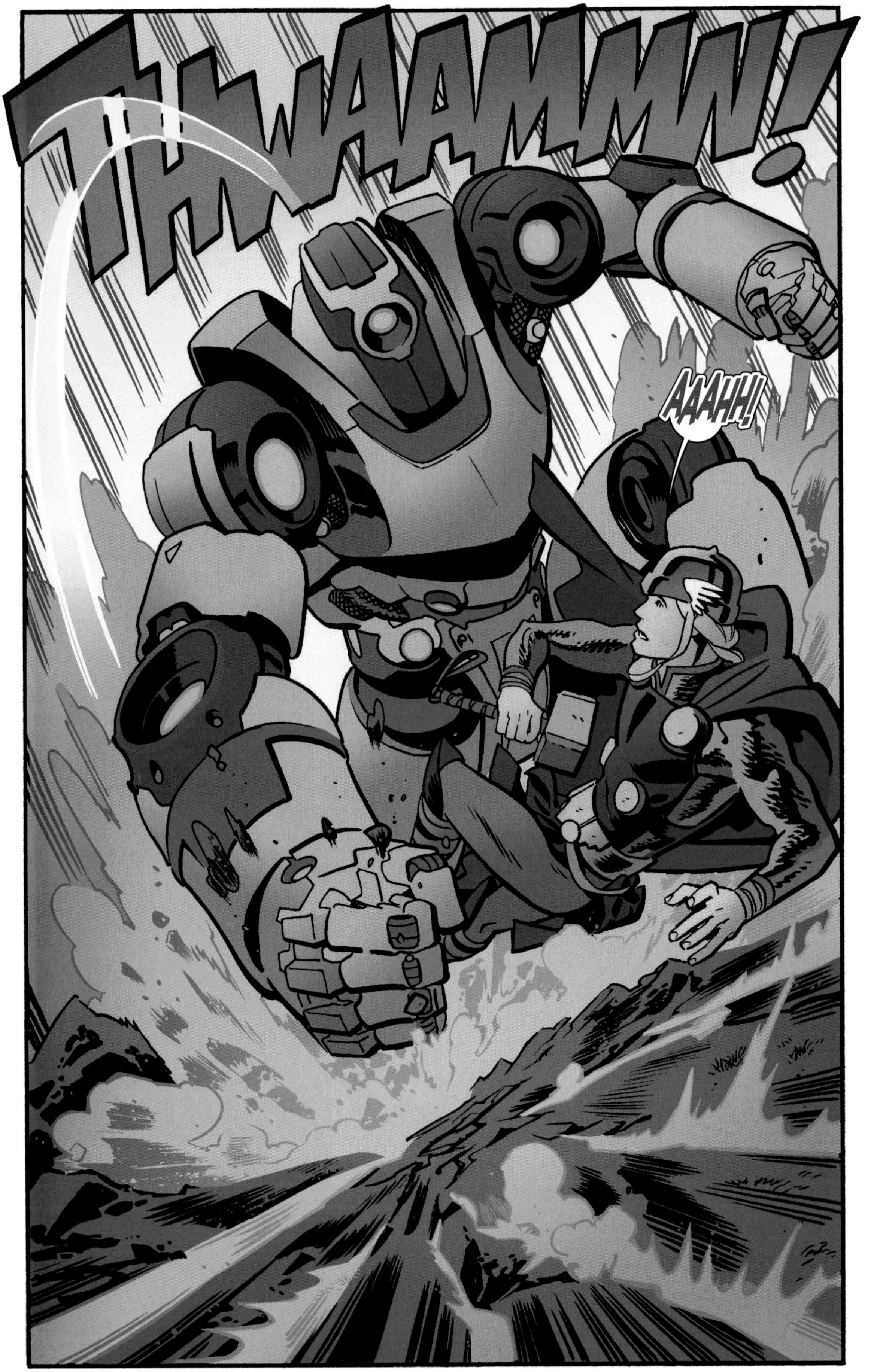
THWAAMMN!
AAAHH!

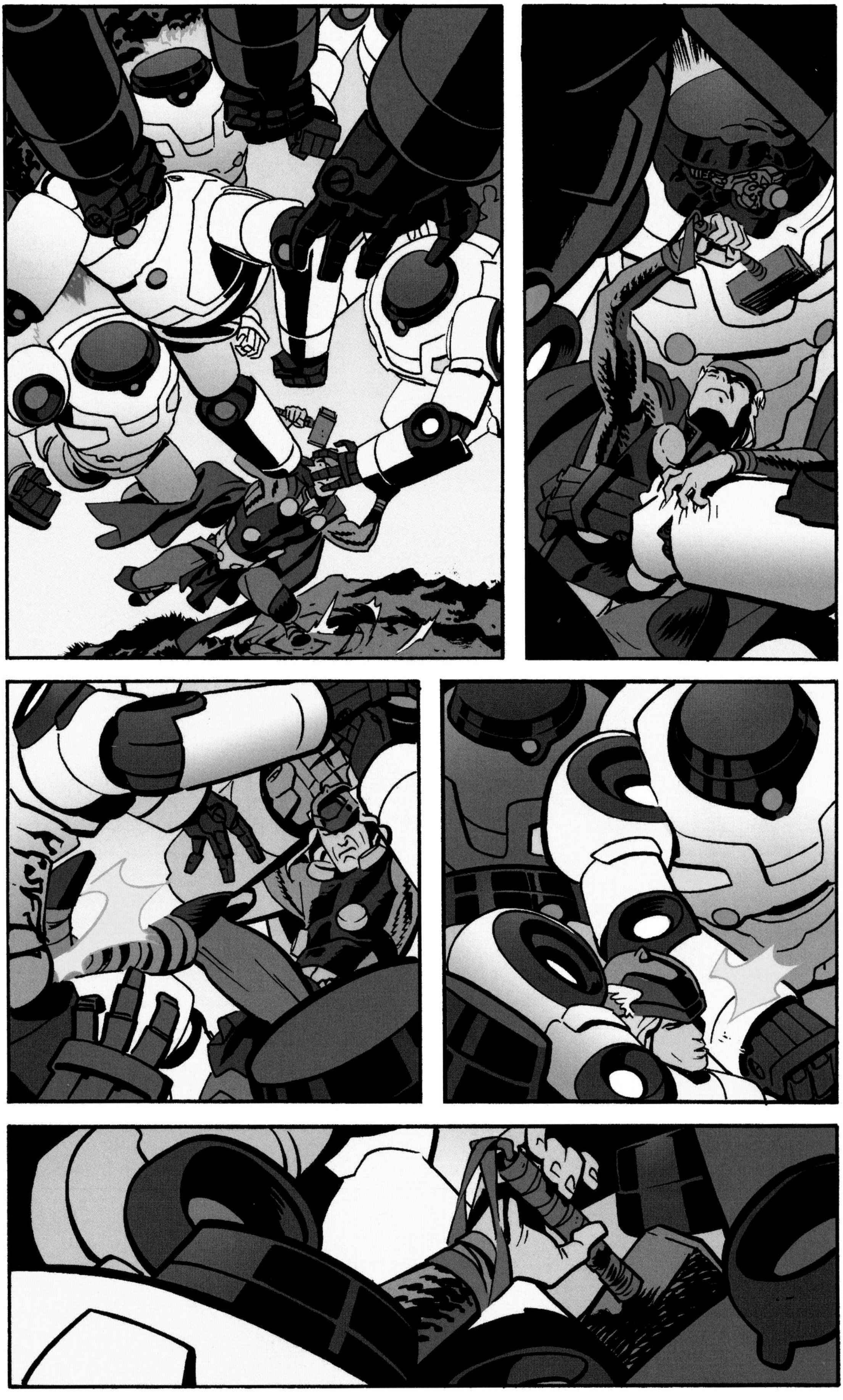

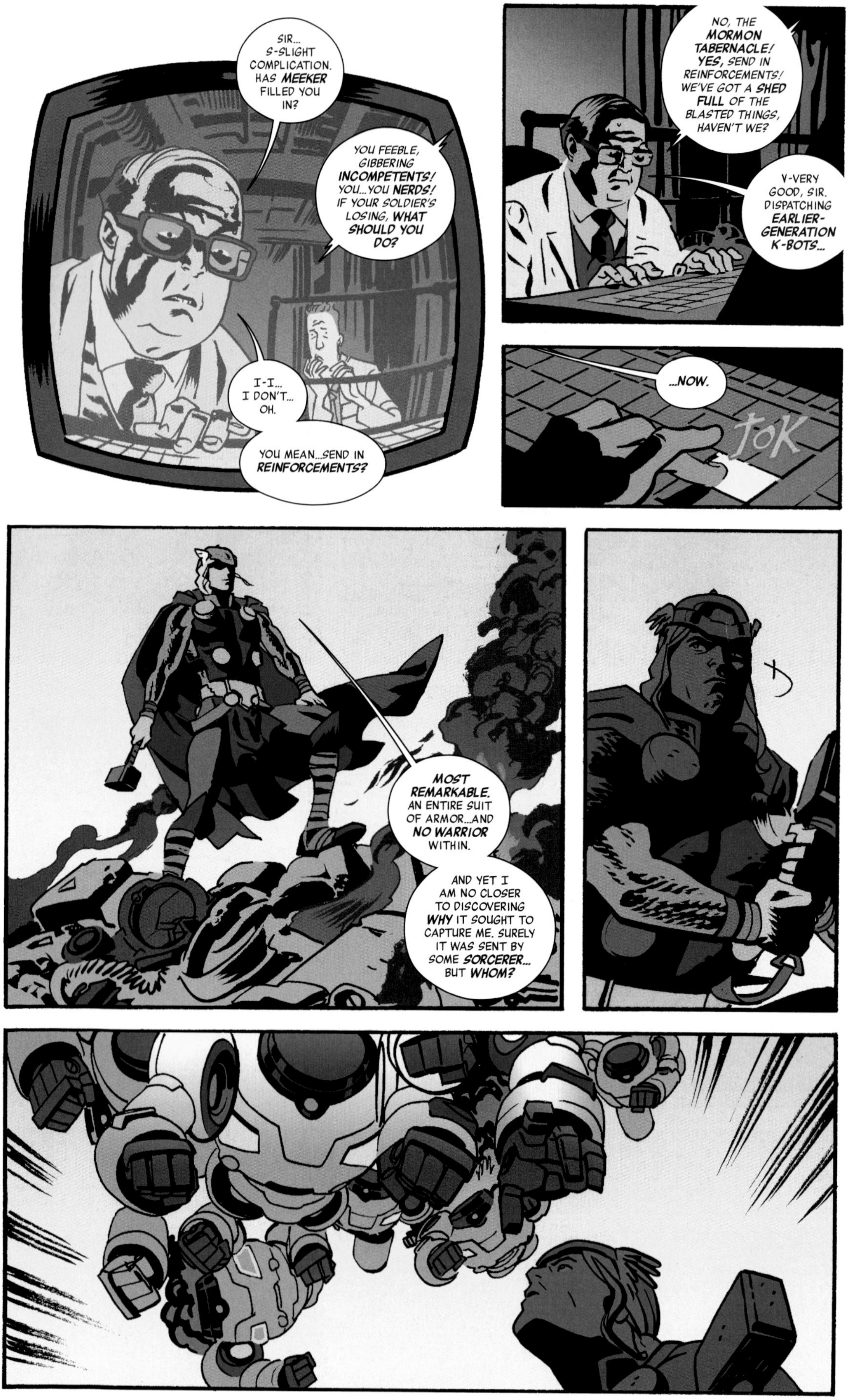
SIR... S-SLIGHT COMPLICATION. HAS MEEKER FILLED YOU IN?
YOU FEEBLE, GIBBERING INCOMPETENTS! YOU...YOU NERDS! IF YOUR SOLDIER'S LOSING, WHAT SHOULD YOU DO?
I-I... I DON'T... OH.
YOU MEAN...SEND IN REINFORCEMENTS?
NO, THE MORMON TABERNACLE! YES, SEND IN REINFORCEMENTS! WE'VE GOT A SHED FULL OF THE BLASTED THINGS, HAVEN'T WE?
V-VERY GOOD, SIR. DISPATCHING EARLIER-GENERATION K-BOTS...
...NOW.
TOK
MOST REMARKABLE. AN ENTIRE SUIT OF ARMOR...AND NO WARRIOR WITHIN.
AND YET I AM NO CLOSER TO DISCOVERING WHY IT SOUGHT TO CAPTURE ME. SURELY IT WAS SENT BY SOME SORCERER... BUT WHOM?

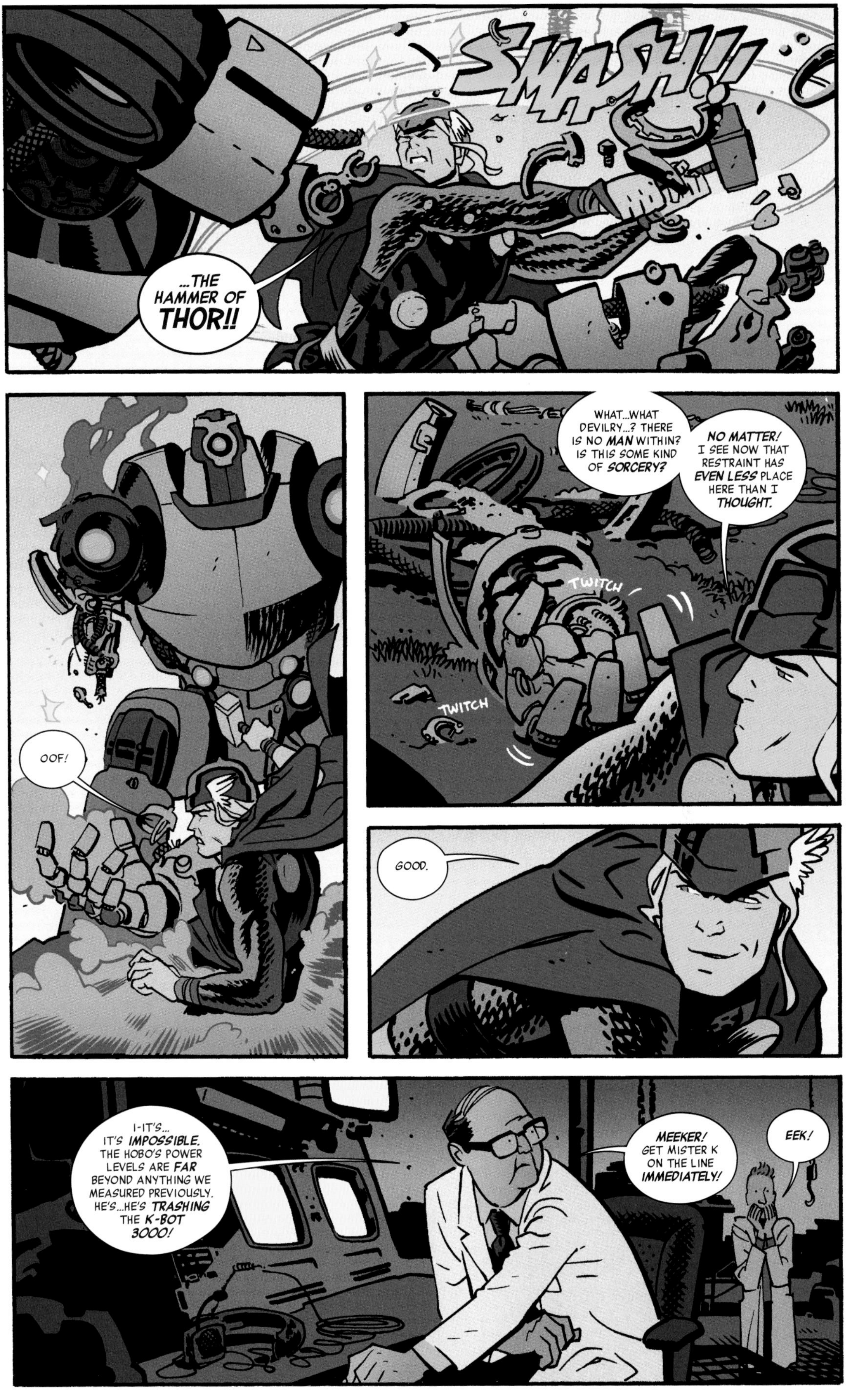
SMASH!!
...THE HAMMER OF THOR!!
OOF!
WHAT...WHAT DEVILRY...? THERE IS NO MAN WITHIN? IS THIS SOME KIND OF SORCERY?
NO MATTER! I SEE NOW THAT RESTRAINT HAS EVEN LESS PLACE HERE THAN I THOUGHT.
TWITCH
TWITCH
GOOD.
I-IT'S... IT'S IMPOSSIBLE. THE HOBO'S POWER LEVELS ARE FAR BEYOND ANYTHING WE MEASURED PREVIOUSLY. HE'S...HE'S TRASHING THE K-BOT 3000!
MEEKER! GET MISTER K ON THE LINE IMMEDIATELY!
EEK!

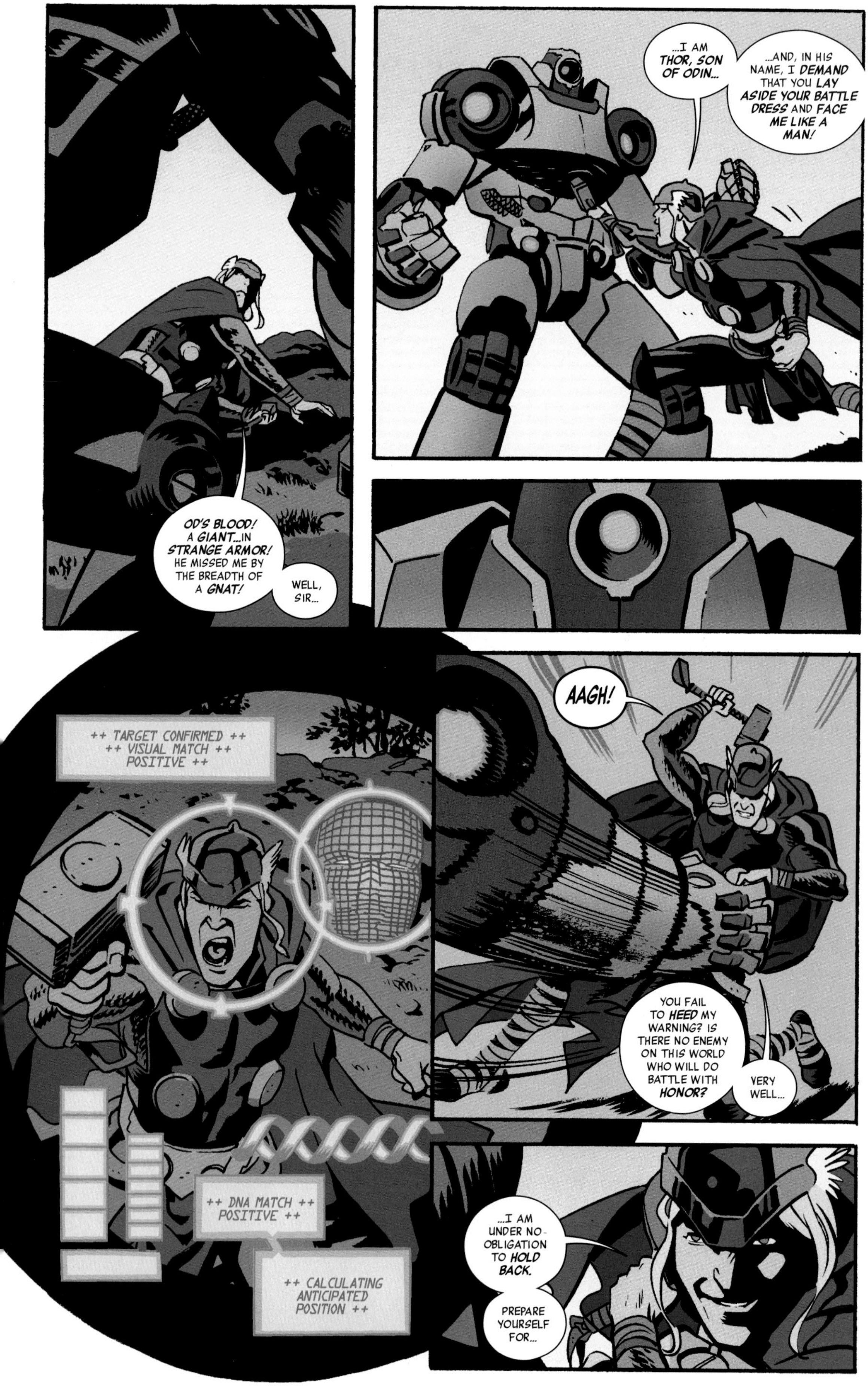
OD'S BLOOD! A GIANT...IN STRANGE ARMOR! HE MISSED ME BY THE BREADTH OF A GNAT!
WELL, SIR...
...I AM THOR, SON OF ODIN...
...AND, IN HIS NAME, I DEMAND THAT YOU LAY ASIDE YOUR BATTLE DRESS AND FACE ME LIKE A MAN!
++ TARGET CONFIRMED ++ ++ VISUAL MATCH ++ POSITIVE ++
++ DNA MATCH ++ POSITIVE ++
++ CALCULATING ANTICIPATED POSITION ++
AAGH!
YOU FAIL TO HEED MY WARNING? IS THERE NO ENEMY ON THIS WORLD WHO WILL DO BATTLE WITH HONOR?
VERY WELL...
...I AM UNDER NO-OBLIGATION TO HOLD BACK.
PREPARE YOURSELF FOR...

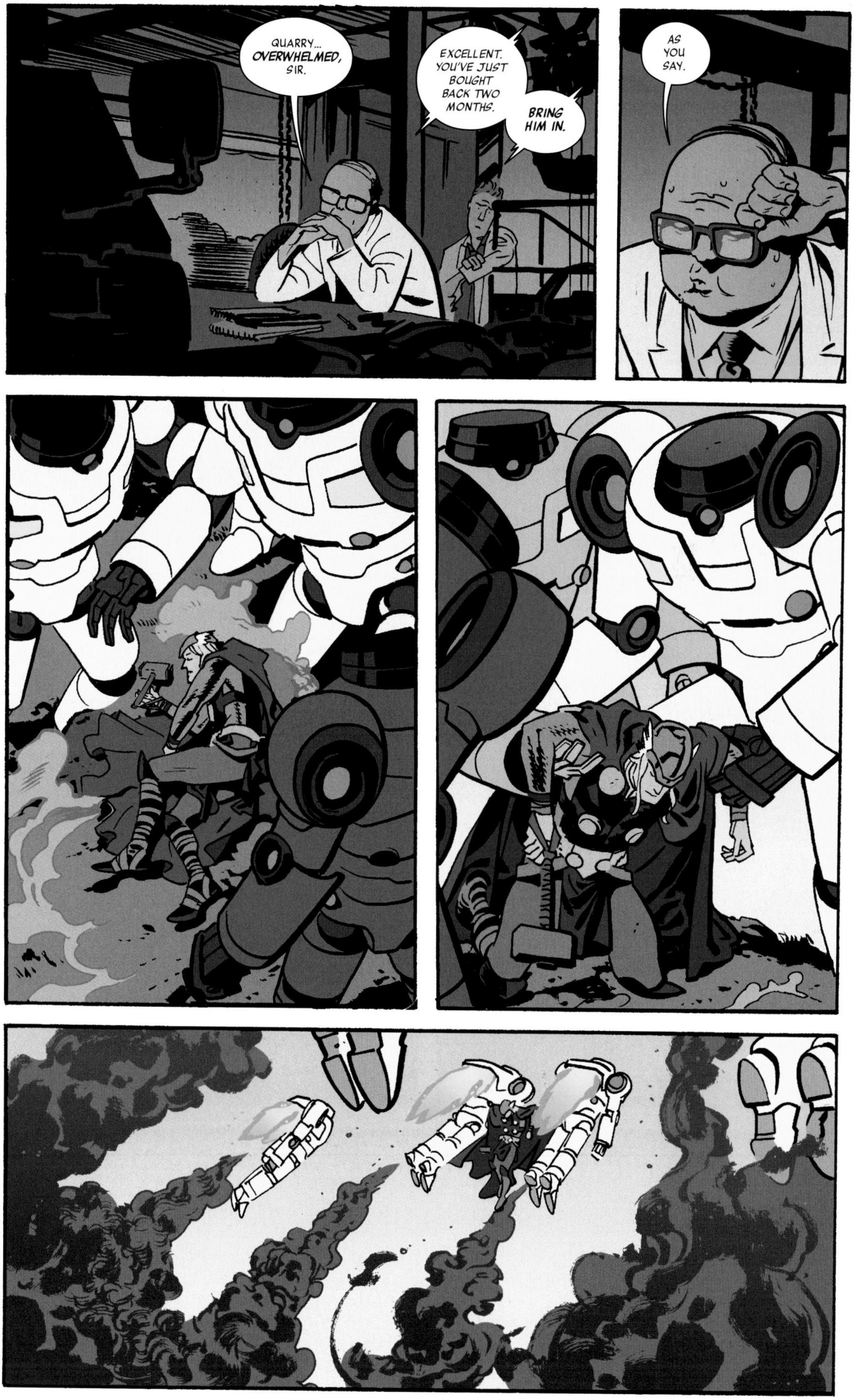
QUARRY... OVERWHELMED, SIR.
EXCELLENT. YOU'VE JUST BOUGHT BACK TWO MONTHS.
BRING HIM IN.
AS YOU SAY.

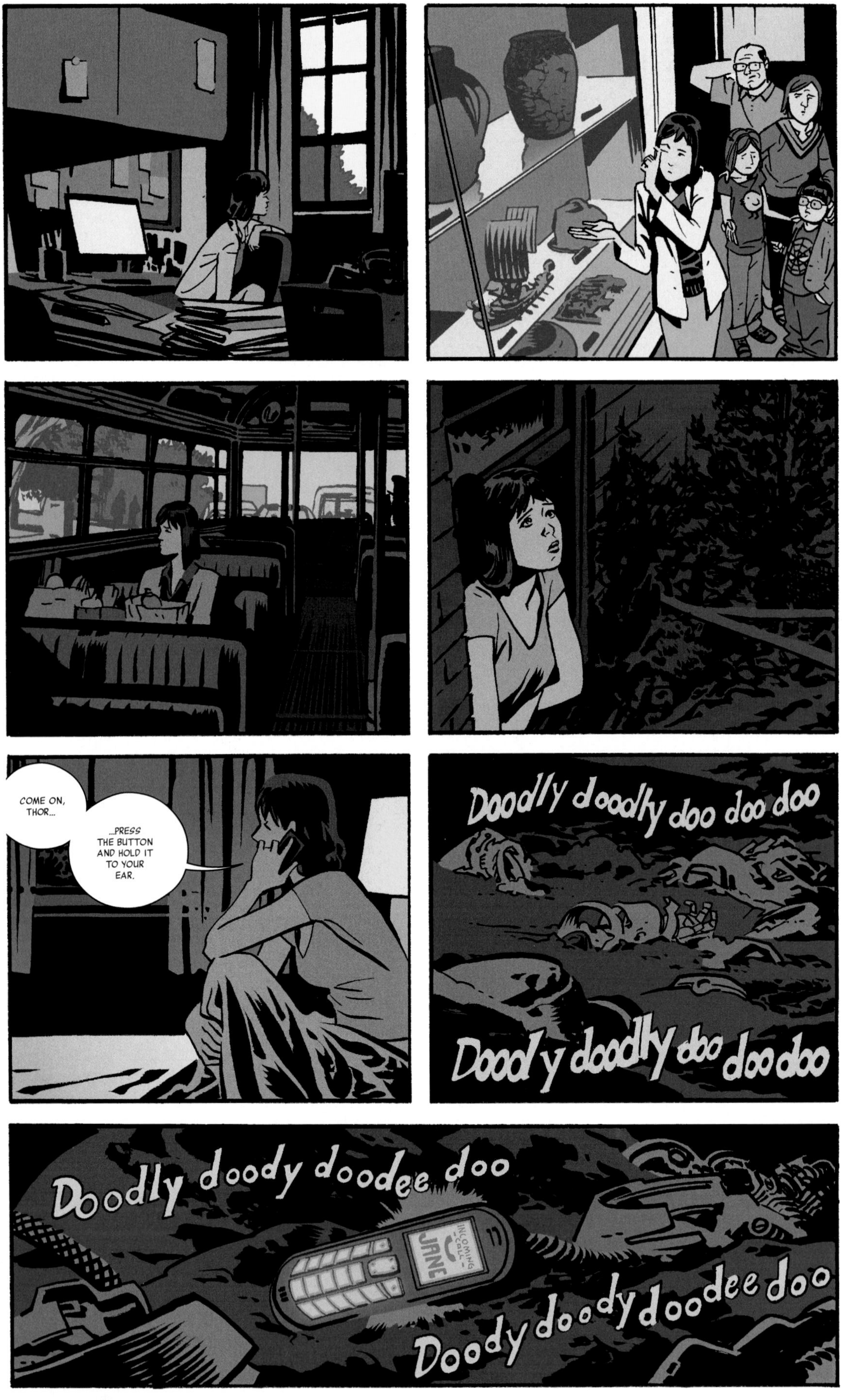
COME ON, THOR...
...PRESS THE BUTTON AND HOLD IT TO YOUR EAR.
Doodly doodly doo doo doo
Doodly doodly doo doo doo
Doodly doody doodee doo
INCOMING CALL
JANE
Doody doody doodee doo

THOR THE MIGHTY AVENGER #8

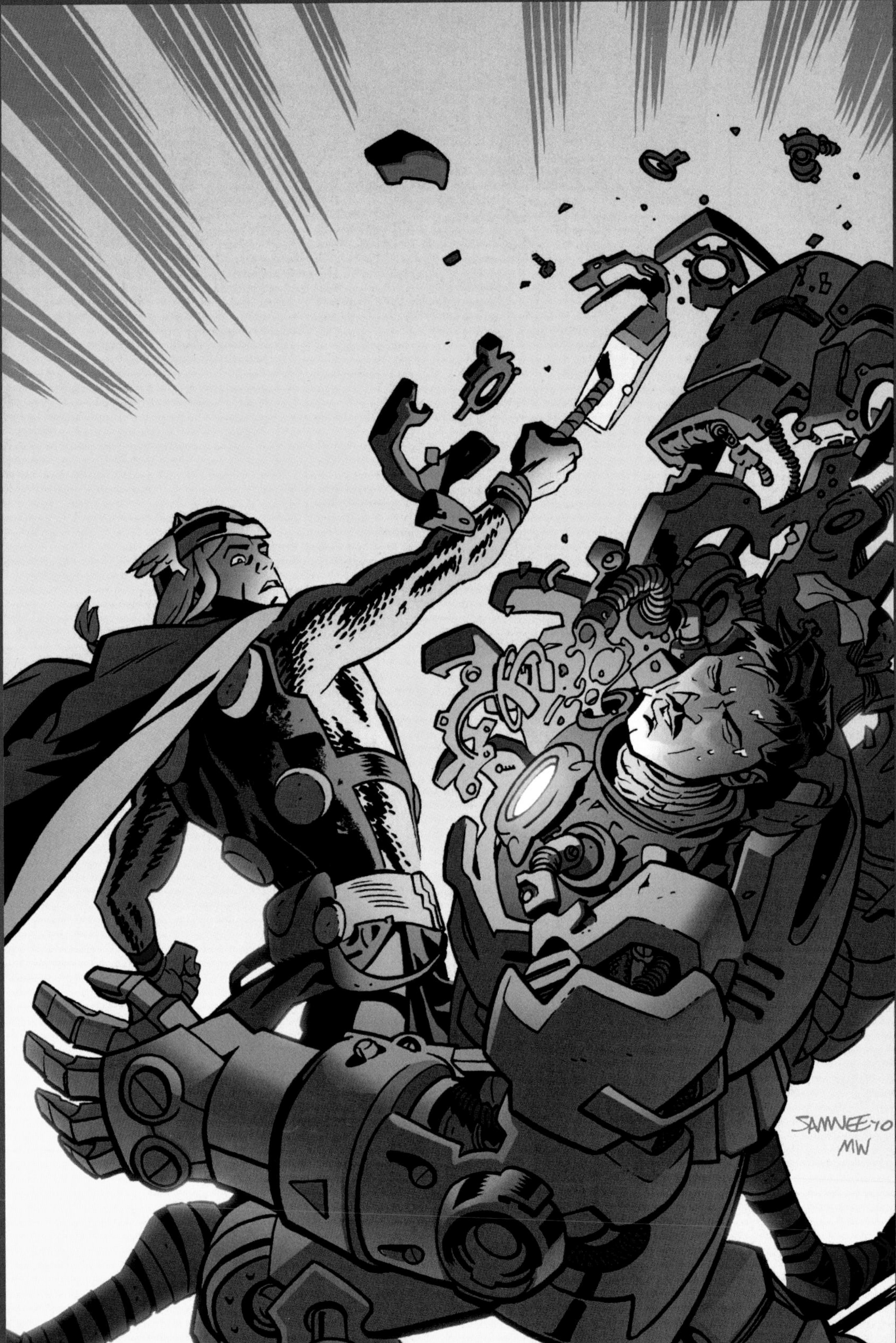
SAMNEE '10
MW

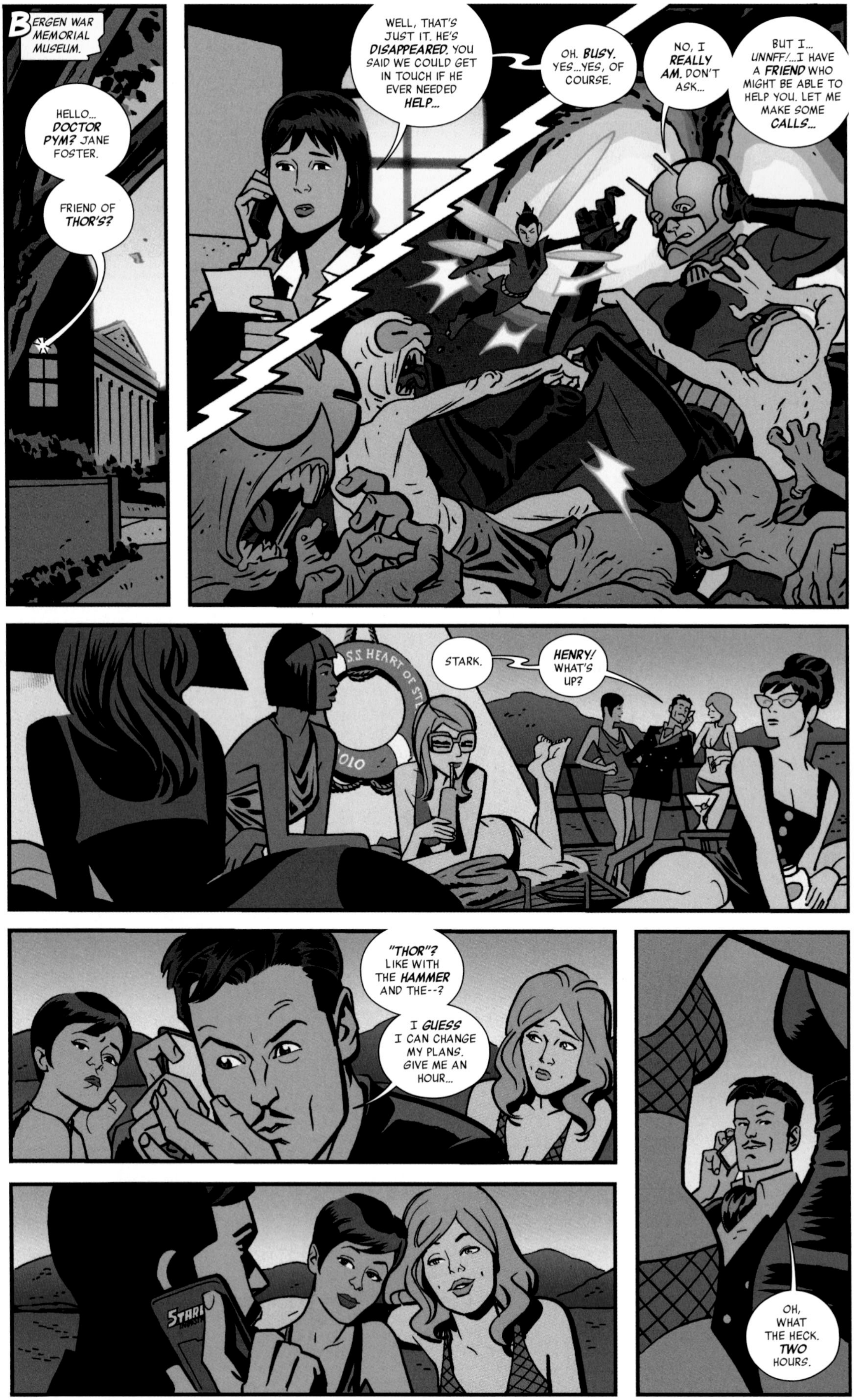
BERGEN WAR MEMORIAL MUSEUM.
HELLO... DOCTOR PYM? JANE FOSTER.
FRIEND OF THOR'S?
WELL, THAT'S JUST IT. HE'S DISAPPEARED. YOU SAID WE COULD GET IN TOUCH IF HE EVER NEEDED HELP...
OH. BUSY. YES...YES, OF COURSE.
NO, I REALLY AM. DON'T ASK...
BUT I... UNNFF!...I HAVE A FRIEND WHO MIGHT BE ABLE TO HELP YOU. LET ME MAKE SOME CALLS...
STARK.
HENRY! WHAT'S UP?
"THOR"? LIKE WITH THE HAMMER AND THE--?
I GUESS I CAN CHANGE MY PLANS. GIVE ME AN HOUR...
OH, WHAT THE HECK. TWO HOURS.

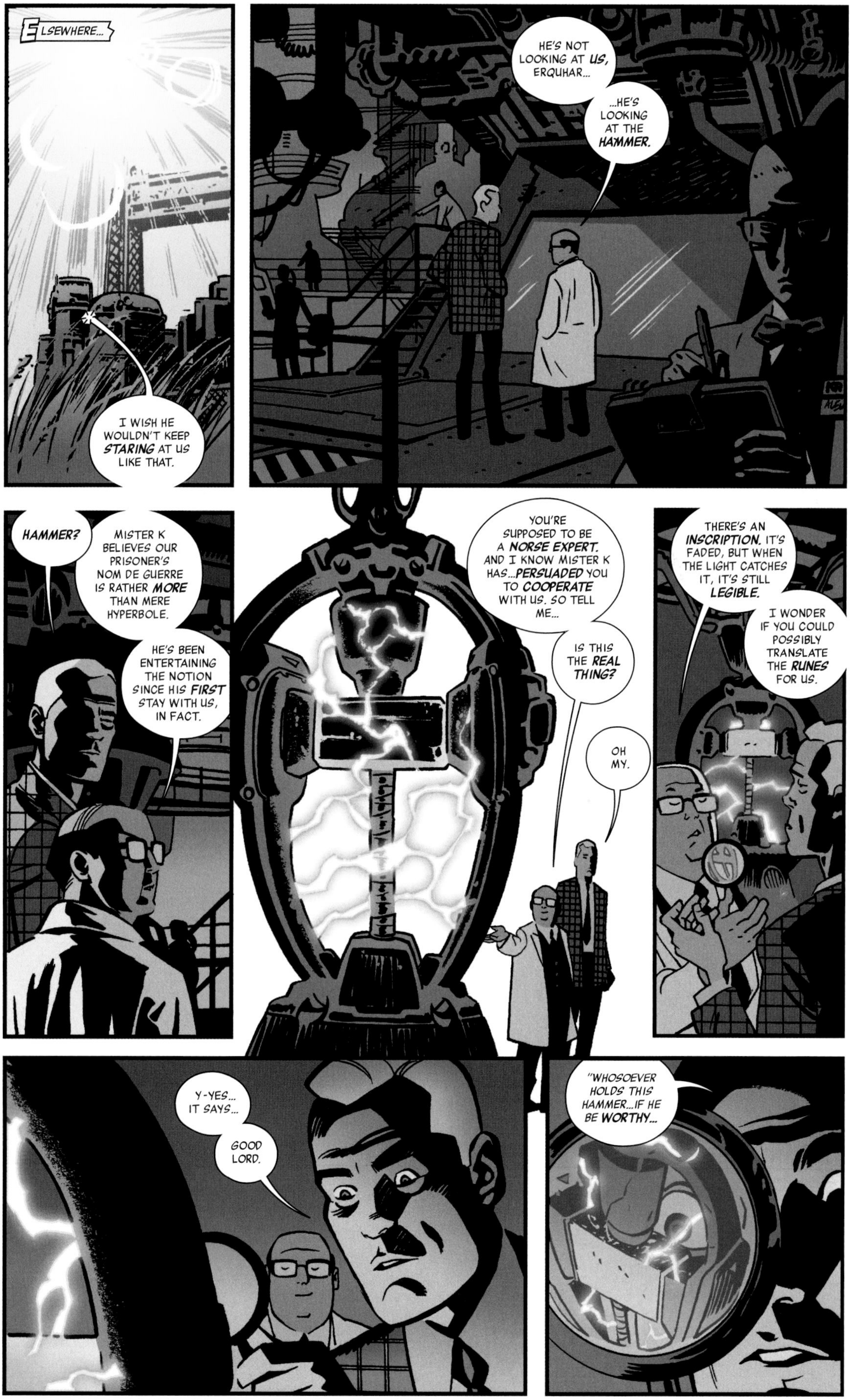
ELSEWHERE...
I WISH HE WOULDN'T KEEP STARING AT US LIKE THAT.
HE'S NOT LOOKING AT US, ERQUHAR...
...HE'S LOOKING AT THE HAMMER.
HAMMER?
MISTER K BELIEVES OUR PRISONER'S NOM DE GUERRE IS RATHER MORE THAN MERE HYPERBOLE.
HE'S BEEN ENTERTAINING THE NOTION SINCE HIS FIRST STAY WITH US, IN FACT.
YOU'RE SUPPOSED TO BE A NORSE EXPERT. AND I KNOW MISTER K HAS...PERSUADED YOU TO COOPERATE WITH US. SO TELL ME...
IS THIS THE REAL THING?
OH MY.
THERE'S AN INSCRIPTION. IT'S FADED, BUT WHEN THE LIGHT CATCHES IT, IT'S STILL LEGIBLE.
I WONDER IF YOU COULD POSSIBLY TRANSLATE THE RUNES FOR US.
Y-YES... IT SAYS...
GOOD LORD.
"WHOSOEVER HOLDS THIS HAMMER...IF HE BE WORTHY...

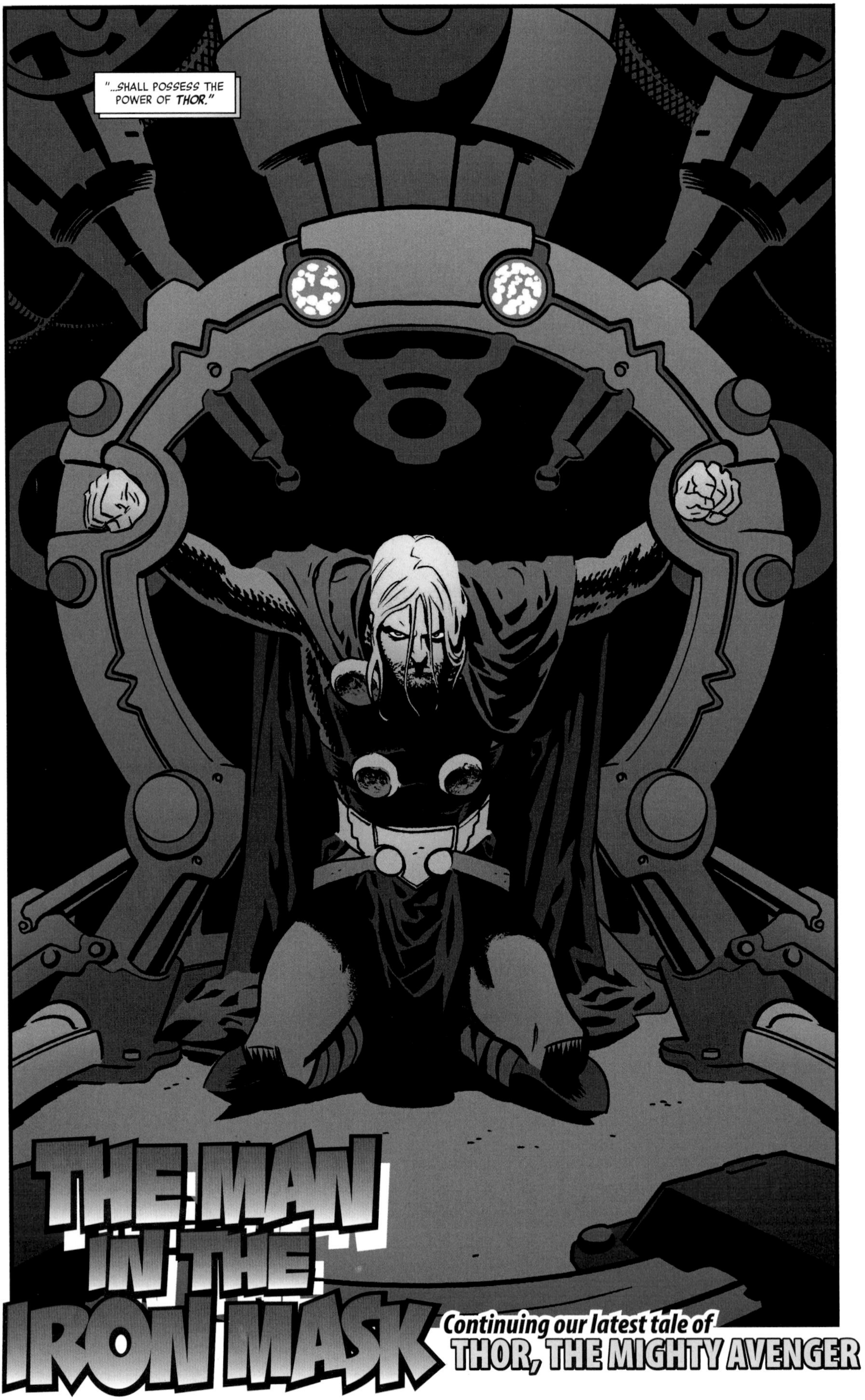
"...SHALL POSSESS THE POWER OF THOR."
THE MAN IN THE IRON MASK
Continuing our latest tale of
THOR, THE MIGHTY AVENGER

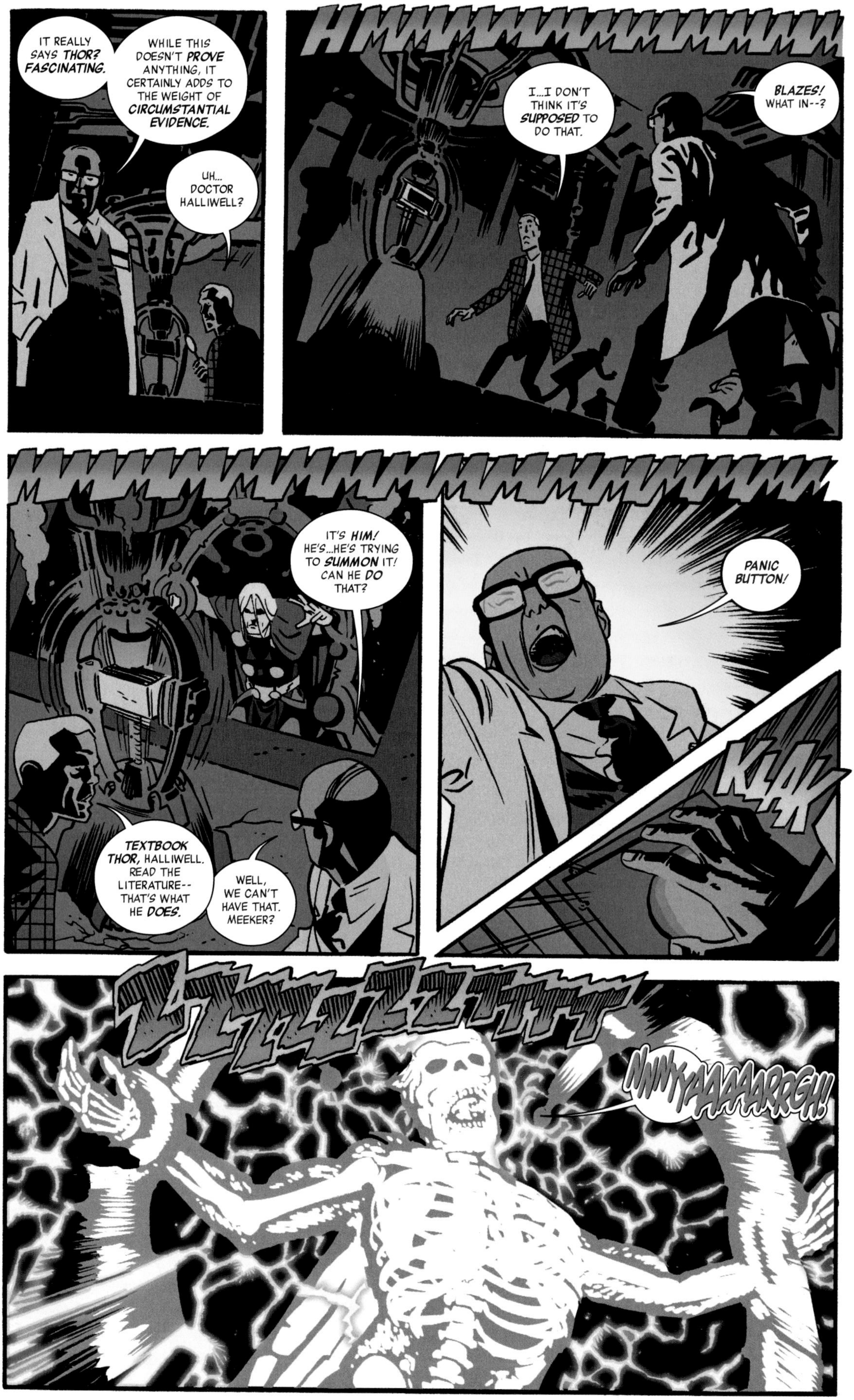
IT REALLY SAYS THOR? FASCINATING.
WHILE THIS DOESN'T PROVE ANYTHING, IT CERTAINLY ADDS TO THE WEIGHT OF CIRCUMSTANTIAL EVIDENCE.
UH... DOCTOR HALLIWELL?
HMMMMMMMMMMMMMMM
I...I DON'T THINK IT'S SUPPOSED TO DO THAT.
BLAZES! WHAT IN--?
MMMMMMMMMMMMMMMMMMMMMMMMM
IT'S HIM! HE'S...HE'S TRYING TO SUMMON IT! CAN HE DO THAT?
TEXTBOOK THOR, HALLIWELL. READ THE LITERATURE-- THAT'S WHAT HE DOES.
WELL, WE CAN'T HAVE THAT. MEEKER?
PANIC BUTTON!
KLAK
ZZZZZZZZTTTTT
NNNYAAAAARRGH!

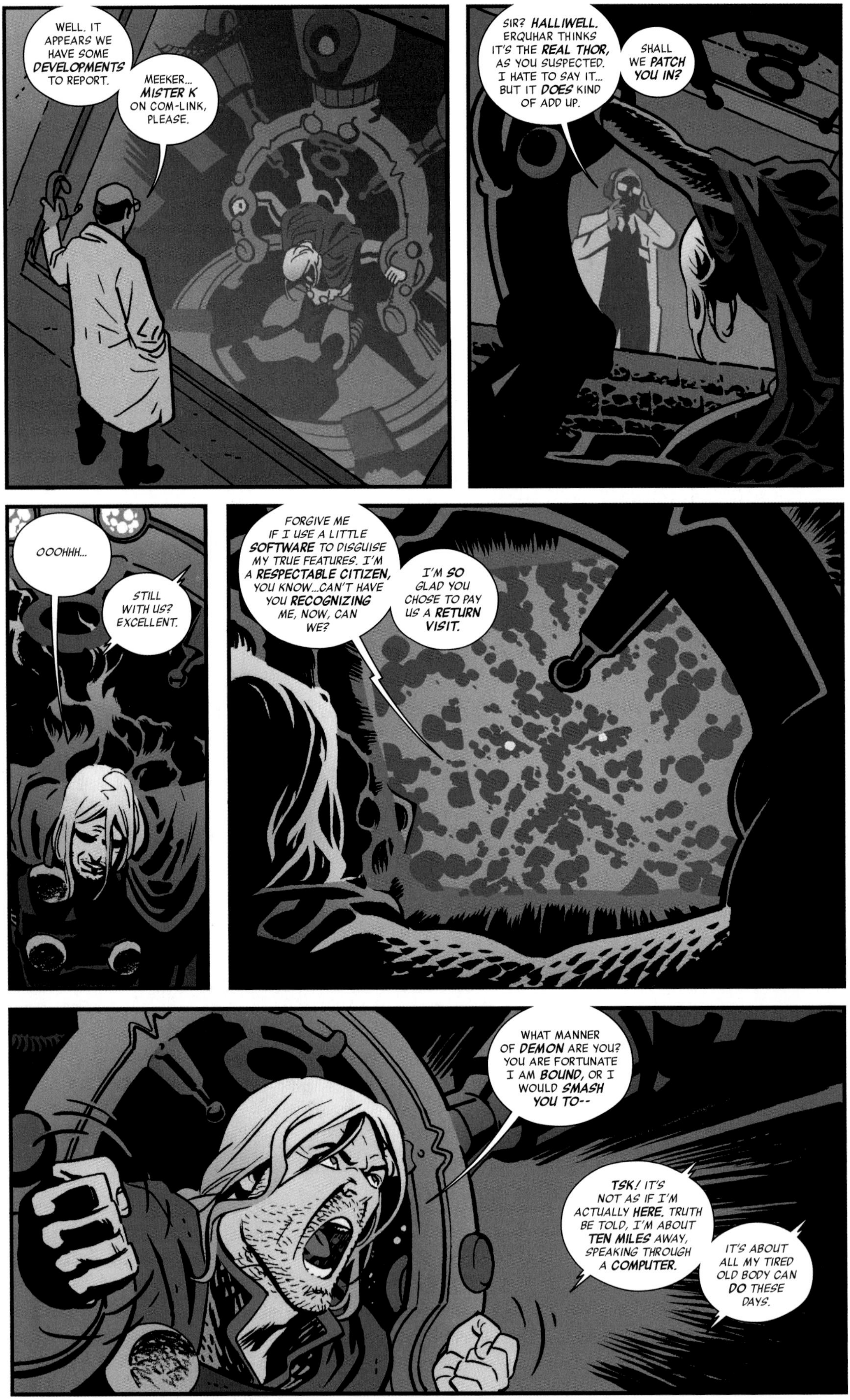
WELL. IT APPEARS WE HAVE SOME DEVELOPMENTS TO REPORT.
MEEKER... MISTER K ON COM-LINK, PLEASE.
SIR? HALLIWELL. ERQUHAR THINKS IT'S THE REAL THOR, AS YOU SUSPECTED. I HATE TO SAY IT... BUT IT DOES KIND OF ADD UP.
SHALL WE PATCH YOU IN?
OOOHHH...
STILL WITH US? EXCELLENT.
FORGIVE ME IF I USE A LITTLE SOFTWARE TO DISGUISE MY TRUE FEATURES. I'M A RESPECTABLE CITIZEN, YOU KNOW...CAN'T HAVE YOU RECOGNIZING ME, NOW, CAN WE?
I'M SO GLAD YOU CHOSE TO PAY US A RETURN VISIT.
WHAT MANNER OF DEMON ARE YOU? YOU ARE FORTUNATE I AM BOUND, OR I WOULD SMASH YOU TO--
TSK! IT'S NOT AS IF I'M ACTUALLY HERE. TRUTH BE TOLD, I'M ABOUT TEN MILES AWAY, SPEAKING THROUGH A COMPUTER.
IT'S ABOUT ALL MY TIRED OLD BODY CAN DO THESE DAYS.

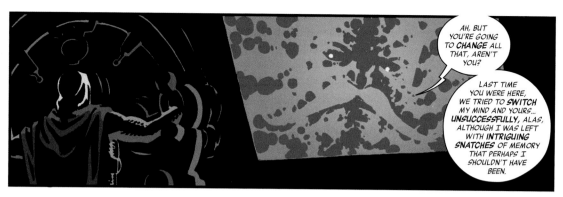

AH, BUT YOU'RE GOING TO *CHANGE* ALL THAT, AREN'T YOU?

LAST TIME YOU WERE HERE, WE TRIED TO *SWITCH* MY MIND AND YOURS... *UNSUCCESSFULLY,* ALAS, ALTHOUGH I WAS LEFT WITH *INTRIGUING SNATCHES* OF MEMORY THAT PERHAPS I SHOULDN'T HAVE BEEN.

YOU... YOU *STOLE* MY MEMORIES?

ALL THESE WEEKS I HAVE THOUGHT MY FATHER WAS *TOYING* WITH ME... OR THAT I WAS *LOSING MY MIND...*AND IT WAS *YOU* ALL ALONG?

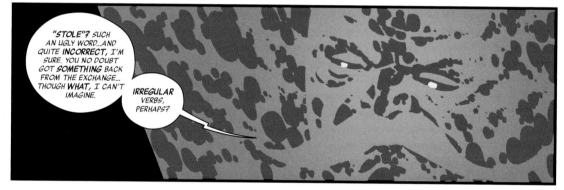

"STOLE"? SUCH AN UGLY WORD...AND QUITE *INCORRECT,* I'M SURE. YOU NO DOUBT GOT *SOMETHING* BACK FROM THE EXCHANGE... THOUGH *WHAT,* I CAN'T IMAGINE.

IRREGULAR VERBS, PERHAPS?

OH, AND I'D *STOP STRAINING* IF I WERE YOU. YOU MIGHT DAMAGE THE *BODY.* THOSE BONDS HAVE BEEN THOROUGHLY TESTED... *ARNOLD SCHWARZENEGGER* AT HIS PEAK COULDN'T BREAK OUT OF--

SNA?P

SNAP

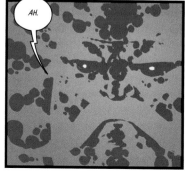

AH.

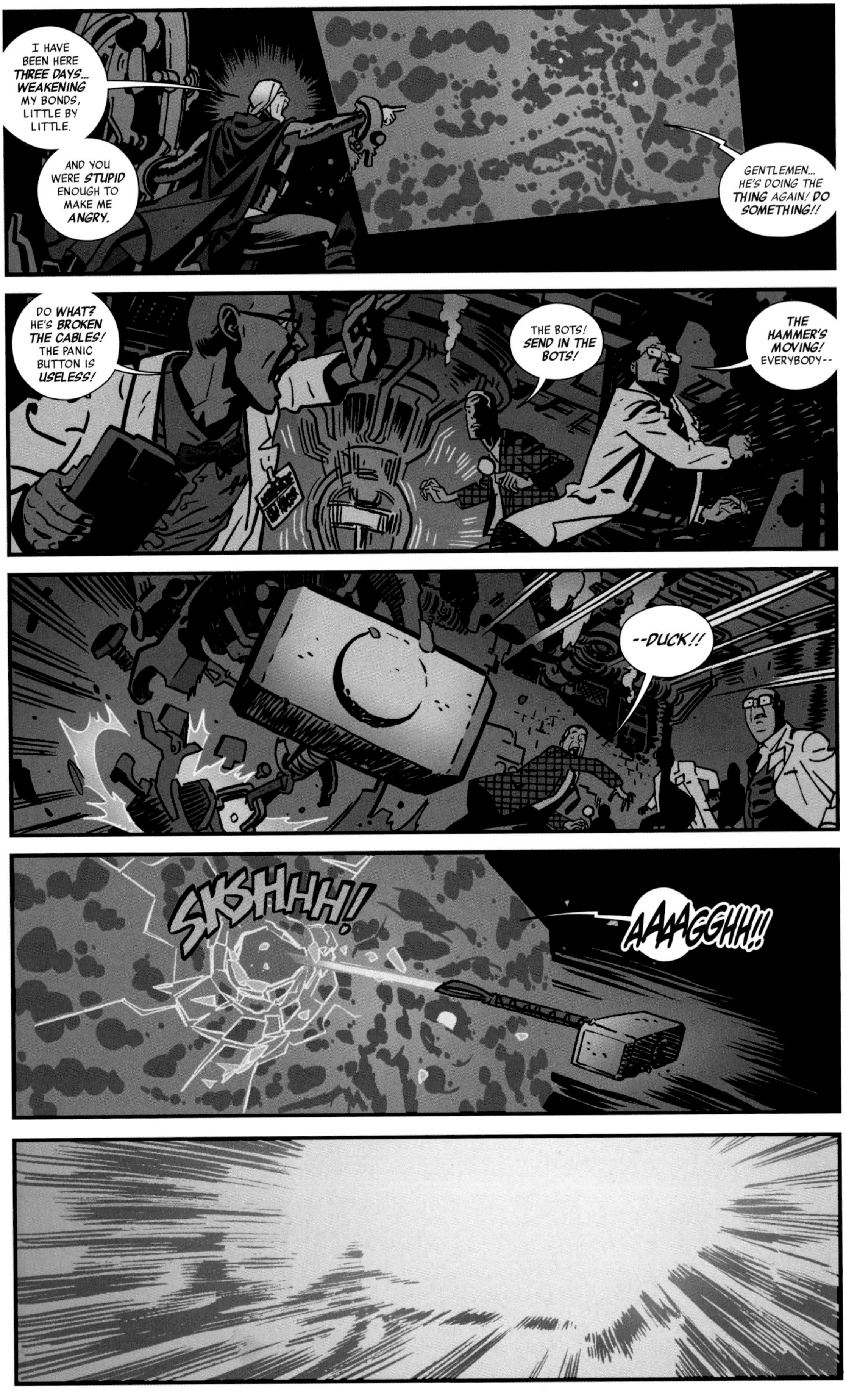
I HAVE BEEN HERE THREE DAYS... WEAKENING MY BONDS, LITTLE BY LITTLE.
AND YOU WERE STUPID ENOUGH TO MAKE ME ANGRY.
GENTLEMEN... HE'S DOING THE THING AGAIN! DO SOMETHING!!
DO WHAT? HE'S BROKEN THE CABLES! THE PANIC BUTTON IS USELESS!
THE BOTS! SEND IN THE BOTS!
THE HAMMER'S MOVING! EVERYBODY--
--DUCK!!
SKSHHH!
AAAAGGHH!!

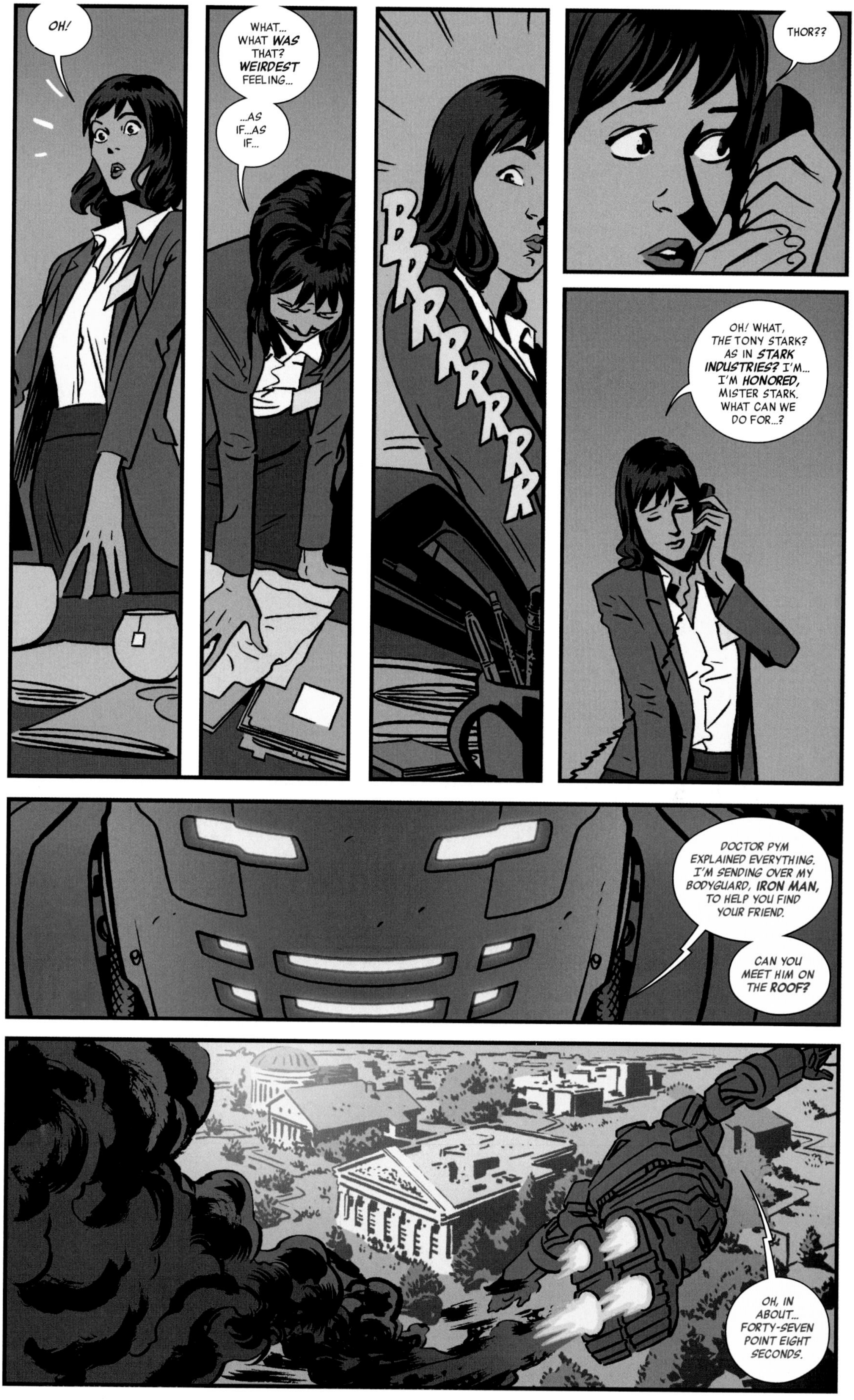

OH!
WHAT... WHAT WAS THAT? WEIRDEST FEELING...
...AS IF...AS IF...
BRRRRRRRR
THOR??
OH! WHAT, THE TONY STARK? AS IN STARK INDUSTRIES? I'M... I'M HONORED, MISTER STARK. WHAT CAN WE DO FOR...?
DOCTOR PYM EXPLAINED EVERYTHING. I'M SENDING OVER MY BODYGUARD, IRON MAN, TO HELP YOU FIND YOUR FRIEND.
CAN YOU MEET HIM ON THE ROOF?
OH, IN ABOUT... FORTY-SEVEN POINT EIGHT SECONDS.

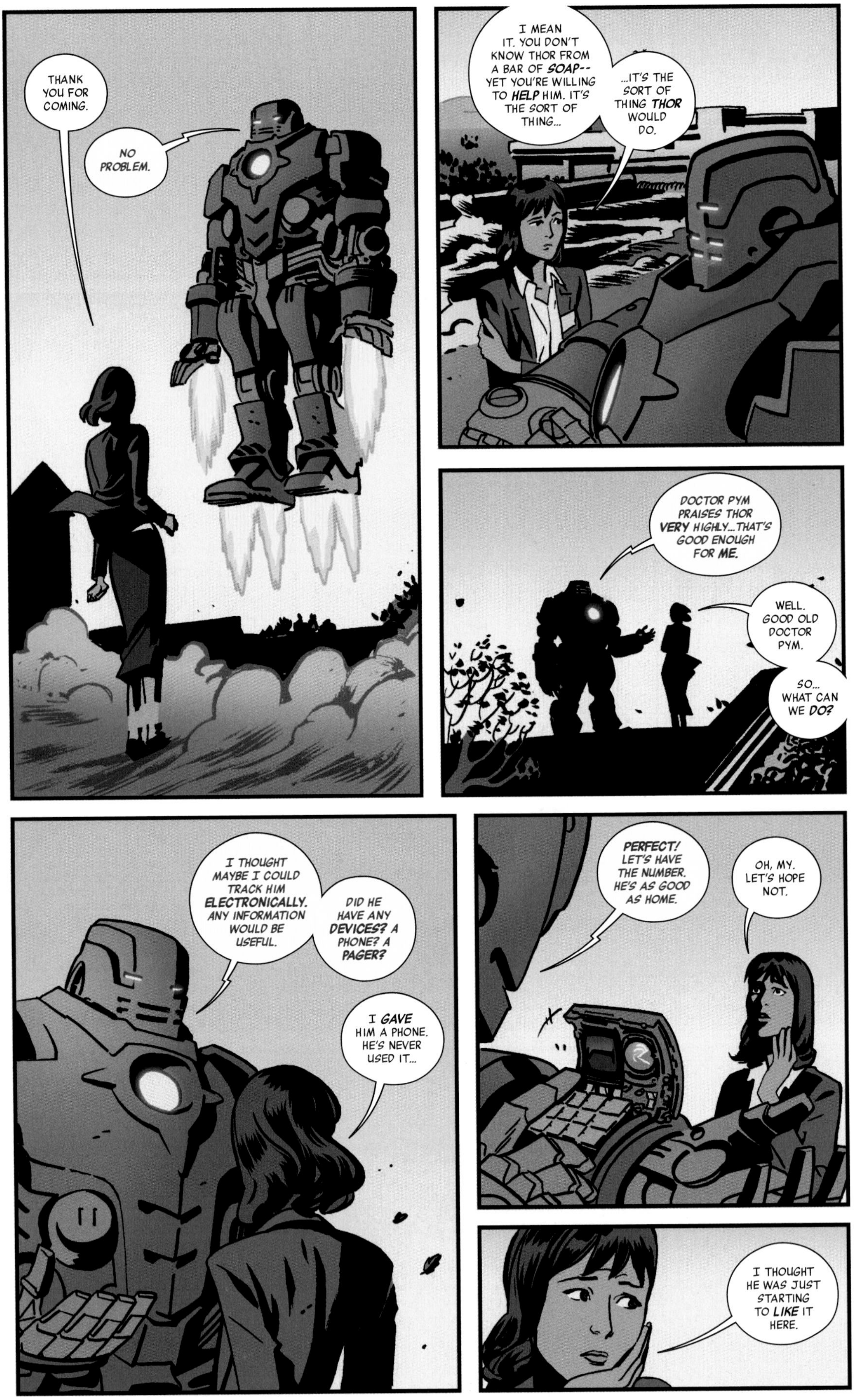
THANK YOU FOR COMING.
NO PROBLEM.
I MEAN IT. YOU DON'T KNOW THOR FROM A BAR OF SOAP-- YET YOU'RE WILLING TO HELP HIM. IT'S THE SORT OF THING...
...IT'S THE SORT OF THING THOR WOULD DO.
DOCTOR PYM PRAISES THOR VERY HIGHLY...THAT'S GOOD ENOUGH FOR ME.
WELL. GOOD OLD DOCTOR PYM.
SO... WHAT CAN WE DO?
I THOUGHT MAYBE I COULD TRACK HIM ELECTRONICALLY. ANY INFORMATION WOULD BE USEFUL.
DID HE HAVE ANY DEVICES? A PHONE? A PAGER?
I GAVE HIM A PHONE. HE'S NEVER USED IT...
PERFECT! LET'S HAVE THE NUMBER. HE'S AS GOOD AS HOME.
OH, MY. LET'S HOPE NOT.
I THOUGHT HE WAS JUST STARTING TO LIKE IT HERE.

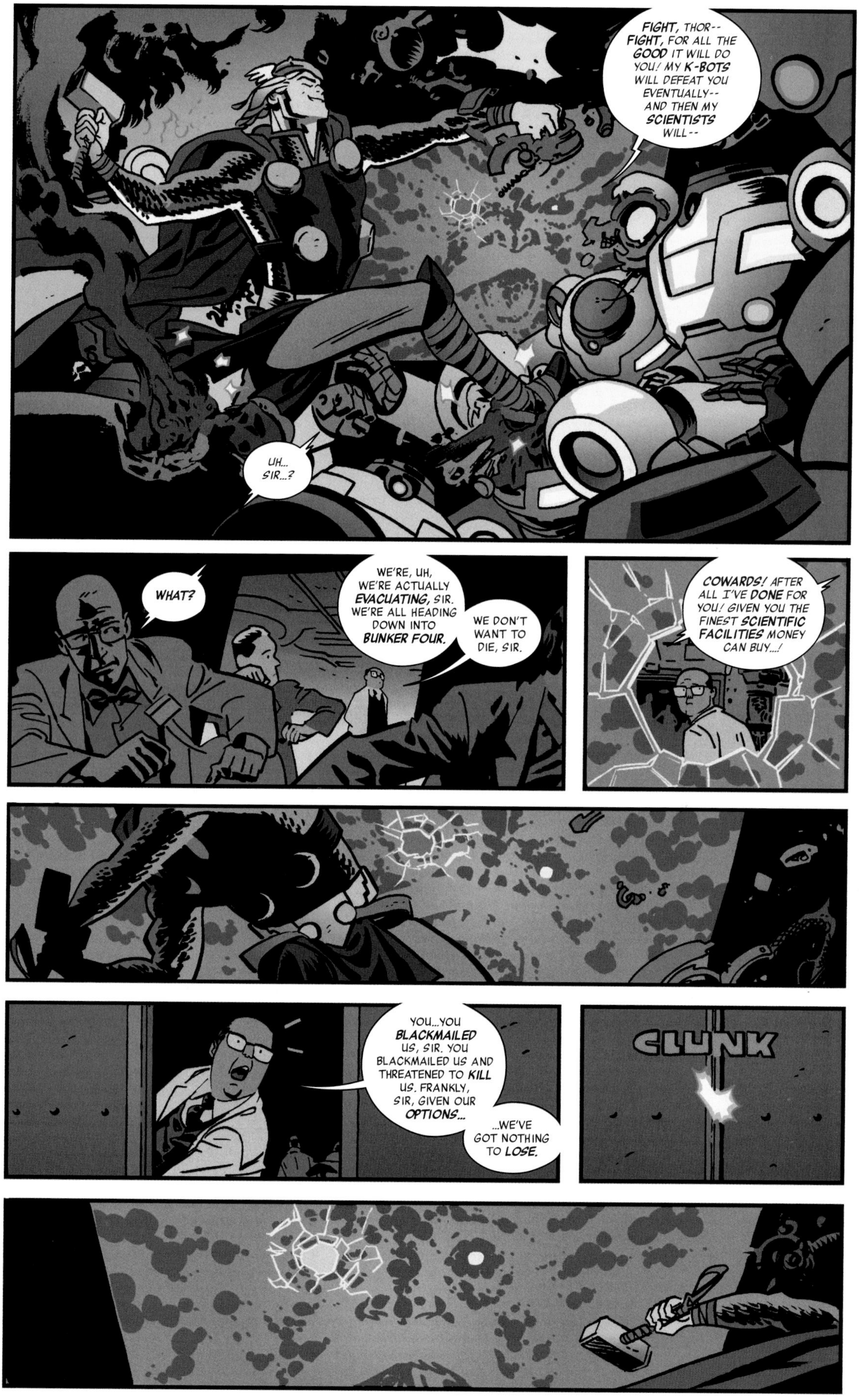
FIGHT, THOR-- FIGHT, FOR ALL THE GOOD IT WILL DO YOU! MY K-BOTS WILL DEFEAT YOU EVENTUALLY-- AND THEN MY SCIENTISTS WILL--
UH... SIR...?
WHAT?
WE'RE, UH, WE'RE ACTUALLY EVACUATING, SIR. WE'RE ALL HEADING DOWN INTO BUNKER FOUR.
WE DON'T WANT TO DIE, SIR.
COWARDS! AFTER ALL I'VE DONE FOR YOU! GIVEN YOU THE FINEST SCIENTIFIC FACILITIES MONEY CAN BUY...!
YOU...YOU BLACKMAILED US, SIR. YOU BLACKMAILED US AND THREATENED TO KILL US. FRANKLY, SIR, GIVEN OUR OPTIONS...
...WE'VE GOT NOTHING TO LOSE.
CLUNK

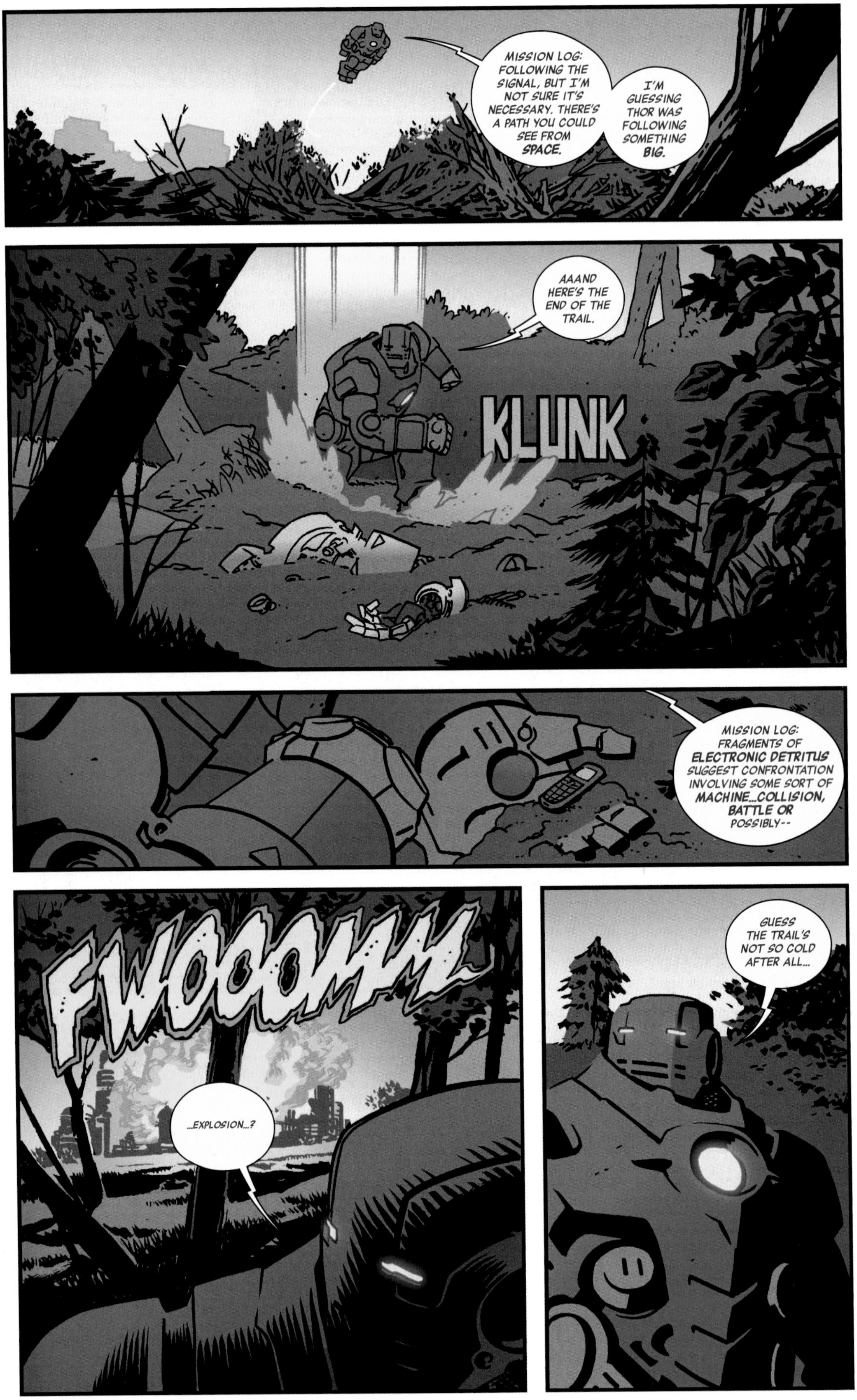
MISSION LOG: FOLLOWING THE SIGNAL, BUT I'M NOT SURE IT'S NECESSARY. THERE'S A PATH YOU COULD SEE FROM SPACE.
I'M GUESSING THOR WAS FOLLOWING SOMETHING BIG.
AAAND HERE'S THE END OF THE TRAIL.
KLUNK
MISSION LOG: FRAGMENTS OF ELECTRONIC DETRITUS SUGGEST CONFRONTATION INVOLVING SOME SORT OF MACHINE...COLLISION, BATTLE OR POSSIBLY--
FWOOOMM
...EXPLOSION...?
GUESS THE TRAIL'S NOT SO COLD AFTER ALL...

=KOFF!
KOFF!= WHAT
IN ODIN'S
NAME--?

SURPRISED?

AFTER YOUR
THOROUGH **TRASHING**
OF MY **K-BOT 3000,**
I HAD SOME
ADJUSTMENTS MADE
TO THE REST OF
THE FLEET.

IF THEIR
CHEST CASINGS
ARE BREACHED,
THEY'RE NOW
PRIMED TO
BLOW UP.

I HAVE NO
DOUBT YOU CAN
SURVIVE **ONE** SUCH
EXPLOSION...
POSSIBLY EVEN **TWO**
OR THREE...

...BUT A
DOZEN?

GIVE UP
QUIETLY AND I'LL
MAKE...**WHATEVER**
FOLLOWS...AS
PAINLESS AS
POSSIBLE.

EEEEEEEEEEEEEEEEEEEEEEEEEEE

+++
111000111100
+++

WHAT... ?

+++
0001110101100
+++

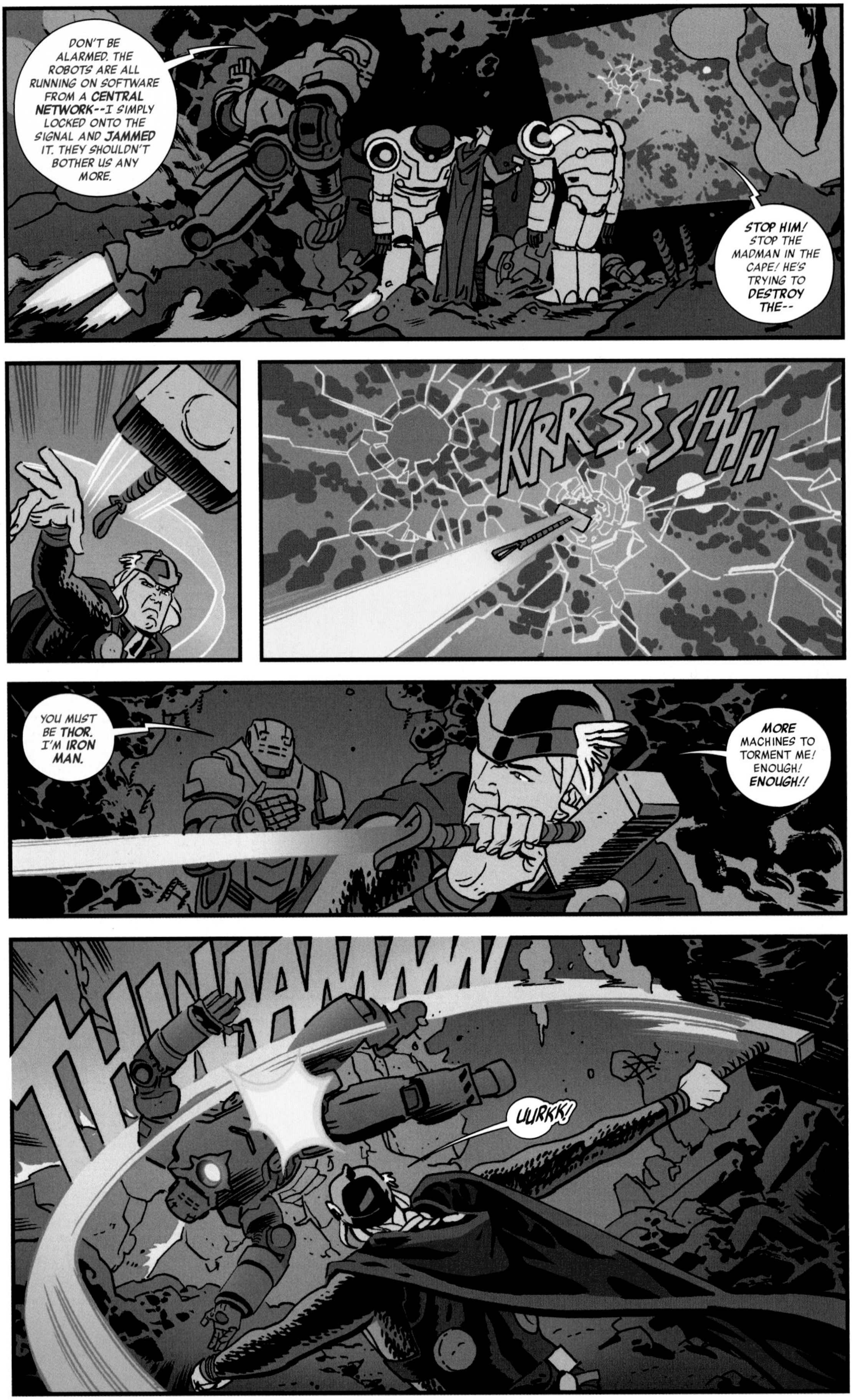
DON'T BE ALARMED. THE ROBOTS ARE ALL RUNNING ON SOFTWARE FROM A CENTRAL NETWORK--I SIMPLY LOCKED ONTO THE SIGNAL AND JAMMED IT. THEY SHOULDN'T BOTHER US ANY MORE.
STOP HIM! STOP THE MADMAN IN THE CAPE! HE'S TRYING TO DESTROY THE--
KRRSSSHHH
YOU MUST BE THOR. I'M IRON MAN.
MORE MACHINES TO TORMENT ME! ENOUGH! ENOUGH!!
UURKK!

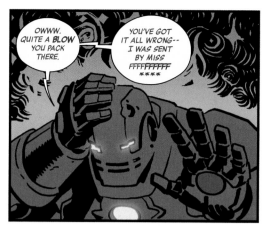

OWWW. QUITE A **BLOW** YOU PACK THERE.

YOU'VE GOT IT ALL WRONG-- I WAS SENT BY MISS FFFFFFFFFF

HACKING INTO THIS METAL SUIT WAS **CHILD'S PLAY!** MAYBE MY K-BOTS ARE OUT OF COMMISSION--BUT THERE'S NOTHING TO STOP ME FROM GETTING YOU TO THE CHAMBER **MYSELF!**

FFFFFFF-FABULOUS!

NOW... WHAT DO THESE DO...?

YOU **AGAIN?!** I THOUGHT I **DESTROYED** YOUR UGLY FACE!

IT APPEARS I MUST ALSO **SMASH** YOUR METAL BODY TO--

ZZZAPP!

UUUNGHH!

OOH. NICE.

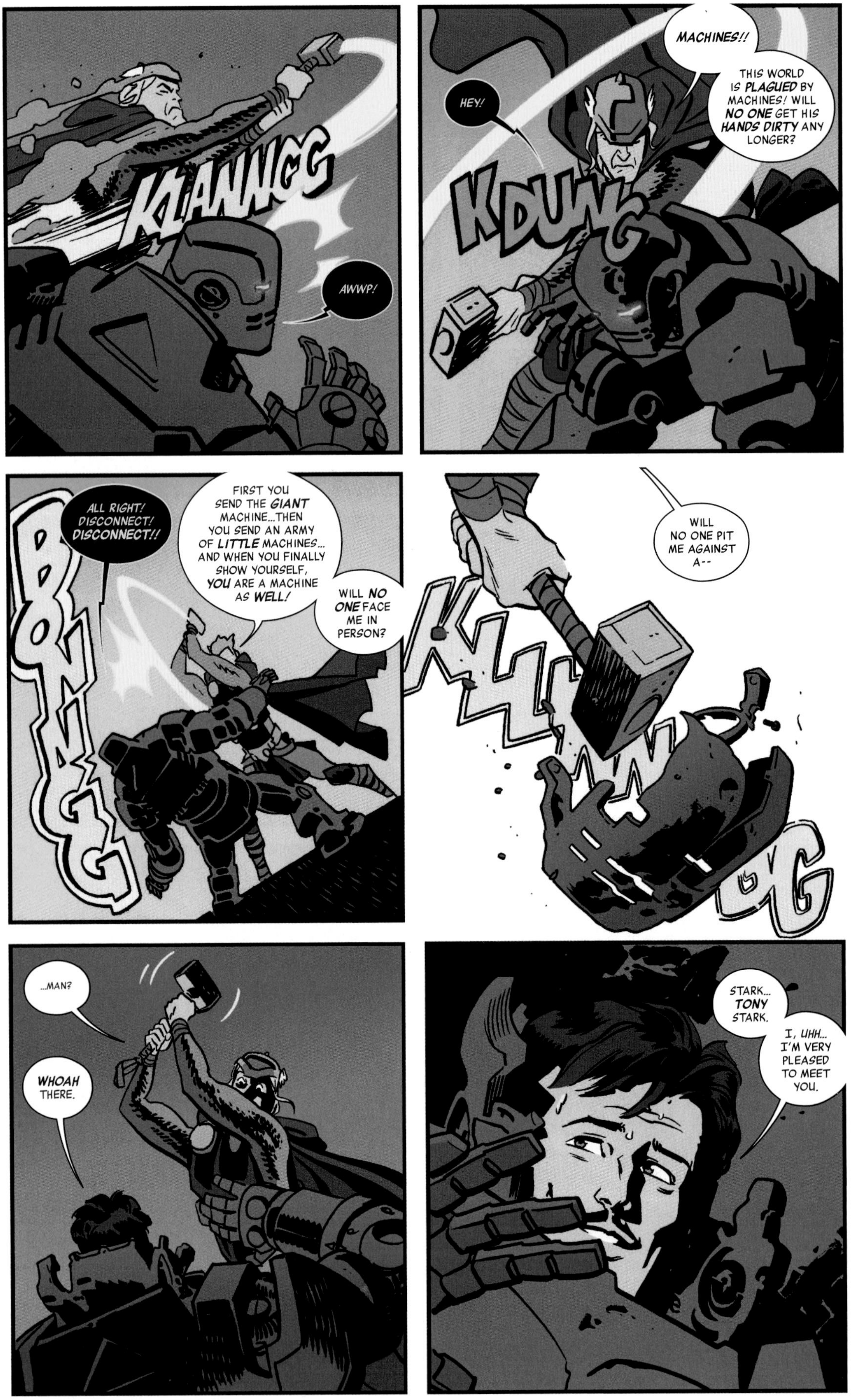
KLANNGG
AWWP!
MACHINES!!
HEY!
THIS WORLD IS PLAGUED BY MACHINES! WILL NO ONE GET HIS HANDS DIRTY ANY LONGER?
KDUNG
ALL RIGHT! DISCONNECT! DISCONNECT!!
FIRST YOU SEND THE GIANT MACHINE...THEN YOU SEND AN ARMY OF LITTLE MACHINES... AND WHEN YOU FINALLY SHOW YOURSELF, YOU ARE A MACHINE AS WELL!
WILL NO ONE FACE ME IN PERSON?
BONNG
WILL NO ONE PIT ME AGAINST A--
...MAN?
WHOAH THERE.
STARK... TONY STARK.
I, UHH... I'M VERY PLEASED TO MEET YOU.

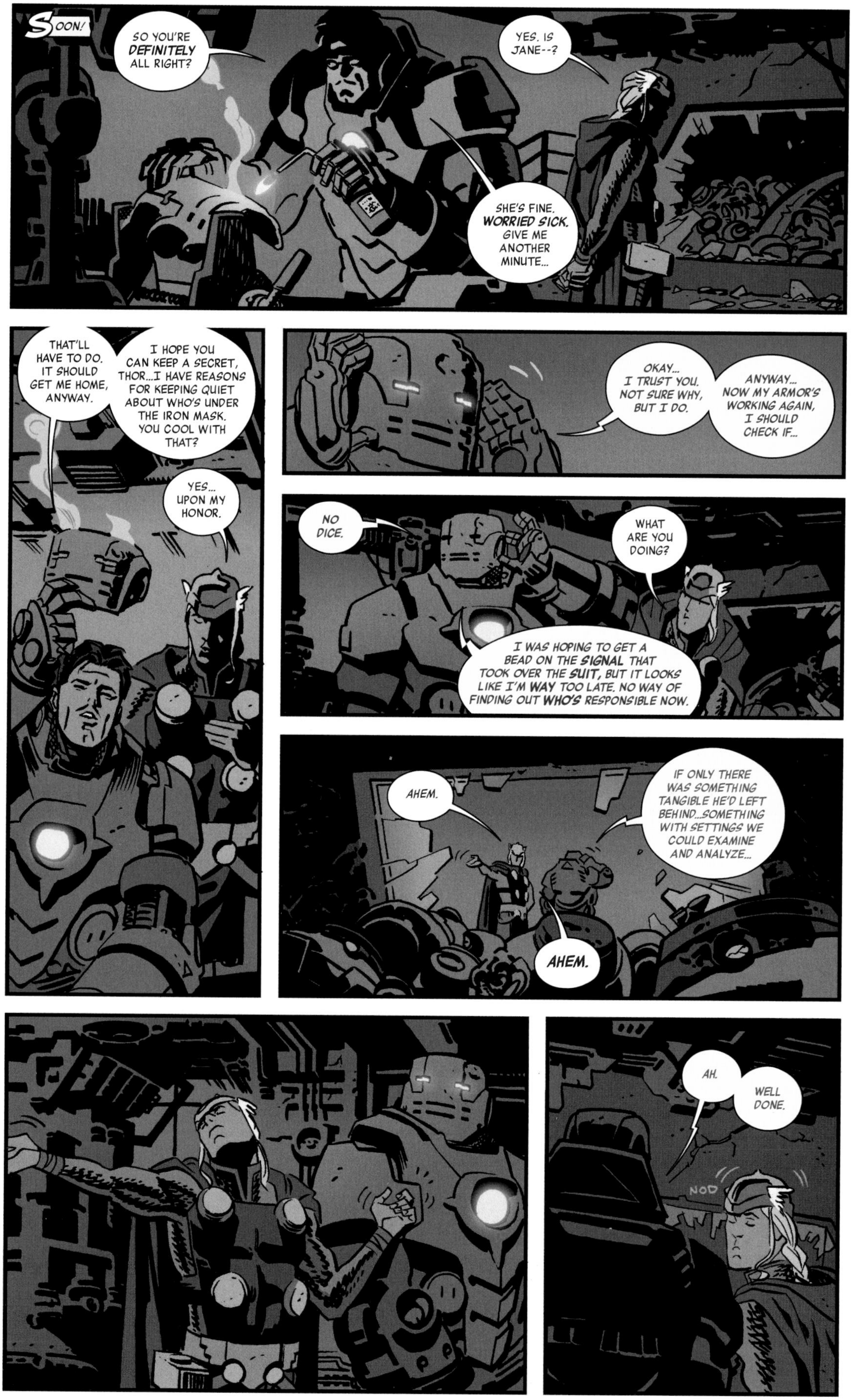
SOON!
SO YOU'RE DEFINITELY ALL RIGHT?
YES. IS JANE--?
SHE'S FINE. WORRIED SICK. GIVE ME ANOTHER MINUTE...
THAT'LL HAVE TO DO. IT SHOULD GET ME HOME, ANYWAY.
I HOPE YOU CAN KEEP A SECRET, THOR...I HAVE REASONS FOR KEEPING QUIET ABOUT WHO'S UNDER THE IRON MASK. YOU COOL WITH THAT?
YES... UPON MY HONOR.
OKAY... I TRUST YOU. NOT SURE WHY, BUT I DO.
ANYWAY... NOW MY ARMOR'S WORKING AGAIN, I SHOULD CHECK IF...
NO DICE.
WHAT ARE YOU DOING?
I WAS HOPING TO GET A BEAD ON THE SIGNAL THAT TOOK OVER THE SUIT, BUT IT LOOKS LIKE I'M WAY TOO LATE. NO WAY OF FINDING OUT WHO'S RESPONSIBLE NOW.
AHEM.
IF ONLY THERE WAS SOMETHING TANGIBLE HE'D LEFT BEHIND...SOMETHING WITH SETTINGS WE COULD EXAMINE AND ANALYZE...
AHEM.
AH.
WELL DONE.
NOD

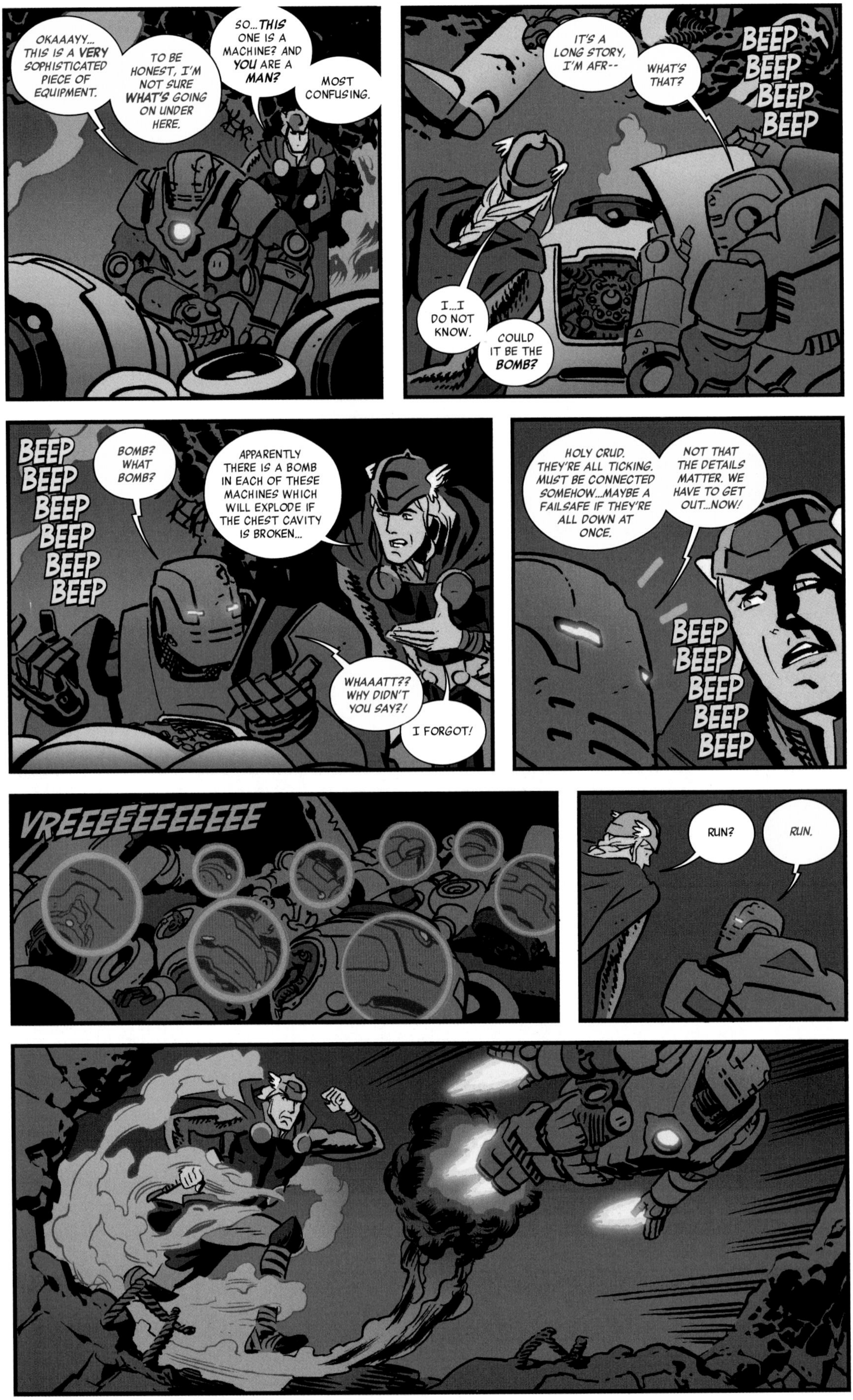
OKAAAYY... THIS IS A VERY SOPHISTICATED PIECE OF EQUIPMENT.
TO BE HONEST, I'M NOT SURE WHAT'S GOING ON UNDER HERE.
SO...THIS ONE IS A MACHINE? AND YOU ARE A MAN?
MOST CONFUSING.
IT'S A LONG STORY, I'M AFR--
BEEP BEEP BEEP BEEP
WHAT'S THAT?
I...I DO NOT KNOW.
COULD IT BE THE BOMB?
BEEP BEEP BEEP BEEP BEEP BEEP
BOMB? WHAT BOMB?
APPARENTLY THERE IS A BOMB IN EACH OF THESE MACHINES WHICH WILL EXPLODE IF THE CHEST CAVITY IS BROKEN...
WHAAATT?? WHY DIDN'T YOU SAY?!
I FORGOT!
HOLY CRUD. THEY'RE ALL TICKING. MUST BE CONNECTED SOMEHOW...MAYBE A FAILSAFE IF THEY'RE ALL DOWN AT ONCE.
NOT THAT THE DETAILS MATTER. WE HAVE TO GET OUT...NOW!
BEEP BEEP BEEP BEEP BEEP
VREEEEEEEEEEE
RUN?
RUN.

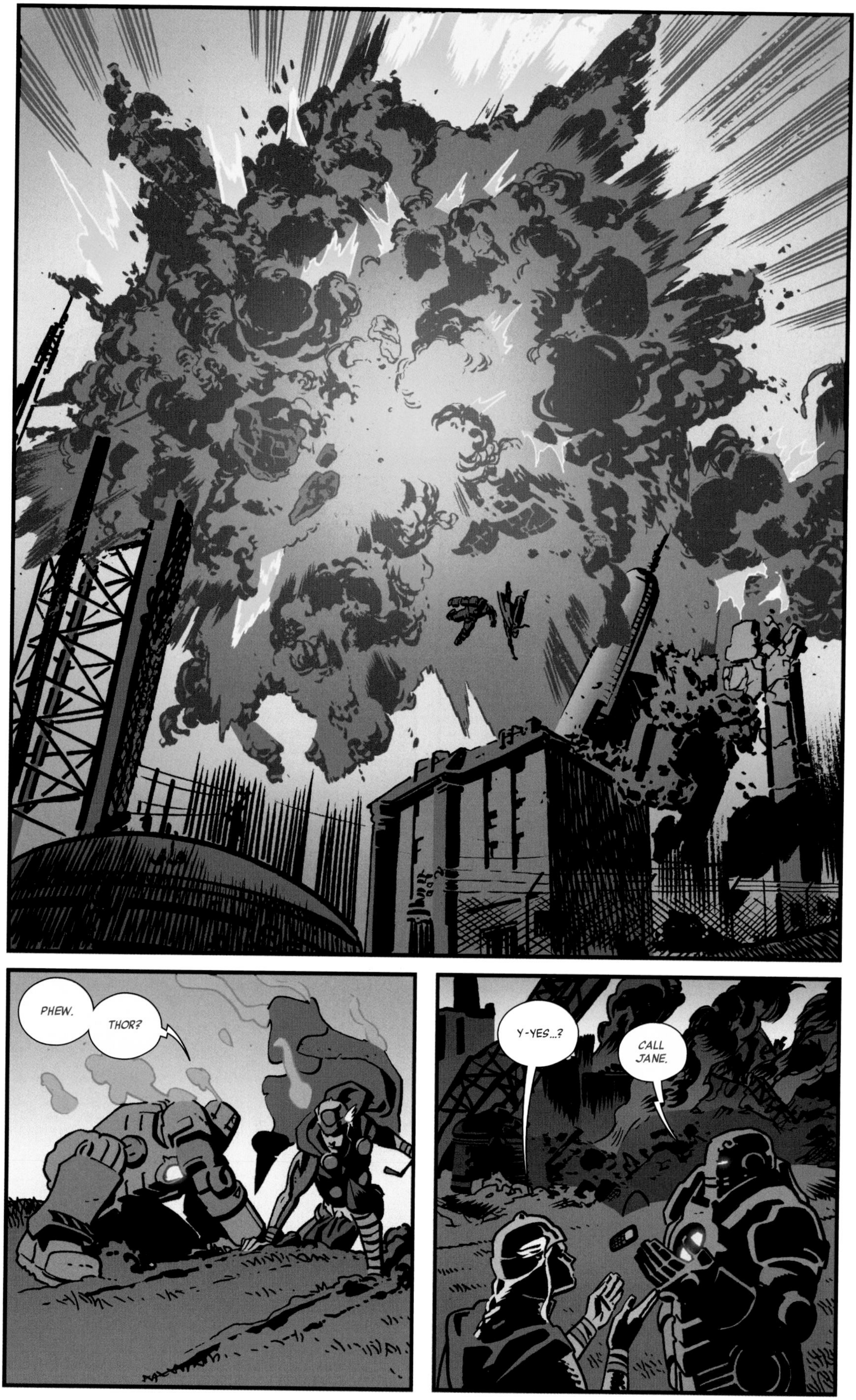
PHEW.
THOR?
Y-YES...?
CALL JANE.

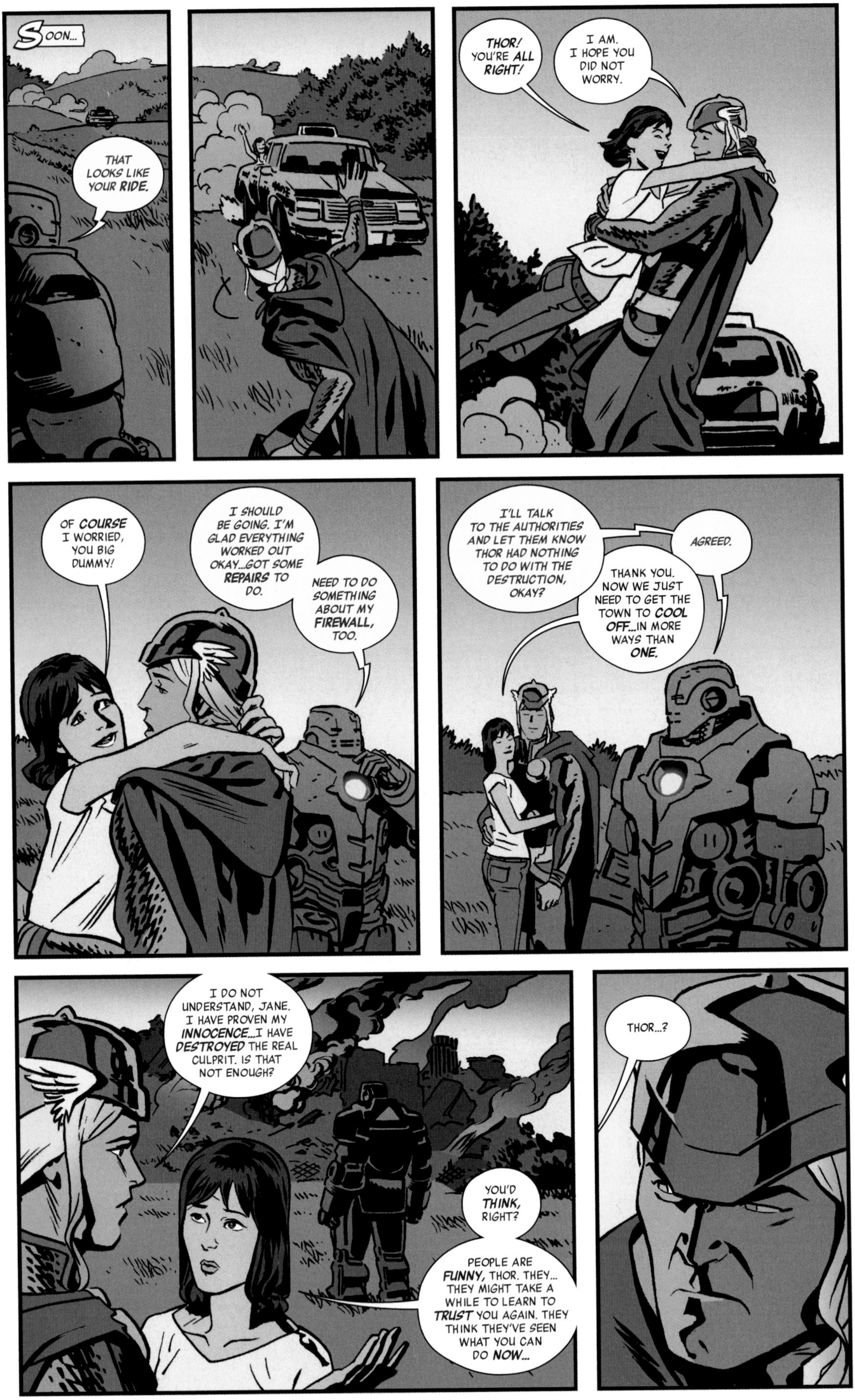
SOON...
THAT LOOKS LIKE YOUR RIDE.
THOR! YOU'RE ALL RIGHT!
I AM. I HOPE YOU DID NOT WORRY.
OF COURSE I WORRIED, YOU BIG DUMMY!
I SHOULD BE GOING. I'M GLAD EVERYTHING WORKED OUT OKAY...GOT SOME REPAIRS TO DO.
NEED TO DO SOMETHING ABOUT MY FIREWALL, TOO.
I'LL TALK TO THE AUTHORITIES AND LET THEM KNOW THOR HAD NOTHING TO DO WITH THE DESTRUCTION, OKAY?
AGREED.
THANK YOU. NOW WE JUST NEED TO GET THE TOWN TO COOL OFF...IN MORE WAYS THAN ONE.
I DO NOT UNDERSTAND, JANE. I HAVE PROVEN MY INNOCENCE...I HAVE DESTROYED THE REAL CULPRIT. IS THAT NOT ENOUGH?
YOU'D THINK, RIGHT?
PEOPLE ARE FUNNY, THOR. THEY... THEY MIGHT TAKE A WHILE TO LEARN TO TRUST YOU AGAIN. THEY THINK THEY'VE SEEN WHAT YOU CAN DO NOW...
THOR...?

DO? DO??

I SHALL **SHOW** THE WORLD WHAT I CAN DO! I SHALL BRING DOWN **STORMS** UPON THEIR **CRACKED AND BLISTERED EARTH!** FOR I AM **THOR**...

...**SON OF ODIN!!**

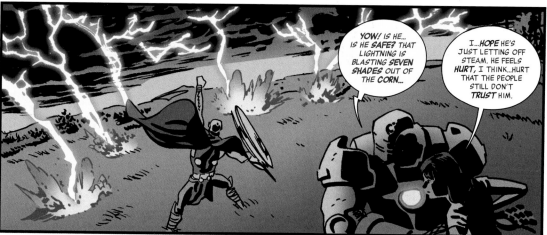

YOW! IS HE... IS HE **SAFE?** THAT LIGHTNING IS BLASTING **SEVEN SHADES** OUT OF THE **CORN**...

I...**HOPE** HE'S JUST LETTING OFF STEAM. HE FEELS **HURT**, I THINK...HURT THAT THE PEOPLE STILL DON'T **TRUST** HIM.

BUT I THOUGHT HE'D GOTTEN OVER THESE...THESE **TANTRUMS**.

I THOUGHT HE'D **GROWN UP** A LITTLE, FRANKLY. WHAT HE THINKS HE'LL ACCOMPLISH BY **TRASHING A CORNFIELD**, I CAN'T...

OH.

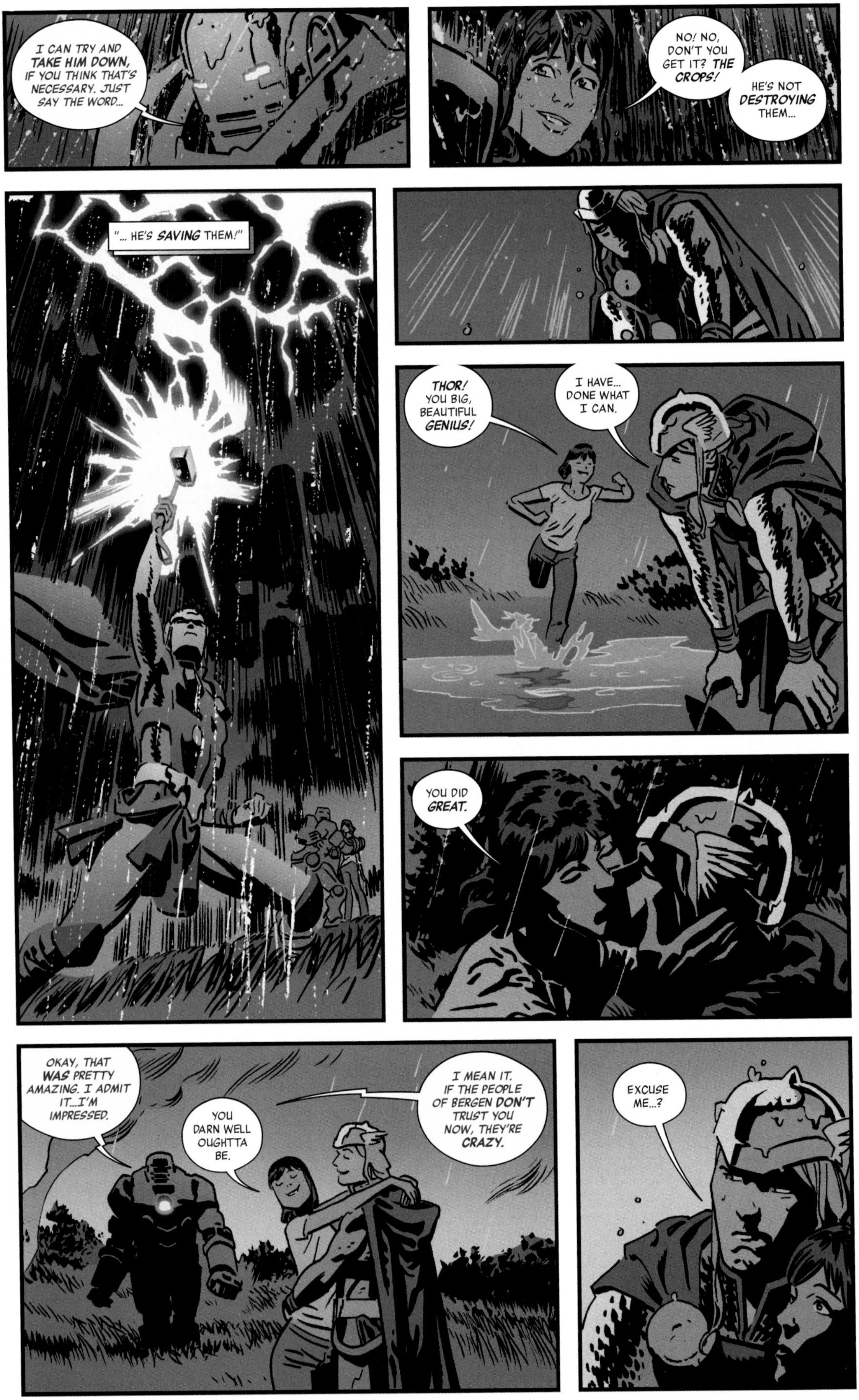
I CAN TRY AND TAKE HIM DOWN, IF YOU THINK THAT'S NECESSARY. JUST SAY THE WORD...
NO! NO, DON'T YOU GET IT? THE CROPS!
HE'S NOT DESTROYING THEM...
"... HE'S SAVING THEM!"
THOR! YOU BIG, BEAUTIFUL GENIUS!
I HAVE... DONE WHAT I CAN.
YOU DID GREAT.
OKAY, THAT WAS PRETTY AMAZING. I ADMIT IT...I'M IMPRESSED.
YOU DARN WELL OUGHTTA BE.
I MEAN IT. IF THE PEOPLE OF BERGEN DON'T TRUST YOU NOW, THEY'RE CRAZY.
EXCUSE ME...?

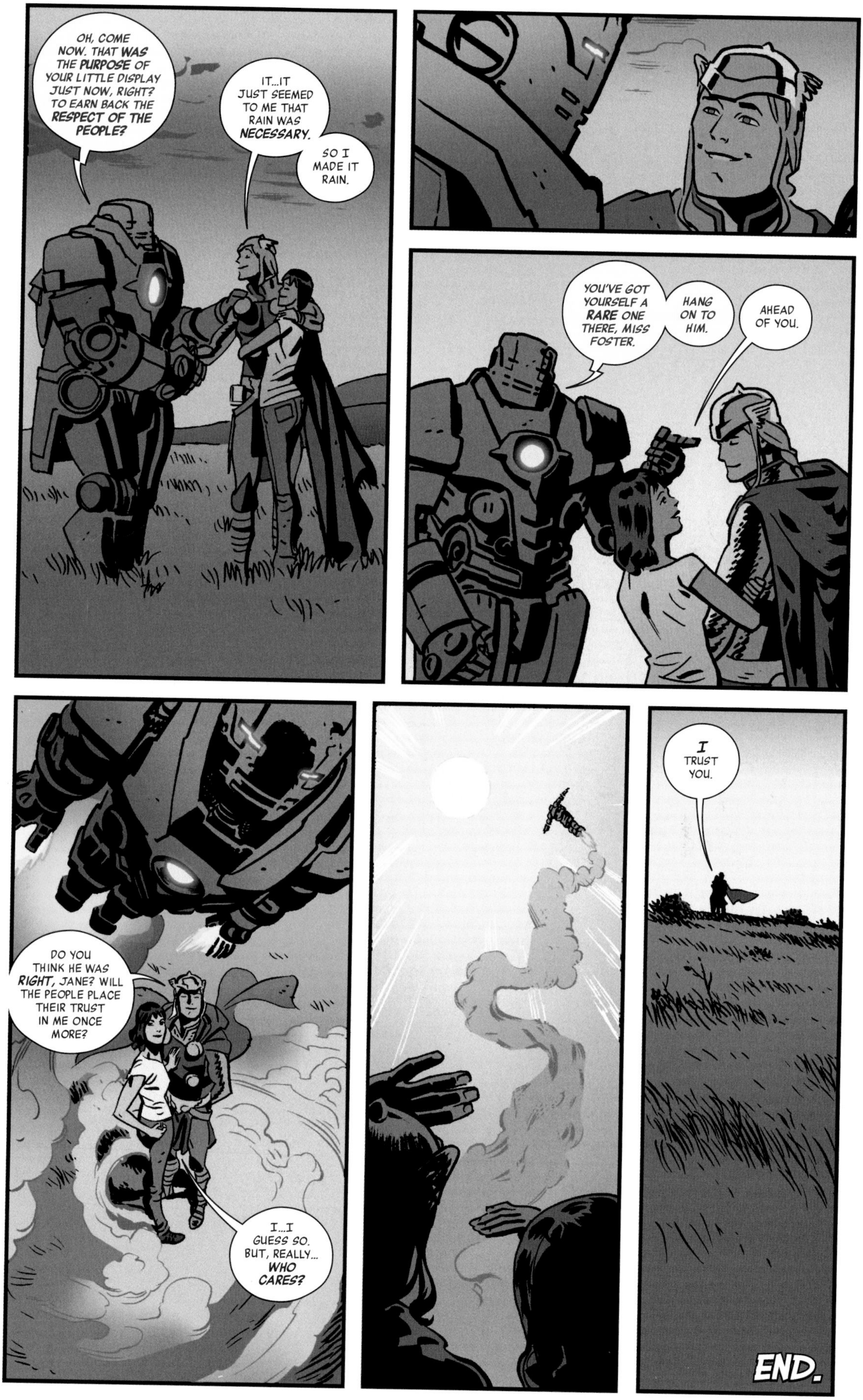
OH, COME NOW. THAT WAS THE PURPOSE OF YOUR LITTLE DISPLAY JUST NOW, RIGHT? TO EARN BACK THE RESPECT OF THE PEOPLE?
IT...IT JUST SEEMED TO ME THAT RAIN WAS NECESSARY.
SO I MADE IT RAIN.
YOU'VE GOT YOURSELF A RARE ONE THERE, MISS FOSTER.
HANG ON TO HIM.
AHEAD OF YOU.
DO YOU THINK HE WAS RIGHT, JANE? WILL THE PEOPLE PLACE THEIR TRUST IN ME ONCE MORE?
I...I GUESS SO. BUT, REALLY... WHO CARES?
I TRUST YOU.
END.

And it came to pass that
THOR: THE MIGHTY AVENGER
did end. And the readers came and they were all a-twitter. And they did open the final issue and turn to the last page, and lo! there they did read these simple inscriptions:

Whosoever holds this comic book, if they should have romance in their hearts, shall possess the everlasting gratitude of THOR, THE MIGHTY AVENGER.
- Roger Langridge

I can't believe this journey is coming to an end. Working on THOR: THE MIGHTY AVENGER with this wonderful team has been the most fun I've ever had making comics. What an amazing experience it has been to have a book that I love so much be so well received by fans. My sincere gratitude to all of you who supported the series.
- Chris Samnee

THOR THE MIGHTY AVENGER will always be a career highlight for me, and that's all thanks to the top notch creative team and the most amazing fans in comics. Thanks so much to all of you!
- Matt Wilson

THOR THE MIGHTY AVENGER has been a blast, and I'm sad to see it end. I'm proud to have been a part of this amazing creative team. Thanks to everyone who supported this book!
- Rus Wooton

Y'know how you think back to when you were a kid, and you fondly remember stories you read that made you laugh, blew your mind, took you on fantastic journeys and made you feel like all the characters were your friends? When the children of today think back in ten years, I think that's how they're gonna remember what Roger, Chris, Matt & Rus did on THOR THE MIGHTY AVENGER. I'm too lucky and so proud that I got to be a part of such a special tale.
- Nate Cosby

FREE COMIC BOOK DAY 2011

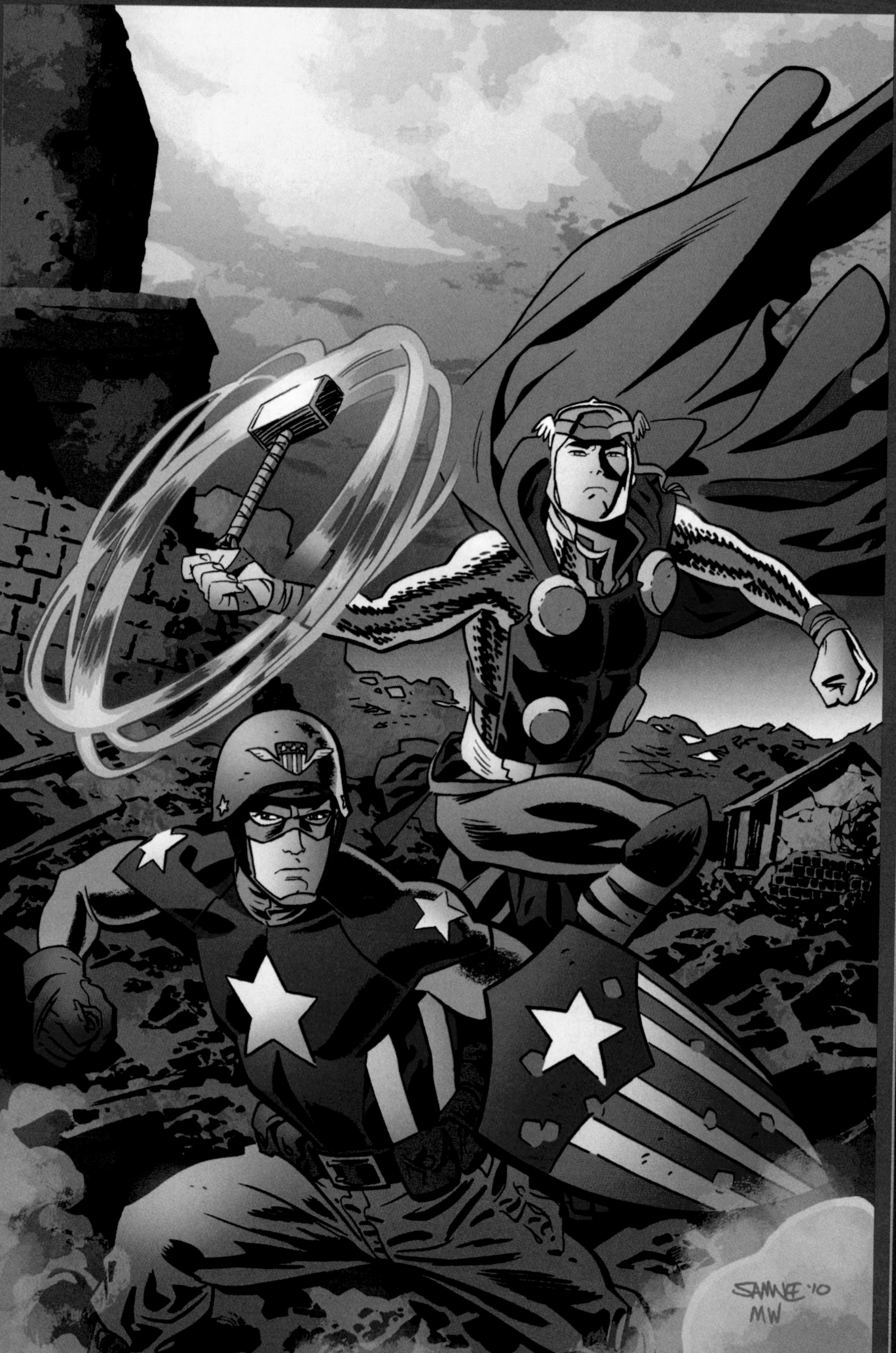
SAMNEE '10
MW

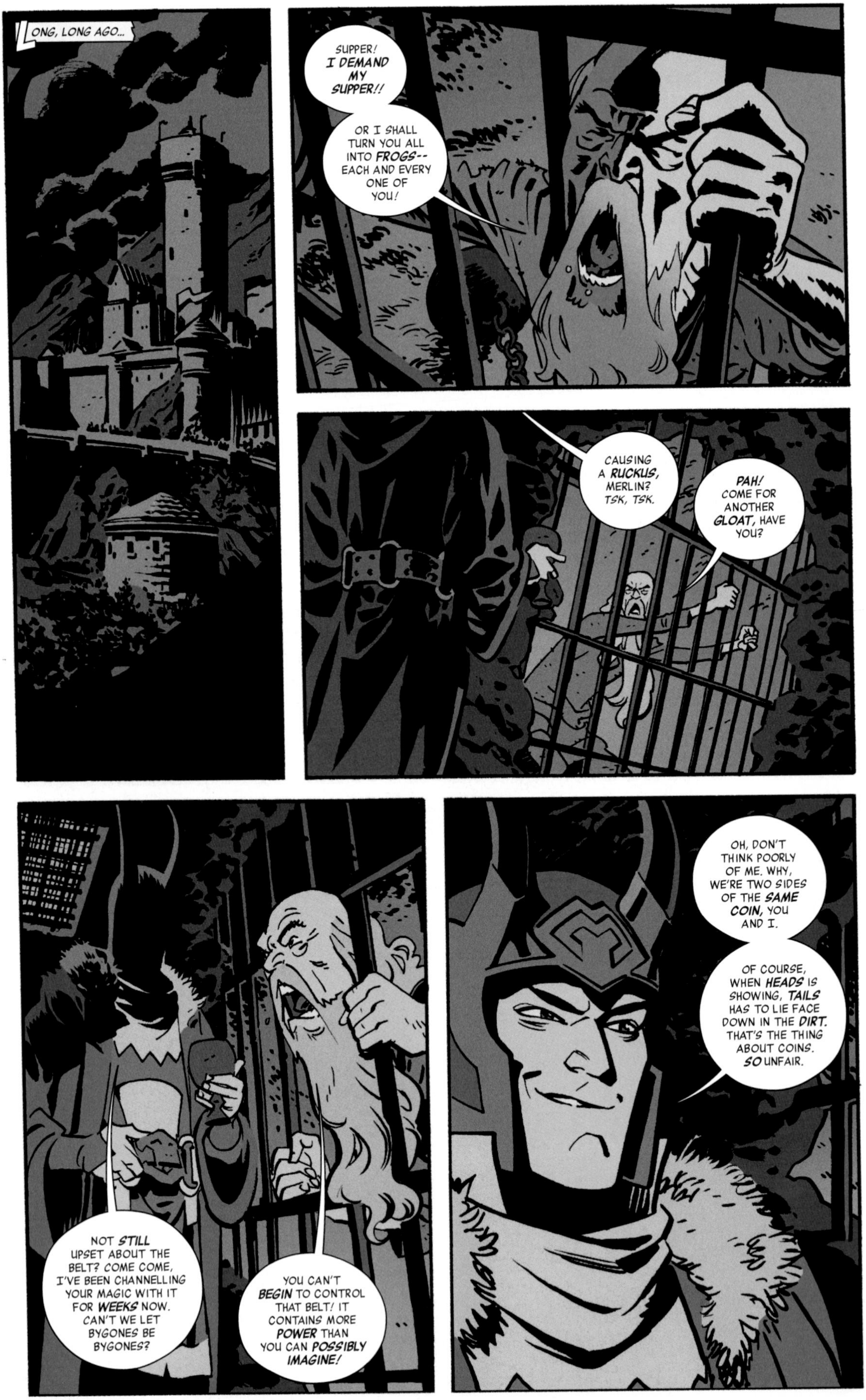
LONG, LONG AGO...
SUPPER! I DEMAND MY SUPPER!!
OR I SHALL TURN YOU ALL INTO FROGS-- EACH AND EVERY ONE OF YOU!
CAUSING A RUCKUS, MERLIN? TSK, TSK.
PAH! COME FOR ANOTHER GLOAT, HAVE YOU?
NOT STILL UPSET ABOUT THE BELT? COME COME, I'VE BEEN CHANNELLING YOUR MAGIC WITH IT FOR WEEKS NOW. CAN'T WE LET BYGONES BE BYGONES?
YOU CAN'T BEGIN TO CONTROL THAT BELT! IT CONTAINS MORE POWER THAN YOU CAN POSSIBLY IMAGINE!
OH, DON'T THINK POORLY OF ME. WHY, WE'RE TWO SIDES OF THE SAME COIN, YOU AND I.
OF COURSE, WHEN HEADS IS SHOWING, TAILS HAS TO LIE FACE DOWN IN THE DIRT. THAT'S THE THING ABOUT COINS. SO UNFAIR.

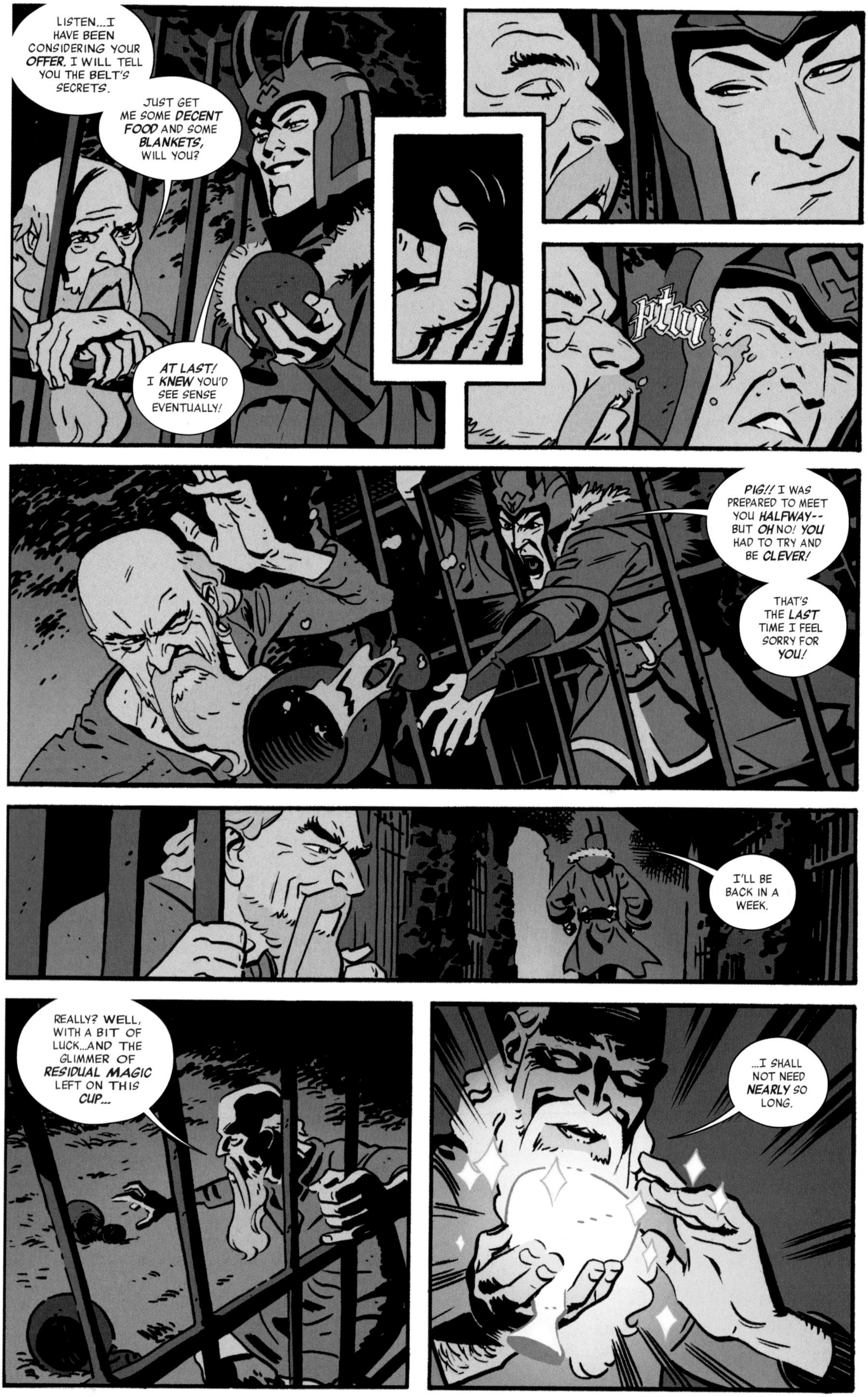
LISTEN...I HAVE BEEN CONSIDERING YOUR OFFER. I WILL TELL YOU THE BELT'S SECRETS.
JUST GET ME SOME DECENT FOOD AND SOME BLANKETS, WILL YOU?
AT LAST! I KNEW YOU'D SEE SENSE EVENTUALLY!
ptui
PIG!! I WAS PREPARED TO MEET YOU HALFWAY--BUT OH NO! YOU HAD TO TRY AND BE CLEVER!
THAT'S THE LAST TIME I FEEL SORRY FOR YOU!
I'LL BE BACK IN A WEEK.
REALLY? WELL, WITH A BIT OF LUCK...AND THE GLIMMER OF RESIDUAL MAGIC LEFT ON THIS CUP...
...I SHALL NOT NEED NEARLY SO LONG.

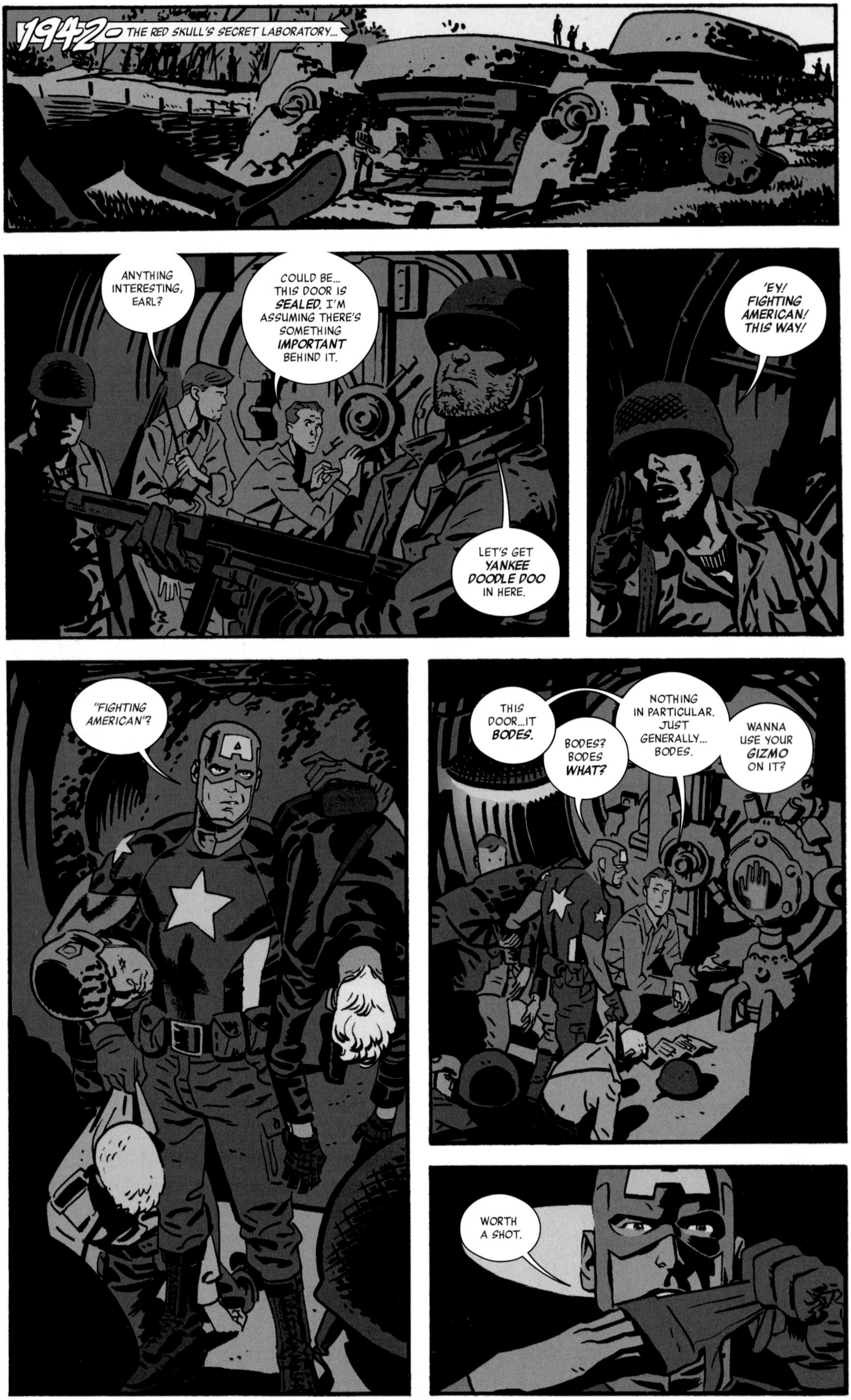
1942 — THE RED SKULL'S SECRET LABORATORY...
ANYTHING INTERESTING, EARL?
COULD BE... THIS DOOR IS SEALED. I'M ASSUMING THERE'S SOMETHING IMPORTANT BEHIND IT.
LET'S GET YANKEE DOODLE DOO IN HERE.
'EY! FIGHTING AMERICAN! THIS WAY!
"FIGHTING AMERICAN"?
THIS DOOR...IT BODES.
BODES? BODES WHAT?
NOTHING IN PARTICULAR. JUST GENERALLY... BODES.
WANNA USE YOUR GIZMO ON IT?
WORTH A SHOT.

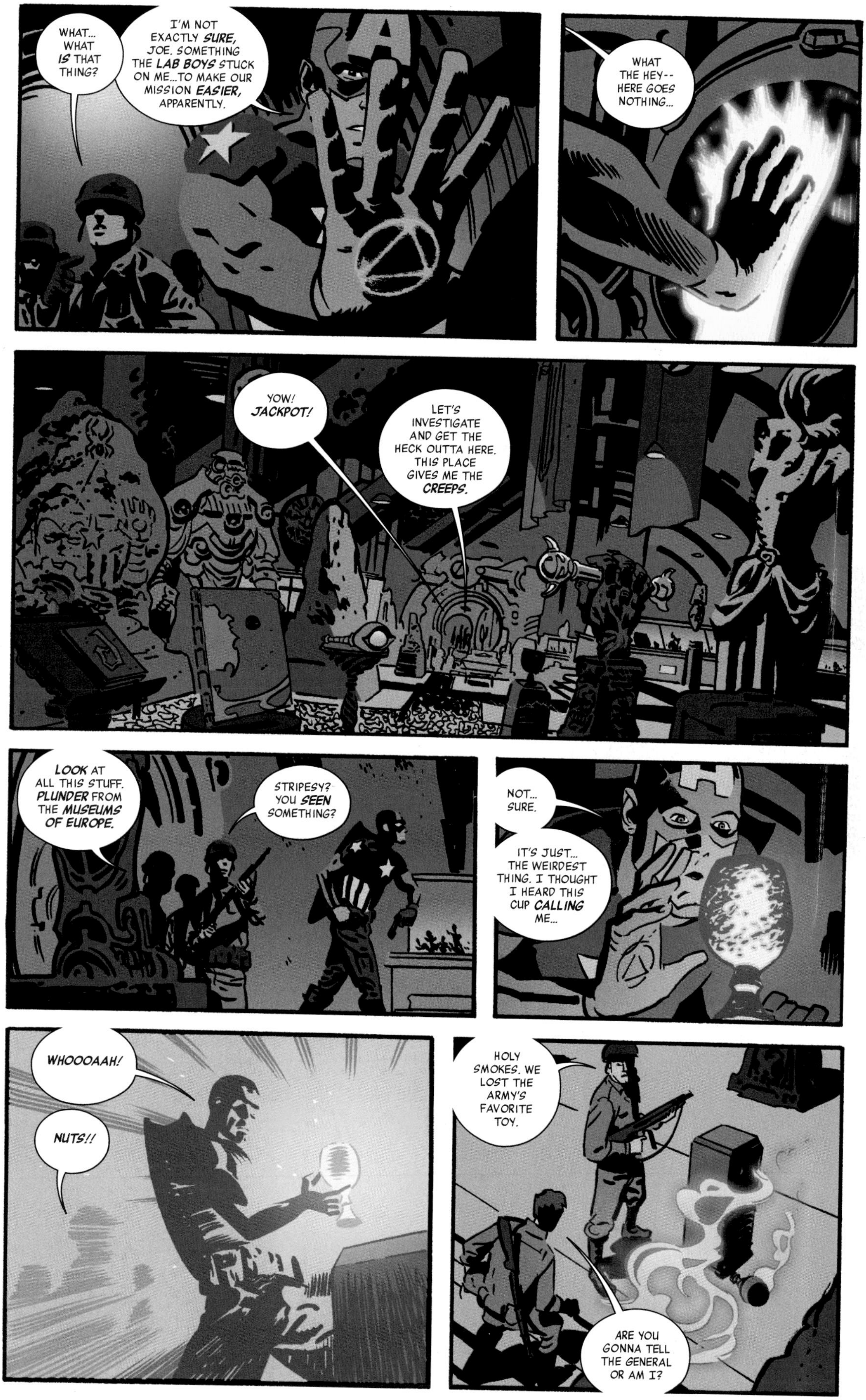
WHAT... WHAT IS THAT THING?
I'M NOT EXACTLY SURE, JOE. SOMETHING THE LAB BOYS STUCK ON ME...TO MAKE OUR MISSION EASIER, APPARENTLY.
WHAT THE HEY-- HERE GOES NOTHING...
YOW! JACKPOT!
LET'S INVESTIGATE AND GET THE HECK OUTTA HERE. THIS PLACE GIVES ME THE CREEPS.
LOOK AT ALL THIS STUFF. PLUNDER FROM THE MUSEUMS OF EUROPE.
STRIPESY? YOU SEEN SOMETHING?
NOT... SURE.
IT'S JUST... THE WEIRDEST THING. I THOUGHT I HEARD THIS CUP CALLING ME...
WHOOOAAH!
NUTS!!
HOLY SMOKES. WE LOST THE ARMY'S FAVORITE TOY.
ARE YOU GONNA TELL THE GENERAL OR AM I?

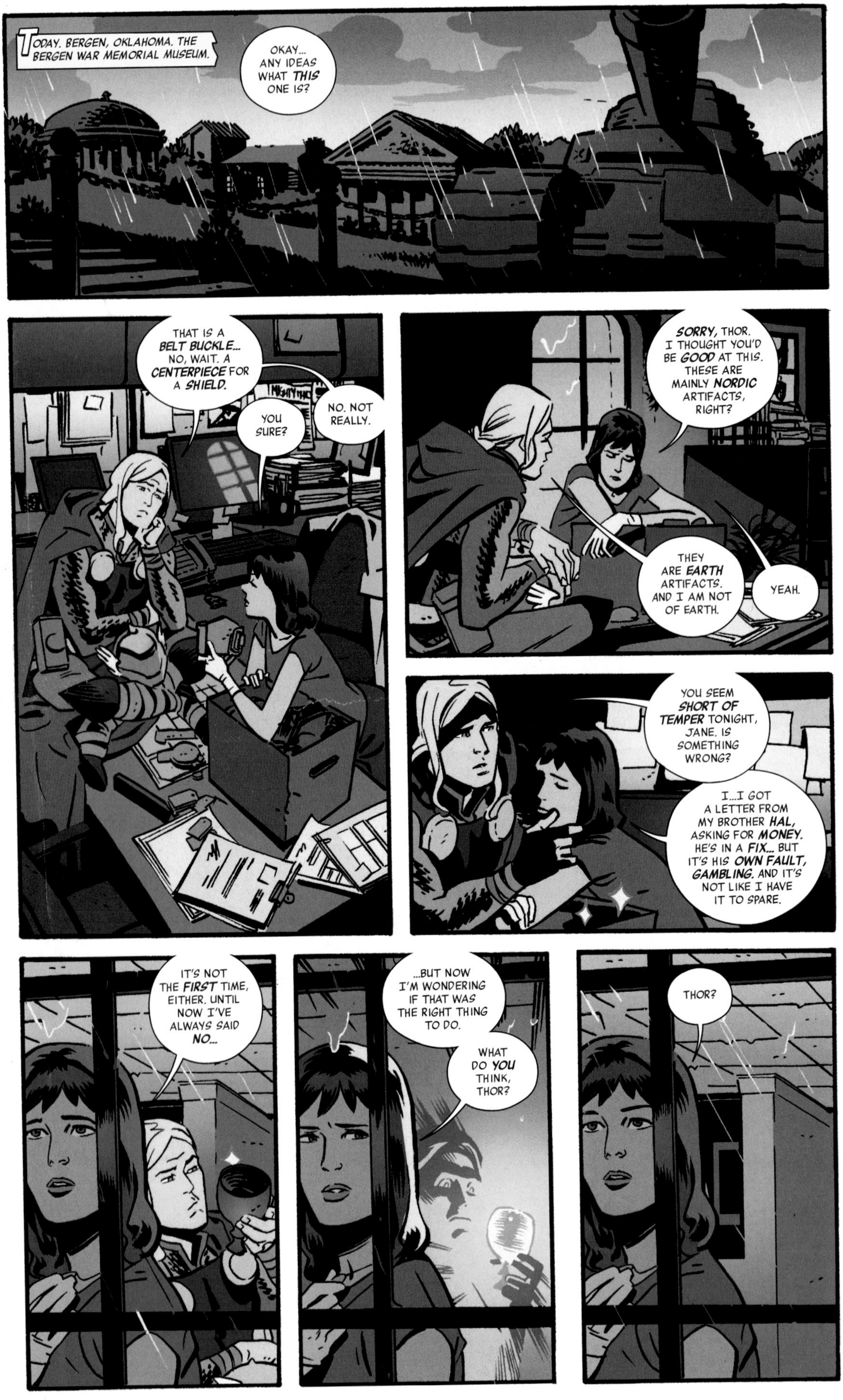
TODAY. BERGEN, OKLAHOMA. THE BERGEN WAR MEMORIAL MUSEUM.
OKAY... ANY IDEAS WHAT THIS ONE IS?
THAT IS A BELT BUCKLE... NO, WAIT. A CENTERPIECE FOR A SHIELD.
YOU SURE?
NO. NOT REALLY.
SORRY, THOR. I THOUGHT YOU'D BE GOOD AT THIS. THESE ARE MAINLY NORDIC ARTIFACTS, RIGHT?
THEY ARE EARTH ARTIFACTS. AND I AM NOT OF EARTH.
YEAH.
YOU SEEM SHORT OF TEMPER TONIGHT, JANE. IS SOMETHING WRONG?
I...I GOT A LETTER FROM MY BROTHER HAL, ASKING FOR MONEY. HE'S IN A FIX... BUT IT'S HIS OWN FAULT, GAMBLING. AND IT'S NOT LIKE I HAVE IT TO SPARE.
IT'S NOT THE FIRST TIME, EITHER. UNTIL NOW I'VE ALWAYS SAID NO...
...BUT NOW I'M WONDERING IF THAT WAS THE RIGHT THING TO DO.
WHAT DO YOU THINK, THOR?
THOR?

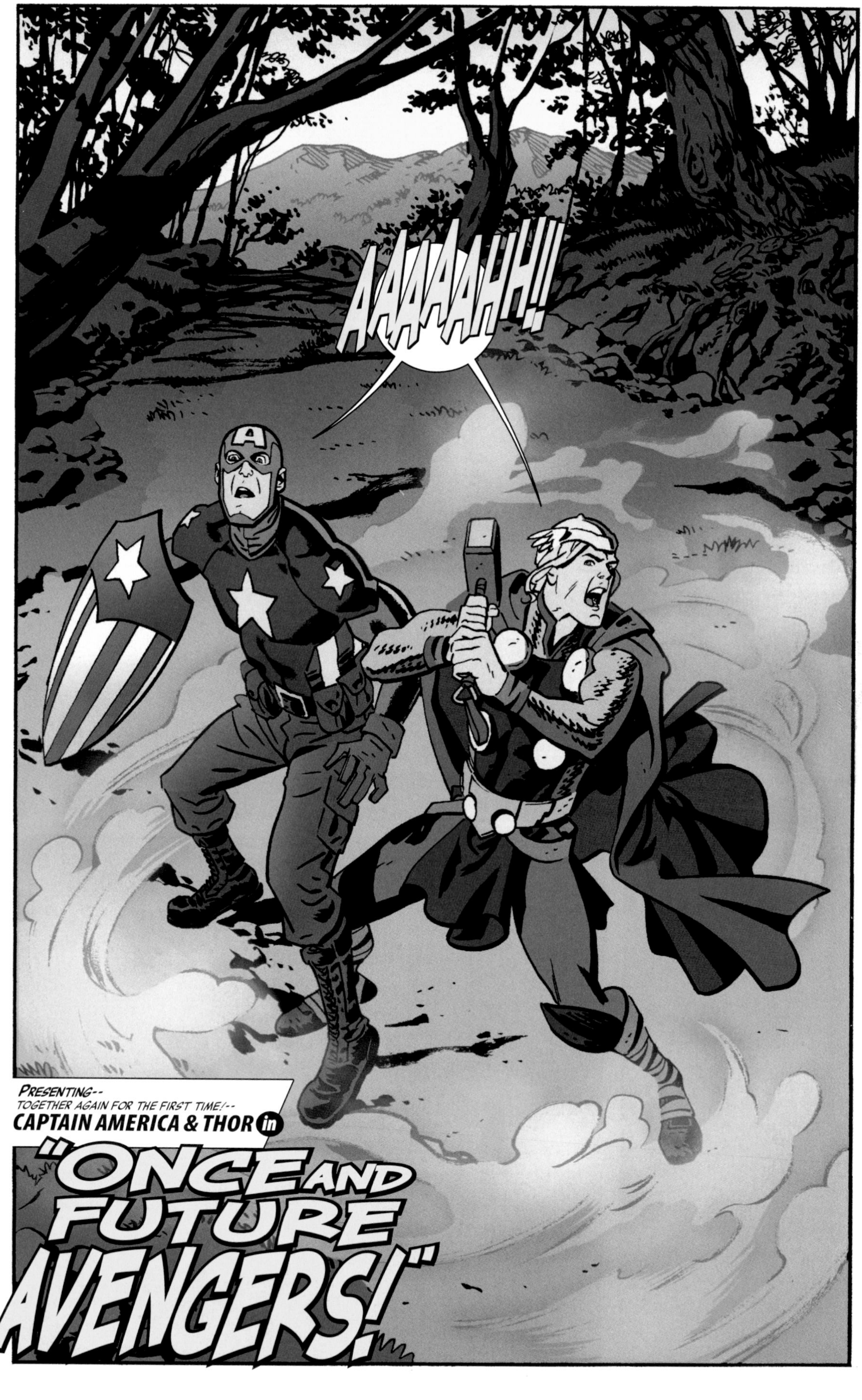
AAAAAHH!!
PRESENTING--
TOGETHER AGAIN FOR THE FIRST TIME!--
CAPTAIN AMERICA & THOR in
"ONCE AND FUTURE AVENGERS!"

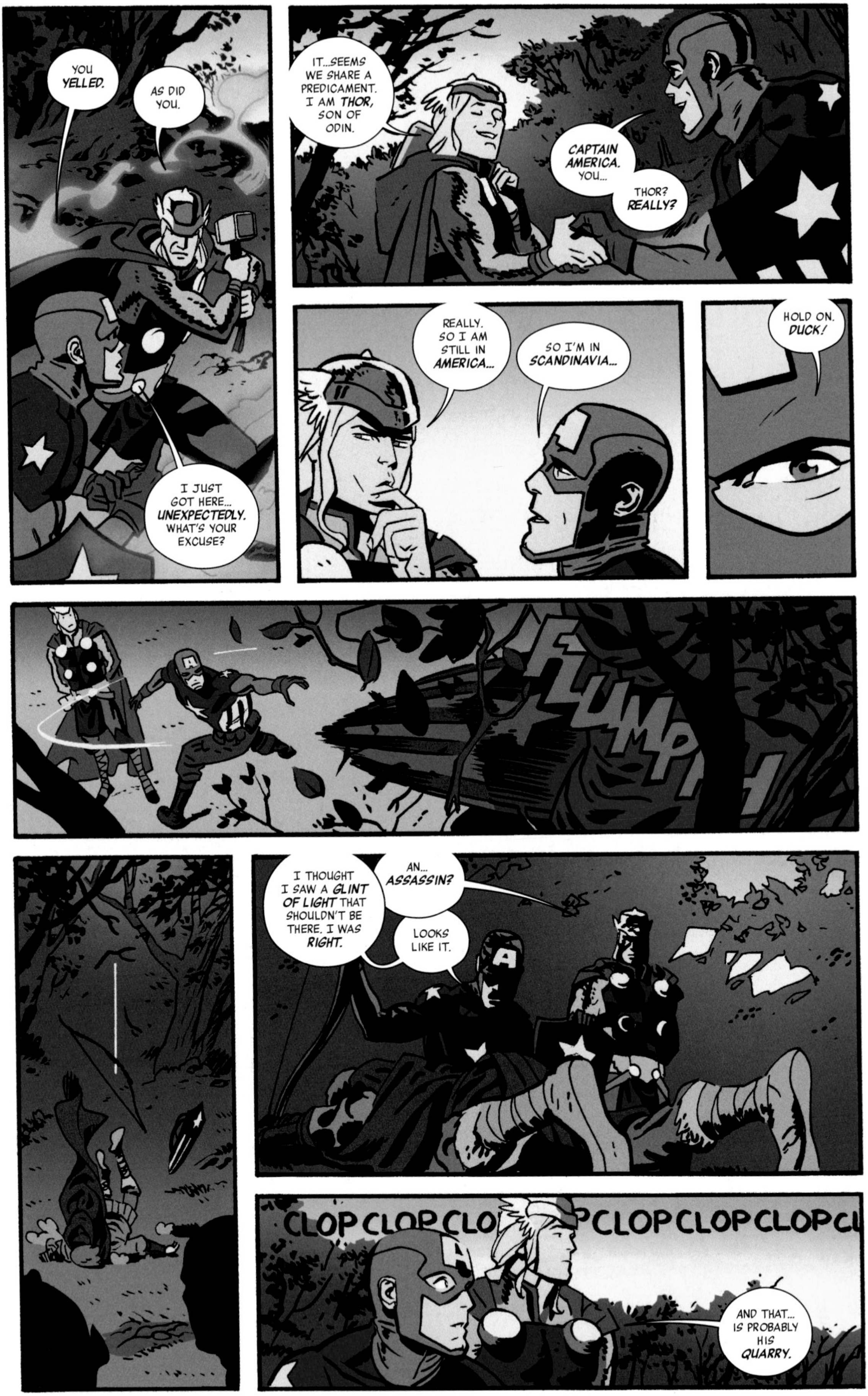
YOU YELLED.
AS DID YOU.
I JUST GOT HERE... UNEXPECTEDLY. WHAT'S YOUR EXCUSE?
IT...SEEMS WE SHARE A PREDICAMENT. I AM THOR, SON OF ODIN.
CAPTAIN AMERICA. YOU...
THOR? REALLY?
REALLY. SO I AM STILL IN AMERICA...
SO I'M IN SCANDINAVIA...
HOLD ON. DUCK!
FLUMPHH
I THOUGHT I SAW A GLINT OF LIGHT THAT SHOULDN'T BE THERE. I WAS RIGHT.
AN... ASSASSIN?
LOOKS LIKE IT.
CLOP CLOP CLOP CLOP CLOP CLOP
AND THAT... IS PROBABLY HIS QUARRY.

THERE MAY BE **MORE** OF THESE GUYS--RUN AHEAD AND **STOP THOSE HORSES** WHILE I...

HOLD.

THROOMM!

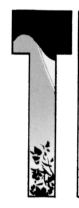

WHUMP

WHUMP

WHUMP

WHUMP

I TRUST THAT WILL BE **SUFFICIENT**, CAPTAIN...

CAPTAIN?

JUST A MOMENT, THOR...

CAMELOT 10 Miles

...I THINK I MIGHT KNOW WHERE WE **ARE**.

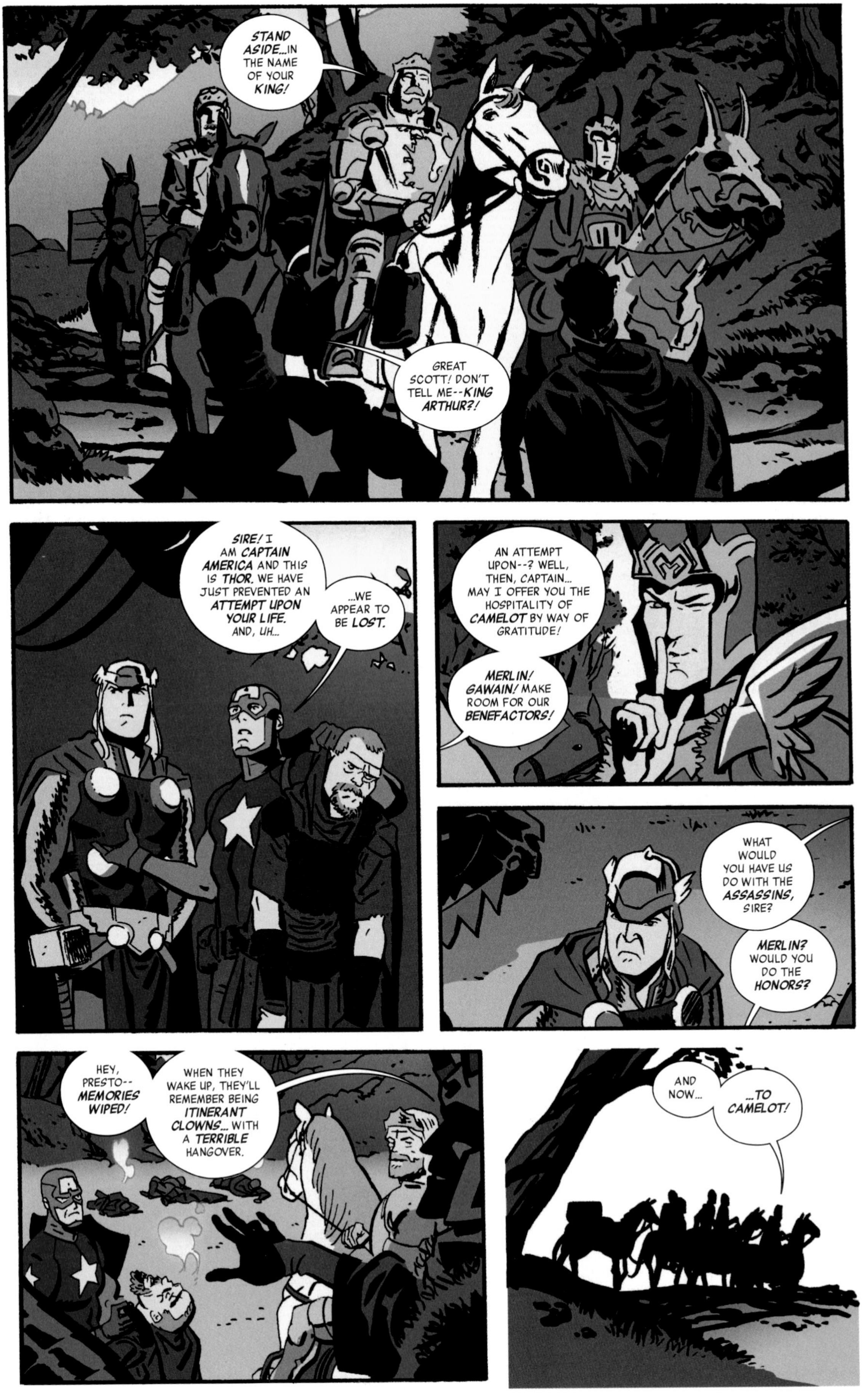

STAND ASIDE...IN THE NAME OF YOUR KING!
GREAT SCOTT! DON'T TELL ME--KING ARTHUR?!
SIRE! I AM CAPTAIN AMERICA AND THIS IS THOR. WE HAVE JUST PREVENTED AN ATTEMPT UPON YOUR LIFE. AND, UH...
...WE APPEAR TO BE LOST.
AN ATTEMPT UPON--? WELL, THEN, CAPTAIN... MAY I OFFER YOU THE HOSPITALITY OF CAMELOT BY WAY OF GRATITUDE!
MERLIN! GAWAIN! MAKE ROOM FOR OUR BENEFACTORS!
WHAT WOULD YOU HAVE US DO WITH THE ASSASSINS, SIRE?
MERLIN? WOULD YOU DO THE HONORS?
HEY, PRESTO-- MEMORIES WIPED!
WHEN THEY WAKE UP, THEY'LL REMEMBER BEING ITINERANT CLOWNS... WITH A TERRIBLE HANGOVER.
AND NOW...
...TO CAMELOT!

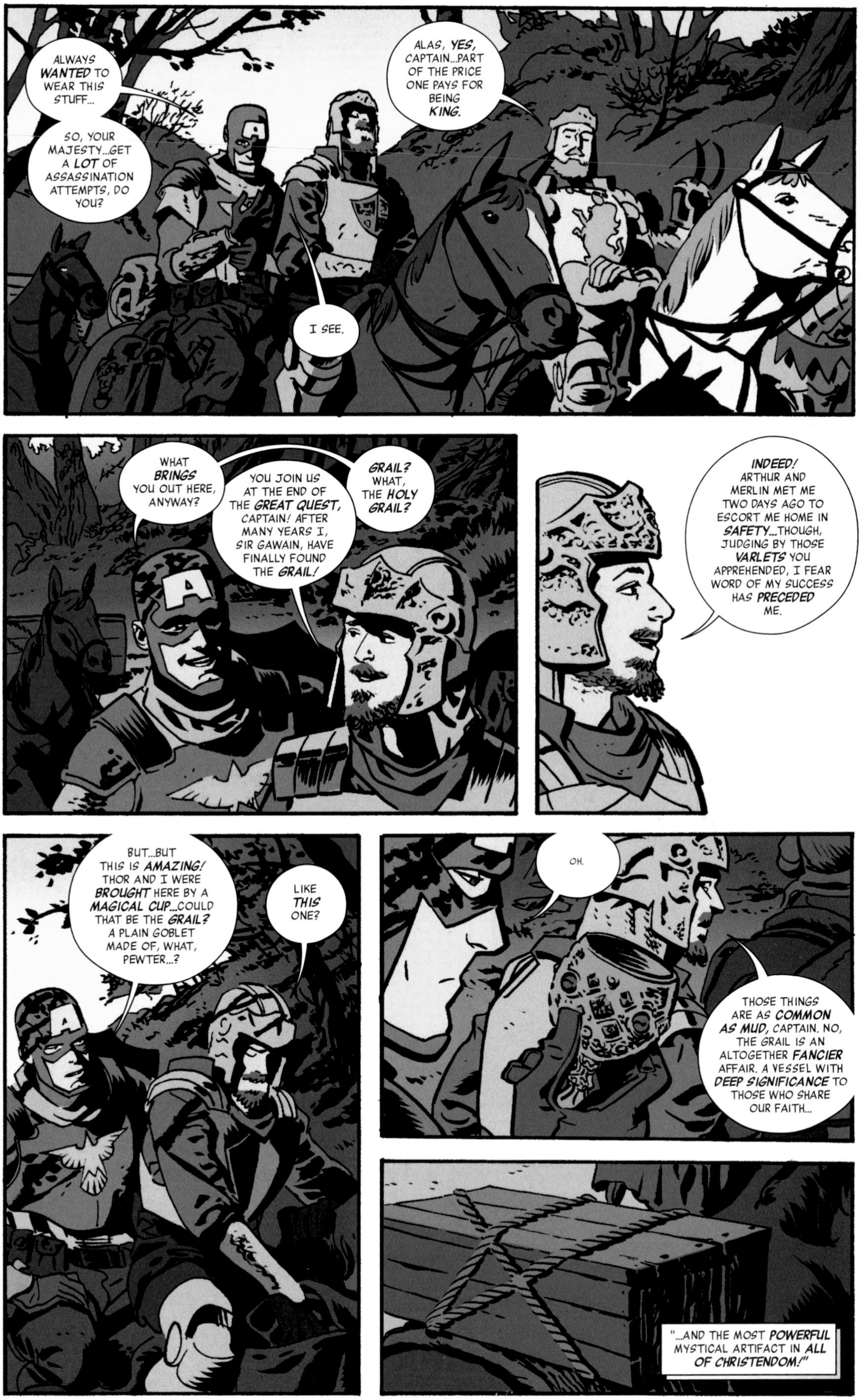
ALWAYS WANTED TO WEAR THIS STUFF...
SO, YOUR MAJESTY...GET A LOT OF ASSASSINATION ATTEMPTS, DO YOU?
ALAS, YES, CAPTAIN...PART OF THE PRICE ONE PAYS FOR BEING KING.
I SEE.
WHAT BRINGS YOU OUT HERE, ANYWAY?
YOU JOIN US AT THE END OF THE GREAT QUEST, CAPTAIN! AFTER MANY YEARS I, SIR GAWAIN, HAVE FINALLY FOUND THE GRAIL!
GRAIL? WHAT, THE HOLY GRAIL?
INDEED! ARTHUR AND MERLIN MET ME TWO DAYS AGO TO ESCORT ME HOME IN SAFETY...THOUGH, JUDGING BY THOSE VARLETS YOU APPREHENDED, I FEAR WORD OF MY SUCCESS HAS PRECEDED ME.
BUT...BUT THIS IS AMAZING! THOR AND I WERE BROUGHT HERE BY A MAGICAL CUP...COULD THAT BE THE GRAIL? A PLAIN GOBLET MADE OF, WHAT, PEWTER...?
LIKE THIS ONE?
OH.
THOSE THINGS ARE AS COMMON AS MUD, CAPTAIN. NO, THE GRAIL IS AN ALTOGETHER FANCIER AFFAIR. A VESSEL WITH DEEP SIGNIFICANCE TO THOSE WHO SHARE OUR FAITH...
"...AND THE MOST POWERFUL MYSTICAL ARTIFACT IN ALL OF CHRISTENDOM!"

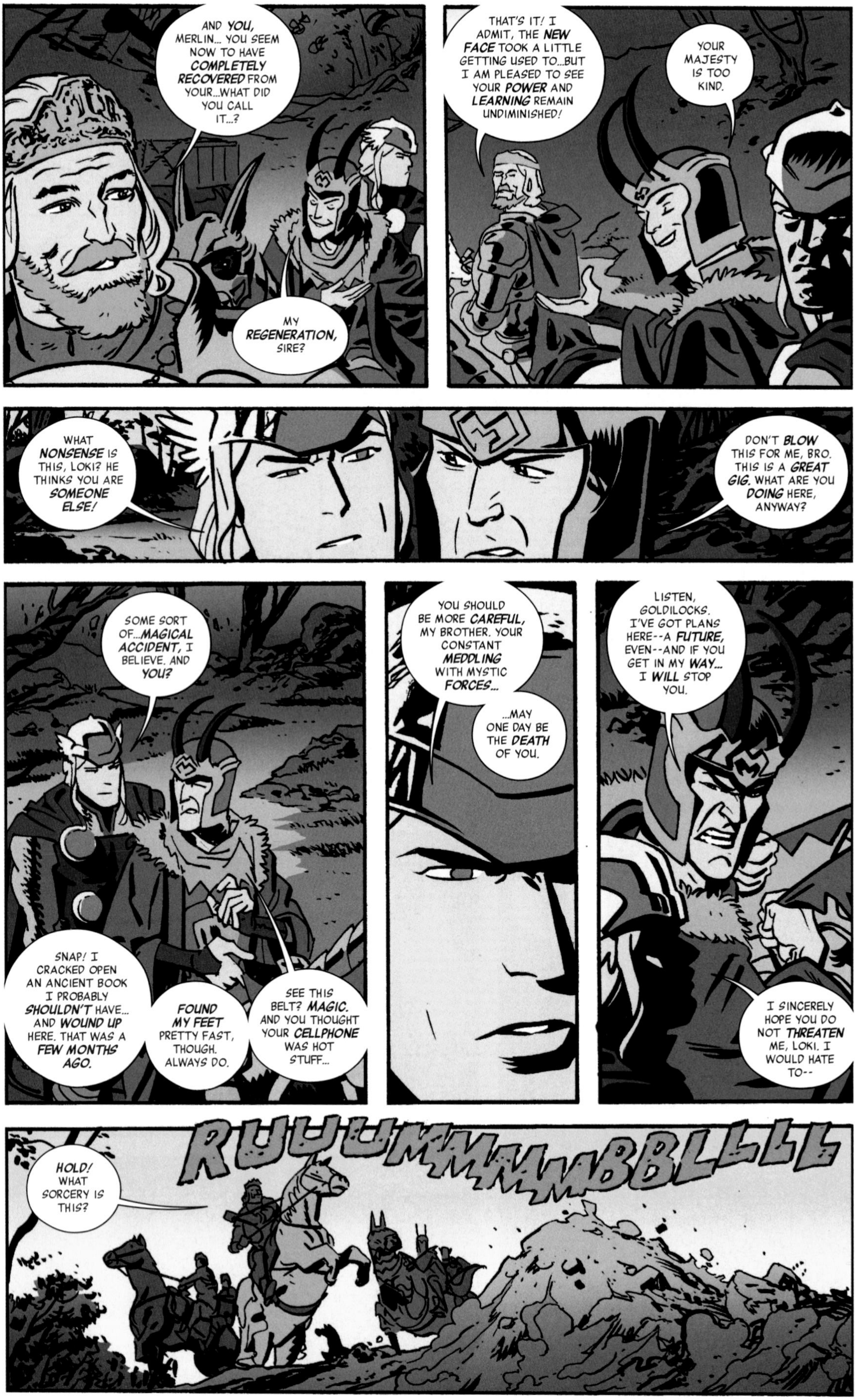
AND YOU, MERLIN... YOU SEEM NOW TO HAVE COMPLETELY RECOVERED FROM YOUR...WHAT DID YOU CALL IT...?
MY REGENERATION, SIRE?
THAT'S IT! I ADMIT, THE NEW FACE TOOK A LITTLE GETTING USED TO...BUT I AM PLEASED TO SEE YOUR POWER AND LEARNING REMAIN UNDIMINISHED!
YOUR MAJESTY IS TOO KIND.
WHAT NONSENSE IS THIS, LOKI? HE THINKS YOU ARE SOMEONE ELSE!
DON'T BLOW THIS FOR ME, BRO. THIS IS A GREAT GIG. WHAT ARE YOU DOING HERE, ANYWAY?
SOME SORT OF...MAGICAL ACCIDENT, I BELIEVE. AND YOU?
SNAP! I CRACKED OPEN AN ANCIENT BOOK I PROBABLY SHOULDN'T HAVE... AND WOUND UP HERE. THAT WAS A FEW MONTHS AGO.
FOUND MY FEET PRETTY FAST, THOUGH. ALWAYS DO.
SEE THIS BELT? MAGIC. AND YOU THOUGHT YOUR CELLPHONE WAS HOT STUFF...
YOU SHOULD BE MORE CAREFUL, MY BROTHER. YOUR CONSTANT MEDDLING WITH MYSTIC FORCES...
...MAY ONE DAY BE THE DEATH OF YOU.
LISTEN, GOLDILOCKS. I'VE GOT PLANS HERE--A FUTURE, EVEN--AND IF YOU GET IN MY WAY... I WILL STOP YOU.
I SINCERELY HOPE YOU DO NOT THREATEN ME, LOKI. I WOULD HATE TO--
RUUUMMMMMBBLLLL
HOLD! WHAT SORCERY IS THIS?

RRAAARRRRRRR

A...A **DRAGON!** IN THE NAME OF OUR LORD...IS SUCH A THING **POSSIBLE?**

SIRE...I SUGGEST WE SAVE THE **PHILOSOPHY**--

T'HWOCK

SCHWAPP

--FOR AFTER THE **FUNERAL!**

TER-RIFIC. **DON'T** DO THAT AG--

T'HWAMM

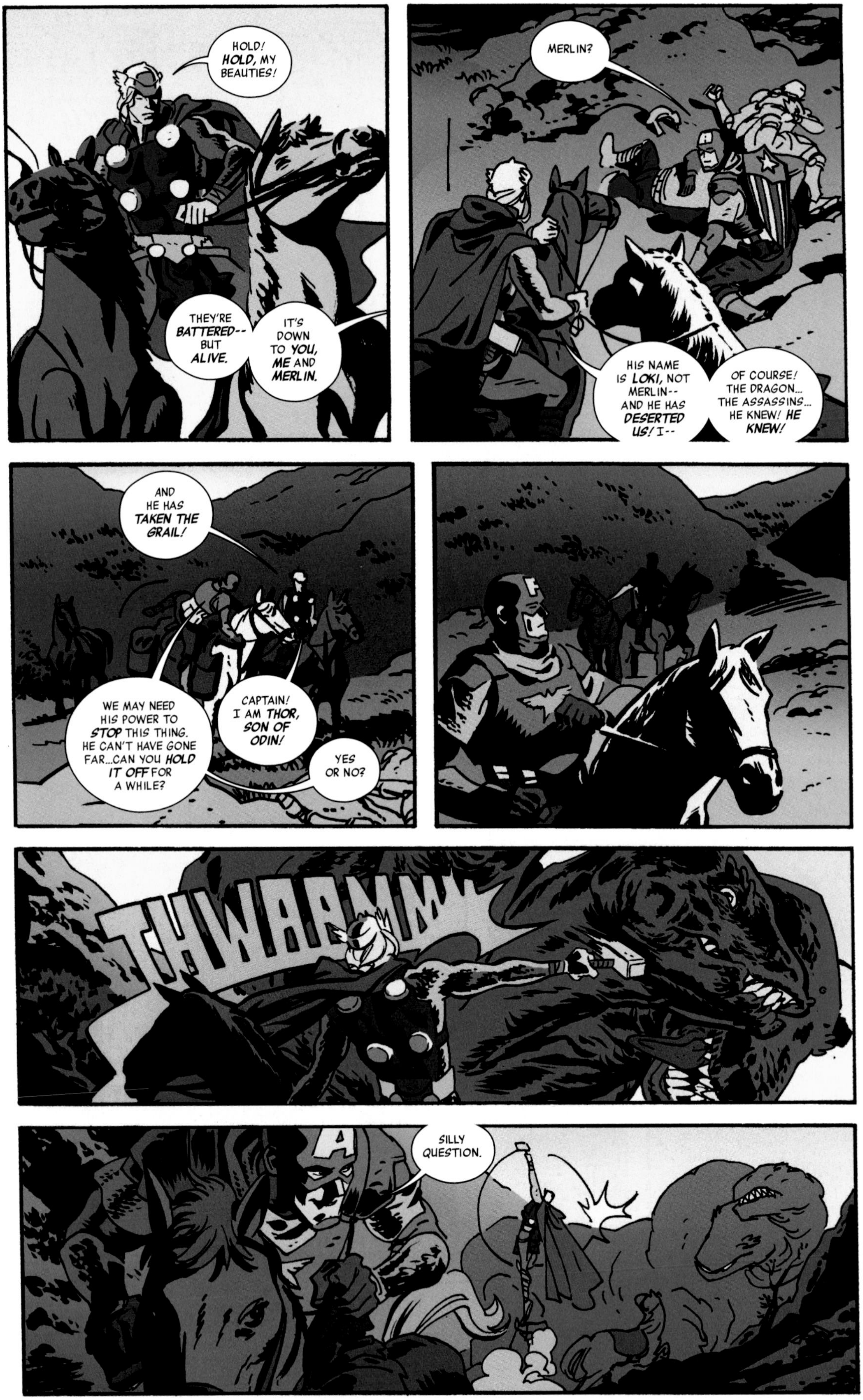
HOLD! HOLD, MY BEAUTIES!
THEY'RE BATTERED--BUT ALIVE.
IT'S DOWN TO YOU, ME AND MERLIN.
MERLIN?
HIS NAME IS LOKI, NOT MERLIN--AND HE HAS DESERTED US! I--
OF COURSE! THE DRAGON... THE ASSASSINS... HE KNEW! HE KNEW!
AND HE HAS TAKEN THE GRAIL!
WE MAY NEED HIS POWER TO STOP THIS THING. HE CAN'T HAVE GONE FAR...CAN YOU HOLD IT OFF FOR A WHILE?
CAPTAIN! I AM THOR, SON OF ODIN!
YES OR NO?
THWAMM
SILLY QUESTION.

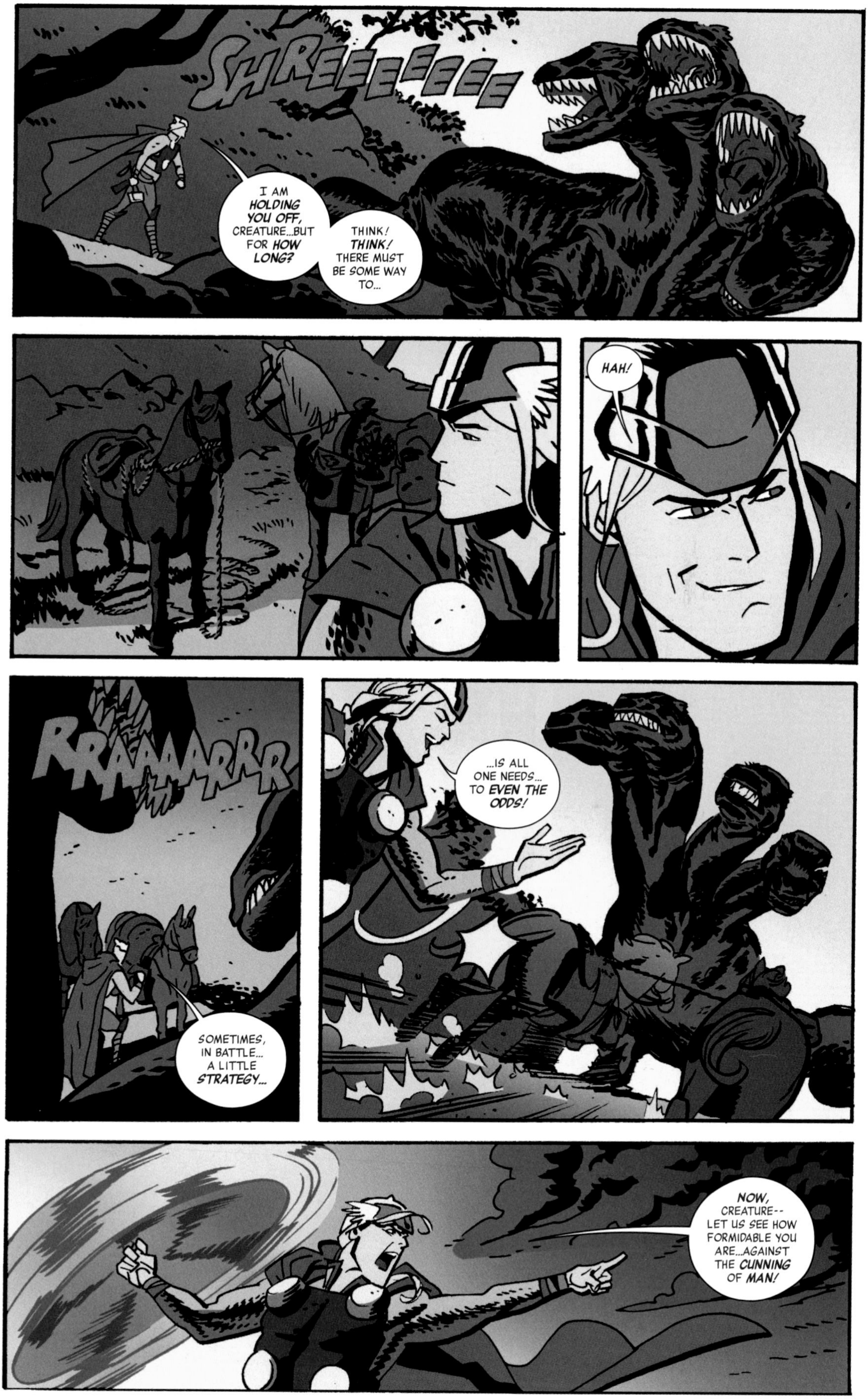

SHREEEEEEE
I AM HOLDING YOU OFF, CREATURE...BUT FOR HOW LONG?
THINK! THINK! THERE MUST BE SOME WAY TO...
HAH!
RRAAAARRR
SOMETIMES, IN BATTLE... A LITTLE STRATEGY...
...IS ALL ONE NEEDS... TO EVEN THE ODDS!
NOW, CREATURE-- LET US SEE HOW FORMIDABLE YOU ARE...AGAINST THE CUNNING OF MAN!

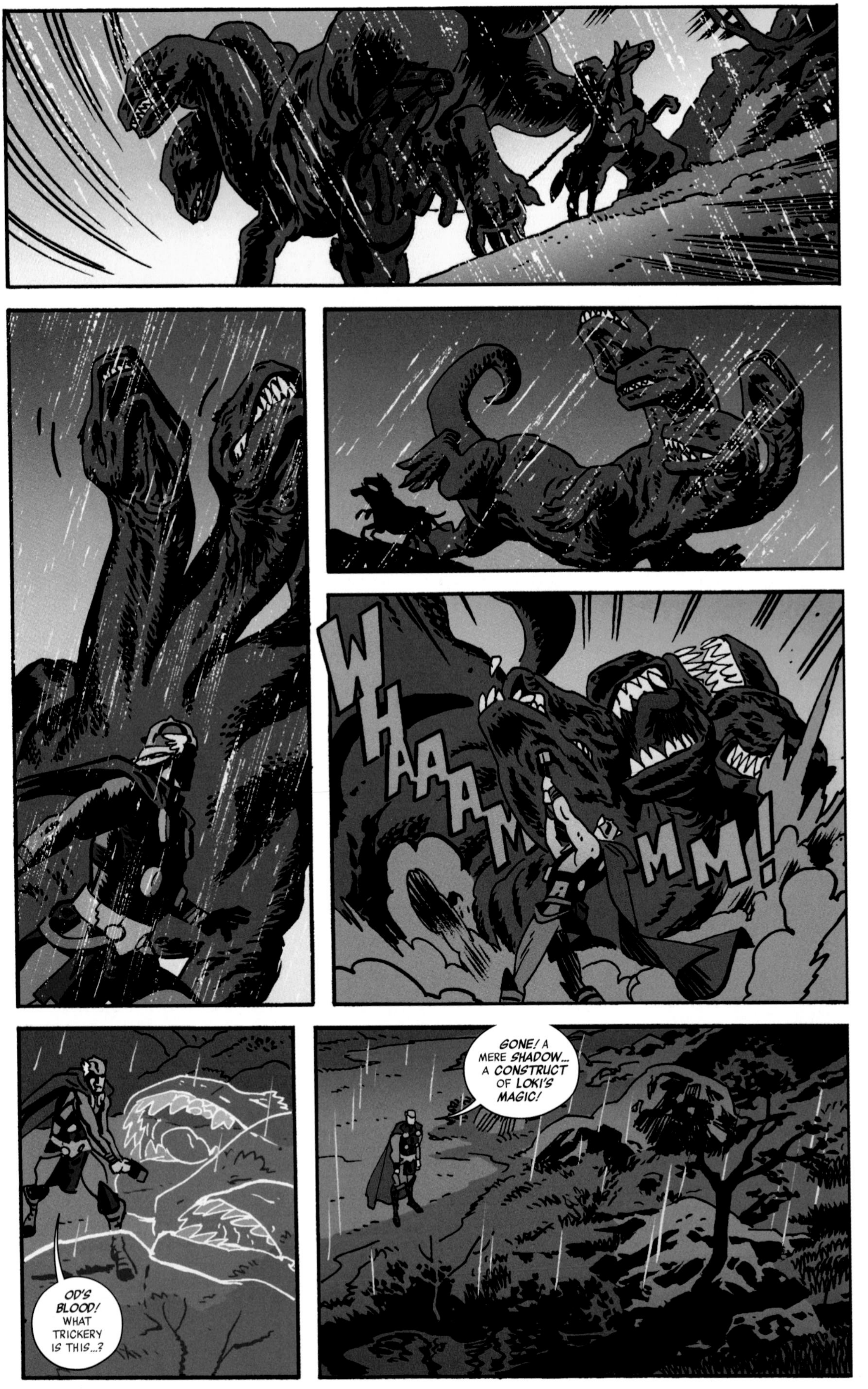
WHAAAMMM!
OD'S BLOOD! WHAT TRICKERY IS THIS...?
GONE! A MERE SHADOW... A CONSTRUCT OF LOKI'S MAGIC!

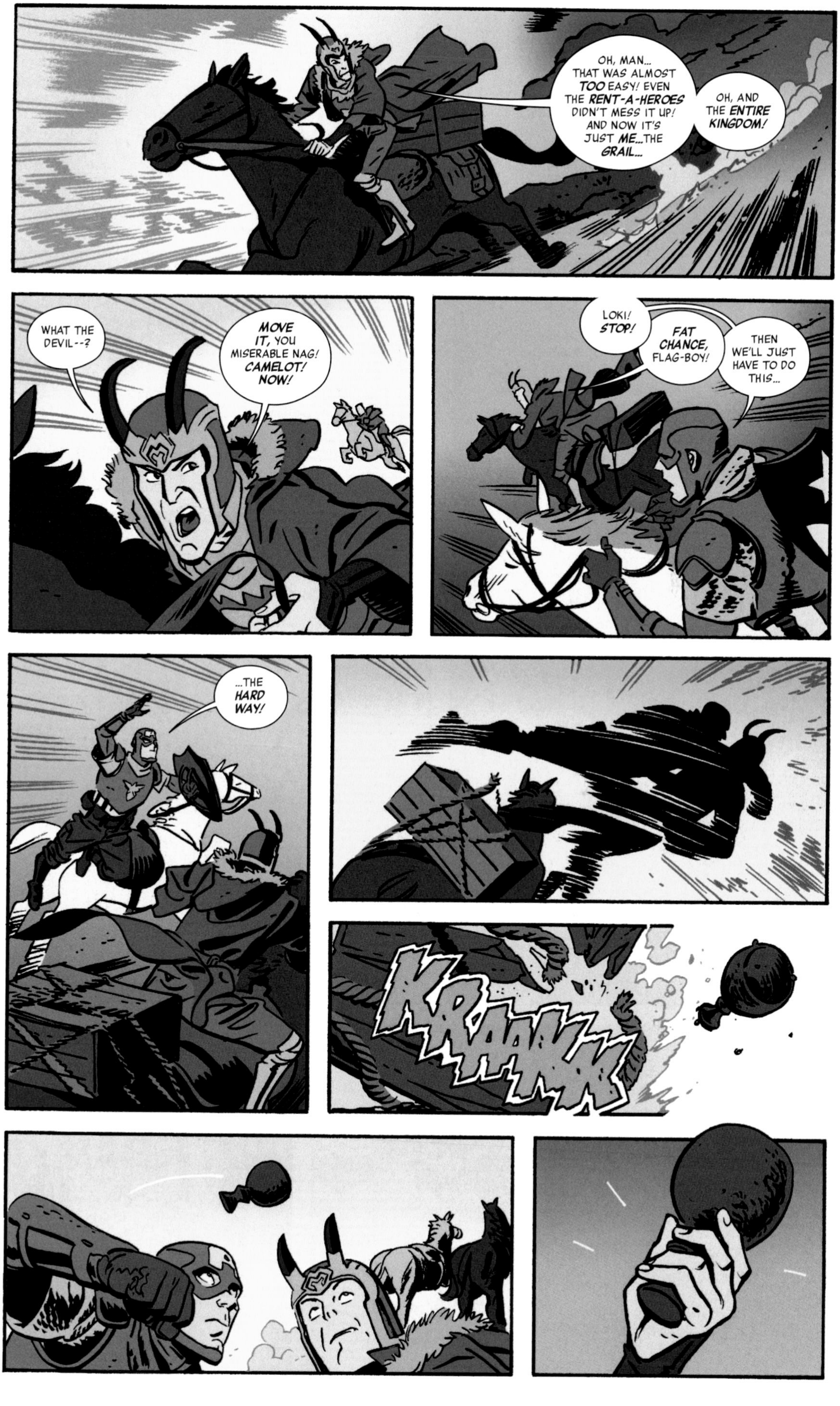
OH, MAN... THAT WAS ALMOST TOO EASY! EVEN THE RENT-A-HEROES DIDN'T MESS IT UP! AND NOW IT'S JUST ME...THE GRAIL...
OH, AND THE ENTIRE KINGDOM!
WHAT THE DEVIL--?
MOVE IT, YOU MISERABLE NAG! CAMELOT! NOW!
LOKI! STOP!
FAT CHANCE, FLAG-BOY!
THEN WE'LL JUST HAVE TO DO THIS...
...THE HARD WAY!
KRAAAKK

AT LAST-- IT'S **MINE!** THE **ULTIMATE SOURCE OF POWER!**

IT'S THE DREAM OF EVERY MAGICIAN SINCE **THE DAWN OF TIME**-- THE ABILITY TO HAVE EVERY COMMAND... **EVERY SLIGHTEST WISH**...INSTANTLY, INFALLIBLY **OBEYED!**

AND NOW IT LOOKS LIKE RAIN.

THIS DAY JUST GETS BETTER AND BETTER.

CAPTAIN! HIS BELT!

THOR! WHAT...?

CAN'T **HEAR** YOU...!

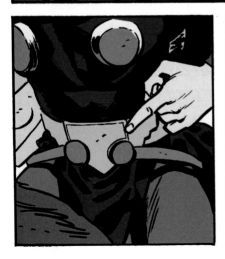

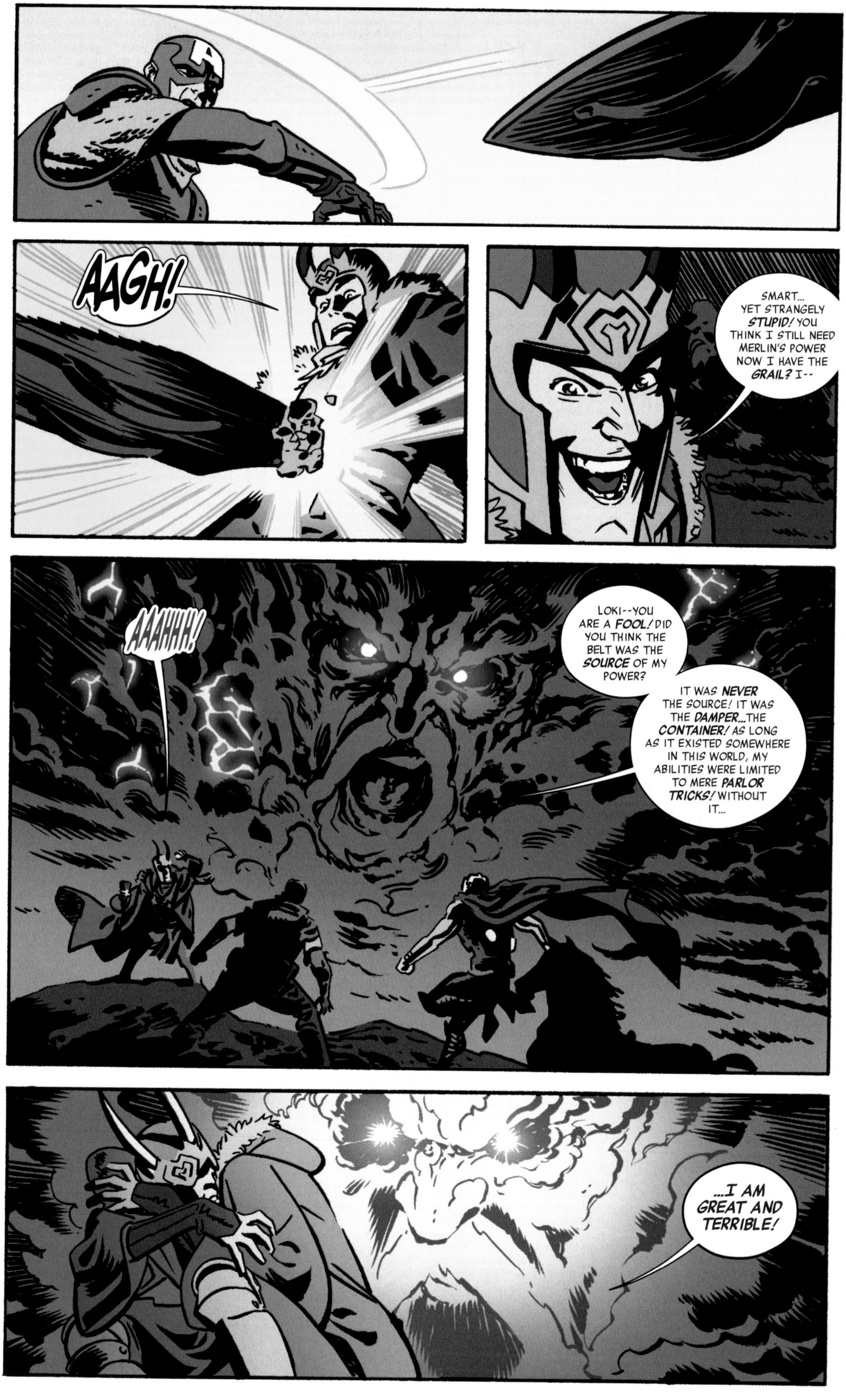

AAGH!
SMART... YET STRANGELY STUPID! YOU THINK I STILL NEED MERLIN'S POWER NOW I HAVE THE GRAIL? I--
AAAHHH!
LOKI--YOU ARE A FOOL! DID YOU THINK THE BELT WAS THE SOURCE OF MY POWER?
IT WAS NEVER THE SOURCE! IT WAS THE DAMPER...THE CONTAINER! AS LONG AS IT EXISTED SOMEWHERE IN THIS WORLD, MY ABILITIES WERE LIMITED TO MERE PARLOR TRICKS! WITHOUT IT...
...I AM GREAT AND TERRIBLE!

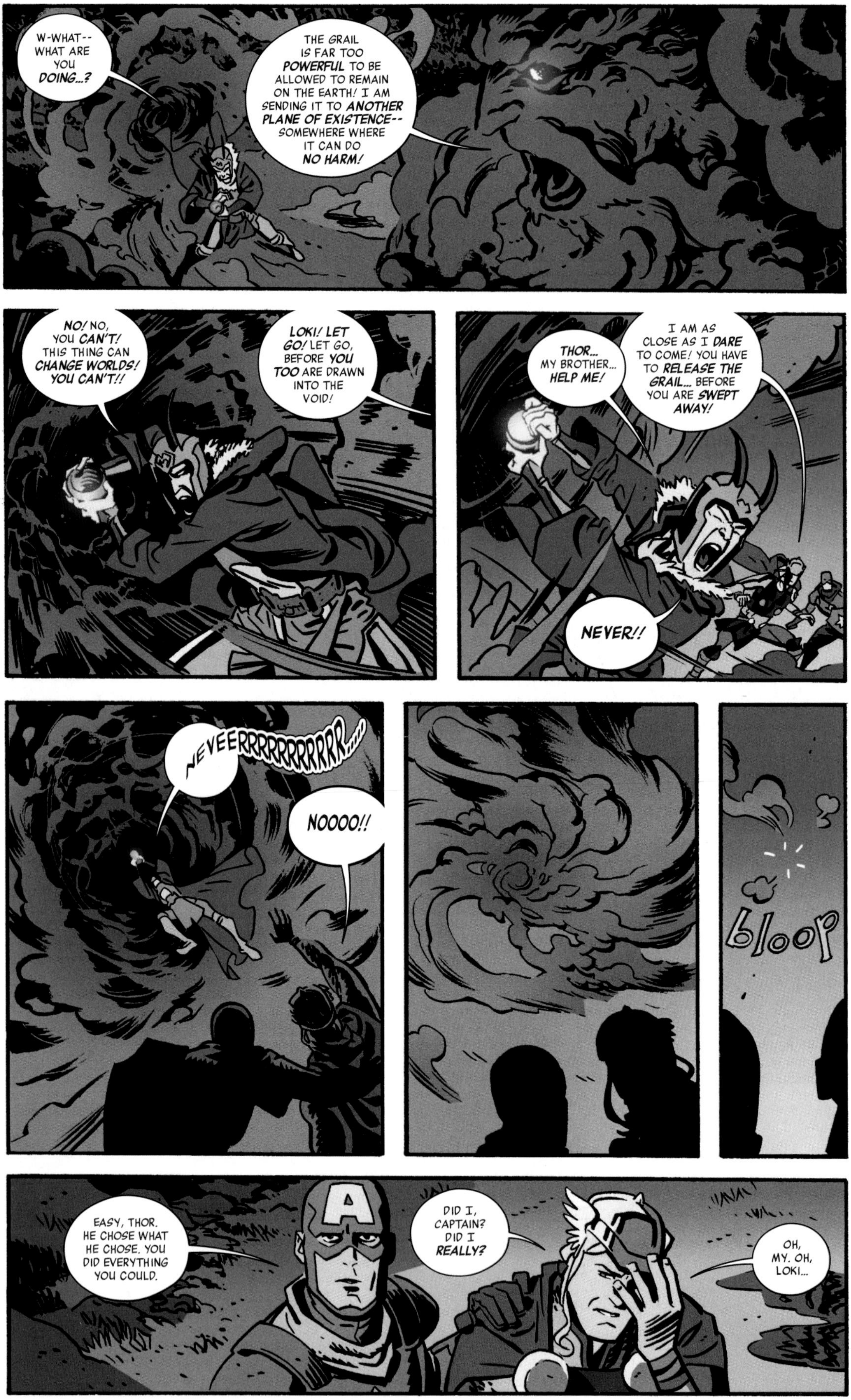
W-WHAT-- WHAT ARE YOU DOING...?
THE GRAIL IS FAR TOO POWERFUL TO BE ALLOWED TO REMAIN ON THE EARTH! I AM SENDING IT TO ANOTHER PLANE OF EXISTENCE-- SOMEWHERE WHERE IT CAN DO NO HARM!
NO! NO, YOU CAN'T! THIS THING CAN CHANGE WORLDS! YOU CAN'T!!
LOKI! LET GO! LET GO, BEFORE YOU TOO ARE DRAWN INTO THE VOID!
THOR... MY BROTHER... HELP ME!
I AM AS CLOSE AS I DARE TO COME! YOU HAVE TO RELEASE THE GRAIL... BEFORE YOU ARE SWEPT AWAY!
NEVER!!
NEVEERRRRRRRRRRR.....
NOOOO!!
bloop
EASY, THOR. HE CHOSE WHAT HE CHOSE. YOU DID EVERYTHING YOU COULD.
DID I, CAPTAIN? DID I REALLY?
OH, MY. OH, LOKI...

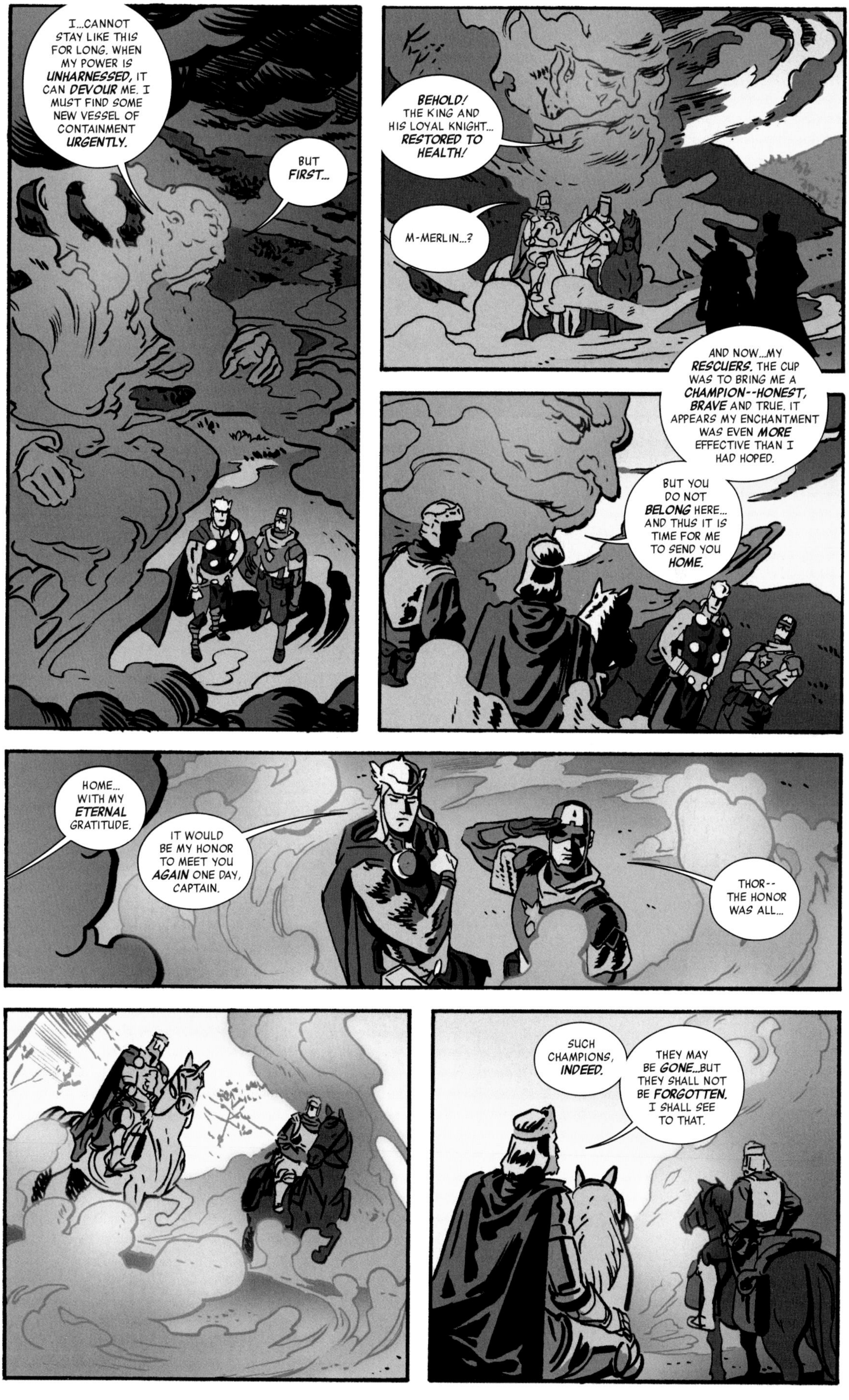
I...CANNOT STAY LIKE THIS FOR LONG. WHEN MY POWER IS UNHARNESSED, IT CAN DEVOUR ME. I MUST FIND SOME NEW VESSEL OF CONTAINMENT URGENTLY.
BUT FIRST...
BEHOLD! THE KING AND HIS LOYAL KNIGHT... RESTORED TO HEALTH!
M-MERLIN...?
AND NOW...MY RESCUERS. THE CUP WAS TO BRING ME A CHAMPION--HONEST, BRAVE AND TRUE. IT APPEARS MY ENCHANTMENT WAS EVEN MORE EFFECTIVE THAN I HAD HOPED.
BUT YOU DO NOT BELONG HERE... AND THUS IT IS TIME FOR ME TO SEND YOU HOME.
HOME... WITH MY ETERNAL GRATITUDE.
IT WOULD BE MY HONOR TO MEET YOU AGAIN ONE DAY, CAPTAIN.
THOR-- THE HONOR WAS ALL...
SUCH CHAMPIONS, INDEED.
THEY MAY BE GONE...BUT THEY SHALL NOT BE FORGOTTEN. I SHALL SEE TO THAT.

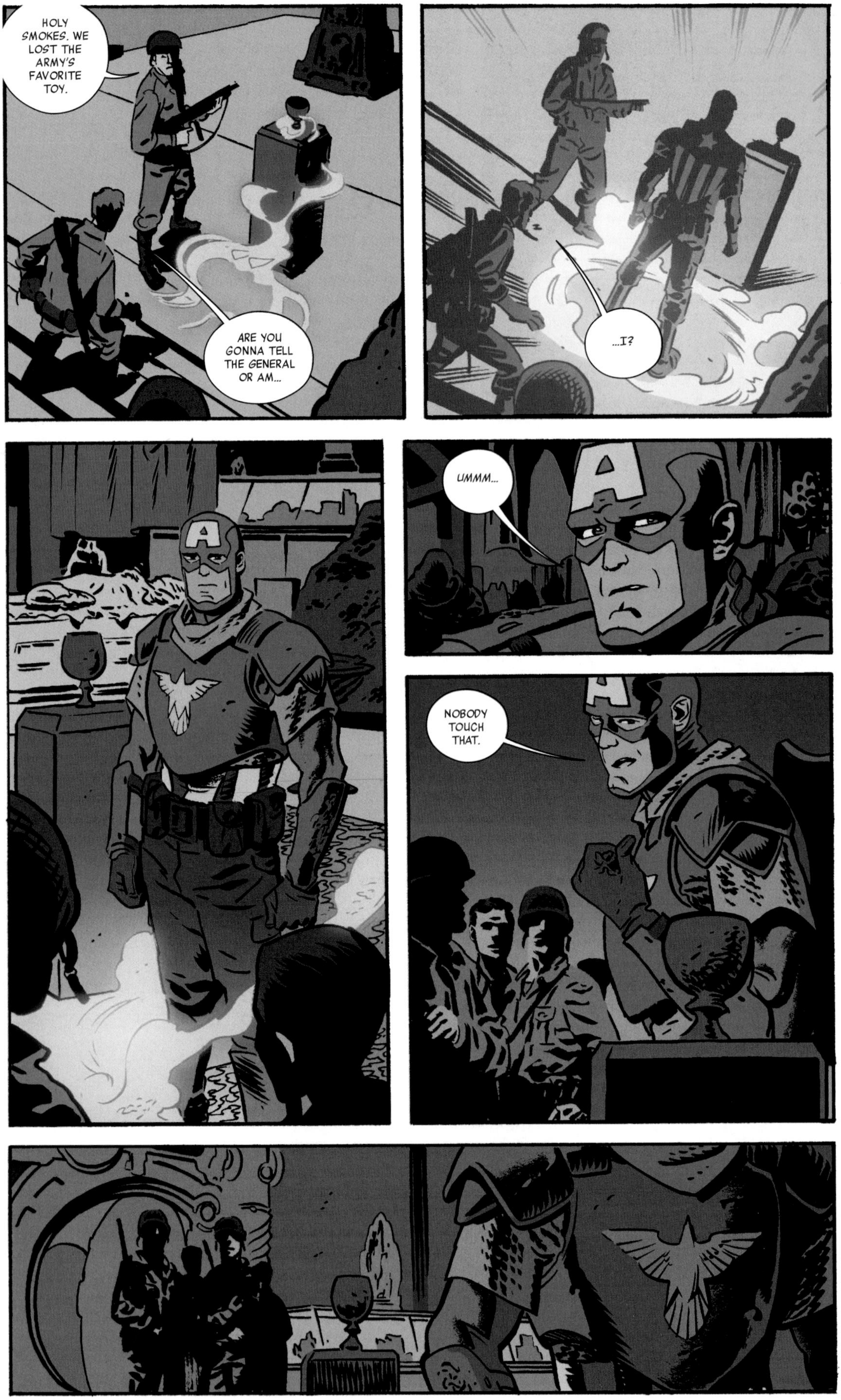

HOLY SMOKES. WE LOST THE ARMY'S FAVORITE TOY.
ARE YOU GONNA TELL THE GENERAL OR AM...
...I?
UMMM...
NOBODY TOUCH THAT.

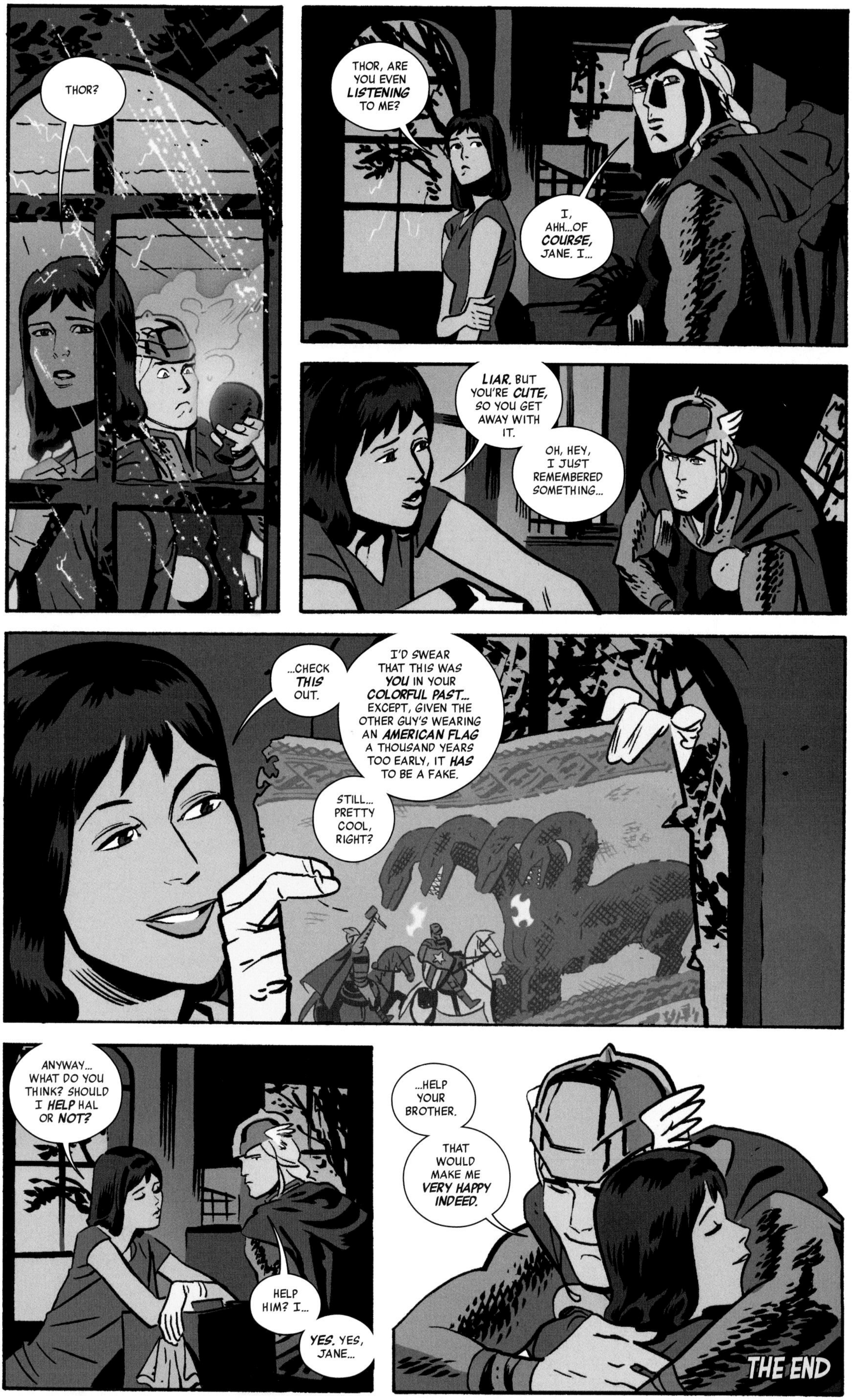
THOR?
THOR, ARE YOU EVEN LISTENING TO ME?
I, AHH...OF COURSE, JANE. I...
LIAR. BUT YOU'RE CUTE, SO YOU GET AWAY WITH IT.
OH, HEY, I JUST REMEMBERED SOMETHING...
...CHECK THIS OUT.
I'D SWEAR THAT THIS WAS YOU IN YOUR COLORFUL PAST... EXCEPT, GIVEN THE OTHER GUY'S WEARING AN AMERICAN FLAG A THOUSAND YEARS TOO EARLY, IT HAS TO BE A FAKE.
STILL... PRETTY COOL, RIGHT?
ANYWAY... WHAT DO YOU THINK? SHOULD I HELP HAL OR NOT?
HELP HIM? I...
YES. YES, JANE...
...HELP YOUR BROTHER.
THAT WOULD MAKE ME VERY HAPPY INDEED.
THE END

THOR: THE MIGHTY AVENGER VOL. 1 GRAPHIC NOVEL COVER BY CHRIS SAMNEE & MATTHEW WILSON

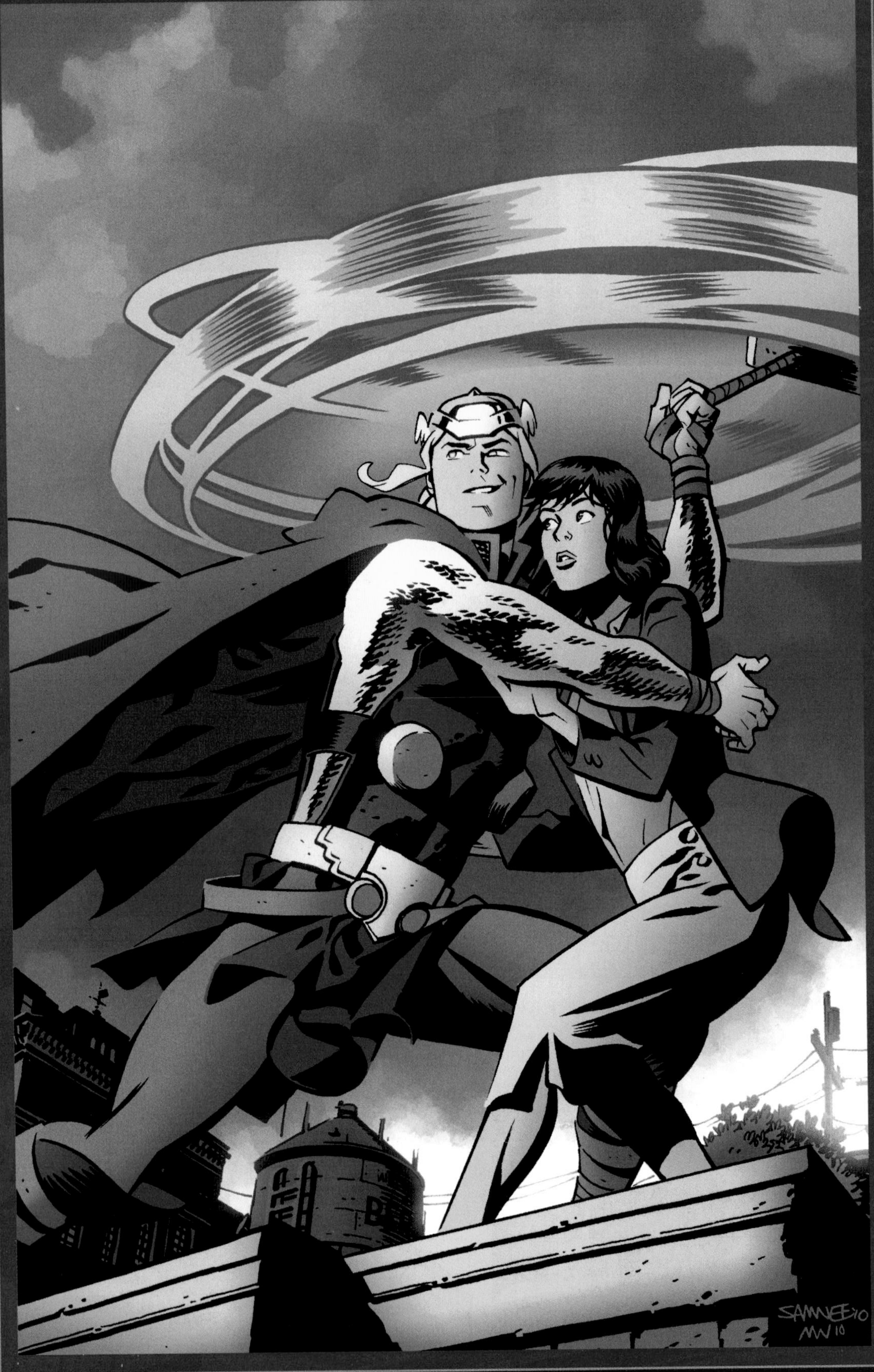
SAMNEE '10
MW 10

THOR: THE MIGHTY AVENGER VOL. 1 GRAPHIC NOVEL COVER
INKS BY CHRIS SAMNEE

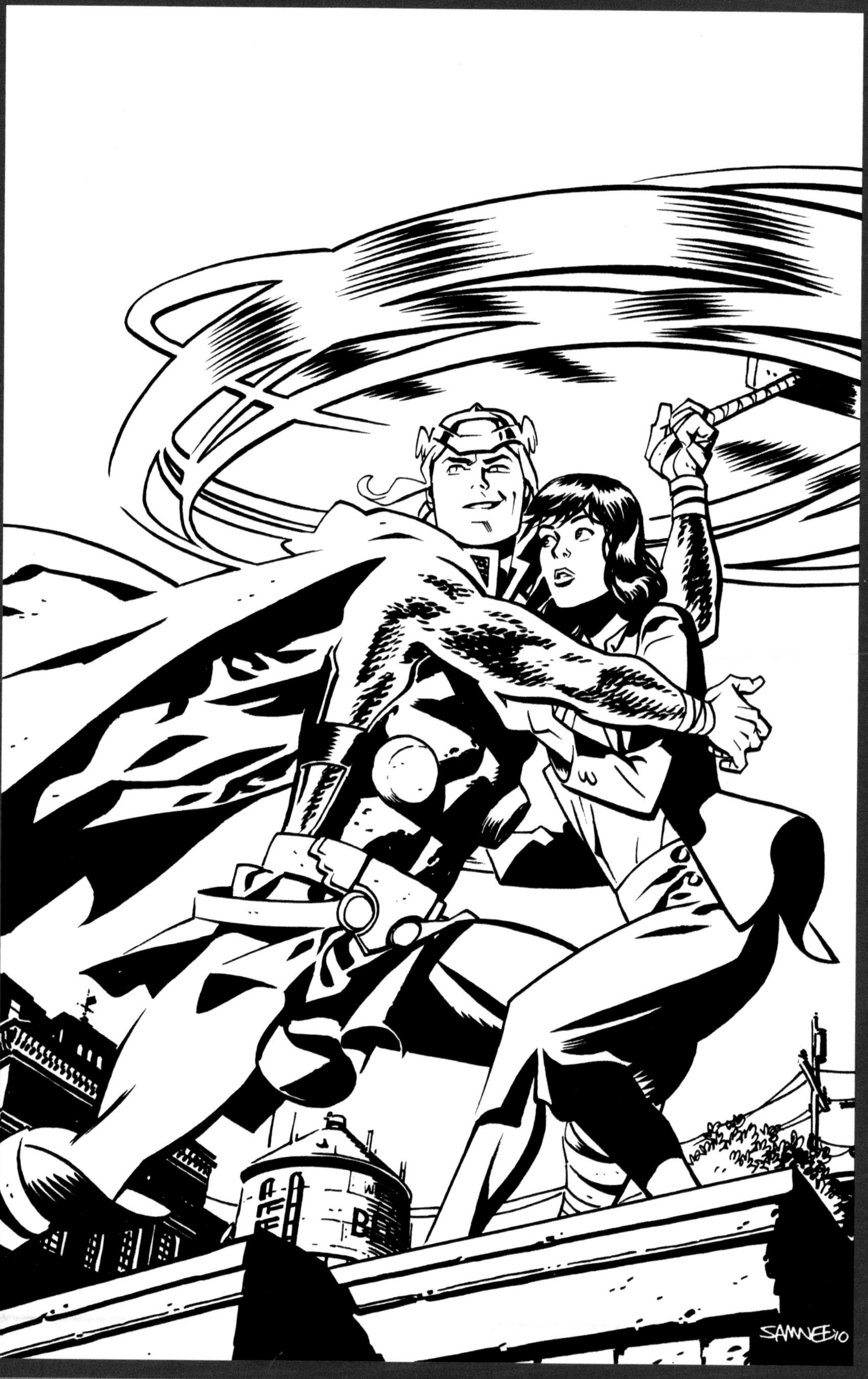
SAMNEE'10

CHARACTER DESIGNS BY CHRIS SAMNEE

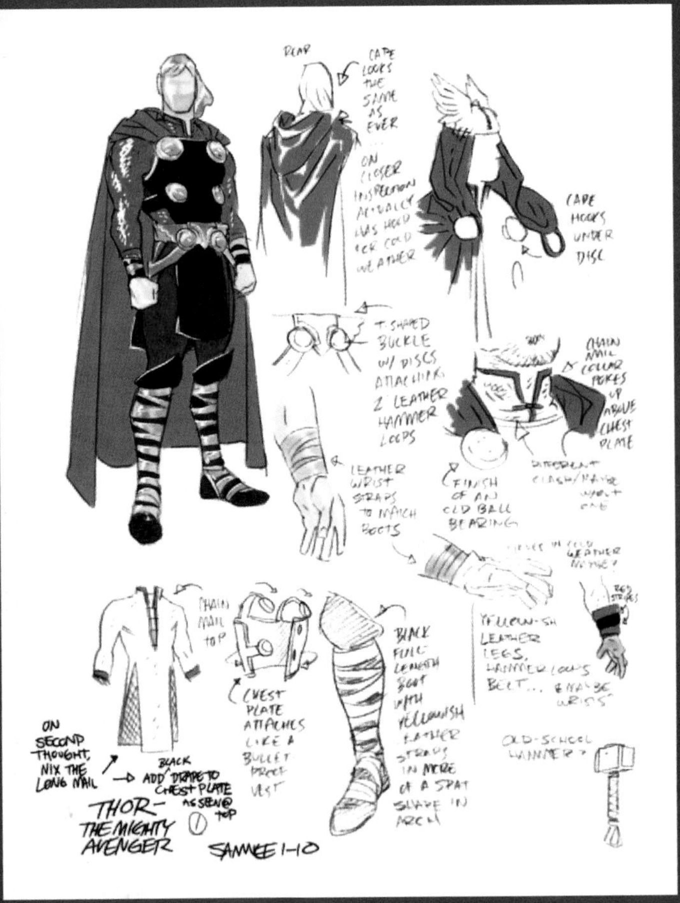
REAR
CAPE LOOKS THE SAME AS EVER
ON CLOSER INSPECTION ACTUALLY HAS HOOD FOR COLD WEATHER
CAPE HOOKS UNDER DISC
T-SHAPED BUCKLE W/ DISCS ATTACHING 2 LEATHER HAMMER LOOPS
CHAIN MAIL COLLAR POKES UP ABOVE CHEST PLATE
LEATHER WRIST STRAPS TO MATCH BOOTS
FINISH OF AN OLD BALL BEARING
CHAIN MAIL TOP
CHEST PLATE ATTACHES LIKE A BULLET PROOF VEST
BLACK FULL LENGTH BOOT WITH YELLOWISH LEATHER STRAPS IN MORE OF A SPAT SHAPE IN ARCH
YELLOWISH LEATHER LEGS, HAMMER LOOPS BELT... MAYBE WRISTS
OLD-SCHOOL HAMMER?
ON SECOND THOUGHT, NIX THE LONG MAIL
ADD BLACK DRAPE TO CHEST PLATE AS SEEN @ TOP
THOR- THE MIGHTY AVENGER ①
SAMNEE 1-10

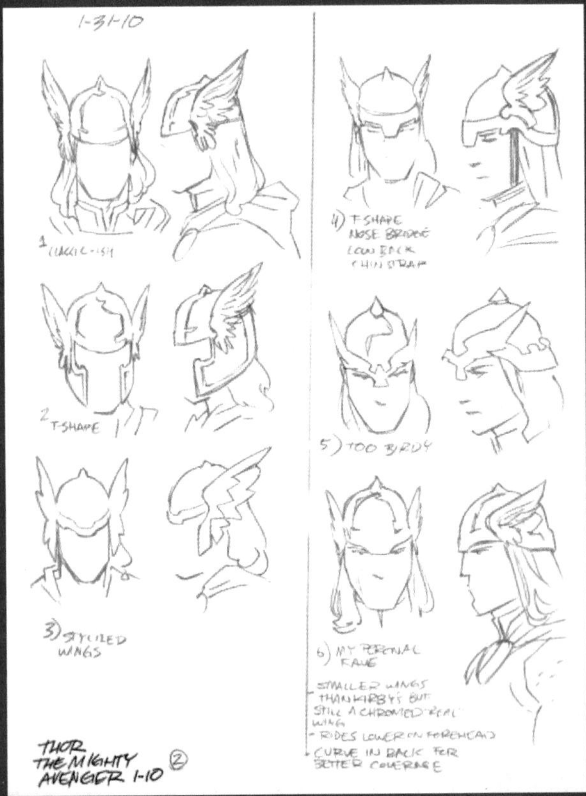
1-31-10
1 CLASSIC-ISH
2 T-SHAPE
3) STYLIZED WINGS
4) T-SHAPE NOSE BRIDGE LOW BACK CHIN STRAP
5) TOO BIRDY
6) MY PERSONAL FAVE
- SMALLER WINGS THAN KIRBY'S BUT STILL A CHROMED 'REAL' WING
- RIDES LOWER ON FOREHEAD
- CURVE IN BACK FOR BETTER COVERAGE
THOR THE MIGHTY AVENGER 1-10 ②

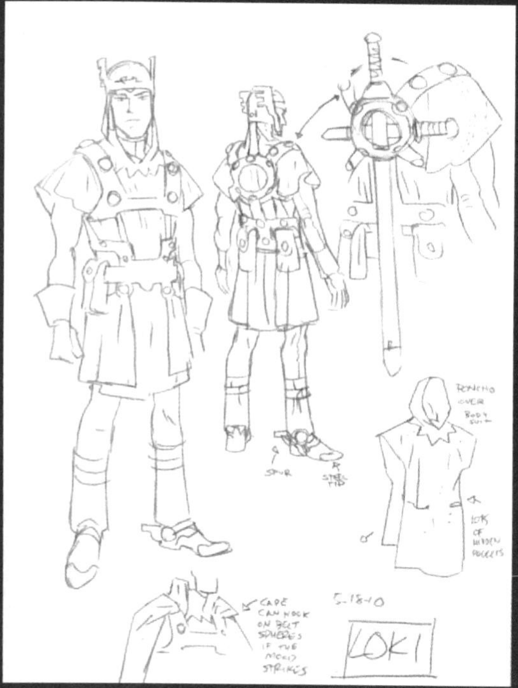
PONCHO OVER BODY SUIT
SPUR
STEEL TIP
LOTS OF HIDDEN POCKETS
CAPE CAN HOOK ON BELT SPHERES IF THE MOOD STRIKES
5-18-10
LOKI

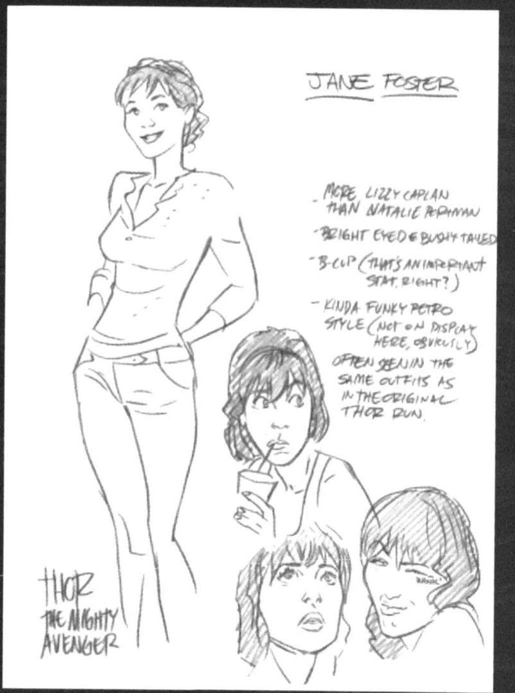
JANE FOSTER
- MORE LIZZY CAPLAN THAN NATALIE PORTMAN
- BRIGHT EYED & BUSHY TAILED
- B-CUP (THAT'S AN IMPORTANT STAT, RIGHT?)
- KINDA FUNKY RETRO STYLE (NOT ON DISPLAY HERE, OBVIOUSLY)
OFTEN SEEN IN THE SAME OUTFITS AS IN THE ORIGINAL THOR RUN.
THOR THE MIGHTY AVENGER

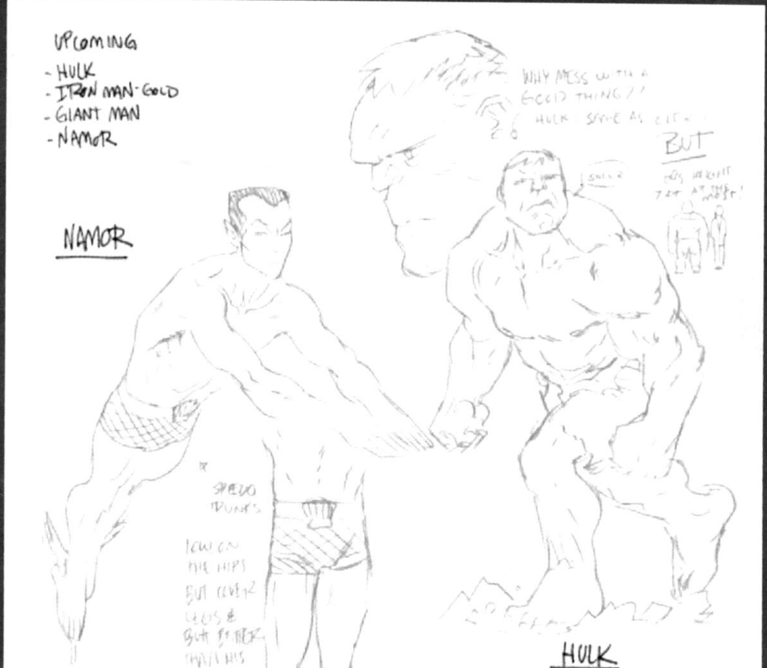
UPCOMING
- HULK
- IRON MAN - GOLD
- GIANT MAN
- NAMOR
WHY MESS WITH A GOOD THING?!
BUT
NAMOR
SPEEDO TRUNKS
LOW ON THE HIPS BUT COVER CHEEKS & BUTT BETTER THAN HIS OLD PAIR OF LADIES PANTIES
HELLO
HULK
- BULKY
- NOT VEINY
- HAIRY?
THOR THE MIGHTY AVENGER ③ 2-1-10

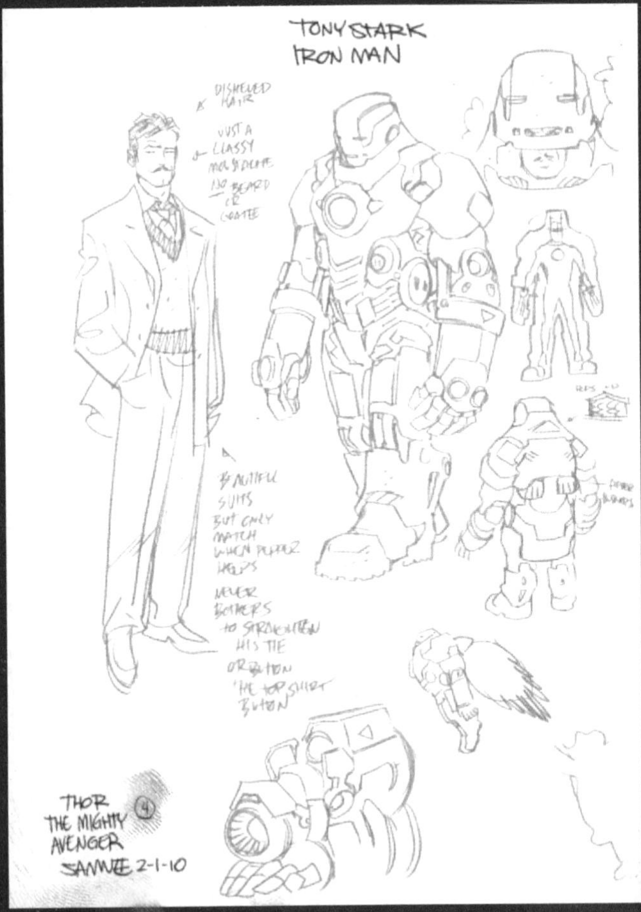
TONY STARK
IRON MAN
NEVER BOTHERS TO STRAIGHTEN HIS TIE
THOR
THE MIGHTY
AVENGER
SAMNEE 2-1-10

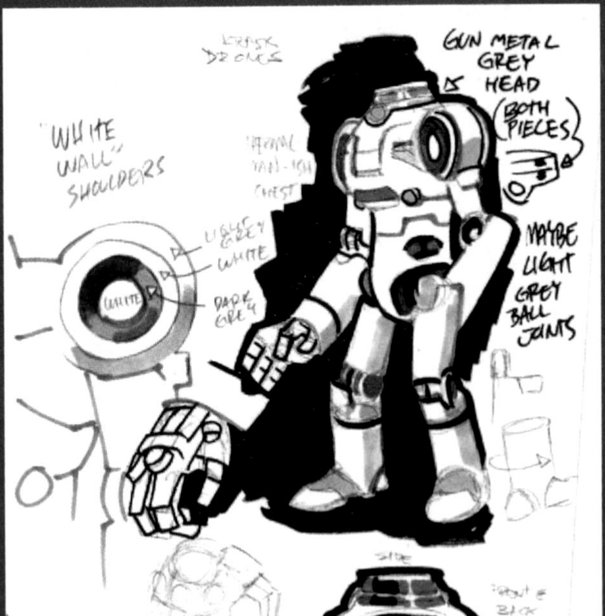
GUN METAL GREY HEAD (BOTH PIECES)
"WHITE WALL" SHOULDERS
LIGHT GREY
WHITE
DARK GREY
MAYBE LIGHT GREY BALL JOINTS